MW00560110

Means Residential Square Foot Costs

Contractor's Pricing Guide 2008

The 2008 Contractor's Pricing Guide: Residential Square Foot Costs, *and all of RSMeans Annual Cost Data Books for 2008, are dedicated to the memory of our respected colleague and friend, Senior Engineering Operations Manager, John Ferguson.*

Senior Editor
Robert W. Mewis, CCC

Contributing Editors
Christopher Babbit
Ted Baker
Barbara Balboni
Robert A. Bastoni
John H. Chiang, PE
Gary W. Christensen
David G. Drain, PE
Cheryl Elsmore
Robert J. Kuchta
Robert C. McNichols
Melville J. Mossman, PE
Jeannene D. Murphy
Stephen C. Plotner
Eugene R. Spencer
Marshall J. Stetson
Phillip R. Waier, PE

*Senior Engineering
Operations Manager*
John H. Ferguson, PE

*Senior Vice President
& General Manager*
John Ware

*Vice President
of Direct Response*
John M. Shea

Director of Sales
Brian Hare

*Director of
Product Development*
Thomas J. Dion

Production Manager
Michael Kokernak

Production Coordinator
Wayne D. Anderson

Technical Support
Jonathan Forgit
Mary Lou Geary
Jill Goodman
Roger Hancock
Gary L. Hoitt
Genevieve Medeiros
Paula Reale-Camelio
Kathryn S. Rodriguez
Sheryl A. Rose

Book & Cover Design
Norman R. Forgit

RSMeans

Means Residential Square Foot Costs

Contractor's Pricing Guide 2008

- Residential Cost Models for All Standard Building Classes
- Costs for Modifications & Additions
- Costs for Hundreds of Residential Building Systems & Components
- Cost Adjustment Factors for Your Location
- Illustrations

$39.95 per copy (in United States)
Price subject to change without prior notice.

Copyright © 2007
Reed Construction Data, Inc.
Construction Publishers & Consultants
63 Smiths Lane
Kingston, MA 02364-0800
781-422-5000
www.rsmeans.com
RS**Means** is a product line of Reed Construction Data.

Printed in the United States of America

ISSN 1074-049X

ISBN 978-0-87629-058-3

Foreword

Our Mission

Since 1942, RSMeans has been actively engaged in construction cost publishing and consulting throughout North America.

Today, over 60 years after RSMeans began, our primary objective remains the same: to provide you, the construction and facilities professional, with the most current and comprehensive construction cost data possible.

Whether you are a contractor, an owner, an architect, an engineer, a facilities manager, or anyone else who needs a reliable construction cost estimate, you'll find this publication to be a highly useful and necessary tool.

With the constant flow of new construction methods and materials today, it's difficult to find the time to look at and evaluate all the different construction cost possibilities. In addition, because labor and material costs keep changing, last year's cost information is not a reliable basis for today's estimate or budget.

That's why so many construction professionals turn to RSMeans. We keep track of the costs for you, along with a wide range of other key information, from city cost indexes . . . to productivity rates . . . to crew composition . . . to contractor's overhead and profit rates.

RSMeans performs these functions by collecting data from all facets of the industry and organizing it in a format that is instantly accessible to you. From the preliminary budget to the detailed unit price estimate, you'll find the data in this book useful for all phases of construction cost determination.

The Staff, the Organization, and Our Services

When you purchase one of RSMeans' publications, you are, in effect, hiring the services of a full-time staff of construction and engineering professionals.

Our thoroughly experienced and highly qualified staff works daily at collecting, analyzing, and disseminating comprehensive cost information for your needs. These staff members have years of practical construction experience and engineering training prior to joining the firm. As a result, you can count on them not only for the cost figures, but also for additional background reference information that will help you create a realistic estimate.

The RSMeans organization is always prepared to help you solve construction problems through its four major divisions: Construction and Cost Data Publishing, Electronic Products and Services, Consulting and Business Solutions, and Professional Development Services.

Besides a full array of construction cost estimating books, RSMeans also publishes a number of other reference works for the construction industry. Subjects include construction estimating and project and business management; special topics such as HVAC, roofing, plumbing, and hazardous waste remediation; and a library of facility management references.

In addition, you can access all of our construction cost data electronically using *Means CostWorks®* CD or on the Web.

What's more, you can increase your knowledge and improve your construction estimating and management performance with an RSMeans Construction Seminar or In-House Training Program. These two-day seminar programs offer unparalleled opportunities for everyone in your organization to get updated on a wide variety of construction-related issues.

RSMeans is also a worldwide provider of construction cost management and analysis services for commercial and government owners.

In short, RSMeans can provide you with the tools and expertise for constructing accurate and dependable construction estimates and budgets in a variety of ways.

Part of a Family of Companies Dedicated to the Construction Industry

RSMeans is owned by Reed Construction Data, a leader in providing information solutions to the construction industry. Headquartered near Atlanta, Georgia, Reed Construction Data is a subsidiary of Reed Business Information, North America's largest business-to-business information provider. With more than 80 market-leading publications and 55 websites, Reed Business Information's wide range of services also includes research, business development, direct marketing lists, training and development programs, and technology solutions. Reed Business Information is a member of the Reed Elsevier PLC group (NYSE: RUK and ENL), a leading provider of global information-driven services and solutions in the science and medical, legal, education, and business-to-business industry sectors.

Robert Snow Means Established a Tradition of Quality That Continues Today

Robert Snow Means spent years building RSMeans, making certain he always delivered a quality product.

Today, at RSMeans, we do more than talk about the quality of our data and the usefulness of our books. We stand behind all of our data, from historical cost indexes to construction materials and techniques to current costs.

If you have any questions about our products or services, please call us toll-free at 1-800-334-3509. Our customer service representatives will be happy to assist you. You can also visit our Web site at www.rsmeans.com.

Table of Contents

How the Book is Built: An Overview

A Powerful Construction Tool

You have in your hands one of the most powerful construction tools available today. A successful project is built on the foundation of an accurate and dependable estimate. This book will enable you to construct just such an estimate.

For the casual user the book is designed to be:

- quickly and easily understood so you can get right to your estimate.
- filled with valuable information so you can understand the necessary factors that go into the cost estimate.

For the regular user, the book is designed to be:

- a handy desk reference that can be quickly referred to for key costs.
- a comprehensive, fully reliable source of current construction costs so you'll be prepared to estimate any project.
- a source book for preliminary project cost, product selections, and alternate materials and methods.

To meet all of these requirements we have organized the book into the following clearly defined sections.

Square Foot Cost Section

This section lists Square Foot costs for typical residential construction projects. The organizational format used divides the projects into basic building classes. These classes are defined at the beginning of the section. The individual projects are further divided into ten common components of construction. A Table of Contents, an explanation of square foot prices, and an outline of a typical page layout are located at the beginning of the section.

Assemblies Cost Section

This section uses an Assemblies (sometimes referred to as systems) format grouping all the functional elements of a building into nine construction divisions.

At the top of each Assemblies cost table is an illustration, a brief description, and the design criteria used to develop the cost. Each of the components and its contributing cost to the system is shown.

Material: These cost figures include a standard 10% markup for profit. They are national average material costs as of January of the current year and include delivery to the job site.

Installation: The installation costs include labor and equipment, plus a markup for the installing contractor's overhead and profit.

For a complete breakdown and explanation of a typical Assemblies page, see "How to Use the Assemblies Section" at the beginning of the Assemblies Section.

Location Factors: You can adjust total project costs to over 900 locations throughout the U.S. and Canada by using the data in this section.

Abbreviations: A listing of the abbreviations used throughout this book, along with the terms they represent, is included in this section.

Index

A comprehensive listing of all terms and subjects in this book to help you find what you need quickly.

The Scope of This Book

This book is designed to be as comprehensive and as easy to use as possible. To that end we have made certain assumptions and limited its scope in three key ways:

1. We have established material prices based on a national average.
2. We have computed labor costs based on a seven major-region average of residential wage rates.

Project Size

This book is intended for use by those involved primarily in Residential construction costing less than $850,000. This includes the construction of homes, row houses, townhouses, condominiums, and apartments.

With reasonable exercise of judgment the figures can be used for any building work. For other types of projects, such as repair and remodeling or commercial buildings, consult the appropriate RSMeans publication for more information.

How to Use the Book: The Details

What's Behind the Numbers? The Development of Cost Data

The staff at RSMeans continuously monitors developments in the construction industry in order to ensure reliable, thorough, and up-to-date cost information.

While *overall* construction costs may vary relative to general economic conditions, price fluctuations within the industry are dependent upon many factors. Individual price variations may, in fact, be opposite to overall economic trends. Therefore, costs are continually monitored and complete updates are published yearly. Also, new items are frequently added in response to changes in materials and methods.

Costs – $ (U.S.)

All costs represent U.S. national averages and are given in U.S. dollars. The RSMeans Location Factors can be used to adjust costs to a particular location. The Location Factors for Canada can be used to adjust U.S. national averages to local costs in Canadian dollars. No exchange rate conversion is necessary.

Material Costs

The RSMeans staff contacts manufacturers, dealers, distributors, and contractors all across the U.S. and Canada to determine national average material costs. If you have access to current material costs for your specific location, you may wish to make adjustments to reflect differences from the national average. Included within material costs are fasteners for a normal installation. RSMeans engineers use manufacturers' recommendations, written specifications, and/or standard construction practice for size and spacing of fasteners. Adjustments to material costs may be required for your specific application or location. Material costs do not include sales tax.

Labor Costs

Labor costs are based on the average of residential wages from across the U.S. for the current year. Rates, along with overhead and profit markups, are listed on the inside back cover of this book.

- If wage rates in your area vary from those used in this book, or if rate increases are expected within a given year, labor costs should be adjusted accordingly.

Labor costs reflect productivity based on actual working conditions. In addition to actual installation, these figures include time spent during a normal workday on tasks such as, as material receiving and handling, mobilization at site, site movement, breaks, and cleanup.

Productivity data is developed over an extended period so as not to be influenced by abnormal variations and reflects a typical average.

Equipment Costs

Equipment costs include not only rental, but also operating costs for equipment under normal use. Equipment and rental rates are obtained from industry sources throughout North America—contractors, suppliers, dealers, manufacturers, and distributers.

Factors Affecting Costs

Costs can vary depending upon a number of variables. Here's how we have handled the main factors affecting costs.

Quality—The prices for materials and the workmanship upon which productivity is based represent sound construction work. They are also in line with U.S. government specifications.

Overtime—We have made no allowance for overtime. If you anticipate premium time or work beyond normal working hours, be sure to make an appropriate adjustment to your labor costs.

Productivity—The productivity, daily output, and labor-hour figures for each line item are based on working an eight-hour day in daylight hours in moderate temperatures. For work that extends beyond normal work hours or is performed under adverse conditions, productivity may decrease.

Size of Project—The size, scope of work, and type of construction project will have a significant impact on cost. Economies of scale can reduce costs for large projects. Unit costs can often run higher for small projects. Costs in this book are intended for the size and type of project as previously described in "How the Book Is Built: An Overview." Costs for projects of a significantly different size or type should be adjusted accordingly.

Location—Material prices in this book are for metropolitan areas. However, in dense urban areas, traffic and site storage limitations may increase costs. Beyond a 20-mile radius of large cities, extra trucking or transportation charges may also increase the material costs slightly. On the other hand, lower wage rates may be in effect. Be sure to consider both of these factors when preparing an estimate, particularly if the job site is located in a central city or remote rural location.

In addition, highly specialized subcontract items may require travel and per-diem expenses for mechanics.

Other Factors–

- season of year
- contractor management
- weather conditions
- local union restrictions
- building code requirements
- availability of:
  - adequate energy
  - skilled labor
  - building materials
- owner's special requirements/ restrictions
- safety requirements
- environmental considerations

Overhead & Profit—The "Assemblies" section of this book uses costs that include the installing contractor's overhead and profit (O&P). An allowance covering the general contractor's markup must be added to these figures. The general contractor can include this price in the bid with a normal markup ranging from 5% to 15%. The markup depends on economic conditions plus the supervision and troubleshooting expected by the general contractor. For purposes of this book, it is best for a general contractor to add an allowance of 10% to the figures in the Assemblies section.

General Conditions

General Conditions, or General Requirements, of the contract should also be added to the Total Cost including O&P when applicable. General Conditions for the *Installing Contractor* may range from 0% to 10% of the Total Cost including O&P. For the *General or Prime Contractor*, costs for General Conditions may range from 5% to 15% of the Total Cost including O&P, with a figure of 10% as the most typical allowance.

Unpredictable Factors—General business conditions influence "in-place" costs of all items. Substitute materials and construction methods may have to be employed. These may affect the installed cost and/or life cycle costs. Such factors may be difficult to evaluate and cannot necessarily be predicted on the basis of the job's location in a particular section of the country. Thus, where these factors apply, you may find significant but unavoidable cost variations for which you will have to apply a measure of judgment to your estimate.

Rounding of Costs

In general, all unit prices in excess of $5.00 have been rounded to make them easier to use and still maintain adequate precision of the results. The rounding rules we have chosen are in the following table.

Prices from . . .	Rounded to the nearest . . .
$.01 to $5.00	$.01
$5.01 to $20.00	$.05
$20.01 to $100.00	$.50
$100.01 to $300.00	$1.00
$300.01 to $1,000.00	$5.00
$1,000.01 to $10,000.00	$25.00
$10,000.01 to $50,000.00	$100.00
$50,000.01 and above	$500.00

Final Checklist

Estimating can be a straightforward process provided you remember the basics. Here's a checklist of some of the steps you should remember to complete before finalizing your estimate.

Did you remember to . . .

* factor in the Location Factor for your locale?
* take into consideration which items have been marked up and by how much?
* mark up the entire estimate sufficiently for your purposes?
* include all components of your project in the final estimate?
* double check your figures for accuracy?
* call RSMeans if you have any questions about your estimate or the data you've found in our publications?

Remember, RSMeans stands behind its publications. If you have any questions about your estimate, about the costs you've used from our books—or even about the technical aspects of the job that may affect your estimate—feel free to call the RSMeans editors at 1-800-334-3509.

Square Foot Cost Section

Table of Contents

How to Use the Square Foot Cost Pages

Introduction: This section contains costs per square foot for four classes of construction in seven building types. Costs are listed for various exterior wall materials which are typical of the class and building type. There are cost tables for wings and ells with modification tables to adjust the base cost of each class of building. Non-standard items can easily be added to the standard structures.

Accompanying each building type in each class is a list of components used in a typical residence. The components are divided into ten primary estimating divisions. The divisions correspond with the "Assemblies" section of this manual.

Cost estimating for a residence is a three-step process:
(1) Identification
(2) Listing dimensions
(3) Calculations

Guidelines and a sample cost estimating form are shown on the following pages.

Identification: To properly identify a residential building, the class of construction, type, and exterior wall material must be determined. Located at the beginning of this section are drawings and guidelines for determining the class of construction. There are also detailed specifications accompanying each type of building, along with additional drawings at the beginning of each set of tables, to further aid in proper building class and type identification.

Sketches for seven types of residential buildings and their configurations are shown along with definitions of living area next to each sketch. Sketches and definitions of garage types follow the residential buildings.

Living Area: Base cost tables are prepared as costs per square foot of living area. The living area of a residence is that area which is suitable and normally designed for full-time living. It does not include basement recreation rooms or finished attics, although these areas are often considered full-time living areas by owners.

Living area is calculated from the exterior dimensions without the need to adjust for exterior wall thickness. When calculating the living area of a 1-1/2-story, two-story, three-story or tri-level residence, overhangs and other differences in size and shape between floors must be considered.

Only the floor area with a ceiling height of six feet or more in a 1-1/2 story-residence is considered living area. In bi-levels and tri-levels, the areas that are below grade are considered living area, even when these areas may not be completely finished.

Base Tables and Modifications: Base cost tables show the base cost per square foot without a basement, with one full bath and one full kitchen. Adjustments for finished and unfinished basements are part of the base cost tables. Adjustments for multi-family residences, additional bathrooms, townhouses, alternative roofs, and air conditioning and heating systems are listed in Modifications, Adjustments, and Alternatives tables below the base cost tables.

The component list for each residence type should also be consulted when preparing an estimate. If the components listed are not appropriate, modifications can be made by consulting the "Assemblies" section of this manual.

Costs for other modifications, adjustments, and alternatives, including garages, breezeways, and site improvements, are in the modification tables at the end of this section.

Listing of Dimensions: To use this section of the manual, only the dimensions used to calculate the horizontal area of the building and additions and modifications are needed. The dimensions, normally the length and width, can come from drawings or field measurements. For ease in calculation, consider measuring in tenths of feet, i.e., 9 ft. 6 in. = 9.5 ft., 9 ft. 4 in. = 9.3 ft.

In all cases, make a sketch of the building. Any protrusions or other variations in shape should be noted on the sketch with dimensions.

Calculations: The calculations portion of the estimate is a two-step activity:
(1) The selection of appropriate costs from the tables
(2) Computations

Selection of Appropriate Costs: To select the appropriate cost from the base tables the following information is needed:
(1) Class of construction
(2) Type of residence
(3) Occupancy
(4) Building configuration
(5) Exterior wall construction
(6) Living area

Consult the tables and accompanying information to make the appropriate selections. Modifications, adjustments, and alternatives are classified by class, type and size. Further modifications can be made using the "Assemblies" Section.

Computations: The computation process should take the following sequence:
(1) Multiply the base cost by the area
(2) Add or subtract the modifications
(3) Apply the location modifier

When selecting costs, interpolate or use the cost that most nearly matches the structure under study. This applies to size, exterior wall construction, and class.

How to Use the Square Foot Cost Pages

Exterior wall system

Specification highlights

Class of construction

Type of residence

Basement additions

Living areas used to compute costs per square foot. (Living areas explained on pages 6–12)

Base cost per square foot of living area for a 2 story wood sided residence without basement with total living area of 2,000 square feet. A detailed breakdown of this cost, typical for all residences of this class and type, appears on the facing page

Addition for unfinished basement

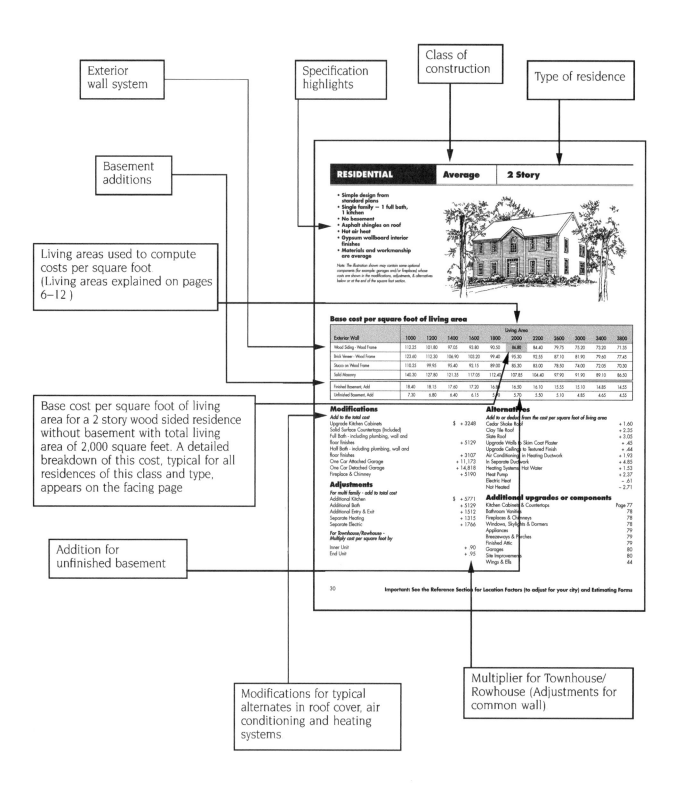

RESIDENTIAL	Average	2 Story

- Simple design from standard plans
- Single family — 1 full bath, 1 kitchen
- No basement
- Asphalt shingles on roof
- Hot air heat
- Gypsum wallboard interior finishes
- Materials and workmanship are average

Note: The illustration shown may contain some optional components (for example: garages and/or fireplaces) whose costs are shown in the modifications, adjustments, & alternatives below or at the end of the square foot section.

Base cost per square foot of living area

Exterior Wall	Living Area										
	1000	1200	1400	1600	1800	2000	2200	2600	3000	3400	3800
Wood Siding - Wood Frame	112.25	101.80	97.05	93.80	90.50	86.80	84.40	79.75	75.20	73.20	71.35
Brick Veneer - Wood Frame	123.60	112.30	106.90	103.20	99.40	95.30	92.55	87.10	81.90	79.60	77.45
Stucco on Wood Frame	110.25	99.95	95.40	92.15	89.00	85.30	83.00	78.50	74.00	72.05	70.30
Solid Masonry	140.30	127.80	121.35	117.05	112.40	107.85	104.40	97.90	91.90	89.10	86.50
Finished Basement, Add	18.40	18.15	17.60	17.20	16.8	16.50	16.10	15.55	15.10	14.85	14.55
Unfinished Basement, Add	7.30	6.80	6.40	6.15	5 0	5.70	5.50	5.10	4.85	4.65	4.55

Modifications

Add to the total cost

Upgrade Kitchen Cabinets	$ + 3248
Solid Surface Countertops (Included)	
Full Bath - including plumbing, wall and floor finishes	+ 5129
Half Bath - including plumbing, wall and floor finishes	+ 3107
One Car Attached Garage	+ 11,173
One Car Detached Garage	+ 14,818
Fireplace & Chimney	+ 5190

Adjustments

For multi family - add to total cost

Additional Kitchen	$ + 5771
Additional Bath	+ 5129
Additional Entry & Exit	+ 1512
Separate Heating	+ 1315
Separate Electric	+ 1766

For Townhouse/Rowhouse -
Multiply cost per square foot by

Inner Unit	+ .90
End Unit	+ .95

Alternatives

Add to or deduct from the cost per square foot of living area

Cedar Shake Roof	+ 1.60
Clay Tile Roof	+ 2.35
Slate Roof	+ 3.05
Upgrade Walls to Skim Coat Plaster	+ .45
Upgrade Ceiling to Textured Finish	+ .44
Air Conditioning in Heating Ductwork	+ 1.93
In Separate Ductwork	+ 4.85
Heating Systems Hot Water	+ 1.53
Heat Pump	+ 2.37
Electric Heat	– .61
Not Heated	– 2.71

Additional upgrades or components

Kitchen Cabinets & Countertops	Page 77
Bathroom Vanities	78
Fireplaces & Chimneys	78
Windows, Skylights & Dormers	78
Appliances	79
Breezeways & Porches	79
Finished Attic	79
Garages	80
Site Improvements	80
Wings & Ells	44

30   **Important: See the Reference Section for Location Factors (to adjust for your city) and Estimating Forms**

Modifications for typical alternates in roof cover, air conditioning and heating systems.

Multiplier for Townhouse/ Rowhouse (Adjustments for common wall)

Components
This page contains the ten components needed to develop the complete square foot cost of the typical dwelling specified. All components are defined with a description of the materials and/or task involved. Use cost figures from each component to estimate the cost per square foot of that section of the project.

Specifications
The parameters for an example dwelling from the facing page are listed here. Included are the square foot dimensions of the proposed building. LIVING AREA takes into account the number of floors and other factors needed to define a building's TOTAL SQUARE FOOTAGE. Perimeter and partition dimensions are defined in terms of linear feet.

Line Totals
The extreme right-hand column lists the sum of two figures. Use this total to determine the sum of MATERIAL COST plus INSTALLATION COST. The result is a convenient total cost for each of the ten components.

Average 2 Story
Living Area - 2000 S.F.
Perimeter - 135 L.F.

		Labor-Hours	Cost Per Square Foot Of Living Area		
			Mat.	Labor	Total
1 Site Work	Site preparation for slab; 4' deep trench excavation for foundation wall.	.034		.63	.63
2 Foundation	Continuous reinforced concrete footing 8" deep x 18" wide; dampproofed and insulated reinforced concrete foundation wall, 8" thick, 4' deep, 4" concrete slab on 4" crushed stone base and polyethylene vapor barrier, trowel finish.	.066	3.01	3.46	6.47
3 Framing	Exterior walls - 2" x 4" wood studs, 16" O.C.; 1/2" plywood sheathing; 2" x 6" rafters 16" O.C. with 1/2" plywood sheathing, 4 in 12 pitch; 2" x 6" ceiling joists 16" O.C.; 2" x 8" floor joists 16" O.C. with 5/8" plywood subfloor; 1/2" plywood subfloor on 1" x 2" wood sleepers 16" O.C.	.131	6.11	7.65	13.76
4 Exterior Walls	Beveled wood siding and building paper on insulated wood frame walls; 6" attic insulation; double hung windows; 3 flush solid core wood exterior doors with storms.	.111	10.88	4.91	15.79
5 Roofing	25 year asphalt shingles; #15 felt building paper; aluminum gutters, downspouts, drip edge and flashings.	.024	.69	1.05	1.74
6 Interiors	Walls and ceilings, 1/2" taped and finished gypsum wallboard, primed and painted with 2 coats; painted baseboard and trim, finished hardwood floor 40%, carpet with 1/2" underlayment 40%, vinyl tile with 1/2" underlayment 15%, ceramic tile with 1/2" underlayment 5%; hollow core and louvered	.232	13.11	12.42	25.53
7 Specialties	Average grade kitchen cabinets - 14 L.F. wall and base with solid surface counter top and kitchen sink; 40 gallon electric water heater.	.021	1.73	.77	2.50
8 Mechanical	1 lavatory, white, wall hung; 1 water closet, white; 1 bathtub with shower; enameled steel, white; gas fired warm air heat.	.060	2.67	2.50	5.17
9 Electrical	200 Amp. service; romex wiring; incandescent lighting fixtures, switches, receptacles.	.039	1.16	1.44	2.60
10 Overhead	Contractor's overhead and profit and plans.		6.69	5.92	12.61
	Total		46.05	40.75	**86.80**

31

Labor-hours
Use this column to determine the unit of measure in LABOR-HOURS needed to perform a task. This figure will give the builder LABOR-HOURS PER SQUARE FOOT of the building. The TOTAL LABOR-HOURS PER COMPONENT are determined by multiplying the LIVING AREA times the LABOR-HOURS listed on that line. (TOTAL LABOR-HOURS PER COMPONENT = LIVING AREA x LABOR-HOURS).

Installation
The labor rates included here incorporate the overhead and profit costs for the installing contractor. The average mark-up used to create these figures is 69.5% over and above BARE LABOR COST including fringe benefits.

Bottom Line Total
This figure is the complete square foot cost for the construction project. To determine TOTAL PROJECT COST, multiply the BOTTOM LINE TOTAL times the LIVING AREA. (TOTAL PROJECT COST = BOTTOM LINE TOTAL x LIVING AREA).

Materials
This column gives the unit needed to develop the COST OF MATERIALS. Note: The figures given here are not BARE COSTS. Ten percent has been added to BARE MATERIAL COST to cover handling.

*NOTE
The components listed on this page are typical of all the sizes of residences from the facing page. Specific quantities of components required would vary with the size of the dwelling and the exterior wall system.

Building Classes

Given below are the four general definitions of building classes. Each building — Economy, Average, Custom and Luxury — is common in residential construction. All four are used in this book to determine costs per square foot.

Economy Class

An economy class residence is usually mass-produced from stock plans. The materials and workmanship are sufficient only to satisfy minimum building codes. Low construction cost is more important than distinctive features. Design is seldom other than square or rectangular.

Average Class

An average class residence is simple in design and is built from standard designer plans. Material and workmanship are average, but often exceed the minimum building codes. There are frequently special features that give the residence some distinctive characteristics.

Custom Class

A custom class residence is usually built from a designer's plans which have been modified to give the building a distinction of design. Material and workmanship are generally above average with obvious attention given to construction details. Construction normally exceeds building code requirements.

Luxury Class

A luxury class residence is built from an architect's plan for a specific owner. It is unique in design and workmanship. There are many special features, and construction usually exceeds all building codes. It is obvious that primary attention is placed on the owner's comfort and pleasure. Construction is supervised by an architect.

Residential Building Types

One Story

This is an example of a one-story dwelling. The living area of this type of residence is confined to the ground floor. The headroom in the attic is usually too low for use as a living area.

One-and-a-half Story

The living area in the upper level of this type of residence is 50% to 90% of the ground floor. This is made possible by a combination of this design's high-peaked roof and/or dormers. Only the upper level area with a ceiling height of 6' or more is considered living area. The living area of this residence is the sum of the ground floor area plus the area on the second level with a ceiling height of 6' or more.

Residential Building Types

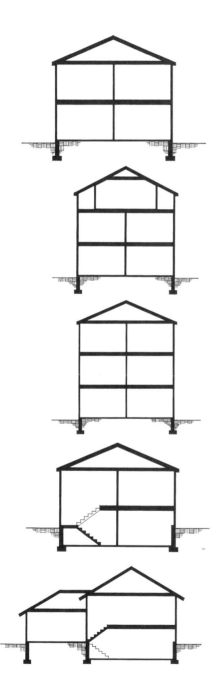

Two Story

This type of residence has a second floor or upper level area which is equal or nearly equal to the ground floor area. The upper level of this type of residence can range from 90% to 110% of the ground floor area, depending on setbacks or overhangs. The living area is the sum of the ground floor area and the upper level floor area.

Two-and-one-half Story

This type of residence has two levels of equal or nearly equal area and a third level which has a living area that is 50% to 90% of the ground floor. This is made possible by a high peaked roof, extended wall heights and/or dormers. Only the upper level area with a ceiling height of 6 feet or more is considered living area. The living area of this residence is the sum of the ground floor area, the second floor area and the area on the third level with a ceiling height of 6 feet or more.

Three Story

This type of residence has three levels which are equal or nearly equal. As in the 2 story residence, the second and third floor areas may vary slightly depending on the setbacks or overhangs. The living area is the sum of the ground floor area and the two upper level floor areas.

Bi-Level

This type of residence has two living areas, one above the other. One area is about 4 feet below grade and the second is about 4 feet above grade. Both are equal in size. The lower level in this type of residence is originally designed and built to serve as a living area and not as a basement. Both levels have full ceiling heights. The living area is the sum of the lower level area and the upper level area.

Tri-Level

This type of residence has three levels of living area. One is at grade level, the second is about 4 feet below grade, and the third is about 4 feet above grade. All levels are originally designed to serve as living areas. All levels have full ceiling heights. The living area is the sum of the areas of each of the three levels.

7

Exterior Wall Construction

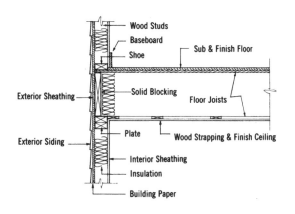

Wood Studs
Baseboard
Shoe
Sub & Finish Floor
Exterior Sheathing
Solid Blocking
Floor Joists
Exterior Siding
Plate
Wood Strapping & Finish Ceiling
Interior Sheathing
Insulation
Building Paper

Typical Frame Construction

Typical wood frame construction consists of wood studs with insulation between them. A typical exterior surface is made up of sheathing, building paper and exterior siding consisting of wood, vinyl, aluminum or stucco over the wood sheathing.

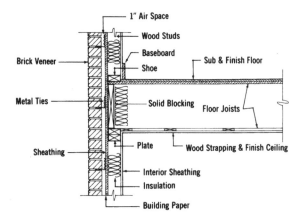

1" Air Space
Wood Studs
Baseboard
Brick Veneer
Shoe
Sub & Finish Floor
Metal Ties
Solid Blocking
Floor Joists
Sheathing
Plate
Wood Strapping & Finish Ceiling
Interior Sheathing
Insulation
Building Paper

Brick Veneer

Typical brick veneer construction consists of wood studs with insulation between them. A typical exterior surface is sheathing, building paper and an exterior of brick tied to the sheathing with metal strips.

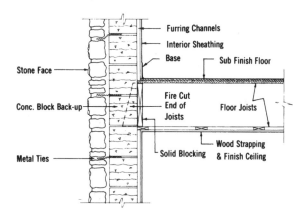

Furring Channels
Interior Sheathing
Base
Sub Finish Floor
Stone Face
Fire Cut End of Joists
Floor Joists
Conc. Block Back-up
Metal Ties
Solid Blocking
Wood Strapping & Finish Ceiling

Stone

Typical solid masonry construction consists of a stone or block wall covered on the exterior with brick, stone or other masonry.

Residential Configurations

Detached House

This category of residence is a freestanding separate building with or without an attached garage. It has four complete walls.

Town/Row House

This category of residence has a number of attached units made up of inner units and end units. The units are joined by common walls. The inner units have only two exterior walls. The common walls are fireproof. The end units have three walls and a common wall. Town houses/row houses can be any of the five types.

Semi-Detached House

This category of residence has two living units side-by-side. The common wall is a fireproof wall. Semi-detached residences can be treated as a row house with two end units. Semi-detached residences can be any of the five types.

Residential Garage Types

Attached Garage

Shares a common wall with the dwelling. Access is typically through a door between dwelling and garage.

Built-In Garage

Constructed under the second floor living space and above basement level of dwelling. Reduces gross square feet of living area.

Basement Garage

Constructed under the roof of the dwelling but below the living area.

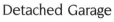

Detached Garage

Constructed apart from the main dwelling. Shares no common area or wall with the dwelling.

RESIDENTIAL
COST ESTIMATE

OWNER'S NAME: _____

RESIDENCE ADDRESS: _____

CITY, STATE, ZIP CODE: _____

APPRAISER: _____

PROJECT: _____

DATE: _____

CLASS OF CONSTRUCTION	RESIDENCE TYPE	CONFIGURATION	EXTERIOR WALL SYSTEM
☐ ECONOMY	☐ 1 STORY	☐ DETACHED	☐ WOOD SIDING - WOOD FRAME
☐ AVERAGE	☐ 1-1/2 STORY	☐ TOWN/ROW HOUSE	☐ BRICK VENEER - WOOD FRAME
☐ CUSTOM	☐ 2 STORY	☐ SEMI-DETACHED	☐ STUCCO ON WOOD FRAME
☐ LUXURY	☐ 2-1/2 STORY		☐ PAINTED CONCRETE BLOCK
	☐ 3 STORY	OCCUPANCY	☐ SOLID MASONRY (AVERAGE & CUSTOM)
	☐ BI-LEVEL	☐ ONE FAMILY	☐ STONE VENEER - WOOD FRAME
	☐ TRI-LEVEL	☐ TWO FAMILY	☐ SOLID BRICK (LUXURY)
		☐ THREE FAMILY	☐ SOLID STONE (LUXURY)
		☐ OTHER _____	

* LIVING AREA (Main Building)		* LIVING AREA (Wing or Ell) ( )		* LIVING AREA (WING or ELL) ( )	
First Level	_____ S.F.	First Level	_____ S.F.	First Level	_____ S.F.
Second level	_____ S.F.	Second level	_____ S.F.	Second level	_____ S.F.
Third Level	_____ S.F.	Third Level	_____ S.F.	Third Level	_____ S.F.
Total	_____ S.F.	Total	_____ S.F.	Total	_____ S.F.

* Basement Area is not part of living area.

MAIN BUILDING	COSTS PER S.F. LIVING AREA
Cost per Square Foot of Living Area, from Page _____	$
Basement Addition: _____ % Finished, _____ % Unfinished	+
Roof Cover Adjustment: _____ Type, Page _____ (Add or Deduct)	( )
Central Air Conditioning: ☐ Separate Ducts ☐ Heating Ducts, Page _____	+
Heating System Adjustment: _____ Type, Page _____ (Add or Deduct)	( )
Main Building: Adjusted Cost per S.F. of Living Area	$

MAIN BUILDING TOTAL COST

$ _____ /S.F. x _____ S.F. x _____ = $ _____

Cost per S.F. Living Area   Living Area   Town/Row House Multiplier (Use 1 for Detached)   TOTAL COST

WING OR ELL ( ) _____ STORY	COSTS PER S.F. LIVING AREA
Cost per Square Foot of Living Area, from Page _____	$
Basement Addition: _____ % Finished, _____ % Unfinished	+
Roof Cover Adjustment: _____ Type, Page _____ (Add or Deduct)	( )
Central Air Conditioning: ☐ Separate Ducts ☐ Heating Ducts, Page _____	+
Heating System Adjustment: _____ Type, Page _____ (Add or Deduct)	( )
Wing or Ell ( ): Adjusted Cost per S.F. of Living Area	$

WING OR ELL ( ) TOTAL COST

$ _____ /S.F. x _____ S.F. x _____ = $ _____

Cost per S.F. Living Area   Living Area   TOTAL COST

WING OR ELL ( ) _____ STORY	COSTS PER S.F. LIVING AREA
Cost per Square Foot of Living Area, from Page _____	$
Basement Addition: _____ % Finished, _____ % Unfinished	+
Roof Cover Adjustment: _____ Type, Page _____ (Add or Deduct)	( )
Central Air Conditioning: ☐ Separate Ducts ☐ Heating Ducts, Page _____	+
Heating System Adjustment: _____ Type, Page _____ (Add or Deduct)	( )
Wing or Ell ( ): Adjusted Cost per S.F. of Living Area	$

WING OR ELL ( ) TOTAL COST

$ _____ /S.F. x _____ S.F. x _____ = $ _____

Cost per S.F. Living Area   Living Area   TOTAL COST

TOTAL THIS PAGE _____

RESIDENTIAL
COST ESTIMATE

		QUANTITY	UNIT COST	$
Total Page 1				$
Additional Bathrooms: _____ Full _____ Half				
Finished Attic: _____ Ft. x _____ Ft.		S.F.		+
Breezeway: ☐ Open ☐ Enclosed _____ Ft. x _____ Ft.		S.F.		+
Covered Porch: ☐ Open ☐ Enclosed _____ Ft. x _____ Ft.		S.F.		+
Fireplace: ☐ Interior Chimney ☐ Exterior Chimney				
☐ No. of Flues ☐ Additional Fireplaces				+
Appliances:				+
Kitchen Cabinets Adjustments: (±)				
☐ Garage ☐ Carport: _____ Car(s) Description _____ (±)				
Miscellaneous:				+

ADJUSTED TOTAL BUILDING COST $ _____

REPLACEMENT COST

ADJUSTED TOTAL BUILDING COST	$	_____
Site Improvements		
(A) Paving & Sidewalks	$	_____
(B) Landscaping	$	_____
(C) Fences	$	_____
(D) Swimming Pools	$	_____
(E) Miscellaneous	$	_____
TOTAL	$	_____
Location Factor	X	_____
Location Replacement Cost	$	_____
Depreciation	- $	_____
LOCAL DEPRECIATED COST	$	_____

INSURANCE COST

ADJUSTED TOTAL BUILDING COST	$	_____
Insurance Exclusions		
(A) Footings, Site work, Underground Piping	- $	_____
(B) Architects Fees	- $	_____
Total Building Cost Less Exclusion	$	_____
Location Factor	X	_____
LOCAL INSURABLE REPLACEMENT COST	$	_____

SKETCH AND ADDITIONAL CALCULATIONS

1 Story

© Home Planners, Inc.

1-1/2 Story

2 Story

Bi-Level

Tri-Level

©Design Basics, Inc.

- **Mass produced from stock plans**
- **Single family — 1 full bath, 1 kitchen**
- **No basement**
- **Asphalt shingles on roof**
- **Hot air heat**
- **Gypsum wallboard interior finishes**
- **Materials and workmanship are sufficient to meet codes**

Note: The illustration shown may contain some optional components (for example: garages and/or fireplaces) whose costs are shown in the modifications, adjustments, & alternatives below or at the end of the square foot section.

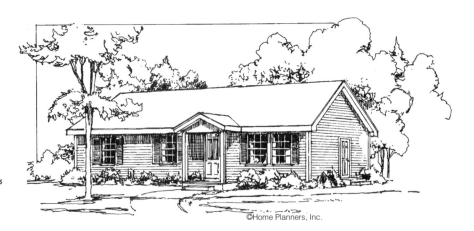

©Home Planners, Inc.

Base cost per square foot of living area

Exterior Wall	Living Area										
	600	800	1000	1200	1400	1600	1800	2000	2400	2800	3200
Wood Siding - Wood Frame	104.15	94.45	87.10	81.05	75.80	72.45	70.90	68.60	63.95	60.60	58.35
Brick Veneer - Wood Frame	113.70	103.00	94.85	88.05	82.15	78.40	76.60	74.00	68.85	65.15	62.60
Stucco on Wood Frame	99.85	90.65	83.60	77.95	72.95	69.80	68.30	66.15	61.75	58.60	56.45
Painted Concrete Block	103.95	94.25	86.95	80.95	75.65	72.30	70.75	68.50	63.85	60.50	58.30
Finished Basement, Add	26.05	24.50	23.35	22.35	21.55	21.00	20.75	20.30	19.70	19.25	18.80
Unfinished Basement, Add	11.80	10.55	9.65	8.85	8.20	7.80	7.55	7.25	6.75	6.35	6.05

Modifications

Add to the total cost

Upgrade Kitchen Cabinets	$ + 727
Solid Surface Countertops	+ 563
Full Bath - including plumbing, wall and floor finishes	+ 4087
Half Bath - including plumbing, wall and floor finishes	+ 2475
One Car Attached Garage	+ 9905
One Car Detached Garage	+ 12,792
Fireplace & Chimney	+ 4670

Adjustments

For multi family - add to total cost

Additional Kitchen	$ + 2975
Additional Bath	+ 4087
Additional Entry & Exit	+ 1512
Separate Heating	+ 1315
Separate Electric	+ 981

For Townhouse/Rowhouse - Multiply cost per square foot by

Inner Unit	+ .95
End Unit	+ .97

Alternatives

Add to or deduct from the cost per square foot of living area

Composition Roll Roofing	– .80
Cedar Shake Roof	+ 3.45
Upgrade Walls and Ceilings to Skim Coat Plaster	+ .61
Upgrade Ceilings to Textured Finish	+ .44
Air Conditioning, in Heating Ductwork	+ 3.09
In Separate Ductwork	+ 5.89
Heating Systems, Hot Water	+ 1.61
Heat Pump	+ 1.95
Electric Heat	– 1.38
Not Heated	– 3.48

Additional upgrades or components

Kitchen Cabinets & Countertops	Page 93
Bathroom Vanities	94
Fireplaces & Chimneys	94
Windows, Skylights & Dormers	94
Appliances	95
Breezeways & Porches	95
Finished Attic	95
Garages	96
Site Improvements	96
Wings & Ells	34

Living Area - 1200 S.F.
Perimeter - 146 L.F.

		Labor-Hours	Cost Per Square Foot Of Living Area		
			Mat.	Labor	Total
1 Site Work	Site preparation for slab; 4' deep trench excavation for foundation wall.	.060		1.02	1.02
2 Foundation	Continuous reinforced concrete footing, 8" deep x 18" wide; dampproofed and insulated 8" thick reinforced concrete block foundation wall, 4' deep; 4" concrete slab on 4" crushed stone base and polyethylene vapor barrier, trowel finish.	.131	5.48	6.20	11.68
3 Framing	Exterior walls - 2" x 4" wood studs, 16" O.C.; 1/2" insulation board sheathing; wood truss roof frame, 24" O.C. with 1/2" plywood sheathing, 4 in 12 pitch.	.098	4.52	5.36	9.88
4 Exterior Walls	Metal lath reinforced stucco exterior on insulated wood frame walls; 6" attic insulation; sliding sash wood windows; 2 flush solid core wood exterior doors with storms.	.110	6.35	5.65	12.00
5 Roofing	20 year asphalt shingles; #15 felt building paper; aluminum gutters, downspouts, drip edge and flashings.	.047	1.34	2.03	3.37
6 Interiors	Walls and ceilings, 1/2" taped and finished gypsum wallboard, primed and painted with 2 coats; painted baseboard and trim; rubber backed carpeting 80%, asphalt tile 20%; hollow core wood interior doors.	.243	8.22	10.45	18.67
7 Specialties	Economy grade kitchen cabinets - 6 L.F. wall and base with plastic laminate counter top and kitchen sink; 30 gallon electric water heater.	.004	1.68	.80	2.48
8 Mechanical	1 lavatory, white, wall hung; 1 water closet, white; 1 bathtub, enameled steel, white; gas fired warm air heat.	.086	3.52	2.94	6.46
9 Electrical	100 Amp. service; romex wiring; incandescent lighting fixtures, switches, receptacles.	.036	.93	1.27	2.20
10 Overhead	Contractor's overhead and profit		4.81	5.38	10.19
	Total		36.85	41.10	**77.95**

- **Mass produced from stock plans**
- **Single family — 1 full bath, 1 kitchen**
- **No basement**
- **Asphalt shingles on roof**
- **Hot air heat**
- **Gypsum wallboard interior finishes**
- **Materials and workmanship are sufficient to meet codes**

Note: The illustration shown may contain some optional components (for example: garages and/or fireplaces) whose costs are shown in the modifications, adjustments, & alternatives below or at the end of the square foot section.

Base cost per square foot of living area

Exterior Wall	Living Area										
	600	800	1000	1200	1400	1600	1800	2000	2400	2800	3200
Wood Siding - Wood Frame	118.45	98.65	88.20	83.35	79.95	74.65	72.10	69.35	63.65	61.55	59.25
Brick Veneer - Wood Frame	131.85	108.35	97.20	91.80	87.95	81.90	79.00	75.95	69.40	67.05	64.35
Stucco on Wood Frame	112.50	94.35	84.20	79.65	76.40	71.40	69.05	66.45	61.05	59.10	57.00
Painted Concrete Block	118.20	98.50	88.00	83.20	79.80	74.50	71.95	69.25	63.55	61.45	59.15
Finished Basement, Add	20.10	17.05	16.25	15.65	15.25	14.65	14.30	14.00	13.35	13.00	12.75
Unfinished Basement, Add	10.35	7.95	7.30	6.90	6.50	6.05	5.75	5.55	5.00	4.80	4.55

Modifications

Add to the total cost

Upgrade Kitchen Cabinets	$ + 727
Solid Surface Countertops	+ 563
Full Bath - including plumbing, wall and floor finishes	+ 4087
Half Bath - including plumbing, wall and floor finishes	+ 2475
One Car Attached Garage	+ 9905
One Car Detached Garage	+ 12,792
Fireplace & Chimney	+ 4670

Adjustments

For multi family - add to total cost

Additional Kitchen	$ + 2975
Additional Bath	+ 4087
Additional Entry & Exit	+ 1512
Separate Heating	+ 1315
Separate Electric	+ 981

For Townhouse/Rowhouse - Multiply cost per square foot by

Inner Unit	+ .95
End Unit	+ .97

Alternatives

Add to or deduct from the cost per square foot of living area

Composition Roll Roofing	– .55
Cedar Shake Roof	+ 2.50
Upgrade Walls and Ceilings to Skim Coat Plaster	+ .61
Upgrade Ceilings to Textured Finish	+ .44
Air Conditioning, in Heating Ductwork	+ 2.31
In Separate Ductwork	+ 5.18
Heating Systems, Hot Water	+ 1.54
Heat Pump	+ 2.15
Electric Heat	– 1.10
Not Heated	– 3.20

Additional upgrades or components

Kitchen Cabinets & Countertops	Page 77
Bathroom Vanities	78
Fireplaces & Chimneys	78
Windows, Skylights & Dormers	78
Appliances	79
Breezeways & Porches	79
Finished Attic	79
Garages	80
Site Improvements	80
Wings & Ells	24

		Labor-Hours	Cost Per Square Foot Of Living Area		
			Mat.	Labor	Total
1 Site Work	Site preparation for slab; 4' deep trench excavation for foundation wall.	.041		.77	.77
2 Foundation	Continuous reinforced concrete footing, 8" deep x 18" wide; dampproofed and insulated 8" thick reinforced concrete block foundation wall, 4' deep; 4" concrete slab on 4" crushed stone base and polyethylene vapor barrier, trowel finish.	.073	3.66	4.21	7.87
3 Framing	Exterior walls - 2" x 4" wood studs, 16" O.C.; 1/2" insulation board sheathing; 2" x 6" rafters, 16" O.C. with 1/2" plywood sheathing, 8 in 12 pitch; 2" x 8" floor joists 16" O.C. with bridging and 5/8" plywood subfloor.	.090	4.44	6.00	10.44
4 Exterior Walls	Beveled wood siding and building paper on insulated wood frame walls; 6" attic insulation; double hung windows; 2 flush solid core wood exterior doors with storms.	.077	9.78	4.47	14.25
5 Roofing	20 year asphalt shingles; #15 felt building paper; aluminum gutters, downspouts, drip edge and flashings.	.029	.84	1.27	2.11
6 Interiors	Walls and ceilings, 1/2" taped and finished gypsum wallboard, primed and painted with 2 coats; painted baseboard and trim; rubber backed carpeting 80%, asphalt tile 20%; hollow core wood interior doors.	.204	9.00	11.08	20.08
7 Specialties	Economy grade kitchen cabinets - 6 L.F. wall and base with plastic laminate counter top and kitchen sink; 30 gallon electric water heater.	.020	1.27	.60	1.87
8 Mechanical	1 lavatory, white, wall hung; 1 water closet, white; 1 bathtub, enameled steel, white; gas fired warm air heat.	.079	2.91	2.63	5.54
9 Electrical	100 Amp. service; romex wiring; incandescent lighting fixtures, switches, receptacles.	.033	.84	1.14	1.98
10 Overhead	Contractor's overhead and profit.		4.91	4.83	9.74
	Total		37.65	37.00	**74.65**

- **Mass produced from stock plans**
- **Single family — 1 full bath, 1 kitchen**
- **No basement**
- **Asphalt shingles on roof**
- **Hot air heat**
- **Gypsum wallboard interior finishes**
- **Materials and workmanship are sufficient to meet codes**

Note: The illustration shown may contain some optional components (for example: garages and/or fireplaces) whose costs are shown in the modifications, adjustments, & alternatives below or at the end of the square foot section.

Base cost per square foot of living area

Exterior Wall	Living Area										
	1000	1200	1400	1600	1800	2000	2200	2600	3000	3400	3800
Wood Siding - Wood Frame	93.70	84.65	80.60	77.80	75.10	71.70	69.55	65.55	61.45	59.65	58.10
Brick Veneer - Wood Frame	104.10	94.25	89.60	86.35	83.15	79.45	76.95	72.20	67.60	65.55	63.70
Stucco on Wood Frame	89.10	80.40	76.60	74.00	71.45	68.20	66.30	62.50	58.65	57.10	55.65
Painted Concrete Block	93.60	84.50	80.40	77.65	74.95	71.55	69.40	65.40	61.30	59.60	58.05
Finished Basement, Add	13.65	13.05	12.55	12.25	11.90	11.70	11.45	11.05	10.70	10.45	10.25
Unfinished Basement, Add	6.35	5.85	5.55	5.25	5.05	4.85	4.65	4.30	4.00	3.85	3.70

Modifications

Add to the total cost

Upgrade Kitchen Cabinets	$ + 727
Solid Surface Countertops	+ 563
Full Bath - including plumbing, wall and floor finishes	+ 4087
Half Bath - including plumbing, wall and floor finishes	+ 2475
One Car Attached Garage	+ 9905
One Car Detached Garage	+ 12,792
Fireplace & Chimney	+ 5160

Adjustments

For multi family - add to total cost

Additional Kitchen	$ + 2975
Additional Bath	+ 4087
Additional Entry & Exit	+ 1512
Separate Heating	+ 1315
Separate Electric	+ 981

For Townhouse/Rowhouse - Multiply cost per square foot by

Inner Unit	+ .93
End Unit	+ .96

Alternatives

Add to or deduct from the cost per square foot of living area

Composition Roll Roofing	– .40
Cedar Shake Roof	+ 1.75
Upgrade Walls and Ceilings to Skim Coat Plaster	+ .62
Upgrade Ceilings to Textured Finish	+ .44
Air Conditioning, in Heating Ductwork	+ 1.87
In Separate Ductwork	+ 4.74
Heating Systems, Hot Water	+ 1.50
Heat Pump	+ 2.28
Electric Heat	– .96
Not Heated	– 3.02

Additional upgrades or components

Kitchen Cabinets & Countertops	Page 77
Bathroom Vanities	78
Fireplaces & Chimneys	78
Windows, Skylights & Dormers	78
Appliances	79
Breezeways & Porches	79
Finished Attic	79
Garages	80
Site Improvements	80
Wings & Ells	24

		Labor-Hours	Cost Per Square Foot Of Living Area		
			Mat.	Labor	Total
1 Site Work	Site preparation for slab; 4' deep trench excavation for foundation wall.	.034		.61	.61
2 Foundation	Continuous reinforced concrete footing, 8" deep x 18" wide; dampproofed and insulated 8" thick reinforced concrete block foundation wall, 4' deep; 4" concrete slab on 4" crushed stone base and polyethylene vapor barrier, trowel finish.	.069	2.93	3.37	6.30
3 Framing	Exterior walls - 2" x 4" wood studs, 16" O.C.; 1/2" insulation board sheathing; wood truss roof frame, 24" O.C. with 1/2" plywood sheathing, 4 in 12 pitch; 2" x 8" floor joists 16" O.C. with bridging and 5/8" plywood subfloor.	.112	4.48	6.29	10.77
4 Exterior Walls	Beveled wood siding and building paper on insulated wood frame walls; 6" attic insulation; double hung windows; 2 flush solid core wood exterior doors with storms.	.107	10.01	4.57	14.58
5 Roofing	20 year asphalt shingles; #15 felt building paper; aluminum gutters, downspouts, drip edge and flashings.	.024	.67	1.02	1.69
6 Interiors	Walls and ceilings, 1/2" taped and finished gypsum wallboard, primed and painted with 2 coats; painted baseboard and trim; rubber backed carpeting 80%, asphalt tile 20%; hollow core wood interior doors.	.219	8.96	11.10	20.06
7 Specialties	Economy grade kitchen cabinets - 6 L.F. wall and base with plastic laminate counter top and kitchen sink; 30 gallon electric water heater.	.017	1.01	.48	1.49
8 Mechanical	1 lavatory, white, wall hung; 1 water closet, white; 1 bathtub, enameled steel, white; gas fired warm air heat.	.061	2.52	2.45	4.97
9 Electrical	100 Amp. service; romex wiring; incandescent lighting fixtures; switches, receptacles.	.030	.80	1.07	1.87
10 Overhead	Contractor's overhead and profit		4.72	4.64	9.36
	Total		36.10	35.60	**71.70**

- **Mass produced from stock plans**
- **Single family — 1 full bath, 1 kitchen**
- **No basement**
- **Asphalt shingles on roof**
- **Hot air heat**
- **Gypsum wallboard interior finishes**
- **Materials and workmanship are sufficient to meet codes**

Note: The illustration shown may contain some optional components (for example: garages and/or fireplaces) whose costs are shown in the modifications, adjustments, & alternatives below or at the end of the square foot section.

Base cost per square foot of living area

Exterior Wall	Living Area										
	1000	1200	1400	1600	1800	2000	2200	2600	3000	3400	3800
Wood Siding - Wood Frame	87.05	78.50	74.80	72.30	69.85	66.65	64.75	61.20	57.45	55.90	54.50
Brick Veneer - Wood Frame	94.85	85.70	81.55	78.70	75.90	72.50	70.35	66.20	62.10	60.35	58.75
Stucco on Wood Frame	83.55	75.25	71.80	69.40	67.20	64.05	62.35	59.00	55.35	53.95	52.65
Painted Concrete Block	86.90	78.30	74.70	72.15	69.75	66.55	64.70	61.10	57.35	55.85	54.45
Finished Basement, Add	13.65	13.05	12.55	12.25	11.90	11.70	11.45	11.05	10.70	10.45	10.25
Unfinished Basement, Add	6.35	5.85	5.55	5.25	5.05	4.85	4.65	4.30	4.00	3.85	3.70

Modifications

Add to the total cost

Upgrade Kitchen Cabinets	$ + 727
Solid Surface Countertops	+ 563
Full Bath - including plumbing, wall and floor finishes	+ 4087
Half Bath - including plumbing, wall and floor finishes	+ 2475
One Car Attached Garage	+ 9905
One Car Detached Garage	+ 12,792
Fireplace & Chimney	+ 4670

Adjustments

For multi family - add to total cost

Additional Kitchen	$ + 2975
Additional Bath	+ 4087
Additional Entry & Exit	+ 1512
Separate Heating	+ 1315
Separate Electric	+ 981

For Townhouse/Rowhouse - Multiply cost per square foot by

Inner Unit	+ .94
End Unit	+ .97

Alternatives

Add to or deduct from the cost per square foot of living area

Composition Roll Roofing	– .40
Cedar Shake Roof	+ 1.75
Upgrade Walls and Ceilings to Skim Coat Plaster	+ .59
Upgrade Ceilings to Textured Finish	+ .44
Air Conditioning, in Heating Ductwork	+ 1.87
In Separate Ductwork	+ 4.74
Heating Systems, Hot Water	+ 1.50
Heat Pump	+ 2.28
Electric Heat	– .96
Not Heated	– 3.02

Additional upgrades or components

Kitchen Cabinets & Countertops	Page 77
Bathroom Vanities	78
Fireplaces & Chimneys	78
Windows, Skylights & Dormers	78
Appliances	79
Breezeways & Porches	79
Finished Attic	79
Garages	80
Site Improvements	80
Wings & Ells	24

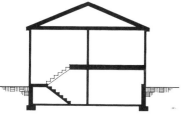

Living Area - 2000 S.F.
Perimeter - 135 L.F.

		Labor-Hours	Cost Per Square Foot Of Living Area		
			Mat.	Labor	Total
1 Site Work	Excavation for lower level, 4' deep. Site preparation for slab.	.029		.61	.61
2 Foundation	Continuous reinforced concrete footing, 8" deep x 18" wide; dampproofed and insulated 8" thick reinforced concrete block foundation wall, 4' deep; 4" concrete slab on 4" crushed stone base and polyethylene vapor barrier, trowel finish.	.069	2.93	3.37	6.30
3 Framing	Exterior walls - 2" x 4" wood studs, 16" O.C.; 1/2" insulation board sheathing; wood truss roof frame, 24" O.C. with 1/2" plywood sheathing, 4 in 12 pitch; 2" x 8" floor joists 16" O.C. with bridging and 5/8" plywood subfloor.	.107	4.21	5.92	10.13
4 Exterior Walls	Beveled wood siding and building paper on insulated wood frame walls; 6" attic insulation; double hung windows; 2 flush solid core wood exterior doors with storms.	.089	7.82	3.58	11.40
5 Roofing	20 year asphalt shingles; #15 felt building paper; aluminum gutters, downspouts, drip edge and flashings.	.024	.67	1.02	1.69
6 Interiors	Walls and ceilings, 1/2" taped and finished gypsum wallboard, primed and painted with 2 coats; painted baseboard and trim, rubber backed carpeting 80%, asphalt tile 20%; hollow core wood interior doors.	.213	8.75	10.74	19.49
7 Specialties	Economy grade kitchen cabinets - 6 L.F. wall and base with plastic laminate counter top and kitchen sink; 30 gallon electric water heater.	.018	1.01	.48	1.49
8 Mechanical	1 lavatory, white, wall hung; 1 water closet, white; 1 bathtub, enameled steel, white; gas fired warm air heat.	.061	2.52	2.45	4.97
9 Electrical	100 Amp. service; romex wiring; incandescent lighting fixtures; switches, receptacles.	.030	.80	1.07	1.87
10 Overhead	Contractor's overhead and profit.		4.29	4.41	8.70
	Total	33.00	33.65		66.65

- **Mass produced from stock plans**
- **Single family — 1 full bath, 1 kitchen**
- **No basement**
- **Asphalt shingles on roof**
- **Hot air heat**
- **Gypsum wallboard interior finishes**
- **Materials and workmanship are sufficient to meet codes**

Note: The illustration shown may contain some optional components (for example: garages and/or fireplaces) whose costs are shown in the modifications, adjustments, & alternatives below or at the end of the square foot section.

©Design Basics, Inc.

Base cost per square foot of living area

Exterior Wall	Living Area										
	1200	1500	1800	2000	2200	2400	2800	3200	3600	4000	4400
Wood Siding - Wood Frame	80.40	73.95	69.10	67.10	64.20	61.90	60.15	57.70	54.75	53.75	51.50
Brick Veneer - Wood Frame	87.50	80.40	74.95	72.65	69.45	66.85	64.90	62.10	58.85	57.75	55.20
Stucco on Wood Frame	77.20	71.05	66.50	64.60	61.80	59.70	58.00	55.70	52.95	52.00	49.80
Solid Masonry	80.25	73.85	69.00	67.00	64.05	61.80	60.10	57.55	54.65	53.70	51.45
Finished Basement, Add*	16.30	15.55	14.90	14.65	14.30	14.00	13.75	13.45	13.10	13.00	12.75
Unfinished Basement, Add*	7.05	6.45	5.90	5.70	5.45	5.20	5.00	4.75	4.50	4.40	4.20

*Basement under middle level only.

Modifications

Add to the total cost

Upgrade Kitchen Cabinets	$ + 727
Solid Surface Countertops	+ 563
Full Bath - including plumbing, wall and floor finishes	+ 4087
Half Bath - including plumbing, wall and floor finishes	+ 2475
One Car Attached Garage	+ 9905
One Car Detached Garage	+ 12,792
Fireplace & Chimney	+ 4670

Adjustments

For multi family - add to total cost

Additional Kitchen	$ + 2975
Additional Bath	+ 4087
Additional Entry & Exit	+ 1512
Separate Heating	+ 1315
Separate Electric	+ 981

For Townhouse/Rowhouse - Multiply cost per square foot by

Inner Unit	+ .93
End Unit	+ .96

Alternatives

Add to or deduct from the cost per square foot of living area

Composition Roll Roofing	– .55
Cedar Shake Roof	+ 2.50
Upgrade Walls and Ceilings to Skim Coat Plaster	+ .53
Upgrade Ceilings to Textured Finish	+ .44
Air Conditioning, in Heating Ductwork	+ 1.60
In Separate Ductwork	+ 4.41
Heating Systems, Hot Water	+ 1.43
Heat Pump	+ 2.37
Electric Heat	– .83
Not Heated	– 2.93

Additional upgrades or components

Kitchen Cabinets & Countertops	Page 77
Bathroom Vanities	78
Fireplaces & Chimneys	78
Windows, Skylights & Dormers	78
Appliances	79
Breezeways & Porches	79
Finished Attic	79
Garages	80
Site Improvements	80
Wings & Ells	24

Important: See the Reference Section for Location Factors (to adjust for your city) and Estimating Forms

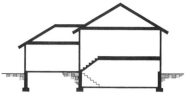

		Labor-Hours	Cost Per Square Foot Of Living Area		
			Mat.	Labor	Total
1 Site Work	Site preparation for slab; 4' deep trench excavation for foundation wall, excavation for lower level, 4' deep.	.027		.51	.51
2 Foundation	Continuous reinforced concrete footing, 8" deep x 18" wide; dampproofed and insulated 8" thick reinforced concrete block foundation wall, 4' deep; 4" concrete slab on 4" crushed stone base and polyethylene vapor barrier, trowel finish.	.071	3.32	3.65	6.97
3 Framing	Exterior walls - 2" x 4" wood studs, 16" O.C.; 1/2" insulation board sheathing; wood truss roof frame, 24" O.C. with 1/2" plywood sheathing, 4 in 12 pitch; 2" x 8" floor joists 16" O.C. with bridging and 5/8" plywood subfloor.	.094	4.03	5.32	9.35
4 Exterior Walls	Beveled wood siding and building paper on insulated wood frame walls; 6" attic insulation; double hung windows; 2 flush solid core wood exterior doors with storms.	.081	6.78	3.09	9.87
5 Roofing	20 year asphalt shingles; #15 felt building paper; aluminum gutters, downspouts, drip edge and flashings.	.032	.89	1.35	2.24
6 Interiors	Walls and ceilings, 1/2" taped and finished gypsum wallboard, primed and painted with 2 coats; painted baseboard and trim, rubber backed carpeting 80%, asphalt tile 20%; hollow core wood interior doors.	.177	7.69	9.55	17.24
7 Specialties	Economy grade kitchen cabinets - 6 L.F. wall and base with plastic laminate counter top and kitchen sink; 30 gallon electric water heater.	.014	.85	.41	1.26
8 Mechanical	1 lavatory, white, wall hung; 1 water closet, white; 1 bathtub, enameled steel, white; gas fired warm air heat.	.057	2.28	2.32	4.60
9 Electrical	100 Amp. service; romex wiring; incandescent lighting fixtures, switches, receptacles.	.029	.76	1.01	1.77
10 Overhead	Contractor's overhead and profit		4.00	4.09	8.09
	Total		30.60	31.30	**61.90**

1 Story — Base cost per square foot of living area

Exterior Wall	Living Area							
	50	100	200	300	400	500	600	700
Wood Siding - Wood Frame	145.25	110.45	95.30	79.25	74.35	71.35	69.35	69.95
Brick Veneer - Wood Frame	169.40	127.75	109.70	88.85	82.95	79.45	77.05	77.35
Stucco on Wood Frame	134.45	102.75	88.90	74.95	70.50	67.75	65.95	66.65
Painted Concrete Block	144.85	110.15	95.05	79.10	74.15	71.25	69.25	69.80
Finished Basement, Add	40.20	32.65	29.55	24.35	23.30	22.70	22.25	21.95
Unfinished Basement, Add	22.60	16.75	14.35	10.30	9.50	9.00	8.70	8.45

1-1/2 Story — Base cost per square foot of living area

Exterior Wall	Living Area							
	100	200	300	400	500	600	700	800
Wood Siding - Wood Frame	114.65	92.05	78.15	69.95	65.75	63.80	61.20	60.45
Brick Veneer - Wood Frame	136.20	109.25	92.55	81.15	76.15	73.55	70.45	69.70
Stucco on Wood Frame	105.00	84.30	71.75	64.95	61.15	59.45	57.10	56.40
Painted Concrete Block	114.25	91.70	77.85	69.70	65.60	63.60	61.05	60.35
Finished Basement, Add	26.80	23.65	21.55	19.25	18.65	18.20	17.85	17.80
Unfinished Basement, Add	13.90	11.50	9.85	8.10	7.60	7.30	6.95	6.95

2 Story — Base cost per square foot of living area

Exterior Wall	Living Area							
	100	200	400	600	800	1000	1200	1400
Wood Siding - Wood Frame	116.60	86.50	73.30	60.50	56.20	53.60	51.90	52.65
Brick Veneer - Wood Frame	140.75	103.75	87.65	70.10	64.80	61.65	59.55	60.05
Stucco on Wood Frame	105.80	78.80	66.85	56.20	52.35	50.00	48.50	49.35
Painted Concrete Block	116.15	86.20	73.00	60.30	56.05	53.50	51.80	52.55
Finished Basement, Add	20.10	16.35	14.80	12.15	11.65	11.35	11.15	10.95
Unfinished Basement, Add	11.30	8.40	7.20	5.15	4.80	4.55	4.35	4.25

Base costs do not include bathroom or kitchen facilities. Use Modifications/Adjustments/Alternatives on pages 77-80 where appropriate.

1 Story

1-1/2 Story

2 Story

2-1/2 Story

Bi-Level

Tri-Level

- **Simple design from standard plans**
- **Single family — 1 full bath, 1 kitchen**
- **No basement**
- **Asphalt shingles on roof**
- **Hot air heat**
- **Gypsum wallboard interior finishes**
- **Materials and workmanship are average**

Note: The illustration shown may contain some optional components (for example: garages and/or fireplaces) whose costs are shown in the modifications, adjustments, & alternatives below or at the end of the square foot section.

©Home Planners, Inc.

Base cost per square foot of living area

Exterior Wall	Living Area										
	600	800	1000	1200	1400	1600	1800	2000	2400	2800	3200
Wood Siding - Wood Frame	126.20	114.55	105.80	98.80	92.80	88.85	86.90	84.30	79.00	75.20	72.70
Brick Veneer - Wood Frame	146.95	134.20	124.60	116.75	110.05	105.70	103.45	100.55	94.65	90.45	87.55
Stucco on Wood Frame	134.60	123.20	114.60	107.75	101.85	97.95	96.00	93.50	88.30	84.55	82.05
Solid Masonry	162.45	148.05	137.15	128.05	120.35	115.35	112.75	109.25	102.65	97.85	94.35
Finished Basement, Add	31.85	30.75	29.25	27.90	26.85	26.15	25.80	25.15	24.40	23.75	23.25
Unfinished Basement, Add	13.30	12.00	11.10	10.25	9.60	9.20	8.90	8.55	8.10	7.70	7.40

Modifications

Add to the total cost

Upgrade Kitchen Cabinets	$ + 3248
Solid Surface Countertops (Included)	
Full Bath - including plumbing, wall and floor finishes	+ 5129
Half Bath - including plumbing, wall and floor finishes	+ 3107
One Car Attached Garage	+ 11,173
One Car Detached Garage	+ 14,818
Fireplace & Chimney	+ 4655

Adjustments

For multi family - add to total cost

Additional Kitchen	$ + 5771
Additional Bath	+ 5129
Additional Entry & Exit	+ 1512
Separate Heating	+ 1315
Separate Electric	+ 1766

For Townhouse/Rowhouse - Multiply cost per square foot by

Inner Unit	+ .92
End Unit	+ .96

Alternatives

Add to or deduct from the cost per square foot of living area

Cedar Shake Roof	+ 3.15
Clay Tile Roof	+ 4.75
Slate Roof	+ 6.05
Upgrade Walls to Skim Coat Plaster	+ .38
Upgrade Ceilings to Textured Finish	+ .44
Air Conditioning, in Heating Ductwork	+ 3.19
In Separate Ductwork	+ 6.11
Heating Systems, Hot Water	+ 1.65
Heat Pump	+ 2.03
Electric Heat	– .77
Not Heated	– 2.90

Additional upgrades or components

Kitchen Cabinets & Countertops	Page 77
Bathroom Vanities	78
Fireplaces & Chimneys	78
Windows, Skylights & Dormers	78
Appliances	79
Breezeways & Porches	79
Finished Attic	79
Garages	80
Site Improvements	80
Wings & Ells	44

Important: See the Reference Section for Location Factors (to adjust for your city) and Estimating Forms

Average 1 Story

Living Area - 1600 S.F.
Perimeter - 163 L.F.

		Labor-Hours	Cost Per Square Foot Of Living Area		
			Mat.	Labor	Total
1 Site Work	Site preparation for slab; 4' deep trench excavation for foundation wall.	.048		.79	.79
2 Foundation	Continuous reinforced concrete footing 8" deep x 18" wide; dampproofed and insulated reinforced concrete foundation wall, 8" thick, 4' deep; 4" concrete slab on 4" crushed stone base and polyethylene vapor barrier, trowel finish.	.113	5.11	5.65	10.76
3 Framing	Exterior walls - 2" x 4" wood studs, 16" O.C.; 1/2" plywood sheathing; 2" x 6" rafters 16" O.C. with 1/2" plywood sheathing, 4 in 12 pitch; 2" x 6" ceiling joists 16" O.C.; 1/2" plywood subfloor on 1" x 2" wood sleepers 16" O.C.	.136	5.25	7.92	13.17
4 Exterior Walls	Beveled wood siding and building paper on insulated wood frame walls; 6" attic insulation; double hung windows; 3 flush solid core wood exterior doors with storms.	.098	9.18	4.18	13.36
5 Roofing	25 year asphalt shingles; #15 felt building paper; aluminum gutters, downspouts, drip edge and flashings.	.047	1.38	2.08	3.46
6 Interiors	Walls and ceilings, 1/2" taped and finished gypsum wallboard, primed and painted with 2 coats; painted baseboard and trim, finished hardwood floor 40%, carpet with 1/2" underlayment 40%, vinyl tile with 1/2" underlayment 15%, ceramic tile with 1/2" underlayment 5%; hollow core and louvered	.251	11.64	11.06	22.70
7 Specialties	Average grade kitchen cabinets - 14 L.F. wall and base with solid surface counter top and kitchen sink; 40 gallon electric water heater.	.009	2.16	.95	3.11
8 Mechanical	1 lavatory, white, wall hung; 1 water closet, white; 1 bathtub with shower, enameled steel, white; gas fired warm air heat.	.098	3.08	2.69	5.77
9 Electrical	200 Amp. service; romex wiring; incandescent lighting fixtures, switches, receptacles.	.041	1.26	1.57	2.83
10 Overhead	Contractor's overhead and profit and plans.		6.64	6.26	12.90
	Total		45.70	43.15	**88.85**

- **Simple design from standard plans**
- **Single family — 1 full bath, 1 kitchen**
- **No basement**
- **Asphalt shingles on roof**
- **Hot air heat**
- **Gypsum wallboard interior finishes**
- **Materials and workmanship are average**

Note: The illustration shown may contain some optional components (for example: garages and/or fireplaces) whose costs are shown in the modifications, adjustments, & alternatives below or at the end of the square foot section.

©By Designer

Base cost per square foot of living area

Exterior Wall	Living Area										
	600	800	1000	1200	1400	1600	1800	2000	2400	2800	3200
Wood Siding - Wood Frame	141.10	118.60	106.35	100.70	96.75	90.60	87.70	84.50	78.05	75.65	73.10
Brick Veneer - Wood Frame	155.80	129.20	116.20	109.95	105.55	98.65	95.30	91.75	84.45	81.65	78.60
Stucco on Wood Frame	138.55	116.70	104.65	99.15	95.20	89.25	86.40	83.25	77.00	74.60	72.10
Solid Masonry	177.35	144.90	130.75	123.55	118.45	110.40	106.45	102.30	93.80	90.55	86.85
Finished Basement, Add	26.15	22.80	21.80	21.00	20.45	19.65	19.20	18.80	17.95	17.60	17.15
Unfinished Basement, Add	11.45	9.00	8.35	7.85	7.50	7.05	6.75	6.50	6.00	5.75	5.45

Modifications

Add to the total cost

Upgrade Kitchen Cabinets	$ + 3248
Solid Surface Countertops (Included)	
Full Bath - including plumbing, wall and floor finishes	+ 5129
Half Bath - including plumbing, wall and floor finishes	+ 3107
One Car Attached Garage	+ 11,173
One Car Detached Garage	+ 14,818
Fireplace & Chimney	+ 4655

Adjustments

For multi family - add to total cost

Additional Kitchen	$ + 5771
Additional Bath	+ 5129
Additional Entry & Exit	+ 1512
Separate Heating	+ 1315
Separate Electric	+ 1766

For Townhouse/Rowhouse - Multiply cost per square foot by

Inner Unit	+ .92
End Unit	+ .96

Alternatives

Add to or deduct from the cost per square foot of living area

Cedar Shake Roof	+ 2.30
Clay Tile Roof	+ 3.40
Slate Roof	+ 4.35
Upgrade Walls to Skim Coat Plaster	+ .43
Upgrade Ceilings to Textured Finish	+ .44
Air Conditioning, in Heating Ductwork	+ 2.43
In Separate Ductwork	+ 5.34
Heating Systems, Hot Water	+ 1.56
Heat Pump	+ 2.25
Electric Heat	- .69
Not Heated	- 2.79

Additional upgrades or components

Important: See the Reference Section for Location Factors (to adjust for your city) and Estimating Forms

Average 1-1/2 Story

Living Area - 1800 S.F.
Perimeter - 144 L.F.

		Labor-Hours	Cost Per Square Foot Of Living Area		
			Mat.	Labor	Total
1 Site Work	Site preparation for slab; 4' deep trench excavation for foundation wall.	.037		.70	.70
2 Foundation	Continuous reinforced concrete footing 8" deep x 18" wide; dampproofed and insulated reinforced concrete foundation wall, 8" thick, 4' deep; 4" concrete slab on 4" crushed stone base and polyethylene vapor barrier, trowel finish.	.073	3.63	4.15	7.78
3 Framing	Exterior walls - 2" x 4" wood studs, 16" O.C.; 1/2" plywood sheathing; 2" x 6" rafters 16" O.C. with 1/2" plywood sheathing, 8 in 12 pitch; 2" x 8" floor joists 16" O.C. with 5/8" plywood subfloor; 1/2" plywood subfloor on 1" x 2" wood sleepers 16" O.C.	.098	5.81	7.39	13.20
4 Exterior Walls	Beveled wood siding and building paper on insulated wood frame walls; 6" attic insulation; double hung windows; 3 flush solid core wood exterior doors with storms.	.078	9.98	4.53	14.51
5 Roofing	25 year asphalt shingles; #15 felt building paper; aluminum gutters, downspouts, drip edge and flashings.	.029	.86	1.31	2.17
6 Interiors	Walls and ceilings, 1/2" taped and finished gypsum wallboard, primed and painted with 2 coats; painted baseboard and trim, finished hardwood floor 40%, carpet with 1/2" underlayment 40%, vinyl tile with 1/2" underlayment 15%, ceramic tile with 1/2" underlayment 5%; hollow core and louvered	.225	13.23	12.43	25.66
7 Specialties	Average grade kitchen cabinets - 14 L.F. wall and base with solid surface counter top and kitchen sink; 40 gallon electric water heater.	.022	1.92	.84	2.76
8 Mechanical	1 lavatory, white, wall hung; 1 water closet, white; 1 bathtub with shower, enameled steel, white; gas fired warm air heat.	.049	2.85	2.60	5.45
9 Electrical	200 Amp. service; romex wiring; incandescent lighting fixtures, switches, receptacles.	.039	1.21	1.50	2.71
10 Overhead	Contractor's overhead and profit and plans.		6.71	6.05	12.76
	Total		46.20	41.50	**87.70**

- **Simple design from standard plans**
- **Single family — 1 full bath, 1 kitchen**
- **No basement**
- **Asphalt shingles on roof**
- **Hot air heat**
- **Gypsum wallboard interior finishes**
- **Materials and workmanship are average**

Note: The illustration shown may contain some optional components (for example: garages and/or fireplaces) whose costs are shown in the modifications, adjustments, & alternatives below or at the end of the square foot section.

Base cost per square foot of living area

Exterior Wall	Living Area										
	1000	1200	1400	1600	1800	2000	2200	2600	3000	3400	3800
Wood Siding - Wood Frame	112.25	101.80	97.05	93.80	90.50	86.80	84.40	79.75	75.20	73.20	71.35
Brick Veneer - Wood Frame	123.60	112.30	106.90	103.20	99.40	95.30	92.55	87.10	81.90	79.60	77.45
Stucco on Wood Frame	110.25	99.95	95.40	92.15	89.00	85.30	83.00	78.50	74.00	72.05	70.30
Solid Masonry	140.30	127.80	121.35	117.05	112.40	107.85	104.40	97.90	91.90	89.10	86.50
Finished Basement, Add	18.40	18.15	17.60	17.20	16.80	16.50	16.10	15.55	15.10	14.85	14.55
Unfinished Basement, Add	7.30	6.80	6.40	6.15	5.90	5.70	5.50	5.10	4.85	4.65	4.55

Modifications

Add to the total cost

Upgrade Kitchen Cabinets	$ + 3248
Solid Surface Countertops (Included)	
Full Bath - including plumbing, wall and floor finishes	+ 5129
Half Bath - including plumbing, wall and floor finishes	+ 3107
One Car Attached Garage	+ 11,173
One Car Detached Garage	+ 14,818
Fireplace & Chimney	+ 5190

Adjustments

For multi family - add to total cost

Additional Kitchen	$ + 5771
Additional Bath	+ 5129
Additional Entry & Exit	+ 1512
Separate Heating	+ 1315
Separate Electric	+ 1766

For Townhouse/Rowhouse - Multiply cost per square foot by

Inner Unit	+ .90
End Unit	+ .95

Alternatives

Add to or deduct from the cost per square foot of living area

Cedar Shake Roof	+ 1.60
Clay Tile Roof	+ 2.35
Slate Roof	+ 3.05
Upgrade Walls to Skim Coat Plaster	+ .45
Upgrade Ceilings to Textured Finish	+ .44
Air Conditioning, in Heating Ductwork	+ 1.93
In Separate Ductwork	+ 4.85
Heating Systems, Hot Water	+ 1.53
Heat Pump	+ 2.37
Electric Heat	– .61
Not Heated	– 2.71

Additional upgrades or components

Kitchen Cabinets & Countertops	Page 77
Bathroom Vanities	78
Fireplaces & Chimneys	78
Windows, Skylights & Dormers	78
Appliances	79
Breezeways & Porches	79
Finished Attic	79
Garages	80
Site Improvements	80
Wings & Ells	44

Important: See the Reference Section for Location Factors (to adjust for your city) and Estimating Forms

		Labor-Hours	Cost Per Square Foot Of Living Area		
			Mat.	Labor	Total
1 Site Work	Site preparation for slab; 4' deep trench excavation for foundation wall.	.034		.63	.63
2 Foundation	Continuous reinforced concrete footing 8" deep x 18" wide; dampproofed and insulated reinforced concrete foundation wall, 8" thick, 4' deep, 4" concrete slab on 4" crushed stone base and polyethylene vapor barrier, trowel finish.	.066	3.01	3.46	6.47
3 Framing	Exterior walls - 2" x 4" wood studs, 16" O.C.; 1/2" plywood sheathing; 2" x 6" rafters 16" O.C. with 1/2" plywood sheathing, 4 in 12 pitch; 2" x 6" ceiling joists 16" O.C.; 2" x 8" floor joists 16" O.C. with 5/8" plywood subfloor; 1/2" plywood subfloor on 1" x 2" wood sleepers 16" O.C.	.131	6.11	7.65	13.76
4 Exterior Walls	Beveled wood siding and building paper on insulated wood frame walls; 6" attic insulation; double hung windows; 3 flush solid core wood exterior doors with storms.	.111	10.88	4.91	15.79
5 Roofing	25 year asphalt shingles; #15 felt building paper; aluminum gutters, downspouts, drip edge and flashings.	.024	.69	1.05	1.74
6 Interiors	Walls and ceilings, 1/2" taped and finished gypsum wallboard, primed and painted with 2 coats; painted baseboard and trim, finished hardwood floor 40%, carpet with 1/2" underlayment 40%, vinyl tile with 1/2" underlayment 15%, ceramic tile with 1/2" underlayment 5%; hollow core and louvered	.232	13.11	12.42	25.53
7 Specialties	Average grade kitchen cabinets - 14 L.F. wall and base with solid surface counter top and kitchen sink; 40 gallon electric water heater.	.021	1.73	.77	2.50
8 Mechanical	1 lavatory, white, wall hung; 1 water closet, white; 1 bathtub with shower; enameled steel, white; gas fired warm air heat.	.060	2.67	2.50	5.17
9 Electrical	200 Amp. service; romex wiring; incandescent lighting fixtures, switches, receptacles.	.039	1.16	1.44	2.60
10 Overhead	Contractor's overhead and profit and plans.		6.69	5.92	12.61
	Total		46.05	40.75	**86.80**

31

- **Simple design from standard plans**
- **Single family — 1 full bath, 1 kitchen**
- **No basement**
- **Asphalt shingles on roof**
- **Hot air heat**
- **Gypsum wallboard interior finishes**
- **Materials and workmanship are average**

Note: The illustration shown may contain some optional components (for example: garages and/or fireplaces) whose costs are shown in the modifications, adjustments, & alternatives below or at the end of the square foot section.

Base cost per square foot of living area

Exterior Wall	Living Area										
	1200	1400	1600	1800	2000	2400	2800	3200	3600	4000	4400
Wood Siding - Wood Frame	111.30	104.70	95.75	94.15	90.85	85.75	81.60	**77.50**	75.40	71.45	70.20
Brick Veneer - Wood Frame	123.45	115.70	105.80	104.25	100.35	94.35	89.80	84.90	82.40	77.95	76.50
Stucco on Wood Frame	109.20	102.85	94.00	92.40	89.25	84.30	80.15	76.15	74.15	70.30	69.10
Solid Masonry	141.20	131.80	120.65	119.10	114.30	106.90	101.80	95.75	92.70	87.55	85.80
Finished Basement, Add	15.65	15.35	14.75	14.70	14.35	13.70	13.45	13.00	12.75	12.40	12.30
Unfinished Basement, Add	6.05	5.60	5.25	5.20	4.90	4.55	4.40	4.10	3.95	3.80	3.65

Modifications

Add to the total cost

Upgrade Kitchen Cabinets	$ + 3248
Solid Surface Countertops (Included)	
Full Bath - including plumbing, wall and floor finishes	+ 5129
Half Bath - including plumbing, wall and floor finishes	+ 3107
One Car Attached Garage	+ 11,173
One Car Detached Garage	+ 14,818
Fireplace & Chimney	+ 5900

Adjustments

For multi family - add to total cost

Additional Kitchen	$ + 5771
Additional Bath	+ 5129
Additional Entry & Exit	+ 1512
Separate Heating	+ 1315
Separate Electric	+ 1766

For Townhouse/Rowhouse - Multiply cost per square foot by

Inner Unit	+ .90
End Unit	+ .95

Alternatives

Add to or deduct from the cost per square foot of living area

Cedar Shake Roof	+ 1.35
Clay Tile Roof	+ 2.05
Slate Roof	+ 2.60
Upgrade Walls to Skim Coat Plaster	+ .43
Upgrade Ceilings to Textured Finish	+ .44
Air Conditioning, in Heating Ductwork	+ 1.76
In Separate Ductwork	+ 4.68
Heating Systems, Hot Water	+ 1.38
Heat Pump	+ 2.43
Electric Heat	– 1.07
Not Heated	– 3.16

Additional upgrades or components

Kitchen Cabinets & Countertops	Page 77
Bathroom Vanities	78
Fireplaces & Chimneys	78
Windows, Skylights & Dormers	78
Appliances	79
Breezeways & Porches	79
Finished Attic	79
Garages	80
Site Improvements	80
Wings & Ells	44

Important: See the Reference Section for Location Factors (to adjust for your city) and Estimating Forms

Average 2-1/2 Story

Living Area - 3200 S.F.
Perimeter - 150 L.F.

		Labor-Hours	Cost Per Square Foot Of Living Area		
			Mat.	Labor	Total
1 Site Work	Site preparation for slab; 4' deep trench excavation for foundation wall.	.046		.39	.39
2 Foundation	Continuous reinforced concrete footing 8" deep x 18" wide, dampproofed and insulated reinforced concrete foundation wall, 8" thick, 4' deep; 4" concrete slab on 4" crushed stone base and polyethylene vapor barrier, trowel finish.	.061	2.17	2.47	4.64
3 Framing	Exterior walls - 2" x 4" wood studs, 16" O.C.; 1/2" plywood sheathing; 2" x 6" rafters 16" O.C. with 1/2" plywood sheathing, 4 in 12 pitch; 2" x 6" ceiling joists 16" O.C.; 2" x 8" floor joists 16" O.C. with 5/8" plywood subfloor; 1/2" plywood subfloor on 1" x 2" wood sleepers 16" O.C.	.127	6.13	7.48	13.61
4 Exterior Walls	Beveled wood siding and building paper on insulated wood frame walls; 6" attic insulation; double hung windows; 3 flush solid core wood exterior doors with storms.	.136	9.15	4.13	13.28
5 Roofing	25 year asphalt shingles; #15 felt building paper; aluminum gutters, downspouts, drip edge and flashings.	.018	.53	.81	1.34
6 Interiors	Walls and ceilings, 1/2" taped and finished gypsum wallboard, primed and painted with 2 coats; painted baseboard and trim, finished hardwood floor 40%, carpet with 1/2" underlayment 40%, vinyl tile with 1/2" underlayment 15%, ceramic tile with 1/2" underlayment 5%; hollow core and louvered in	.286	12.83	12.00	24.83
7 Specialties	Average grade kitchen cabinets - 14 L.F. wall and base with solid surface counter top and kitchen sink; 40 gallon electric water heater.	.030	1.08	.47	1.55
8 Mechanical	1 lavatory, white, wall hung; 1 water closet, white; 1 bathtub with shower, enameled steel, white; gas fired warm air heat.	.072	2.08	2.22	4.30
9 Electrical	200 Amp. service; romex wiring; incandescent lighting fixtures, switches, receptacles.	.046	1.01	1.26	2.27
10 Overhead	Contractor's overhead and profit and plans.		5.97	5.32	11.29
	Total		40.95	36.55	**77.50**

- **Simple design from standard plans**
- **Single family — 1 full bath, 1 kitchen**
- **No basement**
- **Asphalt shingles on roof**
- **Hot air heat**
- **Gypsum wallboard interior finishes**
- **Materials and workmanship are average**

Note: The illustration shown may contain some optional components (for example: garages and/or fireplaces) whose costs are shown in the modifications, adjustments, & alternatives below or at the end of the square foot section.

Base cost per square foot of living area

Exterior Wall	Living Area										
	1500	1800	2100	2500	3000	3500	4000	4500	5000	5500	6000
Wood Siding - Wood Frame	103.55	94.15	90.05	86.90	80.90	78.25	74.55	70.40	69.15	67.75	66.25
Brick Veneer - Wood Frame	114.90	104.60	99.90	96.35	89.40	86.30	81.95	77.20	75.70	74.05	72.20
Stucco on Wood Frame	101.55	92.25	88.40	85.30	79.35	76.90	73.25	69.25	68.00	66.65	65.15
Solid Masonry	131.60	120.10	114.35	110.15	101.95	98.15	92.70	87.20	85.35	83.30	80.90
Finished Basement, Add	13.45	13.35	13.00	12.65	12.20	11.95	11.55	11.30	11.15	11.00	10.85
Unfinished Basement, Add	4.90	4.60	4.35	4.20	3.90	3.70	3.50	3.30	3.25	3.15	3.05

Modifications

Add to the total cost

Upgrade Kitchen Cabinets	$ + 3248
Solid Surface Countertops (Included)	
Full Bath - including plumbing, wall and floor finishes	+ 5129
Half Bath - including plumbing, wall and floor finishes	+ 3107
One Car Attached Garage	+ 11,173
One Car Detached Garage	+ 14,818
Fireplace & Chimney	+ 5900

Adjustments

For multi family - add to total cost

Additional Kitchen	$ + 5771
Additional Bath	+ 5129
Additional Entry & Exit	+ 1512
Separate Heating	+ 1315
Separate Electric	+ 1766

For Townhouse/Rowhouse - Multiply cost per square foot by

Inner Unit	+ .88
End Unit	+ .94

Alternatives

Add to or deduct from the cost per square foot of living area

Cedar Shake Roof	+ 1.05
Clay Tile Roof	+ 1.60
Slate Roof	+ 2.00
Upgrade Walls to Skim Coat Plaster	+ .45
Upgrade Ceilings to Textured Finish	+ .44
Air Conditioning, in Heating Ductwork	+ 1.76
In Separate Ductwork	+ 4.68
Heating Systems, Hot Water	+ 1.38
Heat Pump	+ 2.43
Electric Heat	− .83
Not Heated	− 2.94

Additional upgrades or components

Kitchen Cabinets & Countertops	Page 77
Bathroom Vanities	78
Fireplaces & Chimneys	78
Windows, Skylights & Dormers	78
Appliances	79
Breezeways & Porches	79
Finished Attic	79
Garages	80
Site Improvements	80
Wings & Ells	44

		Labor-Hours	Cost Per Square Foot Of Living Area		
			Mat.	Labor	Total
1 Site Work	Site preparation for slab; 4' deep trench excavation for foundation wall.	.038		.42	.42
2 Foundation	Continuous reinforced concrete footing 8" deep x 18" wide, dampproofed and insulated reinforced concrete foundation wall, 8" thick, 4' deep; 4" concrete slab on 4" crushed stone base and polyethylene vapor barrier, trowel finish.	.053	2.01	2.30	4.31
3 Framing	Exterior walls - 2" x 4" wood studs, 16" O.C.; 1/2" plywood sheathing; 2" x 6" rafters 16" O.C. with 1/2" plywood sheathing, 4 in 12 pitch; 2" x 6" ceiling joists 16" O.C.; 2" x 8" floor joists 16" O.C. with 5/8" plywood subfloor; 1/2" plywood subfloor on 1" x 2" wood sleepers 16" O.C.	.128	6.33	7.71	14.04
4 Exterior Walls	Horizontal beveled wood siding; building paper; 3-1/2" batt insulation; wood double hung windows; 3 flush solid core wood exterior doors; storms and screens.	.139	10.42	4.70	15.12
5 Roofing	25 year asphalt shingles; #15 felt building paper; aluminum gutters, downspouts, drip edge and flashings.	.014	.46	.70	1.16
6 Interiors	Walls and ceilings, 1/2" taped and finished gypsum wallboard, primed and painted with 2 coats; painted baseboard and trim, finished hardwood floor 40%, carpet with 1/2" underlayment 40%, vinyl tile with 1/2" underlayment 15%, ceramic tile with 1/2" underlayment 5%; hollow core and louvered	.280	13.25	12.46	25.71
7 Specialties	Average grade kitchen cabinets - 14 L.F. wall and base with solid surface counter top and kitchen sink; 40 gallon electric water heater.	.025	1.15	.52	1.67
8 Mechanical	1 lavatory, white, wall hung; 1 water closet, white; 1 bathtub with shower, enameled steel, white; gas fired warm air heat.	.065	2.14	2.27	4.41
9 Electrical	200 Amp. service; romex wiring; incandescent lighting fixtures, switches, receptacles.	.042	1.02	1.28	2.30
10 Overhead	Contractor's overhead and profit and plans.		6.27	5.49	11.76
Total			43.05	37.85	**80.90**

- **Simple design from standard plans**
- **Single family — 1 full bath, 1 kitchen**
- **No basement**
- **Asphalt shingles on roof**
- **Hot air heat**
- **Gypsum wallboard interior finishes**
- **Materials and workmanship are average**

Note: The illustration shown may contain some optional components (for example: garages and/or fireplaces) whose costs are shown in the modifications, adjustments, & alternatives below or at the end of the square foot section.

Base cost per square foot of living area

Exterior Wall	Living Area										
	1000	1200	1400	1600	1800	2000	2200	2600	3000	3400	3800
Wood Siding - Wood Frame	104.90	95.00	90.75	87.75	84.80	81.30	79.15	75.10	70.80	69.05	67.45
Brick Veneer - Wood Frame	113.45	102.90	98.15	94.80	91.45	87.65	85.25	80.55	75.90	73.90	72.00
Stucco on Wood Frame	103.45	93.65	89.50	86.55	83.65	80.15	78.10	74.10	69.95	68.20	66.65
Solid Masonry	126.00	114.50	109.00	105.20	101.20	97.05	94.15	88.65	83.35	80.95	78.75
Finished Basement, Add	18.40	18.15	17.60	17.20	16.80	16.50	16.10	15.55	15.10	14.85	14.55
Unfinished Basement, Add	7.30	6.80	6.40	6.15	5.90	5.70	5.50	5.10	4.85	4.65	4.55

Modifications

Add to the total cost

Upgrade Kitchen Cabinets	$ + 3248
Solid Surface Countertops (Included)	
Full Bath - including plumbing, wall and floor finishes	+ 5129
Half Bath - including plumbing, wall and floor finishes	+ 3107
One Car Attached Garage	+ 11,173
One Car Detached Garage	+ 14,818
Fireplace & Chimney	+ 4655

Adjustments

For multi family - add to total cost

Additional Kitchen	$ + 5771
Additional Bath	+ 5129
Additional Entry & Exit	+ 1512
Separate Heating	+ 1315
Separate Electric	+ 1766

For Townhouse/Rowhouse - Multiply cost per square foot by

Inner Unit	+ .91
End Unit	+ .96

Alternatives

Add to or deduct from the cost per square foot of living area

Cedar Shake Roof	+ 1.60
Clay Tile Roof	+ 2.35
Slate Roof	+ 3.05
Upgrade Walls to Skim Coat Plaster	+ .42
Upgrade Ceilings to Textured Finish	+ .44
Air Conditioning, in Heating Ductwork	+ 1.93
In Separate Ductwork	+ 4.85
Heating Systems, Hot Water	+ 1.53
Heat Pump	+ 2.37
Electric Heat	– .61
Not Heated	– 2.71

Additional upgrades or components

Kitchen Cabinets & Countertops	Page 77
Bathroom Vanities	78
Fireplaces & Chimneys	78
Windows, Skylights & Dormers	78
Appliances	79
Breezeways & Porches	79
Finished Attic	79
Garages	80
Site Improvements	80
Wings & Ells	44

Important: See the Reference Section for Location Factors (to adjust for your city) and Estimating Forms

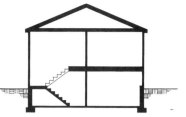

		Labor-Hours	Cost Per Square Foot Of Living Area		
			Mat.	Labor	Total
1 Site Work	Excavation for lower level, 4' deep. Site preparation for slab.	.029		.63	.63
2 Foundation	Continuous reinforced concrete footing 8" deep x 18" wide, dampproofed and insulated reinforced concrete foundation wall, 8" thick, 4' deep; 4" concrete slab on 4" crushed stone base and polyethylene vapor barrier, trowel finish.	.066	3.01	3.46	6.47
3 Framing	Exterior walls - 2" x 4" wood studs, 16" O.C.; 1/2" plywood sheathing; 2" x 6" rafters 16" O.C. with 1/2" plywood sheathing, 4 in 12 pitch; 2" x 6" ceiling joists 16" O.C.; 2" x 8" floor joists 16" O.C. with 5/8" plywood subfloor; 1/2" plywood subfloor on 1" x 2" wood sleepers 16" O.C.	.118	5.83	7.27	13.10
4 Exterior Walls	Horizontal beveled wood siding; building paper; 3-1/2" batt insulation; wood double hung windows; 3 flush solid core wood exterior doors; storms and screens.	.091	8.49	3.81	12.30
5 Roofing	25 year asphalt shingles; #15 felt building paper; aluminum gutters, downspouts, drip edge and flashings.	.024	.69	1.05	1.74
6 Interiors	Walls and ceilings, 1/2" taped and finished gypsum wallboard, primed and painted with 2 coats; painted baseboard and trim, finished hardwood floor 40%, carpet with 1/2" underlayment 40%, vinyl tile with 1/2" underlayment 15%, ceramic tile with 1/2" underlayment 5%; hollow core and louvered in	.217	12.90	12.05	24.95
7 Specialties	Average grade kitchen cabinets - 14 L.F. wall and base with solid surface counter top and kitchen sink; 40 gallon electric water heater.	.021	1.73	.77	2.50
8 Mechanical	1 lavatory, white, wall hung; 1 water closet, white; 1 bathtub with shower, enameled steel, white; gas fired warm air heat.	.061	2.67	2.50	5.17
9 Electrical	200 Amp. service; romex wiring; incandescent lighting fixtures, switches, receptacles.	.039	1.16	1.44	2.60
10 Overhead	Contractor's overhead and profit and plans.		6.22	5.62	11.84
	Total		42.70	38.60	**81.30**

- Simple design from standard plans
- Single family — 1 full bath, 1 kitchen
- No basement
- Asphalt shingles on roof
- Hot air heat
- Gypsum wallboard interior finishes
- Materials and workmanship are average

Note: The illustration shown may contain some optional components (for example: garages and/or fireplaces) whose costs are shown in the modifications, adjustments, & alternatives below or at the end of the square foot section.

©Design Basics, Inc.

Base cost per square foot of living area

Exterior Wall	Living Area										
	1200	1500	1800	2100	2400	2700	3000	3400	3800	4200	4600
Wood Siding - Wood Frame	99.70	92.25	86.65	81.65	78.55	76.75	74.80	72.90	69.75	67.15	65.95
Brick Veneer - Wood Frame	107.55	99.40	93.10	87.50	84.00	82.05	79.75	77.70	74.15	71.35	69.95
Stucco on Wood Frame	98.35	91.00	85.50	80.65	77.60	75.85	73.95	72.05	68.95	66.40	65.20
Solid Masonry	119.05	109.80	102.50	96.10	92.00	89.80	87.05	84.75	80.65	77.50	75.90
Finished Basement, Add*	21.10	20.70	19.80	19.10	18.65	18.35	18.00	17.80	17.40	17.05	16.85
Unfinished Basement, Add*	8.05	7.50	6.90	6.45	6.20	6.05	5.80	5.70	5.40	5.25	5.15

*Basement under middle level only.

Modifications

Add to the total cost

Upgrade Kitchen Cabinets	$ + 3248
Solid Surface Countertops (Included)	
Full Bath - including plumbing, wall and floor finishes	+ 5129
Half Bath - including plumbing, wall and floor finishes	+ 3107
One Car Attached Garage	+ 11,173
One Car Detached Garage	+ 14,818
Fireplace & Chimney	+ 4655

Adjustments

For multi family - add to total cost

Additional Kitchen	$ + 5771
Additional Bath	+ 5129
Additional Entry & Exit	+ 1512
Separate Heating	+ 1315
Separate Electric	+ 1766

For Townhouse/Rowhouse - Multiply cost per square foot by

Inner Unit	+ .90
End Unit	+ .95

Alternatives

Add to or deduct from the cost per square foot of living area

Cedar Shake Roof	+ 2.30
Clay Tile Roof	+ 3.40
Slate Roof	+ 4.35
Upgrade Walls to Skim Coat Plaster	+ .36
Upgrade Ceilings to Textured Finish	+ .44
Air Conditioning, in Heating Ductwork	+ 1.63
In Separate Ductwork	+ 4.57
Heating Systems, Hot Water	+ 1.48
Heat Pump	+ 2.46
Electric Heat	– .49
Not Heated	– 2.61

Additional upgrades or components

Kitchen Cabinets & Countertops	Page 77
Bathroom Vanities	78
Fireplaces & Chimneys	78
Windows, Skylights & Dormers	78
Appliances	79
Breezeways & Porches	79
Finished Attic	79
Garages	80
Site Improvements	80
Wings & Ells	44

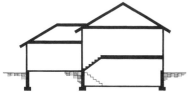

		Labor-Hours	Cost Per Square Foot Of Living Area		
			Mat.	Labor	Total
1 Site Work	Site preparation for slab; 4' deep trench excavation for foundation wall, excavation for lower level, 4' deep.	.029		.52	.52
2 Foundation	Continuous reinforced concrete footing 8" deep x 18" wide; dampproofed and insulated reinforced concrete foundation wall, 8" thick, 4' deep; 4" concrete slab on 4" crushed stone base and polyethylene vapor barrier, trowel finish.	.080	3.41	3.75	7.16
3 Framing	Exterior walls - 2" x 4" wood studs, 16" O.C.; 1/2" plywood sheathing; 2" x 6" rafters 16" O.C. with 1/2" plywood sheathing, 4 in 12 pitch; 2" x 6" ceiling joists 16" O.C.; 2" x 8" floor joists 16" O.C. with 5/8" plywood subfloor; 1/2" plywood subfloor on 1" x 2" wood sleepers 16" O.C.	.124	5.38	6.84	12.22
4 Exterior Walls	Horizontal beveled wood siding: building paper; 3-1/2" batt insulation; wood double hung windows; 3 flush solid core wood exterior doors; storms and screens.	.083	7.36	3.32	10.68
5 Roofing	25 year asphalt shingles; #15 felt building paper; aluminum gutters, downspouts, drip edge and flashings.	.032	.91	1.39	2.30
6 Interiors	Walls and ceilings, 1/2" taped and finished gypsum wallboard, primed and painted with 2 coats; painted baseboard and trim, finished hardwood floor 40%, carpet with 1/2" underlayment 40%, vinyl tile with 1/2" underlayment 15%, ceramic tile with 1/2" underlayment 5%; hollow core and louvered in	.186	13.19	11.79	24.98
7 Specialties	Average grade kitchen cabinets - 14 L.F. wall and base with solid surface counter top and kitchen sink; 40 gallon electric water heater.	.012	1.44	.64	2.08
8 Mechanical	1 lavatory, white, wall hung; 1 water closet, white; 1 bathtub with shower, enameled steel, white; gas fired warm air heat.	.059	2.35	2.37	4.72
9 Electrical	200 Amp. service; romex wiring; incandescent lighting fixtures, switches, receptacles.	.036	1.09	1.36	2.45
10 Overhead	Contractor's overhead and profit and plans.		5.97	5.47	11.44
	Total	41.10	37.45		**78.55**

- **Post and beam frame**
- **Log exterior walls**
- **Simple design from standard plans**
- **Single family — 1 full bath, 1 kitchen**
- **No basement**
- **Asphalt shingles on roof**
- **Hot air heat**
- **Gypsum wallboard interior finishes**
- **Materials and workmanship are average**

Note: The illustration shown may contain some optional components (for example: garages and/or fireplaces) whose costs are shown in the modifications, adjustments, & alternatives below or at the end of the square foot section.

Base cost per square foot of living area

Exterior Wall	Living Area										
	600	800	1000	1200	1400	1600	1800	2000	2400	2800	3200
6" Log - Solid Wall	146.10	133.30	123.65	115.70	108.95	104.55	102.35	99.35	93.55	89.30	86.30
8" Log - Solid Wall	146.80	133.95	124.20	116.20	109.45	105.00	102.75	99.80	93.85	89.65	86.65
Finished Basement, Add	31.85	30.75	29.25	27.90	26.85	26.15	25.80	25.15	24.40	23.75	23.25
Unfinished Basement, Add	13.30	12.00	11.10	10.25	9.60	9.20	8.90	8.55	8.10	7.70	7.40

Modifications

Add to the total cost

Upgrade Kitchen Cabinets	$ + 3248
Solid Surface Countertops (Included)	
Full Bath - including plumbing, wall and floor finishes	+ 5129
Half Bath - including plumbing, wall and floor finishes	+ 3107
One Car Attached Garage	+ 11,173
One Car Detached Garage	+ 14,818
Fireplace & Chimney	+ 4655

Adjustments

For multi family - add to total cost

Additional Kitchen	$ + 5771
Additional Bath	+ 5129
Additional Entry & Exit	+ 1512
Separate Heating	+ 1315
Separate Electric	+ 1766

For Townhouse/Rowhouse - Multiply cost per square foot by

Inner Unit	+ .92
End Unit	+ .96

Alternatives

Add to or deduct from the cost per square foot of living area

Cedar Shake Roof	+ 1.60
Air Conditioning, in Heating Ductwork	+ 3.19
In Separate Ductwork	+ 6.10
Heating Systems, Hot Water	+ 1.65
Heat Pump	+ 2.02
Electric Heat	– .80
Not Heated	– 2.90

Additional upgrades or components

Kitchen Cabinets & Countertops	Page 77
Bathroom Vanities	78
Fireplaces & Chimneys	78
Windows, Skylights & Dormers	78
Appliances	79
Breezeways & Porches	79
Finished Attic	79
Garages	80
Site Improvements	80
Wings & Ells	44

		Labor-Hours	Cost Per Square Foot Of Living Area		
			Mat.	Labor	Total
1 Site Work	Site preparation for slab; 4' deep trench excavation for foundation wall.	.048		.79	.79
2 Foundation	Continuous reinforced concrete footing 8" deep x 18" wide; dampproofed and insulated reinforced concrete foundation wall, 8" thick, 4' deep; 4" concrete slab on 4" crushed stone base and polyethylene vapor barrier, trowel finish.	.113	5.11	5.65	10.76
3 Framing	Exterior walls - Precut traditional log home. Handcrafted white cedar or pine logs. Delivery included.	.136	21.95	12.20	34.15
4 Exterior Walls	Wood double-hung windows, solid wood exterior doors	.098	5.16	2.43	7.59
5 Roofing	25 year asphalt shingles; #15 felt building paper; aluminum gutters, downspouts, drip edge and flashings.	.047	1.38	2.08	3.46
6 Interiors	Walls and ceilings, 1/2" taped and finished gypsum wallboard, primed and painted with 2 coats; painted baseboard and trim, finished hardwood floor 40%, carpet with 1/2" underlayment 40%, vinyl tile with 1/2" underlayment 15%, ceramic tile with 1/2" underlayment 5%; hollow core and louvered	.251	10.98	9.95	20.93
7 Specialties	Average grade kitchen cabinets - 14 L.F. wall and base with solid surface counter top and kitchen sink; 40 gallon electric water heater.	.009	2.16	.95	3.11
8 Mechanical	1 lavatory, white, wall hung; 1 water closet, white; 1 bathtub with shower, enameled steel, white; gas fired warm air heat.	.098	3.08	2.69	5.77
9 Electrical	200 Amp. service; romex wiring; incandescent lighting fixtures, switches, receptacles.	.041	1.26	1.57	2.83
10 Overhead	Contractor's overhead and profit and plans.		8.67	6.49	15.16
	Total		59.75	44.80	**104.55**

- **Post and beam frame**
- **Log exterior walls**
- **Simple design from standard plans**
- **Single family — 1 full bath, 1 kitchen**
- **No basement**
- **Asphalt shingles on roof**
- **Hot air heat**
- **Gypsum wallboard interior finishes**
- **Materials and workmanship are average**

Note: The illustration shown may contain some optional components (for example: garages and/or fireplaces) whose costs are shown in the modifications, adjustments, & alternatives below or at the end of the square foot section.

Base cost per square foot of living area

Exterior Wall	Living Area										
	1000	1200	1400	1600	1800	2000	2200	2600	3000	3400	3800
6" Log-Solid	130.55	119.20	113.80	110.05	106.15	102.10	99.25	93.80	88.65	86.30	84.15
8" Log-Solid	112.25	101.80	97.05	93.80	90.50	86.80	84.40	79.75	75.20	73.20	71.35
Finished Basement, Add	18.40	18.15	17.60	17.20	16.80	16.50	16.10	15.55	15.10	14.85	14.55
Unfinished Basement, Add	7.30	6.80	6.40	6.15	5.90	5.70	5.50	5.10	4.85	4.65	4.55

Modifications

Add to the total cost

Upgrade Kitchen Cabinets	$ + 3248
Solid Surface Countertops (Included)	
Full Bath - including plumbing, wall and floor finishes	+ 5129
Half Bath - including plumbing, wall and floor finishes	+ 3107
One Car Attached Garage	+ 11,173
One Car Detached Garage	+ 14,818
Fireplace & Chimney	+ 5190

Adjustments

For multi family - add to total cost

Additional Kitchen	$ + 5771
Additional Bath	+ 5129
Additional Entry & Exit	+ 1512
Separate Heating	+ 1315
Separate Electric	+ 1766

For Townhouse/Rowhouse - Multiply cost per square foot by

Inner Unit	+ .92
End Unit	+ .96

Alternatives

Add to or deduct from the cost per square foot of living area

Cedar Shake Roof	+ 2.30
Air Conditioning, in Heating Ductwork	+ 1.93
In Separate Ductwork	+ 4.85
Heating Systems, Hot Water	+ 1.53
Heat Pump	+ 2.37
Electric Heat	− .61
Not Heated	− 2.71

Additional upgrades or components

Kitchen Cabinets & Countertops	Page 77
Bathroom Vanities	78
Fireplaces & Chimneys	78
Windows, Skylights & Dormers	78
Appliances	79
Breezeways & Porches	79
Finished Attic	79
Garages	80
Site Improvements	80
Wings & Ells	44

Important: See the Reference Section for Location Factors (to adjust for your city) and Estimating Forms

Solid Wall 2 Story

Living Area - 2000 S.F.
Perimeter - 135 L.F.

		Labor-Hours	Cost Per Square Foot Of Living Area		
			Mat.	Labor	Total
1 Site Work	Site preparation for slab; 4' deep trench excavation for foundation wall.	.034		.63	.63
2 Foundation	Continuous reinforced concrete footing 8" deep x 18" wide; dampproofed and insulated reinforced concrete foundation wall, 8" thick, 4' deep, 4" concrete slab on 4" crushed stone base and polyethylene vapor barrier, trowel finish.	.066	3.01	3.46	6.47
3 Framing	Exterior walls - Precut traditional log home. Handcrafted white cedar or pine logs. Delivery included.	.131	24.01	12.65	36.66
4 Exterior Walls	Wood double-hung windows, solid wood exterior doors	.111	5.65	2.61	8.26
5 Roofing	25 year asphalt shingles; #15 felt building paper; aluminum gutters, downspouts, drip edge and flashings.	.024	.69	1.05	1.74
6 Interiors	Walls and ceilings, 1/2" taped and finished gypsum wallboard, primed and painted with 2 coats; painted baseboard and trim, finished hardwood floor 40%, carpet with 1/2" underlayment 40%, vinyl tile with 1/2" underlayment 15%, ceramic tile with 1/2" underlayment 5%; hollow core and louvered	.232	12.25	10.97	23.22
7 Specialties	Average grade kitchen cabinets - 14 L.F. wall and base with solid surface counter top and kitchen sink; 40 gallon electric water heater.	.021	1.73	.77	2.50
8 Mechanical	1 lavatory, white, wall hung; 1 water closet, white; 1 bathtub with shower; enameled steel, white; gas fired warm air heat.	.060	2.67	2.50	5.17
9 Electrical	200 Amp. service; romex wiring; incandescent lighting fixtures, switches, receptacles.	.039	1.16	1.44	2.60
10 Overhead	Contractor's overhead and profit and plans.		8.68	6.17	14.85
	Total		59.85	42.25	**102.10**

1 Story — Base cost per square foot of living area

Exterior Wall	Living Area							
	50	100	200	300	400	500	600	700
Wood Siding - Wood Frame	168.15	129.75	112.95	95.75	90.30	87.00	84.85	85.65
Brick Veneer - Wood Frame	184.40	138.45	118.50	96.05	89.50	85.60	83.00	83.55
Stucco on Wood Frame	163.30	126.25	110.00	93.75	88.50	85.30	83.20	84.10
Solid Masonry	233.70	176.55	151.95	121.80	113.70	108.85	107.20	107.05
Finished Basement, Add	51.35	42.45	38.10	30.90	29.45	28.60	28.05	27.65
Unfinished Basement, Add	24.40	18.40	15.90	11.80	10.90	10.45	10.05	9.90

1-1/2 Story — Base cost per square foot of living area

Exterior Wall	Living Area							
	100	200	300	400	500	600	700	800
Wood Siding - Wood Frame	135.35	109.00	93.25	84.35	79.60	77.40	74.55	73.65
Brick Veneer - Wood Frame	191.75	144.35	119.95	104.85	97.50	93.55	89.35	87.75
Stucco on Wood Frame	163.90	122.05	101.45	90.40	84.15	80.95	77.45	75.95
Solid Masonry	226.55	172.20	143.20	123.00	114.20	109.35	104.25	102.60
Finished Basement, Add	34.60	31.20	28.35	25.25	24.35	23.75	23.25	23.15
Unfinished Basement, Add	15.30	12.80	11.15	9.35	8.85	8.45	8.20	8.10

2 Story — Base cost per square foot of living area

Exterior Wall	Living Area							
	100	200	400	600	800	1000	1200	1400
Wood Siding - Wood Frame	134.85	101.35	86.55	72.80	68.05	65.10	63.25	64.25
Brick Veneer - Wood Frame	195.95	137.65	111.05	89.10	81.80	77.45	74.50	74.85
Stucco on Wood Frame	164.80	115.35	92.50	76.75	70.70	67.05	64.65	65.30
Solid Masonry	234.95	165.50	134.25	104.60	95.75	90.45	86.90	86.80
Finished Basement, Add	27.50	23.10	20.90	17.30	16.65	16.15	15.85	15.70
Unfinished Basement, Add	12.30	9.35	8.10	6.05	5.60	5.40	5.20	5.05

Base costs do not include bathroom or kitchen facilities. Use Modifications/Adjustments/Alternatives on pages 77-80 where appropriate.

Important: See the Reference Section for Location Factors (to adjust for your city) and Estimating Forms

1 Story

1 - 1/2 Story

2 Story

2 - 1/2 Story

Bi-Level

Tri-Level

- **A distinct residence from designer's plans**
- **Single family — 1 full bath, 1 half bath, 1 kitchen**
- **No basement**
- **Asphalt shingles on roof**
- **Forced hot air heat/air conditioning**
- **Gypsum wallboard interior finishes**
- **Materials and workmanship are above average**

Note: The illustration shown may contain some optional components (for example: garages and/or fireplaces) whose costs are shown in the modifications, adjustments, & alternatives below or at the end of the square foot section.

©Design Basics, Inc.

Base cost per square foot of living area

Exterior Wall	Living Area										
	800	1000	1200	1400	1600	1800	2000	2400	2800	3200	3600
Wood Siding - Wood Frame	155.55	141.40	129.95	120.75	114.45	111.10	107.00	99.30	93.75	89.90	85.80
Brick Veneer - Wood Frame	175.40	160.35	148.15	138.30	131.55	127.95	123.50	115.25	109.35	105.15	100.70
Stone Veneer - Wood Frame	179.00	163.65	151.10	140.95	134.05	130.40	125.75	117.35	111.30	106.90	102.40
Solid Masonry	183.30	167.55	154.65	144.15	137.05	133.25	128.50	119.80	113.55	109.00	104.35
Finished Basement, Add	48.70	48.60	46.50	44.75	43.70	43.05	42.15	40.90	39.95	39.15	38.35
Unfinished Basement, Add	20.75	19.60	18.50	17.65	17.10	16.75	16.30	15.65	15.20	14.75	14.40

Modifications

Add to the total cost

Upgrade Kitchen Cabinets	$ + 971
Solid Surface Countertops (Included)	
Full Bath - including plumbing, wall and floor finishes	+ 6078
Half Bath - including plumbing, wall and floor finishes	+ 3681
Two Car Attached Garage	+ 21,925
Two Car Detached Garage	+ 25,012
Fireplace & Chimney	+ 4970

Adjustments

For multi family - add to total cost

Additional Kitchen	$ + 12,567
Additional Full Bath & Half Bath	+ 9759
Additional Entry & Exit	+ 1512
Separate Heating & Air Conditioning	+ 5762
Separate Electric	+ 1766

For Townhouse/Rowhouse - Multiply cost per square foot by

Inner Unit	+ .90
End Unit	+ .95

Alternatives

Add to or deduct from the cost per square foot of living area

Cedar Shake Roof	+ 2.70
Clay Tile Roof	+ 4.30
Slate Roof	+ 5.60
Upgrade Ceilings to Textured Finish	+ .44
Air Conditioning, in Heating Ductwork	Base System
Heating Systems, Hot Water	+ 1.68
Heat Pump	+ 2.01
Electric Heat	– 2.24
Not Heated	– 3.63

Additional upgrades or components

Kitchen Cabinets & Countertops	Page 77
Bathroom Vanities	78
Fireplaces & Chimneys	78
Windows, Skylights & Dormers	78
Appliances	79
Breezeways & Porches	79
Finished Attic	79
Garages	80
Site Improvements	80
Wings & Ells	60

		Labor-Hours	Cost Per Square Foot Of Living Area		
			Mat.	Labor	Total
1 Site Work	Site preparation for slab; 4' deep trench excavation for foundation wall.	.028		.63	.63
2 Foundation	Continuous reinforced concrete footing 8" deep x 18" wide; dampproofed and insulated reinforced concrete foundation wall, 8" thick, 4' deep; 4" concrete slab on 4" crushed stone base and polyethylene vapor barrier, trowel finish.	.113	5.71	6.21	11.92
3 Framing	Exterior walls - 2" x 6" wood studs, 16" O.C.; 1/2" plywood sheathing; 2" x 8" rafters 16" O.C. with 1/2" plywood sheathing, 4 in 12 pitch; 2" x 6" ceiling joists 16" O.C.; 5/8" plywood subfloor on 1" x 3" wood sleepers 16" O.C.	.190	3.62	5.71	9.33
4 Exterior Walls	Horizontal beveled wood siding; building paper; 6" batt insulation; wood double hung windows; 3 solid core wood exterior doors; storms and screens.	.085	9.03	2.92	11.95
5 Roofing	30 year asphalt shingles; #15 felt building paper; aluminum gutters, downspouts and drip edge; copper flashings.	.082	4.60	3.01	7.61
6 Interiors	Walls and ceilings - 5/8" gypsum wallboard, skim coat plaster, painted with primer and 2 coats; hardwood baseboard and trim, sanded and finished; hardwood floor 70%, ceramic tile with underlayment 20%, vinyl tile with underlayment 10%; wood panel interior doors, primed and painted with 2 coat	.292	13.87	10.97	24.84
7 Specialties	Custom grade kitchen cabinets - 20 L.F. wall and base with solid surface counter top and kitchen sink; 4 L.F. bathroom vanity; 75 gallon electric water heater, medicine cabinet.	.019	4.54	1.07	5.61
8 Mechanical	Gas fired warm air heat/air conditioning; one full bath including: bathtub, corner shower, built in lavatory and water closet; one 1/2 bath including: built in lavatory and water closet.	.092	5.37	2.77	8.14
9 Electrical	200 Amp. service; romex wiring; fluorescent and incandescent lighting fixtures, switches, receptacles.	.039	1.24	1.53	2.77
10 Overhead	Contractor's overhead and profit and design.		9.62	6.88	16.50
	Total		57.60	41.70	**99.30**

- **A distinct residence from designer's plans**
- **Single family — 1 full bath, 1 half bath, 1 kitchen**
- **No basement**
- **Asphalt shingles on roof**
- **Forced hot air heat/air conditioning**
- **Gypsum wallboard interior finishes**
- **Materials and workmanship are above average**

Note: The illustration shown may contain some optional components (for example: garages and/or fireplaces) whose costs are shown in the modifications, adjustments, & alternatives below or at the end of the square foot section.

•Donald A. Gardner Architects, Inc.

Base cost per square foot of living area

Exterior Wall	Living Area										
	1000	1200	1400	1600	1800	2000	2400	2800	3200	3600	4000
Wood Siding - Wood Frame	140.40	130.90	124.20	115.95	111.35	106.75	97.85	93.90	90.20	87.40	83.35
Brick Veneer - Wood Frame	150.05	139.95	132.80	123.75	118.75	113.80	104.05	99.75	95.65	92.60	88.20
Stone Veneer - Wood Frame	153.85	143.50	136.20	126.80	121.65	116.55	106.45	102.10	97.85	94.70	90.15
Solid Masonry	158.35	147.70	140.25	130.45	125.15	119.80	109.40	104.80	100.35	97.10	92.45
Finished Basement, Add	32.30	32.50	31.60	30.40	29.60	28.95	27.65	27.05	26.30	26.00	25.40
Unfinished Basement, Add	13.90	13.30	12.90	12.25	11.85	11.55	10.85	10.55	10.20	10.05	9.75

Modifications

Add to the total cost

Upgrade Kitchen Cabinets	$ + 971
Solid Surface Countertops (Included)	
Full Bath - including plumbing, wall and floor finishes	+ 6078
Half Bath - including plumbing, wall and floor finishes	+ 3681
Two Car Attached Garage	+ 21,925
Two Car Detached Garage	+ 25,012
Fireplace & Chimney	+ 4970

Adjustments

For multi family - add to total cost

Additional Kitchen	$ + 12,567
Additional Full Bath & Half Bath	+ 9759
Additional Entry & Exit	+ 1512
Separate Heating & Air Conditioning	+ 5762
Separate Electric	+ 1766

For Townhouse/Rowhouse - Multiply cost per square foot by

Inner Unit	+ .90
End Unit	+ .95

Alternatives

Add to or deduct from the cost per square foot of living area

Cedar Shake Roof	+ 1.95
Clay Tile Roof	+ 3.10
Slate Roof	+ 4.05
Upgrade Ceilings to Textured Finish	+ .44
Air Conditioning, in Heating Ductwork	Base System
Heating Systems, Hot Water	+ 1.60
Heat Pump	+ 2.11
Electric Heat	– 1.98
Not Heated	– 3.35

Additional upgrades or components

Kitchen Cabinets & Countertops	Page 77
Bathroom Vanities	78
Fireplaces & Chimneys	78
Windows, Skylights & Dormers	78
Appliances	79
Breezeways & Porches	79
Finished Attic	79
Garages	80
Site Improvements	80
Wings & Ells	60

		Labor-Hours	Cost Per Square Foot Of Living Area		
			Mat.	Labor	Total
1 Site Work	Site preparation for slab; 4' deep trench excavation for foundation wall.	.028		.54	.54
2 Foundation	Continuous reinforced concrete footing 8" deep x 18" wide; dampproofed and insulated reinforced concrete foundation wall, 8" thick, 4' deep; 4" concrete slab on 4" crushed stone base and polyethylene vapor barrier, trowel finish.	.065	3.99	4.43	8.42
3 Framing	Exterior walls - 2" x 6" wood studs, 16" O.C.; 1/2" plywood sheathing; 2" x 8" rafters 16" O.C. with 1/2" plywood sheathing, 8 in 12 pitch; 2" x 10" floor joists 16" O.C. with 5/8" plywood subfloor; 5/8" plywood subfloor on 1" x 3" wood sleepers 16" O.C.	.192	4.76	6.04	10.80
4 Exterior Walls	Horizontal beveled wood siding; building paper; 6" batt insulation; wood double hung windows; 3 solid core wood exterior doors; storms and screens.	.064	9.11	2.96	12.07
5 Roofing	30 year asphalt shingles; #15 felt building paper; aluminum gutters, downspouts and drip edge; copper flashings.	.048	2.87	1.89	4.76
6 Interiors	Walls and ceilings - 5/8" gypsum wallboard, skim coat plaster, painted with primer and 2 coats; hardwood baseboard and trim, sanded and finished; hardwood floor 70%, ceramic tile with underlayment 20%, vinyl tile with underlayment 10%; wood panel interior doors, primed and painted with 2 coat	.259	15.01	11.98	26.99
7 Specialties	Custom grade kitchen cabinets - 20 L.F. wall and base with solid surface counter top and kitchen sink; 4 L.F. bathroom vanity; 75 gallon electric water heater, medicine cabinet.	.030	3.88	.94	4.82
8 Mechanical	Gas fired warm air heat/air conditioning; one full bath including: bathtub, corner shower, built in lavatory and water closet; one 1/2 bath including: built in lavatory and water closet.	.084	4.66	2.58	7.24
9 Electrical	200 Amp. service; romex wiring; fluorescent and incandescent lighting fixtures, switches, receptacles.	.038	1.18	1.48	2.66
10 Overhead	Contractor's overhead and profit and design.		9.09	6.51	15.60
	Total		54.55	39.35	**93.90**

- **A distinct residence from designer's plans**
- **Single family — 1 full bath, 1 half bath, 1 kitchen**
- **No basement**
- **Asphalt shingles on roof**
- **Forced hot air heat/air conditioning**
- **Gypsum wallboard interior finishes**
- **Materials and workmanship are above average**

Note: The illustration shown may contain some optional components (for example: garages and/or fireplaces) whose costs are shown in the modifications, adjustments, & alternatives below or at the end of the square foot section.

Base cost per square foot of living area

Exterior Wall	Living Area										
	1200	1400	1600	1800	2000	2400	2800	3200	3600	4000	4400
Wood Siding - Wood Frame	131.85	124.25	118.85	114.00	108.85	101.35	95.00	90.75	88.30	85.65	83.45
Brick Veneer - Wood Frame	142.10	133.85	128.00	122.70	117.20	108.90	101.85	97.15	94.50	91.50	89.10
Stone Veneer - Wood Frame	146.15	137.65	131.65	126.10	120.50	111.80	104.50	99.70	96.95	93.80	91.30
Solid Masonry	150.95	142.10	135.95	130.15	124.40	115.35	107.65	102.70	99.80	96.50	93.90
Finished Basement, Add	25.95	26.10	25.50	24.75	24.30	23.25	22.40	21.90	21.55	21.10	20.85
Unfinished Basement, Add	11.20	10.70	10.40	10.00	9.80	9.25	8.80	8.55	8.40	8.20	8.05

Modifications

Add to the total cost

Upgrade Kitchen Cabinets	$ + 971
Solid Surface Countertops (Included)	
Full Bath - including plumbing, wall and floor finishes	+ 6078
Half Bath - including plumbing, wall and floor finishes	+ 3681
Two Car Attached Garage	+ 21,925
Two Car Detached Garage	+ 25,012
Fireplace & Chimney	+ 5610

Adjustments

For multi family - add to total cost

Additional Kitchen	$ + 12,567
Additional Full Bath & Half Bath	+ 9759
Additional Entry & Exit	+ 1512
Separate Heating & Air Conditioning	+ 5762
Separate Electric	+ 1766

For Townhouse/Rowhouse - Multiply cost per square foot by

Inner Unit	+ .87
End Unit	+ .93

Alternatives

Add to or deduct from the cost per square foot of living area

Cedar Shake Roof	+ 1.35
Clay Tile Roof	+ 2.15
Slate Roof	+ 2.80
Upgrade Ceilings to Textured Finish	+ .44
Air Conditioning, in Heating Ductwork	Base System
Heating Systems, Hot Water	+ 1.56
Heat Pump	+ 2.35
Electric Heat	– 1.98
Not Heated	– 3.17

Additional upgrades or components

Kitchen Cabinets & Countertops	Page 77
Bathroom Vanities	78
Fireplaces & Chimneys	78
Windows, Skylights & Dormers	78
Appliances	79
Breezeways & Porches	79
Finished Attic	79
Garages	80
Site Improvements	80
Wings & Ells	60

Important: See the Reference Section for Location Factors (to adjust for your city) and Estimating Forms

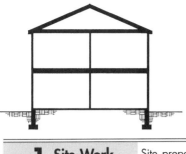

Custom 2 Story

Living Area - 2800 S.F.
Perimeter - 156 L.F.

		Labor-Hours	Cost Per Square Foot Of Living Area		
			Mat.	Labor	Total
1 Site Work	Site preparation for slab; 4' deep trench excavation for foundation wall.	.024		.54	.54
2 Foundation	Continuous reinforced concrete footing 8" deep x 18" wide; dampproofed and insulated reinforced concrete foundation wall, 8" thick, 4' deep; 4" concrete slab on 4" crushed stone base and polyethylene vapor barrier, trowel finish.	.058	3.38	3.81	7.19
3 Framing	Exterior walls - 2" x 6" wood studs, 16" O.C.; 1/2" plywood sheathing; 2" x 8" rafters 16" O.C. with 1/2" plywood sheathing, 6 in 12 pitch; 2" x 8" ceiling joists 16" O.C.; 2" x 10" floor joists 16" O.C. with 5/8" plywood subfloor; 5/8" plywood subfloor on 1" x 3" wood sleepers 16" O.C.	.159	5.24	6.23	11.47
4 Exterior Walls	Horizontal beveled wood siding; building paper; 6" batt insulation; wood double hung windows; 3 solid core wood exterior doors; storms and screens.	.091	10.37	3.38	13.75
5 Roofing	30 year asphalt shingles; #15 felt building paper; aluminum gutters, downspouts and drip edge; copper flashings.	.042	2.30	1.51	3.81
6 Interiors	Walls and ceilings - 5/8" gypsum wallboard, skim coat plaster, painted with primer and 2 coats; hardwood baseboard and trim, sanded and finished; hardwood floor 70%, ceramic tile with underlayment 20%, vinyl tile with underlayment 10%; wood panel interior doors, primed and painted with 2 coat	.271	15.27	12.24	27.51
7 Specialties	Custom grade kitchen cabinets - 20 L.F. wall and base with solid surface counter top and kitchen sink; 4 L.F. bathroom vanity; 75 gallon electric water heater, medicine cabinet.	.028	3.88	.94	4.82
8 Mechanical	Gas fired warm air heat/air conditioning; one full bath including: bathtub, corner shower; built in lavatory and water closet; one 1/2 bath including: built in lavatory and water closet.	.078	4.79	2.63	7.42
9 Electrical	200 Amp. service; romex wiring; fluorescent and incandescent lighting fixtures, switches, receptacles.	.038	1.18	1.48	2.66
10 Overhead	Contractor's overhead and profit and design.		9.29	6.54	15.83
	Total		55.70	39.30	**95.00**

- **A distinct residence from designer's plans**
- **Single family — 1 full bath, 1 half bath, 1 kitchen**
- **No basement**
- **Asphalt shingles on roof**
- **Forced hot air heat/air conditioning**
- **Gypsum wallboard interior finishes**
- **Materials and workmanship are above average**

Note: The illustration shown may contain some optional components (for example: garages and/or fireplaces) whose costs are shown in the modifications, adjustments, & alternatives below or at the end of the square foot section.

Base cost per square foot of living area

Exterior Wall	Living Area										
	1500	1800	2100	2400	2800	3200	3600	4000	4500	5000	5500
Wood Siding - Wood Frame	129.80	117.15	109.80	105.30	99.55	94.10	91.05	86.15	83.50	81.30	78.95
Brick Veneer - Wood Frame	140.50	127.05	118.60	113.70	107.60	101.30	97.90	92.50	89.60	87.05	84.45
Stone Veneer - Wood Frame	144.70	130.90	122.05	116.95	110.75	104.15	100.55	95.00	91.95	89.35	86.60
Solid Masonry	149.70	135.50	126.20	120.90	114.45	107.55	103.80	98.00	94.75	92.00	89.15
Finished Basement, Add	20.60	20.60	19.50	19.05	18.55	17.85	17.45	17.00	16.65	16.35	16.05
Unfinished Basement, Add	8.95	8.50	7.95	7.70	7.45	7.10	6.90	6.70	6.55	6.35	6.20

Modifications

Add to the total cost

Upgrade Kitchen Cabinets	$ + 971
Solid Surface Countertops (Included)	
Full Bath - including plumbing, wall and floor finishes	+ 6078
Half Bath - including plumbing, wall and floor finishes	+ 3681
Two Car Attached Garage	+ 21,925
Two Car Detached Garage	+ 25,012
Fireplace & Chimney	+ 6335

Adjustments

For multi family - add to total cost

Additional Kitchen	$ + 12,567
Additional Full Bath & Half Bath	+ 9759
Additional Entry & Exit	+ 1512
Separate Heating & Air Conditioning	+ 5762
Separate Electric	+ 1766

For Townhouse/Rowhouse -
Multiply cost per square foot by

Inner Unit	+ .87
End Unit	+ .94

Alternatives

Add to or deduct from the cost per square foot of living area

Cedar Shake Roof	+ 1.15
Clay Tile Roof	+ 1.85
Slate Roof	+ 2.45
Upgrade Ceilings to Textured Finish	+ .44
Air Conditioning, in Heating Ductwork	Base System
Heating Systems, Hot Water	+ 1.41
Heat Pump	+ 2.43
Electric Heat	– 3.47
Not Heated	– 3.17

Additional upgrades or components

Kitchen Cabinets & Countertops	Page 77
Bathroom Vanities	78
Fireplaces & Chimneys	78
Windows, Skylights & Dormers	78
Appliances	79
Breezeways & Porches	79
Finished Attic	79
Garages	80
Site Improvements	80
Wings & Ells	60

		Labor-Hours	Cost Per Square Foot Of Living Area		
			Mat.	Labor	Total
1 Site Work	Site preparation for slab; 4' deep trench excavation for foundation wall.	.048		.47	.47
2 Foundation	Continuous reinforced concrete footing 8" deep x 18" wide; dampproofed and insulated reinforced concrete foundation wall, 8" thick, 4' deep; 4" concrete slab on 4" crushed stone base and polyethylene vapor barrier, trowel finish.	.063	2.78	3.17	5.95
3 Framing	Exterior walls - 2" x 6" wood studs, 16" O.C.; 1/2" plywood sheathing; 2" x 8" rafters 16" O.C. with 1/2" plywood sheathing, 6 in 12 pitch; 2" x 8" ceiling joists 16" O.C.; 2" x 10" floor joists 16" O.C. with 5/8" plywood subfloor; 5/8" plywood subfloor on 1" x 3" wood sleepers 16" O.C.	.177	5.68	6.50	12.18
4 Exterior Walls	Horizontal beveled wood siding; building paper; 6" batt insulation; wood double hung windows; 3 solid core wood exterior doors; storms and screens.	.134	10.75	3.54	14.29
5 Roofing	30 year asphalt shingles; #15 felt building paper; aluminum gutters, downspouts and drip edge; copper flashings.	.032	1.77	1.16	2.93
6 Interiors	Walls and ceilings - 5/8" gypsum wallboard, skim coat plaster, painted with primer and 2 coats; hardwood baseboard and trim, sanded and finished; hardwood floor 70%, ceramic tile with underlayment 20%, vinyl tile with underlayment 10%; wood panel interior doors, primed and painted with 2 coat	.354	15.97	12.94	28.91
7 Specialties	Custom grade kitchen cabinets - 20 L.F. wall and base with solid surface counter top and kitchen sink; 4 L.F. bathroom vanity; 75 gallon electric water heater, medicine cabinet.	.053	3.40	.80	4.20
8 Mechanical	Gas fired warm air heat/air conditioning; one full bath including: bathtub, corner shower; built in lavatory and water closet; one 1/2 bath including: built in lavatory and water closet.	.104	4.36	2.52	6.88
9 Electrical	200 Amp. service; romex wiring; fluorescent and incandescent lighting fixtures, switches, receptacles.	.048	1.15	1.44	2.59
10 Overhead	Contractor's overhead and profit and design.		9.19	6.51	15.70
	Total		55.05	39.05	**94.10**

RESIDENTIAL — Custom — 3 Story

- A distinct residence from designer's plans
- Single family — 1 full bath, 1 half bath, 1 kitchen
- No basement
- Asphalt shingles on roof
- Forced hot air heat/air conditioning
- Gypsum wallboard interior finishes
- Materials and workmanship are above average

Note: The illustration shown may contain some optional components (for example: garages and/or fireplaces) whose costs are shown in the modifications, adjustments, & alternatives below or at the end of the square foot section.

Base cost per square foot of living area

Exterior Wall	Living Area										
	1500	1800	2100	2500	3000	3500	4000	4500	5000	5500	6000
Wood Siding - Wood Frame	129.25	116.70	110.75	105.80	97.95	94.10	89.30	84.15	82.40	80.45	78.45
Brick Veneer - Wood Frame	140.40	127.00	120.35	115.00	106.30	102.00	96.45	90.80	88.75	86.60	84.25
Stone Veneer - Wood Frame	144.75	131.05	124.15	118.60	109.60	105.10	99.30	93.40	91.30	89.05	86.55
Solid Masonry	149.90	135.85	128.65	122.95	113.45	108.75	102.60	96.50	94.30	91.90	89.30
Finished Basement, Add	18.10	18.10	17.45	16.95	16.20	15.75	15.20	14.75	14.55	14.35	14.05
Unfinished Basement, Add	7.85	7.45	7.10	6.90	6.50	6.30	6.05	5.80	5.70	5.60	5.45

Modifications

Add to the total cost

Upgrade Kitchen Cabinets	$ + 971
Solid Surface Countertops (Included)	
Full Bath - including plumbing, wall and floor finishes	+ 6078
Half Bath - including plumbing, wall and floor finishes	+ 3681
Two Car Attached Garage	+ 21,925
Two Car Detached Garage	+ 25,012
Fireplace & Chimney	+ 6335

Adjustments

For multi family - add to total cost

Additional Kitchen	$ + 12,567
Additional Full Bath & Half Bath	+ 9759
Additional Entry & Exit	+ 1512
Separate Heating & Air Conditioning	+ 5762
Separate Electric	+ 1766

For Townhouse/Rowhouse - Multiply cost per square foot by

Inner Unit	+ .85
End Unit	+ .93

Alternatives

Add to or deduct from the cost per square foot of living area

Cedar Shake Roof	+ .90
Clay Tile Roof	+ 1.45
Slate Roof	+ 1.85
Upgrade Ceilings to Textured Finish	+ .44
Air Conditioning, in Heating Ductwork	Base System
Heating Systems, Hot Water	+ 1.41
Heat Pump	+ 2.43
Electric Heat	– 3.47
Not Heated	– 3.07

Additional upgrades or components

Kitchen Cabinets & Countertops	Page 77
Bathroom Vanities	78
Fireplaces & Chimneys	78
Windows, Skylights & Dormers	78
Appliances	79
Breezeways & Porches	79
Finished Attic	79
Garages	80
Site Improvements	80
Wings & Ells	60

Important: See the Reference Section for Location Factors (to adjust for your city) and Estimating Forms

		Labor-Hours	Cost Per Square Foot Of Living Area		
			Mat.	Labor	Total
1 Site Work	Site preparation for slab; 4' deep trench excavation for foundation wall.	.048		.50	.50
2 Foundation	Continuous reinforced concrete footing 8" deep x 18" wide; dampproofed and insulated reinforced concrete foundation wall, 8" thick, 4' deep; 4" concrete slab on 4" crushed stone base and polyethylene vapor barrier, trowel finish.	.060	2.58	2.99	5.57
3 Framing	Exterior walls - 2" x 6" wood studs, 16" O.C.; 1/2" plywood sheathing; 2" x 8" rafters 16" O.C. with 1/2" plywood sheathing, 6 in 12 pitch; 2" x 8" ceiling joists 16" O.C.; 2" x 10" floor joists 16" O.C. with 5/8" plywood subfloor; 5/8" plywood subfloor on 1" x 3" wood sleepers 16" O.C.	.191	5.98	6.72	12.70
4 Exterior Walls	Horizontal beveled wood siding; building paper; 6" batt insulation; wood double hung windows; 3 solid core wood exterior doors; storms and screens.	.150	12.27	4.03	16.30
5 Roofing	30 year asphalt shingles; #15 felt building paper; aluminum gutters, downspouts and drip edge; copper flashings.	.028	1.54	1.00	2.54
6 Interiors	Walls and ceilings - 5/8" gypsum wallboard, skim coat plaster, painted with primer and 2 coats; hardwood baseboard and trim, sanded and finished; hardwood floor 70%, ceramic tile with underlayment 20%, vinyl tile with underlayment 10%; wood panel interior doors, primed and painted with 2 coat	.409	16.42	13.40	29.82
7 Specialties	Custon grade kitchen cabinets - 20 L.F. wall and base with solid surface counter top and kitchen sink; 4 L.F. bathroom vanity; 75 gallon electric water heater, medicine cabinet.	.053	3.63	.86	4.49
8 Mechanical	Gas fired warm air heat/air conditioning; one full bath including: bathtub, corner shower; built in lavatory and water closet; one 1/2 bath including: built in lavatory and water closet.	.105	4.56	2.57	7.13
9 Electrical	200 Amp. service; romex wiring; fluorescent and incandescent lighting fixtures, switches, receptacles.	.048	1.16	1.46	2.62
10 Overhead	Contractor's overhead and profit and design.		9.61	6.67	16.28
	Total		57.75	40.20	**97.95**

- **A distinct residence from designer's plans**
- **Single family — 1 full bath, 1 half bath, 1 kitchen**
- **No basement**
- **Asphalt shingles on roof**
- **Forced hot air heat/air conditioning**
- **Gypsum wallboard interior finishes**
- **Materials and workmanship are above average**

Note: The illustration shown may contain some optional components (for example: garages and/or fireplaces) whose costs are shown in the modifications, adjustments, & alternatives below or at the end of the square foot section.

Base cost per square foot of living area

Exterior Wall	Living Area										
	1200	1400	1600	1800	2000	2400	2800	3200	3600	4000	4400
Wood Siding - Wood Frame	124.50	117.35	112.25	107.85	102.90	95.95	90.05	86.10	83.90	81.50	79.40
Brick Veneer - Wood Frame	132.20	124.60	119.10	114.35	109.15	101.60	95.15	90.90	88.55	85.80	83.60
Stone Veneer - Wood Frame	135.20	127.40	121.80	116.90	111.60	103.80	97.15	92.80	90.35	87.55	85.25
Solid Masonry	138.85	130.75	125.00	119.90	114.50	106.45	99.60	95.00	92.50	89.60	87.20
Finished Basement, Add	25.95	26.10	25.50	24.75	24.30	23.25	22.40	21.90	21.55	21.10	20.85
Unfinished Basement, Add	11.20	10.70	10.40	10.00	9.80	9.25	8.80	8.55	8.40	8.20	8.05

Modifications

Add to the total cost

Upgrade Kitchen Cabinets	$ + 971
Solid Surface Countertops (Included)	
Full Bath - including plumbing, wall and floor finishes	+ 6078
Half Bath - including plumbing, wall and floor finishes	+ 3681
Two Car Attached Garage	+ 21,925
Two Car Detached Garage	+ 25,012
Fireplace & Chimney	+ 4970

Adjustments

For multi family - add to total cost

Additional Kitchen	$ + 12,567
Additional Full Bath & Half Bath	+ 9759
Additional Entry & Exit	+ 1512
Separate Heating & Air Conditioning	+ 5762
Separate Electric	+ 1766

*For Townhouse/Rowhouse -
Multiply cost per square foot by*

Inner Unit	+ .89
End Unit	+ .95

Alternatives

Add to or deduct from the cost per square foot of living area

Cedar Shake Roof	+ 1.35
Clay Tile Roof	+ 2.15
Slate Roof	+ 2.80
Upgrade Ceilings to Textured Finish	+ .44
Air Conditioning, in Heating Ductwork	Base System
Heating Systems, Hot Water	+ 1.56
Heat Pump	+ 2.35
Electric Heat	– 1.98
Not Heated	– 3.07

Additional upgrades or components

Kitchen Cabinets & Countertops	Page 77
Bathroom Vanities	78
Fireplaces & Chimneys	78
Windows, Skylights & Dormers	78
Appliances	79
Breezeways & Porches	79
Finished Attic	79
Garages	80
Site Improvements	80
Wings & Ells	60

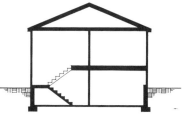

		Labor-Hours	Cost Per Square Foot Of Living Area		
			Mat.	Labor	Total
1 Site Work	Excavation for lower level, 4' deep. Site preparation for slab.	.024		.54	.54
2 Foundation	Continuous reinforced concrete footing 8" deep x 18" wide; dampproofed and insulated reinforced concrete foundation wall, 8" thick, 4' deep; 4" concrete slab on 4" crushed stone base and polyethylene vapor barrier, trowel finish.	.058	3.38	3.81	7.19
3 Framing	Exterior walls - 2" x 6" wood studs, 16" O.C.; 1/2" plywood sheathing; 2" x 8" rafters 16" O.C. with 1/2" plywood sheathing, 6 in 12 pitch; 2" x 8" ceiling joists 16" O.C.; 2" x 10" floor joists 16" O.C. with 5/8" plywood subfloor; 5/8" plywood subfloor on 1" x 3" wood sleepers 16" O.C.	.147	4.96	5.95	10.91
4 Exterior Walls	Horizontal beveled wood siding; building paper; 6" batt insulation; wood double hung windows; 3 solid core wood exterior doors; storms and screens.	.079	8.09	2.65	10.74
5 Roofing	30 year asphalt shingles; #15 felt building paper; aluminum gutters, downspouts and drip edge; copper flashings.	.033	2.30	1.51	3.81
6 Interiors	Walls and ceilings - 5/8" gypsum wallboard, skim coat plaster, painted with primer and 2 coats; hardwood baseboard and trim, sanded and finished; hardwood floor 70%, ceramic tile with underlayment 20%, vinyl tile with underlayment 10%; wood panel interior doors, primed and painted with 2 coat	.257	15.08	11.92	27.00
7 Specialties	Custom grade kitchen cabinets - 20 L.F. wall and base with solid surface counter top and kitchen sink; 4 L.F. bathroom vanity; 75 gallon electric water heater, medicine cabinet.	.028	3.88	.94	4.82
8 Mechanical	Gas fired warm air heat/air conditioning; one full bath including: bathtub, corner shower, built in lavatory and water closet; one 1/2 bath including: built in lavatory and water closet.	.078	4.79	2.63	7.42
9 Electrical	200 Amp. service; romex wiring; fluorescent and incandescent lighting fixtures, switches, receptacles.	.038	1.18	1.48	2.66
10 Overhead	Contractor's overhead and profit and design.		8.74	6.22	14.96
	Total		52.40	37.65	**90.05**

- **A distinct residence from designer's plans**
- **Single family — 1 full bath, 1 half bath, 1 kitchen**
- **No basement**
- **Asphalt shingles on roof**
- **Forced hot air heat/air conditioning**
- **Gypsum wallboard interior finishes**
- **Materials and workmanship are above average**

Note: The illustration shown may contain some optional components (for example: garages and/or fireplaces) whose costs are shown in the modifications, adjustments, & alternatives below or at the end of the square foot section.

©Design Basics, Inc.

Base cost per square foot of living area

Exterior Wall	Living Area										
	1200	1500	1800	2100	2400	2800	3200	3600	4000	4500	5000
Wood Siding - Wood Frame	128.15	116.85	108.30	101.10	96.30	92.90	88.75	84.45	82.60	78.35	76.20
Brick Veneer - Wood Frame	135.80	123.75	114.55	106.80	101.65	98.05	93.50	88.85	86.85	82.35	79.95
Stone Veneer - Wood Frame	138.85	126.55	117.00	109.00	103.75	100.05	95.40	90.60	88.50	83.85	81.40
Solid Masonry	142.40	129.80	119.95	111.70	106.20	102.45	97.60	92.65	90.55	85.75	83.15
Finished Basement, Add*	32.45	32.35	30.95	29.85	29.15	28.60	27.85	27.25	27.00	26.35	25.95
Unfinished Basement, Add*	13.85	13.05	12.35	11.75	11.35	11.15	10.80	10.45	10.35	10.00	9.80

*Basement under middle level only.

Modifications

Add to the total cost

Upgrade Kitchen Cabinets	$ + 971
Solid Surface Countertops (Included)	
Full Bath - including plumbing, wall and floor finishes	+ 6078
Half Bath - including plumbing, wall and floor finishes	+ 3681
Two Car Attached Garage	+ 21,925
Two Car Detached Garage	+ 25,012
Fireplace & Chimney	+ 4970

Adjustments

For multi family - add to total cost

Additional Kitchen	$ + 12,567
Additional Full Bath & Half Bath	+ 9759
Additional Entry & Exit	+ 1512
Separate Heating & Air Conditioning	+ 5762
Separate Electric	+ 1766

*For Townhouse/Rowhouse -
Multiply cost per square foot by*

Inner Unit	+ .87
End Unit	+ .94

Alternatives

Add to or deduct from the cost per square foot of living area

Cedar Shake Roof	+ 1.95
Clay Tile Roof	+ 3.10
Slate Roof	+ 4.05
Upgrade Ceilings to Textured Finish	+ .44
Air Conditioning, in Heating Ductwork	Base System
Heating Systems, Hot Water	+ 1.51
Heat Pump	+ 2.45
Electric Heat	– 1.76
Not Heated	– 3.07

Additional upgrades or components

Kitchen Cabinets & Countertops	Page 77
Bathroom Vanities	78
Fireplaces & Chimneys	78
Windows, Skylights & Dormers	78
Appliances	79
Breezeways & Porches	79
Finished Attic	79
Garages	80
Site Improvements	80
Wings & Ells	60

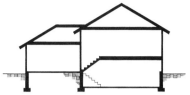

	Labor-Hours	Cost Per Square Foot Of Living Area		
		Mat.	Labor	Total
1 Site Work Site preparation for slab; 4' deep trench excavation for foundation wall, excavation for lower level, 4' deep.	.023		.47	.47
2 Foundation Continuous reinforced concrete footing 8" deep x 18" wide; dampproofed and insulated reinforced concrete foundation wall, 8" thick, 4' deep; 4" concrete slab on 4" crushed stone base and polyethylene vapor barrier, trowel finish.	.073	3.98	4.38	8.36
3 Framing Exterior walls - 2" x 6" wood studs, 16" O.C.; 1/2" plywood sheathing; 2" x 8" rafters 16" O.C. with 1/2" plywood sheathing, 6 in 12 pitch; 2" x 8" ceiling joists 16" O.C.; 2" x 10" floor joists 16" O.C. with 5/8" plywood subfloor; 5/8" plywood subfloor on 1" x 3" wood sleepers 16" O.C.	.162	4.47	5.84	10.31
4 Exterior Walls Horizontal beveled wood siding; building paper; 6" batt insulation; wood double hung windows; 3 solid core wood exterior doors; storms and screens.	.076	7.79	2.54	10.33
5 Roofing 30 year asphalt shingles; #15 felt building paper; aluminum gutters, downspouts and drip edge; copper flashings.	.045	3.06	2.01	5.07
6 Interiors Walls and ceilings - 5/8" gypsum wallboard, skim coat plaster, painted with primer and 2 coats; hardwood baseboard and trim, sanded and finished; hardwood floor 70%, ceramic tile with underlayment 20%, vinyl tile with underlayment 10%; wood panel interior doors, primed and painted with 2 coat	.242	14.41	11.40	25.81
7 Specialties Custom grade kitchen cabinets - 20 L.F. wall and base with solid surface counter top and kitchen sink; 4 L.F. bathroom vanity; 75 gallon electric water heater, medicine cabinet.	.026	3.40	.80	4.20
8 Mechanical Gas fired warm air heat/air conditioning; one full bath including: bathtub, corner shower, built in lavatory and water closet; one 1/2 bath including: built in lavatory and water closet.	.073	4.36	2.52	6.88
9 Electrical 200 Amp. service; romex wiring; fluorescent and incandescent lighting fixtures, switches, receptacles.	.036	1.15	1.44	2.59
10 Overhead Contractor's overhead and profit and design.		8.53	6.20	14.73
Total		51.15	37.60	**88.75**

1 Story   Base cost per square foot of living area

Exterior Wall	Living Area							
	50	100	200	300	400	500	600	700
Wood Siding - Wood Frame	204.40	159.45	139.80	118.75	112.35	108.45	105.90	106.70
Brick Veneer - Wood Frame	230.30	177.95	155.25	129.00	121.60	117.10	114.15	114.65
Stone Veneer - Wood Frame	240.50	185.25	161.35	133.10	125.20	120.50	117.40	117.75
Solid Masonry	252.65	193.95	168.50	137.85	129.55	124.60	121.25	121.45
Finished Basement, Add	77.90	66.45	60.30	49.90	47.85	46.55	45.75	45.15
Unfinished Basement, Add	56.40	39.05	31.10	23.85	22.00	20.85	20.10	19.55

1-1/2 Story   Base cost per square foot of living area

Exterior Wall	Living Area							
	100	200	300	400	500	600	700	800
Wood Siding - Wood Frame	163.45	134.55	116.90	106.30	100.95	98.35	95.15	94.20
Brick Veneer - Wood Frame	186.60	153.05	132.35	118.35	112.10	108.85	105.05	104.05
Stone Veneer - Wood Frame	195.70	160.35	138.35	123.05	116.45	113.00	108.95	107.90
Solid Masonry	206.55	169.05	145.60	128.65	121.60	117.90	113.60	112.55
Finished Basement, Add	52.10	48.20	44.05	39.45	38.20	37.40	36.60	36.50
Unfinished Basement, Add	33.75	25.75	22.00	18.70	17.55	16.80	16.20	15.95

2 Story   Base cost per square foot of living area

Exterior Wall	Living Area							
	100	200	400	600	800	1000	1200	1400
Wood Siding - Wood Frame	163.10	125.05	108.35	92.15	86.70	83.45	81.30	82.30
Brick Veneer - Wood Frame	189.00	143.55	123.75	102.45	96.00	92.10	89.45	90.30
Stone Veneer - Wood Frame	199.20	150.85	129.85	106.50	99.65	95.50	92.70	93.40
Solid Masonry	211.35	159.55	137.05	111.30	103.95	99.55	96.65	97.10
Finished Basement, Add	38.95	33.25	30.15	25.00	23.90	23.30	22.95	22.55
Unfinished Basement, Add	28.20	19.55	15.55	11.95	11.00	10.45	10.10	9.80

Base costs do not include bathroom or kitchen facilities. Use Modifications/Adjustments/Alternatives on pages 77-80 where appropriate.

1 Story

1-1/2 Story

2 Story

2-1/2 Story

Bi-Level

Tri-Level

- **Unique residence built from an architect's plan**
- **Single family — 1 full bath, 1 half bath, 1 kitchen**
- **No basement**
- **Cedar shakes on roof**
- **Forced hot air heat/air conditioning**
- **Gypsum wallboard interior finishes**
- **Many special features**
- **Extraordinary materials and workmanship**

Note: The illustration shown may contain some optional components (for example: garages and/or fireplaces) whose costs are shown in the modifications, adjustments, & alternatives below or at the end of the square foot section.

eHome Planners, Inc.

Base cost per square foot of living area

Exterior Wall	Living Area										
	1000	1200	1400	1600	1800	2000	2400	2800	3200	3600	4000
Wood Siding - Wood Frame	177.75	164.20	153.40	145.95	141.80	136.90	127.90	121.40	116.80	112.10	108.15
Brick Veneer - Wood Frame	187.35	172.85	161.20	153.25	148.85	143.55	133.95	127.00	122.00	116.90	112.65
Solid Brick	203.50	187.35	174.45	165.65	160.80	154.80	144.15	136.45	130.80	125.10	120.30
Solid Stone	198.35	182.80	170.25	161.70	157.05	151.25	140.95	133.50	128.00	122.50	117.95
Finished Basement, Add	46.70	50.20	48.05	46.75	45.90	44.85	43.30	42.10	41.00	40.15	39.30
Unfinished Basement, Add	20.50	19.25	18.20	17.55	17.15	16.60	15.80	15.20	14.65	14.20	13.80

Modifications

Add to the total cost

Upgrade Kitchen Cabinets	$ + 1281
Solid Surface Countertops (Included)	
Full Bath - including plumbing, wall and floor finishes	+ 7050
Half Bath - including plumbing, wall and floor finishes	+ 4270
Two Car Attached Garage	+ 25,754
Two Car Detached Garage	+ 28,975
Fireplace & Chimney	+ 6965

Adjustments

For multi family - add to total cost

Additional Kitchen	$ + 16,194
Additional Full Bath & Half Bath	+ 11,320
Additional Entry & Exit	+ 2172
Separate Heating & Air Conditioning	+ 5762
Separate Electric	+ 1766

For Townhouse/Rowhouse - Multiply cost per square foot by

Inner Unit	+ .90
End Unit	+ .95

Alternatives

Add to or deduct from the cost per square foot of living area

Heavyweight Asphalt Shingles	– 2.70
Clay Tile Roof	+ 1.55
Slate Roof	+ 2.90
Upgrade Ceilings to Textured Finish	+ .44
Air Conditioning, in Heating Ductwork	Base System
Heating Systems, Hot Water	+ 1.80
Heat Pump	+ 2.16
Electric Heat	– 1.96
Not Heated	– 3.93

Additional upgrades or components

Kitchen Cabinets & Countertops	Page 77
Bathroom Vanities	78
Fireplaces & Chimneys	78
Windows, Skylights & Dormers	78
Appliances	79
Breezeways & Porches	79
Finished Attic	79
Garages	80
Site Improvements	80
Wings & Ells	76

		Labor-Hours	Cost Per Square Foot Of Living Area		
			Mat.	Labor	Total
1 Site Work	Site preparation for slab; 4' deep trench excavation for foundation wall.	.028		.59	.59
2 Foundation	Continuous reinforced concrete footing 8" deep x 18" wide; dampproofed and insulated reinforced concrete foundation wall, 12" thick, 4' deep; 4" concrete slab on 4" crushed stone base and polyethylene vapor barrier, trowel finish.	.098	6.75	6.45	13.20
3 Framing	Exterior walls - 2" x 6" wood studs, 16" O.C.; 5/8" plywood sheathing; 2" x 10" rafters 16" O.C. with 5/8" plywood sheathing, 6 in 12 pitch; 2" x 8" ceiling joists 16" O.C.; 5/8" plywood subfloor on 1" x 3" wood sleepers 16" O.C.	.260	9.50	11.76	21.26
4 Exterior Walls	Horizontal beveled wood siding; building paper; 6" batt insulation; wood double hung windows; 3 solid core wood exterior doors; storms and screens.	.204	8.94	2.87	11.81
5 Roofing	Red cedar shingles; #15 felt building paper; aluminum gutters, downspouts and drip edge; copper flashings.	.082	5.37	3.51	8.88
6 Interiors	Walls and ceilings - 5/8" gypsum wallboard, skim coat plaster, painted with primer and 2 coats; hardwood baseboard and trim, sanded and finished; hardwood floor 70%, ceramic tile with underlayment 20%, vinyl tile with underlayment 10%; wood panel interior doors, primed and painted with 2 coat	.287	12.38	12.05	24.43
7 Specialties	Luxury grade kitchen cabinets - 25 L.F. wall and base with solid surface counter top and kitchen sink; 6 L.F. bathroom vanity; 75 gallon electric water heater; medicine cabinet.	.052	5.02	1.18	6.20
8 Mechanical	Gas fired warm air heat/air conditioning; one full bath including: bathtub, corner shower; built in lavatory and water closet; one 1/2 bath including: built in lavatory and water closet.	.078	5.49	2.89	8.38
9 Electrical	200 Amp. service; romex wiring; fluorescent and incandescent lighting fixtures; intercom, switches, receptacles.	.044	1.42	1.75	3.17
10 Overhead	Contractor's overhead and profit and architect's fees.		13.18	10.30	23.48
	Total		68.05	53.35	**121.40**

- **Unique residence built from an architect's plan**
- **Single family — 1 full bath, 1 half bath, 1 kitchen**
- **No basement**
- **Cedar shakes on roof**
- **Forced hot air heat/air conditioning**
- **Gypsum wallboard interior finishes**
- **Many special features**
- **Extraordinary materials and workmanship**

Note: The illustration shown may contain some optional components (for example: garages and/or fireplaces) whose costs are shown in the modifications, adjustments, & alternatives below or at the end of the square foot section.

eLarry E. Belk Designs

Base cost per square foot of living area

Exterior Wall	Living Area										
	1000	1200	1400	1600	1800	2000	2400	2800	3200	3600	4000
Wood Siding - Wood Frame	164.75	153.15	145.05	135.25	129.70	124.25	113.70	109.10	104.60	101.35	96.60
Brick Veneer - Wood Frame	175.80	163.50	154.90	144.20	138.15	132.35	120.85	115.85	110.90	107.30	102.20
Solid Brick	194.45	181.00	171.55	159.35	152.50	145.95	132.90	127.20	121.40	117.50	111.70
Solid Stone	188.50	175.45	166.30	154.55	147.95	141.60	129.10	123.60	118.05	114.30	108.70
Finished Basement, Add	32.90	35.70	34.60	33.05	32.15	31.35	29.65	28.95	28.10	27.65	26.90
Unfinished Basement, Add	14.85	14.15	13.65	12.85	12.40	12.00	11.20	10.85	10.40	10.20	9.85

Modifications

Add to the total cost

Upgrade Kitchen Cabinets	$ + 1281
Solid Surface Countertops (Included)	
Full Bath - including plumbing, wall and floor finishes	+ 7050
Half Bath - including plumbing, wall and floor finishes	+ 4270
Two Car Attached Garage	+ 25,754
Two Car Detached Garage	+ 28,975
Fireplace & Chimney	+ 6965

Adjustments

For multi family - add to total cost

Additional Kitchen	$ + 16,194
Additional Full Bath & Half Bath	+ 11,320
Additional Entry & Exit	+ 2172
Separate Heating & Air Conditioning	+ 5762
Separate Electric	+ 1766

For Townhouse/Rowhouse -
Multiply cost per square foot by

Inner Unit	+ .90
End Unit	+ .95

Alternatives

Add to or deduct from the cost per square foot of living area

Heavyweight Asphalt Shingles	– 1.95
Clay Tile Roof	+ 1.15
Slate Roof	+ 2.10
Upgrade Ceilings to Textured Finish	+ .44
Air Conditioning, in Heating Ductwork	Base System
Heating Systems, Hot Water	+ 1.72
Heat Pump	+ 2.39
Electric Heat	– 1.96
Not Heated	– 3.62

Additional upgrades or components

Kitchen Cabinets & Countertops	Page 77
Bathroom Vanities	78
Fireplaces & Chimneys	78
Windows, Skylights & Dormers	78
Appliances	79
Breezeways & Porches	79
Finished Attic	79
Garages	80
Site Improvements	80
Wings & Ells	76

Luxury 1-1/2 Story

Living Area - 2800 S.F.
Perimeter - 175 L.F.

		Labor-Hours	Cost Per Square Foot Of Living Area		
			Mat.	Labor	Total
1 Site Work	Site preparation for slab; 4' deep trench excavation for foundation wall.	.025		.59	.59
2 Foundation	Continuous reinforced concrete footing 8" deep x 18" wide; dampproofed and insulated reinforced concrete foundation wall, 12" thick, 4' deep; 4" concrete slab on 4" crushed stone base and polyethylene vapor barrier, trowel finish.	.066	4.85	4.89	9.74
3 Framing	Exterior walls - 2" x 6" wood studs, 16" O.C.; 5/8" plywood sheathing; 2" x 10" rafters 16" O.C. with 5/8" plywood sheathing, 8 in 12 pitch; 2" x 8" ceiling joists 16" O.C.; 2" x 12" floor joists 16" O.C. with 5/8" plywood subfloor; 5/8" plywood subfloor on 1" x 3" wood sleepers 16" O.C.	.189	5.94	7.58	13.52
4 Exterior Walls	Horizontal beveled wood siding; building paper; 6" batt insulation; wood double hung windows; 3 solid core wood exterior doors; storms and screens.	.174	9.95	3.18	13.13
5 Roofing	Red cedar shingles; #15 felt building paper; aluminum gutters, downspouts and drip edge; copper flashings.	.065	3.36	2.19	5.55
6 Interiors	Walls and ceilings - 5/8" gypsum wallboard, skim coat plaster, painted with primer and 2 coats; hardwood baseboard and trim, sanded and finished; hardwood floor 70%, ceramic tile with underlayment 20%, vinyl tile with underlayment 10%; wood panel interior doors, primed and painted with 2 coa	.260	14.05	13.66	27.71
7 Specialties	Luxury grade kitchen cabinets - 25 L.F. wall and base with solid surface counter top and kitchen sink; 6 L.F. bathroom vanity; 75 gallon electric water heater; medicine cabinet.	.062	5.02	1.18	6.20
8 Mechanical	Gas fired warm air heat/air conditioning; one full bath including: bathtub, corner shower; built in lavatory and water closet; one 1/2 bath including: built in lavatory and water closet.	.080	5.49	2.89	8.38
9 Electrical	200 Amp. service; romex wiring; fluorescent and incandescent lighting fixtures; intercom, switches, receptacles.	.044	1.42	1.75	3.17
10 Overhead	Contractor's overhead and profit and architect's fees.		12.02	9.09	21.11
	Total		62.10	47.00	**109.10**

- **Unique residence built from an architect's plan**
- **Single family — 1 full bath, 1 half bath, 1 kitchen**
- **No basement**
- **Cedar shakes on roof**
- **Forced hot air heat/air conditioning**
- **Gypsum wallboard interior finishes**
- **Many special features**
- **Extraordinary materials and workmanship**

Note: The illustration shown may contain some optional components (for example: garages and/or fireplaces) whose costs are shown in the modifications, adjustments, & alternatives below or at the end of the square foot section.

Base cost per square foot of living area

Exterior Wall	Living Area										
	1200	1400	1600	1800	2000	2400	2800	3200	3600	4000	4400
Wood Siding - Wood Frame	152.70	143.65	137.15	131.45	125.30	116.45	109.00	104.05	101.25	98.05	95.45
Brick Veneer - Wood Frame	164.50	154.70	147.70	141.35	134.90	125.00	116.85	111.40	108.25	104.70	101.90
Solid Brick	184.45	173.25	165.45	158.05	151.00	139.60	130.05	123.80	120.25	115.95	112.75
Solid Stone	178.10	167.40	159.85	152.80	145.85	134.95	125.90	119.85	116.45	112.35	109.30
Finished Basement, Add	26.45	28.65	27.90	27.05	26.45	25.10	24.10	23.45	23.00	22.50	22.15
Unfinished Basement, Add	11.95	11.35	11.00	10.50	10.25	9.60	9.10	8.80	8.55	8.30	8.15

Modifications

Add to the total cost

Upgrade Kitchen Cabinets	$ + 1281
Solid Surface Countertops (Included)	
Full Bath - including plumbing, wall and floor finishes	+ 7050
Half Bath - including plumbing, wall and floor finishes	+ 4270
Two Car Attached Garage	+ 25,754
Two Car Detached Garage	+ 28,975
Fireplace & Chimney	+ 7635

Adjustments

For multi family - add to total cost

Additional Kitchen	$ + 16,194
Additional Full Bath & Half Bath	+ 11,320
Additional Entry & Exit	+ 2172
Separate Heating & Air Conditioning	+ 5762
Separate Electric	+ 1766

For Townhouse/Rowhouse - Multiply cost per square foot by

Inner Unit	+ .86
End Unit	+ .93

Alternatives

Add to or deduct from the cost per square foot of living area

Heavyweight Asphalt Shingles	– 1.35
Clay Tile Roof	+ .80
Slate Roof	+ 1.45
Upgrade Ceilings to Textured Finish	+ .44
Air Conditioning, in Heating Ductwork	Base System
Heating Systems, Hot Water	+ 1.67
Heat Pump	+ 2.52
Electric Heat	– 1.76
Not Heated	– 3.42

Additional upgrades or components

Kitchen Cabinets & Countertops	Page 77
Bathroom Vanities	78
Fireplaces & Chimneys	78
Windows, Skylights & Dormers	78
Appliances	79
Breezeways & Porches	79
Finished Attic	79
Garages	80
Site Improvements	80
Wings & Ells	76

Important: See the Reference Section for Location Factors (to adjust for your city) and Estimating Forms

Luxury 2 Story

Living Area - 3200 S.F.
Perimeter - 163 L.F.

		Labor-Hours	Cost Per Square Foot Of Living Area		
			Mat.	Labor	Total
1 Site Work	Site preparation for slab; 4' deep trench excavation for foundation wall.	.024		.51	.51
2 Foundation	Continuous reinforced concrete footing 8" deep x 18" wide; dampproofed and insulated reinforced concrete foundation wall, 12" thick, 4' deep; 4" concrete slab on 4" crushed stone base and polyethylene vapor barrier, trowel finish.	.058	3.93	3.96	7.89
3 Framing	Exterior walls - 2" x 6" wood studs, 16" O.C.; 5/8" plywood sheathing; 2" x 10" rafters 16" O.C. with 5/8" plywood sheathing, 6 in 12 pitch; 2" x 8" ceiling joists 16" O.C.; 2" x 12" floor joists 16" O.C. with 5/8" plywood subfloor; 5/8" plywood subfloor on 1" x 3" wood sleepers 16" O.C.	.193	5.92	7.56	13.48
4 Exterior Walls	Horizontal beveled wood siding, building paper; 6" batt insulation; wood double hung windows; 3 solid core wood exterior doors; storms and screens.	.247	10.53	3.39	13.92
5 Roofing	Red cedar shingles; #15 felt building paper; aluminum gutters, downspouts and drip edge; copper flashings.	.049	2.69	1.76	4.45
6 Interiors	Walls and ceilings - 5/8" gypsum wallboard, skim coat plaster, painted with primer and 2 coats; hardwood baseboard and trim, sanded and finished; hardwood floor 70%, ceramic tile with underlayment 20%, vinyl tile with underlayment 10%; wood panel interior doors, primed and painted with 2 coat	.252	13.87	13.57	27.44
7 Specialties	Luxury grade kitchen cabinets - 25 L.F. wall and base with solid surface counter top and kitchen sink; 6 L.F. bathroom vanity; 75 gallon electric water heater; medicine cabinet.	.057	4.38	1.03	5.41
8 Mechanical	Gas fired warm air heat/air conditioning; one full bath including: bathtub, corner shower; built in lavatory and water closet; one 1/2 bath including: built in lavatory and water closet.	.071	4.96	2.76	7.72
9 Electrical	200 Amp. service; romex wiring; fluorescent and incandescent lighting fixtures; intercom, switches, receptacles.	.042	1.38	1.71	3.09
10 Overhead	Contractor's overhead and profit and architect's fee.		11.44	8.70	20.14
	Total		59.10	44.95	**104.05**

- **Unique residence built from an architect's plan**
- **Single family — 1 full bath, 1 half bath, 1 kitchen**
- **No basement**
- **Cedar shakes on roof**
- **Forced hot air heat/air conditioning**
- **Gypsum wallboard interior finishes**
- **Many special features**
- **Extraordinary materials and workmanship**

Note: The illustration shown may contain some optional components (for example: garages and/or fireplaces) whose costs are shown in the modifications, adjustments, & alternatives below or at the end of the square foot section.

©Larry W. Garnett & Associates, Inc

Base cost per square foot of living area

Exterior Wall	Living Area										
	1500	1800	2100	2500	3000	3500	4000	4500	5000	5500	6000
Wood Siding - Wood Frame	148.55	133.90	125.10	118.80	109.90	103.65	97.50	94.45	91.85	89.10	86.25
Brick Veneer - Wood Frame	160.85	145.15	135.20	128.35	118.60	111.55	104.80	101.40	98.40	95.35	92.30
Solid Brick	181.55	164.30	152.25	144.50	133.20	124.85	117.15	113.10	109.50	105.95	102.40
Solid Stone	175.00	158.20	146.85	139.40	128.65	120.60	113.25	109.35	105.95	102.65	99.20
Finished Basement, Add	21.10	22.70	21.35	20.65	19.65	18.80	18.20	17.80	17.40	17.05	16.80
Unfinished Basement, Add	9.65	9.05	8.40	8.10	7.65	7.20	6.85	6.65	6.50	6.30	6.20

Modifications

Add to the total cost

Upgrade Kitchen Cabinets	$ + 1281
Solid Surface Countertops (Included)	
Full Bath - including plumbing, wall and floor finishes	+ 7050
Half Bath - including plumbing, wall and floor finishes	+ 4270
Two Car Attached Garage	+ 25,754
Two Car Detached Garage	+ 28,975
Fireplace & Chimney	+ 8355

Adjustments

For multi family - add to total cost

Additional Kitchen	$ + 16,194
Additional Full Bath & Half Bath	+ 11,320
Additional Entry & Exit	+ 2172
Separate Heating & Air Conditioning	+ 5762
Separate Electric	+ 1766

For Townhouse/Rowhouse - Multiply cost per square foot by

Inner Unit	+ .86
End Unit	+ .93

Alternatives

Add to or deduct from the cost per square foot of living area

Heavyweight Asphalt Shingles	– 1.15
Clay Tile Roof	+ .70
Slate Roof	+ 1.25
Upgrade Ceilings to Textured Finish	+ .44
Air Conditioning, in Heating Ductwork	Base System
Heating Systems, Hot Water	+ 1.51
Heat Pump	+ 2.60
Electric Heat	– 3.47
Not Heated	– 3.42

Additional upgrades or components

Kitchen Cabinets & Countertops	Page 77
Bathroom Vanities	78
Fireplaces & Chimneys	78
Windows, Skylights & Dormers	78
Appliances	79
Breezeways & Porches	79
Finished Attic	79
Garages	80
Site Improvements	80
Wings & Ells	76

	Labor-Hours	Cost Per Square Foot Of Living Area		
		Mat.	Labor	Total
1 Site Work Site preparation for slab; 4' deep trench excavation for foundation wall.	.055		.54	.54
2 Foundation Continuous reinforced concrete footing 8" deep x 18" wide; dampproofed and insulated reinforced concrete foundation wall, 12" thick, 4' deep; 4" concrete slab on 4" crushed stone base and polyethylene vapor barrier, trowel finish.	.067	3.43	3.59	7.02
3 Framing Exterior walls - 2" x 6" wood studs, 16" O.C.; 5/8" plywood sheathing; 2" x 10" rafters 16" O.C. with 5/8" plywood sheathing, 6 in 12 pitch; 2" x 8" ceiling joists 16" O.C.; 2" x 12" floor joists 16" O.C. with 5/8" plywood subfloor; 5/8" plywood subfloor on 1" x 3" wood sleepers 16" O.C.	.209	6.12	7.77	13.89
4 Exterior Walls Horizontal beveled wood siding; building paper; 6" batt insulation; wood double hung windows; 3 solid core wood exterior doors; storms and screens.	.405	12.27	3.95	16.22
5 Roofing Red cedar shingles; #15 felt building paper; aluminum gutters, downspouts and drip edge; copper flashings.	.039	2.07	1.36	3.43
6 Interiors Walls and ceilings - 5/8" gypsum wallboard, skim coat plaster, painted with primer and 2 coats; hardwood baseboard and trim, sanded and finished; hardwood floor 70%, ceramic tile with underlayment 20%, vinyl tile with underlayment 10%; wood panel interior doors, primed and painted with 2 coat	.341	15.54	15.12	30.66
7 Specialties Luxury grade kitchen cabinets - 25 L.F. wall and base with solid surface counter top and kitchen sink; 6 L.F. bathroom vanity; 75 gallon electric water heater; medicine cabinet.	.119	4.69	1.09	5.78
8 Mechanical Gas fired warm air heat/air conditioning; one full bath including: bathtub, corner shower; built in lavatory and water closet; one 1/2 bath including: built in lavatory and water closet.	.103	5.22	2.80	8.02
9 Electrical 200 Amp. service; romex wiring; fluorescent and incandescent lighting fixtures; intercom, switches, receptacles.	.054	1.40	1.73	3.13
10 Overhead Contractor's overhead and profit and architect's fee.		12.16	9.05	21.21
Total		62.90	47.00	**109.90**

- **Unique residence built from an architect's plan**
- **Single family — 1 full bath, 1 half bath, 1 kitchen**
- **No basement**
- **Cedar shakes on roof**
- **Forced hot air heat/air conditioning**
- **Gypsum wallboard interior finishes**
- **Many special features**
- **Extraordinary materials and workmanship**

Note: The illustration shown may contain some optional components (for example: garages and/or fireplaces) whose costs are shown in the modifications, adjustments, & alternatives below or at the end of the square foot section.

Base cost per square foot of living area

Exterior Wall	Living Area										
	1500	1800	2100	2500	3000	3500	4000	4500	5000	5500	6000
Wood Siding - Wood Frame	147.55	133.00	125.85	119.95	110.75	106.25	100.60	94.85	92.60	90.35	88.00
Brick Veneer - Wood Frame	160.30	144.80	136.90	130.50	120.30	115.30	108.80	102.40	100.00	97.40	94.65
Solid Brick	181.85	164.75	155.45	148.25	136.40	130.55	122.70	115.20	112.35	109.30	105.90
Solid Stone	175.00	158.40	149.55	142.65	131.30	125.75	118.30	111.15	108.45	105.55	102.35
Finished Basement, Add	18.55	19.90	19.10	18.50	17.55	17.05	16.35	15.75	15.50	15.25	14.95
Unfinished Basement, Add	8.45	7.95	7.55	7.25	6.85	6.60	6.25	5.95	5.85	5.70	5.55

Modifications

Add to the total cost

Upgrade Kitchen Cabinets	$ + 1281
Solid Surface Countertops (Included)	
Full Bath - including plumbing, wall and floor finishes	+ 7050
Half Bath - including plumbing, wall and floor finishes	+ 4270
Two Car Attached Garage	+ 25,754
Two Car Detached Garage	+ 28,975
Fireplace & Chimney	+ 8355

Adjustments

For multi family - add to total cost

Additional Kitchen	$ + 16,194
Additional Full Bath & Half Bath	+ 11,320
Additional Entry & Exit	+ 2172
Separate Heating & Air Conditioning	+ 5762
Separate Electric	+ 1766

For Townhouse/Rowhouse - Multiply cost per square foot by

Inner Unit	+ .84
End Unit	+ .92

Alternatives

Add to or deduct from the cost per square foot of living area

Heavyweight Asphalt Shingles	– .90
Clay Tile Roof	+ .50
Slate Roof	+ .95
Upgrade Ceilings to Textured Finish	+ .44
Air Conditioning, in Heating Ductwork	Base System
Heating Systems, Hot Water	+ 1.51
Heat Pump	+ 2.60
Electric Heat	– 3.47
Not Heated	– 3.32

Additional upgrades or components

Kitchen Cabinets & Countertops	Page 77
Bathroom Vanities	78
Fireplaces & Chimneys	78
Windows, Skylights & Dormers	78
Appliances	79
Breezeways & Porches	79
Finished Attic	79
Garages	80
Site Improvements	80
Wings & Ells	76

Luxury 3 Story

Living Area - 3000 S.F.
Perimeter - 135 L.F.

		Labor-Hours	Cost Per Square Foot Of Living Area		
			Mat.	Labor	Total
1 Site Work	Site preparation for slab; 4' deep trench excavation for foundation wall.	.055		.54	.54
2 Foundation	Continuous reinforced concrete footing 8" deep x 18" wide; dampproofed and insulated reinforced concrete foundation wall, 12" thick, 4' deep; 4" concrete slab on 4" crushed stone base and polyethylene vapor barrier, trowel finish.	.063	3.08	3.28	6.36
3 Framing	Exterior walls - 2" x 6" wood studs, 16" O.C.; 5/8" plywood sheathing; 2" x 10" rafters 16" O.C. with 5/8" plywood sheathing, 6 in 12 pitch; 2" x 8" ceiling joists 16" O.C.; 2" x 12" floor joists 16" O.C. with 5/8" plywood subfloor; 5/8" plywood subfloor on 1" x 3" wood sleepers 16" O.C.	.225	6.21	7.89	14.10
4 Exterior Walls	Horizontal beveled wood siding; building paper; 6" batt insulation; wood double hung windows; 3 solid core wood exterior doors; storms and screens.	.454	13.39	4.32	17.71
5 Roofing	Red cedar shingles; #15 felt building paper; aluminum gutters, downspouts and drip edge; copper flashings.	.034	1.79	1.17	2.96
6 Interiors	Walls and ceilings - 5/8" gypsum wallboard, skim coat plaster, painted with primer and 2 coats; hardwood baseboard and trim, sanded and finished; hardwood floor 70%, ceramic tile with underlayment 20%, vinyl tile with underlayment 10%; wood panel interior doors, primed and painted with 2 coat	.390	15.55	15.23	30.78
7 Specialties	Luxury grade kitchen cabinets - 25 L.F. wall and base with solid surface counter top and kitchen sink; 6 L.F. bathroom vanity; 75 gallon electric water heater; medicine cabinet.	.119	4.69	1.09	5.78
8 Mechanical	Gas fired warm air heat/air conditioning; one full bath including: bathtub, corner shower; built in lavatory and water closet; one 1/2 bath including: built in lavatory and water closet.	.103	5.22	2.80	8.02
9 Electrical	200 Amp. service; romex wiring; fluorescent and incandescent lighting fixtures; intercom, switches, receptacles.	.053	1.40	1.73	3.13
10 Overhead	Contractor's overhead and profit and architect's fees.		12.32	9.05	21.37
Total			63.65	47.10	**110.75**

- **Unique residence built from an architect's plan**
- **Single family — 1 full bath, 1 half bath, 1 kitchen**
- **No basement**
- **Cedar shakes on roof**
- **Forced hot air heat/air conditioning**
- **Gypsum wallboard interior finishes**
- **Many special features**
- **Extraordinary materials and workmanship**

Note: The illustration shown may contain some optional components (for example: garages and/or fireplaces) whose costs are shown in the modifications, adjustments, & alternatives below or at the end of the square foot section.

Base cost per square foot of living area

Exterior Wall	Living Area										
	1200	1400	1600	1800	2000	2400	2800	3200	3600	4000	4400
Wood Siding - Wood Frame	144.20	135.70	129.55	124.35	118.45	110.20	103.40	98.75	96.10	93.25	90.85
Brick Veneer - Wood Frame	153.10	143.95	137.40	131.75	125.60	116.70	109.20	104.20	101.45	98.25	95.70
Solid Brick	168.05	157.95	150.70	144.30	137.70	127.60	119.20	113.50	110.40	106.70	103.80
Solid Stone	163.30	153.50	146.50	140.30	133.90	124.15	116.00	110.60	107.55	104.05	101.25
Finished Basement, Add	26.45	28.65	27.90	27.05	26.45	25.10	24.10	23.45	23.00	22.50	22.15
Unfinished Basement, Add	11.95	11.35	11.00	10.50	10.25	9.60	9.10	8.80	8.55	8.30	8.15

Modifications

Add to the total cost

Upgrade Kitchen Cabinets	$ + 1281
Solid Surface Countertops (Included)	
Full Bath - including plumbing, wall and floor finishes	+ 7050
Half Bath - including plumbing, wall and floor finishes	+ 4270
Two Car Attached Garage	+ 25,754
Two Car Detached Garage	+ 28,975
Fireplace & Chimney	+ 6965

Adjustments

For multi family - add to total cost

Additional Kitchen	$ + 16,194
Additional Full Bath & Half Bath	+ 11,320
Additional Entry & Exit	+ 2172
Separate Heating & Air Conditioning	+ 5762
Separate Electric	+ 1766

For Townhouse/Rowhouse -
Multiply cost per square foot by

Inner Unit	+ .89
End Unit	+ .94

Alternatives

Add to or deduct from the cost per square foot of living area

Heavyweight Asphalt Shingles	− 1.35
Clay Tile Roof	+ .80
Slate Roof	+ 1.45
Upgrade Ceilings to Textured Finish	+ .44
Air Conditioning, in Heating Ductwork	Base System
Heating Systems, Hot Water	+ 1.67
Heat Pump	+ 2.52
Electric Heat	− 1.76
Not Heated	− 3.42

Additional upgrades or components

Kitchen Cabinets & Countertops	Page 77
Bathroom Vanities	78
Fireplaces & Chimneys	78
Windows, Skylights & Dormers	78
Appliances	79
Breezeways & Porches	79
Finished Attic	79
Garages	80
Site Improvements	80
Wings & Ells	76

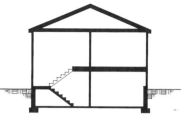

		Labor-Hours	Cost Per Square Foot Of Living Area		
			Mat.	Labor	Total
1 Site Work	Excavation for lower level, 4' deep. Site preparation for slab.	.024		.51	.51
2 Foundation	Continuous reinforced concrete footing 8" deep x 18" wide; dampproofed and insulated reinforced concrete foundation wall, 12" thick, 4' deep; 4" concrete slab on 4" crushed stone base and polyethylene vapor barrier, trowel finish.	.058	3.93	3.96	7.89
3 Framing	Exterior walls - 2" x 6" wood studs, 16" O.C.; 5/8" plywood sheathing; 2" x 10" rafters 16" O.C. with 5/8" plywood sheathing, 6 in 12 pitch; 2" x 8" ceiling joists 16" O.C.; 2" x 12" floor joists 16" O.C. with 5/8" plywood subfloor; 5/8" plywood subfloor on 1" x 3" wood sleepers 16" O.C.	.232	5.62	7.20	12.82
4 Exterior Walls	Horizontal beveled wood siding; building paper; 6" batt insulation; wood double hung windows; 3 solid core wood exterior doors; storms and screens.	.185	8.19	2.64	10.83
5 Roofing	Red cedar shingles: #15 felt building paper; aluminum gutters, downspouts and drip edge; copper flashings.	.042	2.69	1.76	4.45
6 Interiors	Walls and ceilings - 5/8" gypsum wallboard, skim coat plaster, painted with primer and 2 coats; hardwood baseboard and trim, sanded and finished; hardwood floor 70%, ceramic tile with underlayment 20%; vinyl tile with underlayment 10%; wood panel interior doors, primed and painted with 2 coat	.238	13.68	13.24	26.92
7 Specialties	Luxury grade kitchen cabinets - 25 L.F. wall and base with solid surface counter top and kitchen sink; 6 L.F. bathroom vanity; 75 gallon electric water heater; medicine cabinet.	.056	4.38	1.03	5.41
8 Mechanical	Gas fired warm air heat/air conditioning; one full bath including: bathtub, corner shower; built in lavatory and water closet; one 1/2 bath including: built in lavatory and water closet.	.071	4.96	2.76	7.72
9 Electrical	200 Amp. service; romex wiring; fluorescent and incandescent lighting fixtures; intercom, switches, receptacles.	.042	1.38	1.71	3.09
10 Overhead	Contractor's overhead and profit and architect's fees.		10.77	8.34	19.11
	Total		55.60	43.15	**98.75**

- **Unique residence built from an architect's plan**
- **Single family — 1 full bath, 1 half bath, 1 kitchen**
- **No basement**
- **Cedar shakes on roof**
- **Forced hot air heat/air conditioning**
- **Gypsum wallboard interior finishes**
- **Many special features**
- **Extraordinary materials and workmanship**

Note: The illustration shown may contain some optional components (for example: garages and/or fireplaces) whose costs are shown in the modifications, adjustments, & alternatives below or at the end of the square foot section.

©Home Planners, Inc.

Base cost per square foot of living area

Exterior Wall	Living Area										
	1500	1800	2100	2400	2800	3200	3600	4000	4500	5000	5500
Wood Siding - Wood Frame	136.30	126.20	117.75	112.15	108.10	103.15	98.25	95.95	91.10	88.55	85.50
Brick Veneer - Wood Frame	144.30	133.45	124.25	118.25	114.00	108.60	103.30	100.80	95.65	92.80	89.50
Solid Brick	157.75	145.55	135.25	128.55	123.90	117.80	111.80	109.10	103.30	99.95	96.35
Solid Stone	153.50	141.70	131.80	125.35	120.80	114.90	109.10	106.55	100.85	97.70	94.20
Finished Basement, Add*	31.10	33.45	32.05	31.15	30.55	29.65	28.85	28.55	27.70	27.20	26.75
Unfinished Basement, Add*	13.65	12.85	12.10	11.70	11.40	10.95	10.55	10.40	9.95	9.70	9.50

*Basement under middle level only.

Modifications

Add to the total cost

Upgrade Kitchen Cabinets	$ + 1281
Solid Surface Countertops (Included)	
Full Bath - including plumbing, wall and floor finishes	+ 7050
Half Bath - including plumbing, wall and floor finishes	+ 4270
Two Car Attached Garage	+ 25,754
Two Car Detached Garage	+ 28,975
Fireplace & Chimney	+ 6965

Adjustments

For multi family - add to total cost

Additional Kitchen	$ + 16,194
Additional Full Bath & Half Bath	+ 11,320
Additional Entry & Exit	+ 2172
Separate Heating & Air Conditioning	+ 5762
Separate Electric	+ 1766

*For Townhouse/Rowhouse -
Multiply cost per square foot by*

Inner Unit	+ .86
End Unit	+ .93

Alternatives

Add to or deduct from the cost per square foot of living area

Heavyweight Asphalt Shingles	– 1.95
Clay Tile Roof	+ 1.15
Slate Roof	+ 2.10
Upgrade Ceilings to Textured Finish	+ .44
Air Conditioning, in Heating Ductwork	Base System
Heating Systems, Hot Water	+ 1.62
Heat Pump	+ 2.63
Electric Heat	– 1.56
Not Heated	– 3.32

Additional upgrades or components

Kitchen Cabinets & Countertops	Page 77
Bathroom Vanities	78
Fireplaces & Chimneys	78
Windows, Skylights & Dormers	78
Appliances	79
Breezeways & Porches	79
Finished Attic	79
Garages	80
Site Improvements	80
Wings & Ells	76

Luxury Tri-Level

Living Area - 3600 S.F.
Perimeter - 207 L.F.

		Labor-Hours	Cost Per Square Foot Of Living Area		
			Mat.	Labor	Total
1 Site Work	Site preparation for slab; 4' deep trench excavation for foundation wall, excavation for lower level, 4' deep.	.021		.45	.45
2 Foundation	Continuous reinforced concrete footing 8" deep x 18" wide; dampproofed and insulated reinforced concrete foundation wall, 12" thick, 4' deep; 4" concrete slab on 4" crushed stone base and polyethylene vapor barrier, trowel finish.	.109	4.70	4.54	9.24
3 Framing	Exterior walls - 2" x 6" wood studs, 16" O.C.; 5/8" plywood sheathing; 2" x 10" rafters 16" O.C. with 5/8" plywood sheathing, 6 in 12 pitch; 2" x 8" ceiling joists 16" O.C.; 2" x 12" floor joists 16" O.C. with 5/8" plywood subfloor; 5/8" plywood subfloor on 1" x 3" wood sleepers 16" O.C.	.204	5.62	7.20	12.82
4 Exterior Walls	Horizontal beveled wood siding; building paper; 6" batt insulation; wood double hung windows; 3 solid core wood exterior doors; storms and screens.	.181	7.86	2.52	10.38
5 Roofing	Red cedar shingles; #15 felt building paper; aluminum gutters, downspouts and drip edge; copper flashings.	.056	3.58	2.34	5.92
6 Interiors	Walls and ceilings - 5/8" gypsum wallboard, skim coat plaster, painted with primer and 2 coats; hardwood baseboard and trim, sanded and finished; hardwood floor 70%, ceramic tile with underlayment 20%, vinyl tile with underlayment 10%; wood panel interior doors, primed and painted with 2 coat	.217	12.86	12.37	25.23
7 Specialties	Luxury grade kitchen cabinets - 25 L.F. wall and base with solid surface counter top and kitchen sink; 6 L.F. bathroom vanity; 75 gallon electric water heater; medicine cabinet.	.048	3.90	.92	4.82
8 Mechanical	Gas fired warm air heat/air conditioning; one full bath including: bathtub, corner shower; built in lavatory and water closet; one 1/2 bath including: built in lavatory and water closet.	.057	4.59	2.65	7.24
9 Electrical	200 Amp. service; romex wiring; fluorescent and incandescent lighting fixtures; intercom, switches, receptacles.	.039	1.35	1.68	3.03
10 Overhead	Contractor's overhead and profit and architect's fees.		10.69	8.43	19.12
	Total		55.15	43.10	**98.25**

1 Story   Base cost per square foot of living area

Exterior Wall	Living Area							
	50	100	200	300	400	500	600	700
Wood Siding - Wood Frame	224.40	173.35	151.15	127.10	119.90	115.50	112.60	113.40
Brick Veneer - Wood Frame	254.10	194.60	168.85	138.85	130.50	125.40	122.00	122.50
Solid Brick	304.25	230.45	198.75	158.80	148.40	142.10	137.95	137.85
Solid Stone	288.35	219.10	189.25	152.50	142.70	136.85	132.90	133.00
Finished Basement, Add	84.00	76.00	68.05	54.85	52.20	50.60	49.65	48.85
Unfinished Basement, Add	43.40	33.35	29.15	22.20	20.80	19.95	19.40	18.95

1-1/2 Story   Base cost per square foot of living area

Exterior Wall	Living Area							
	100	200	300	400	500	600	700	800
Wood Siding - Wood Frame	179.05	146.25	126.30	114.15	108.05	105.10	101.45	100.40
Brick Veneer - Wood Frame	205.55	167.55	144.00	127.90	120.80	117.15	112.80	111.65
Solid Brick	250.35	203.35	173.85	151.20	142.35	137.50	132.00	130.65
Solid Stone	236.20	192.05	164.40	143.75	135.50	131.05	125.90	124.70
Finished Basement, Add	55.15	54.45	49.15	43.35	41.80	40.75	39.75	39.65
Unfinished Basement, Add	27.50	23.30	20.50	17.45	16.60	16.00	15.50	15.45

2 Story   Base cost per square foot of living area

Exterior Wall	Living Area							
	100	200	400	600	800	1000	1200	1400
Wood Siding - Wood Frame	176.20	133.00	114.15	95.45	89.30	85.60	83.10	84.20
Brick Veneer - Wood Frame	205.95	154.20	131.80	107.25	99.95	95.45	92.50	93.30
Solid Brick	256.10	190.05	161.65	127.20	117.85	112.20	108.45	108.65
Solid Stone	240.25	178.70	152.15	120.85	112.10	106.90	103.40	103.80
Finished Basement, Add	42.05	38.00	34.10	27.50	26.15	25.40	24.85	24.50
Unfinished Basement, Add	21.70	16.70	14.60	11.15	10.40	10.00	9.70	9.50

Base costs do not include bathroom or kitchen facilities. Use Modifications/Adjustments/Alternatives on pages 77-80 where appropriate.

Kitchen cabinets -
Base units, hardwood *(Cost per Unit)*

	Economy	Average	Custom	Luxury
24″ deep, 35″ high,				
One top drawer,				
One door below				
12″ wide	$ 189	$ 252	$ 335	$ 441
15″ wide	198	264	351	462
18″ wide	214	286	380	500
21″ wide	232	310	412	542
24″ wide	255	340	452	595
Four drawers				
12″ wide	322	430	571	752
15″ wide	270	360	478	630
18″ wide	296	395	525	691
24″ wide	322	430	571	752
Two top drawers,				
Two doors below				
27″ wide	281	375	498	656
30″ wide	300	400	532	700
33″ wide	330	440	585	770
36″ wide	341	455	605	796
42″ wide	360	480	638	840
48″ wide	382	510	678	892
Range or sink base				
(Cost per unit)				
Two doors below				
30″ wide	273	365	485	638
33″ wide	288	385	512	673
36″ wide	300	400	532	700
42″ wide	318	425	565	743
48″ wide	333	445	591	778
Corner Base Cabinet				
(Cost per unit)				
36″ wide	390	520	691	910
Lazy Susan *(Cost per unit)*				
With revolving door	390	520	691	910

Kitchen cabinets -
Wall cabinets, hardwood *(Cost per Unit)*

	Economy	Average	Custom	Luxury
12″ deep, 2 doors				
12″ high				
30″ wide	$ 156	$ 208	$ 276	$ 364
36″ wide	179	239	317	418
15″ high				
30″ wide	165	221	293	386
33″ wide	177	237	315	414
36″ wide	186	248	329	434
24″ high				
30″ wide	201	268	356	469
36″ wide	220	294	391	514
42″ wide	240	320	425	560
30″ high, 1 door				
12″ wide	144	193	256	337
15″ wide	161	215	285	376
18″ wide	174	233	309	407
24″ wide	194	259	344	453
30″ high, 2 doors				
27″ wide	228	305	405	533
30″ wide	228	305	405	533
36″ wide	258	345	458	603
42″ wide	281	375	498	656
48″ wide	311	415	551	726
Corner wall, 30″ high				
24″ wide	166	222	295	388
30″ wide	197	263	349	460
36″ wide	212	283	376	495
Broom closet				
84″ high, 24″ deep				
18″ wide	423	565	751	988
Oven Cabinet				
84″ high, 24″ deep				
27″ wide	607	810	1077	1417

Kitchen countertops *(Cost per L.F.)*

	Economy	Average	Custom	Luxury
Solid Surface				
24″ wide, no backsplash	90	120	159	210
with backsplash	97	130	172	227
Stock plastic laminate, 24″ wide				
with backsplash	17	23	30	40
Custom plastic laminate, no splash				
7/8″ thick, alum. molding	25	33	44	58
1-1/4″ thick, no splash	33	45	59	78
Marble				
1/2″ - 3/4″ thick w/splash	45	61	81	106
Maple, laminated				
1-1/2″ thick w/splash	67	90	119	157
Stainless steel				
(per S.F.)	122	163	216	285
Cutting blocks, recessed				
16″ x 20″ x 1″ (each)	90	120	159	210

Vanity bases *(Cost per Unit)*

2 door, 30" high, 21" deep	Economy	Average	Custom	Luxury
24" wide	195	261	347	456
30" wide	228	305	405	533
36" wide	300	400	532	700
48" wide	356	475	631	831

Solid surface vanity tops *(Cost Each)*

Center bowl	Economy	Average	Custom	Luxury
22" x 25"	$ 252	$ 272	$ 293	$ 317
22" x 31"	288	311	335	362
22" x 37"	330	356	384	415
22" x 49"	405	437	472	510

Fireplaces & Chimneys *(Cost per Unit)*

	1-1/2 Story	2 Story	3 Story
Economy (prefab metal)			
Exterior chimney & 1 fireplace	$ 4735	$ 5232	$ 5739
Interior chimney & 1 fireplace	4537	5044	5277
Average (masonry)			
Exterior chimney & 1 fireplace	4701	5241	5959
Interior chimney & 1 fireplace	4403	4943	5383
For more than 1 flue, add	338	575	964
For more than 1 fireplace, add	3333	3333	3333
Custom (masonry)			
Exterior chimney & 1 fireplace	5168	5834	6588
Interior chimney & 1 fireplace	4846	5486	5912
For more than 1 flue, add	405	702	951
For more than 1 fireplace, add	3712	3712	3712
Luxury (masonry)			
Exterior chimney & 1 fireplace	7243	7940	8689
Interior chimney & 1 fireplace	6910	7555	7997
For more than 1 flue, add	598	998	1393
For more than 1 fireplace, add	5709	5709	5709

Windows and Skylights *(Cost Each)*

	Economy	Average	Custom	Luxury
Fixed Picture Windows				
3'-6" x 4'-0"	$ 505	$ 546	$ 590	$ 637
4'-0" x 6'-0"	921	995	1075	1161
5'-0" x 6'-0"	1007	1087	1175	1269
6'-0" x 6'-0"	1028	1111	1200	1296
Bay/Bow Windows				
8'-0" x 5'-0"	1264	1365	1475	1593
10'-0" x 5'-0"	1478	1597	1725	1863
10'-0" x 6'-0"	2314	2500	2700	2916
12'-0" x 6'-0"	2936	3171	3425	3699
Palladian Windows				
3'-2" x 6'-4"		1782	1925	2079
4'-0" x 6'-0"		2106	2275	2457
5'-5" x 6'-10"		2523	2725	2943
8'-0" x 6'-0"		3032	3275	3537
Skylights				
46" x 21-1/2"	406	439	590	637
46" x 28"	439	474	630	680
57" x 44"	535	578	765	826

Dormers *(Cost/S.F. of plan area)*

	Economy	Average	Custom	Luxury
Framing and Roofing Only				
Gable dormer, 2" x 6" roof frame	$ 24	$ 27	$ 31	$ 49
2" x 8" roof frame	25	28	32	52
Shed dormer, 2" x 6" roof frame	15	17	20	32
2" x 8" roof frame	17	18	21	33
2" x 10" roof frame	18	20	22	34

Appliances (Cost per Unit)

	Economy	Average	Custom	Luxury
Range				
30" free standing, 1 oven	$ 350	$ 1225	$ 1662	$ 2100
2 oven	1725	1862	1931	2000
30" built-in, 1 oven	595	1285	1630	1975
2 oven	1650	1912	2043	2175
21" free standing				
1 oven	410	455	477	500
Counter Top Ranges				
4 burner standard	310	562	688	815
As above with griddle	970	1285	1442	1600
Microwave Oven	194	432	551	670
Combination Range,				
Refrigerator, Sink				
30" wide	1250	2350	2900	3450
60" wide	2775	3191	3399	3607
72" wide	3950	4542	4838	5135
Comb. Range, Refrig., Sink,				
Microwave Oven & Ice Maker	6324	7272	7746	8221
Compactor				
4 to 1 compaction	595	665	700	735
Deep Freeze				
15 to 23 C.F.	605	672	706	740
30 C.F.	950	1062	1118	1175
Dehumidifier, portable, auto.				
15 pint	165	183	192	202
30 pint	202	232	247	263
Washing Machine, automatic	475	1075	1375	1675
Water Heater				
Electric, glass lined				
30 gal.	405	500	547	595
80 gal.	805	1040	1157	1275
Water Heater, Gas, glass lined				
30 gal.	755	927	1013	1100
50 gal.	1250	1537	1681	1825
Water Softener, automatic				
30 grains/gal.	685	788	839	891
100 grains/gal.	965	1110	1182	1255
Dishwasher, built-in				
2 cycles	420	505	547	590
4 or more cycles	450	725	862	1000
Dryer, automatic	535	1105	1390	1675
Garage Door Opener	390	467	506	545
Garbage Disposal	119	192	229	266
Heater, Electric, built-in				
1250 watt ceiling type	182	225	246	268
1250 watt wall type	212	250	269	289
Wall type w/blower				
1500 watt	246	340	387	435
3000 watt	435	478	500	522
Hood For Range, 2 speed				
30" wide	146	648	899	1150
42" wide	365	1195	1610	2025
Humidifier, portable				
7 gal. per day	176	202	215	228
15 gal. per day	212	243	259	275
Ice Maker, automatic				
13 lb. per day	995	1144	1218	1293
51 lb. per day	1275	1466	1561	1657
Refrigerator, no frost				
10-12 C.F.	590	697	751	805
14-16 C.F.	625	695	730	765
18-20 C.F.	735	930	1027	1125
21-29 C.F.	920	1910	2405	2900
Sump Pump, 1/3 H.P.	262	371	425	480

Breezeway (Cost per S.F.)

Class	Type	Area (S.F.)			
		50	100	150	200
Economy	Open	$ 21.55	$ 18.30	$ 15.36	$ 15.11
	Enclosed	103.33	79.80	66.26	58.05
Average	Open	28.88	25.46	22.28	20.24
	Enclosed	112.77	84.03	68.73	60.50
Custom	Open	39.99	35.20	30.63	28.03
	Enclosed	164.27	122.20	99.89	87.83
Luxury	Open	41.29	36.19	32.60	31.67
	Enclosed	166.24	123.29	99.74	89.28

Porches (Cost per S.F.)

Class	Type	Area (S.F.)				
		25	50	100	200	300
Economy	Open	$ 61.75	$ 41.32	$ 32.30	$ 27.33	$ 23.32
	Enclosed	123.40	85.99	65.00	50.70	43.40
Average	Open	81.29	51.76	39.71	33.00	33.00
	Enclosed	147.51	99.94	75.60	58.53	49.59
Custom	Open	102.13	67.76	51.01	44.56	39.94
	Enclosed	203.06	138.74	105.56	82.21	70.82
Luxury	Open	109.30	71.45	52.78	47.42	42.28
	Enclosed	213.98	150.28	111.49	86.63	74.57

Finished attic (Cost per S.F.)

Class	Area (S.F.)				
	400	500	600	800	1000
Economy	$ 16.48	$ 15.92	$ 15.26	$ 15.01	$ 14.45
Average	25.25	24.69	24.09	23.79	23.13
Custom	32.55	31.82	31.10	30.63	30.00
Luxury	41.03	40.04	39.10	38.17	37.54

Alarm system (Cost per System)

	Burglar Alarm	Smoke Detector
Economy	$ 375	$ 65
Average	430	79
Custom	979	178
Luxury	1075	178

Sauna, prefabricated
(Cost per unit, including heater and controls—7' high)

Size	Cost
6' x 4'	$ 5025
6' x 5'	5625
6' x 6'	6025
6' x 9'	7475
8' x 10'	9800
8' x 12'	11,500
10' x 12'	12,200

Garages *

(Costs include exterior wall systems comparable with the quality of the residence. Included in the cost is an allowance for one personnel door, manual overhead door(s) and electrical fixture.)

Class	Type									
	Detached			Attached			Built-in		Basement	
	One Car	Two Car	Three Car	One Car	Two Car	Three Car	One Car	Two Car	One Car	Two Car
Economy										
Wood	$12,792	$19,492	$26,191	$ 9904	$17,056	$23,756	$−1716	$−3433	$1295	$1692
Masonry	18,876	27,106	35,335	13,712	22,393	30,623	−2463	−4927		
Average										
Wood	14,818	22,028	29,237	11,173	18,834	26,043	−1965	−3930	1474	2050
Masonry	19,056	27,331	35,605	13,824	22,551	30,825	−2485	−4260		
Custom										
Wood	16,445	25,012	33,579	12,752	21,925	30,492	−3279	−3422	2263	3628
Masonry	21,149	30,899	40,649	15,695	26,052	35,801	−3856	−4577		
Luxury										
Wood	18,561	28,975	39,389	14,733	25,754	36,168	−3323	−3510	3095	4931
Masonry	24,317	36,178	48,039	18,335	30,803	42,664	−4030	−4923		

*See the Introduction to this section for definitions of garage types.

Swimming pools (Cost per S.F.)

Residential	(includes equipment)
Inground	$22.00 - 58.00
Deck equipment	1.30
Paint pool, preparation & 3 coats (epoxy)	4.18
Rubber base paint	3.56
Pool Cover	.82
Swimming Pool Heaters	(Cost per unit)
(not including wiring, external piping, base or pad)	
Gas	
155 MBH	$ 2425
190 MBH	2925
500 MBH	10,100
Electric	
15 KW 7200 gallon pool	2675
24 KW 9600 gallon pool	3525
54 KW 24,000 gallon pool	5300

Wood and coal stoves

Wood Only	
Free Standing (minimum)	$ 1725
Fireplace Insert (minimum)	1739
Coal Only	
Free Standing	$ 1965
Fireplace Insert	2151
Wood and Coal	
Free Standing	$ 4041
Fireplace Insert	4141

Sidewalks (Cost per S.F.)

Concrete, 3000 psi with wire mesh	4" thick	$ 3.43
	5" thick	4.20
	6" thick	4.73
Precast concrete patio blocks (natural)	2" thick	7.81
Precast concrete patio blocks (colors)	2" thick	8.36
Flagstone, bluestone	1" thick	14.55
Flagstone, bluestone	1-1/2" thick	19.55
Slate (natural, irregular)	3/4" thick	14.35
Slate (random rectangular)	1/2" thick	22.00
Seeding		
Fine grading & seeding includes lime, fertilizer & seed per S.Y.		2.21
Lawn Sprinkler System	per S.F.	.87

Fencing (Cost per L.F.)

Chain Link, 4' high, galvanized	$ 16.55
Gate, 4' high (each)	170.00
Cedar Picket, 3' high, 2 rail	11.40
Gate (each)	168.00
3 Rail, 4' high	14.00
Gate (each)	178.00
Cedar Stockade, 3 Rail, 6' high	14.20
Gate (each)	178.00
Board & Battens, 2 sides 6' high, pine	20.00
6' high, cedar	28.00
No. 1 Cedar, basketweave, 6' high	16.15
Gate, 6' high (each)	204.00

Carport (Cost per S.F.)

Economy	$ 7.66
Average	11.61
Custom	17.77
Luxury	20.17

Assemblies Section

Table of Contents

How to Use the Assemblies Section

Illustration
Each building assembly system is accompanied by a detailed, illustrated description. Each individual component is labeled. Every element involved in the total system function is shown.

Description
Each page includes a brief outline of any special conditions to be used when pricing a system. All units of measure are defined here.

System Definition
Not only are all components broken down for each system, but alternative components can be found on the opposite page. Simply insert any chosen new element into the chart to develop a custom system.

Labor-hours
Total labor-hours for a system can be found by simply multiplying the quantity of the system required times LABOR-HOURS. The resulting figure is the total labor-hours needed to complete the system.
(QUANTITY OF SYSTEM x LABOR-HOURS = TOTAL SYSTEM LABOR-HOURS)

Materials
This column contains the MATERIAL COST of each element. These cost figures include 10% for profit.

Installation
Labor rates include both the INSTALLATION COST of the contractor and the standard contractor's O&P. On the average, the LABOR COST will be 70.6% over the above BARE LABOR COST.

Totals
This row provides the necessary system cost totals. TOTAL SYSTEM COST can be derived by multiplying the TOTAL times each system's SQUARE FOOT ESTIMATE (TOTAL x SQUARE FEET = TOTAL SYSTEM COST).

Work Sheet
Using the SELECTIVE PRICE SHEET on the page opposite each system, it is possible to create estimates with alternative items for any number of systems.

Note:
Throughout this section, the words assembly and system are used interchangeably.

Quantities
Each material in a system is shown with the quantity required for the system unit. For example, the rafters in this system have 1.170 L.F. per S.F. of ceiling area.

Unit of Measure
In the three right-hand columns, each cost figure is adjusted to agree with the unit of measure for the entire system. In this case, COST PER SQUARE FOOT (S.F.) is the common unit of measure. NOTE: In addition, under the UNIT heading, all the elements of each system are defined in relation to the product as a selling commodity. For example, "fascia board" is defined in linear feet, instead of in board feet.

Total
MATERIAL COST + INSTALLATION COST = TOTAL. Work on the table from left to right across cost columns to derive totals.

3 | FRAMING   12 | Gable End Roof Framing Systems

System Description	QUAN.	UNIT	LABOR HOURS	COST PER S.F. MAT.	COST PER S.F. INST.	COST PER S.F. TOTAL
2" X 6" RAFTERS, 16" O.C., 4/12 PITCH						
Rafters, 2" x 6", 16" O.C., 4/12 pitch	1.170	L.F.	.019	.70	.84	1.54
Ceiling joists, 2" x 4", 16" O.C.	1.000	L.F.	.013	.39	.58	.97
Ridge board, 2" x 6"	.050	L.F.	.002	.03	.07	.10
Fascia board, 2" x 6"	.100	L.F.	.005	.06	.24	.30
Rafter tie, 1" x 4", 4' O.C.	.060	L.F.	.001	.03	.05	.08
Soffit nailer (outrigger), 2" x 4", 24" O.C.	.170	L.F.	.004	.07	.20	.27
Sheathing, exterior, plywood, CDX, 1/2" thick	1.170	S.F.	.013	.67	.61	1.28
Furring strips, 1" x 3", 16" O.C.	1.000	L.F.	.023	.19	1.03	1.22
TOTAL		S.F.	.080	2.14	3.62	5.76
2" X 8" RAFTERS, 16" O.C., 4/12 PITCH						
Rafters, 2" x 8", 16" O.C., 4/12 pitch	1.170	L.F.	.020	.97	.89	1.86
Ceiling joists, 2" x 6", 16" O.C.	1.000	L.F.	.013	.60	.58	1.18
Ridge board, 2" x 8"	.050	L.F.	.002	.04	.08	.12
Fascia board, 2" x 8"	.100	L.F.	.007	.08	.32	.40
Rafter tie, 1" x 4", 4' O.C.	.060	L.F.	.001	.03	.05	.08
Soffit nailer (outrigger), 2" x 4", 24" O.C.	.170	L.F.	.004	.07	.20	.27
Sheathing, exterior, plywood, CDX, 1/2" thick	1.170	S.F.	.013	.67	.61	1.28
Furring strips, 1" x 3", 16" O.C.	1.000	L.F.	.023	.19	1.03	1.22
TOTAL		S.F.	.083	2.65	3.76	6.41

The cost of this system is based on the square foot of plan area.
All quantities have been adjusted accordingly.

Description	QUAN.	UNIT	LABOR HOURS	COST PER S.F. MAT.	COST PER S.F. INST.	COST PER S.F. TOTAL

Division 1
Site Work

Backfill

Excavate

System Description	QUAN.	UNIT	LABOR HOURS	COST EACH		
				MAT.	INST.	TOTAL
BUILDING, 24′ X 38′, 4′ DEEP						
Cut & chip light trees to 6″ diam.	.190	Acre	9.120		574.75	574.75
Excavator, hydraulic, crawler mtd., 1 C.Y. cap. = 100 C.Y./hr.	174.000	C.Y.	3.480		294.06	294.06
Backfill, dozer, 4″ lifts, no compaction	87.000	C.Y.	.580		111.36	111.36
Rough grade, dozer, 30′ from building	87.000	C.Y.	.580		111.36	111.36
TOTAL		Ea.	13.760		1,091.53	1,091.53
BUILDING, 26′ X 46′, 4′ DEEP						
Cut & chip light trees to 6″ diam.	.210	Acre	10.080		635.25	635.25
Excavator, hydraulic, crawler mtd., 1 C.Y. cap. = 100 C.Y./hr.	201.000	C.Y.	4.020		339.69	339.69
Backfill, dozer, 4″ lifts, no compaction	100.000	C.Y.	.667		128	128
Rough grade, dozer, 30′ from building	100.000	C.Y.	.667		128	128
TOTAL		Ea.	15.434		1,230.94	1,230.94
BUILDING, 26′ X 60′, 4′ DEEP						
Cut & chip light trees to 6″ diam.	.240	Acre	11.520		726	726
Excavator, hydraulic, crawler mtd., 1 C.Y. cap. = 100 C.Y./hr.	240.000	C.Y.	4.800		405.60	405.60
Backfill, dozer, 4″ lifts, no compaction	120.000	C.Y.	.800		153.60	153.60
Rough grade, dozer, 30′ from building	120.000	C.Y.	.800		153.60	153.60
TOTAL		Ea.	17.920		1,438.80	1,438.80
BUILDING, 30′ X 66′, 4′ DEEP						
Cut & chip light trees to 6″ diam.	.260	Acre	12.480		786.50	786.50
Excavator, hydraulic, crawler mtd., 1 C.Y. cap. = 100 C.Y./hr.	268.000	C.Y.	5.360		452.92	452.92
Backfill, dozer, 4″ lifts, no compaction	134.000	C.Y.	.894		171.52	171.52
Rough grade, dozer, 30′ from building	134.000	C.Y.	.894		171.52	171.52
TOTAL		Ea.	19.628		1,582.46	1,582.46

The costs in this system are on a cost each basis.
Quantities are based on 1′-0″ clearance on each side of footing.

Description	QUAN.	UNIT	LABOR HOURS	COST EACH		
				MAT.	INST.	TOTAL

Reed Construction Data®

Reed Construction Data is your all-inclusive source of information encompassing all phases of the construction process. Our products and services are designed specifically to help industry professionals advance their businesses with timely, accurate and actionable project, product and cost data.

Reed Bulletin and Reed Connect™ deliver the most comprehensive, timely and reliable project information to support contractors, distributors and building product manufacturers in identifying, bidding, and tracking projects — private and public, general building and civil. Reed Construction Data also offers in-depth construction activity statistics and forecasts covering major project categories, many at the county and metropolitan level.

For more information about Reed Construction Data, please call **877-REED411** or visit our website at **www.reedconstructiondata.com**.

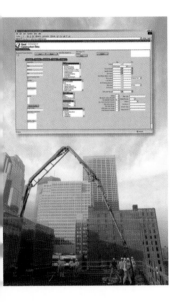

Reed Connect

- Customized web-based project lead delivery service featuring advanced search capabilities.

- Manage and track actionable leads from planning to quote through winning the job.

- Competitive analysis tool to analyze lost sales opportunities.

- Potential integration with your CRM application.

Reed Research & Analytics

Reed Construction Forecast
- Delivers timely construction industry activity combining historical data, current year projections and forecasts.

- Modeled at the individual MSA-level to capture changing local market conditions.

- Covers 21 major project categories.

Reed Construction Starts
- Available in a monthly report or as an interactive database.

- Data provided in square footage and dollar value.

- Highly effective and efficient business planning tool.

Market Fundamentals
- Metropolitan area-specific reporting.

- Five-year forecast of industry performance including major projects in development and underway.

- Property types include office, retail, hotel, warehouse and apartment.

Reed Bulletin

- Project leads targeted by geographic region and formatted by construction stage — available online or in print.

- Locate those hard-to-find jobs that are more profitable to your business.

- Optional automatic e-mail updates sent whenever project details change.

- Download plans and specs online or order print copies.

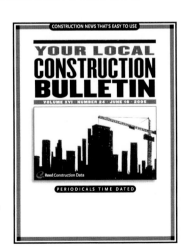

CONSTRUCTION NEWS THAT'S EASY TO USE

YOUR LOCAL CONSTRUCTION BULLETIN

VOLUME XVI · NUMBER 24 · JUNE 16 · 2008

Reed Construction Data

PERIODICALS TIME DATED

Reed Construction Data ®

Reed Construction Data is a leading provider of information resources to the design community. Through our products and services we offer many ways for architects, engineers, designers, and contractors to better serve their clients and build their businesses.

For more information about Reed Construction Data, please call **877-REED411** or visit our website at **www.reedconstructiondata.com**.

Reed Registry
The Premier Source of Architectural Firms

The Reed Registry contains over 30,000 architecture firms and is used by industry professionals to find architects throughout the U.S. and Canada.

Architecture firms can add or update their listing, or enhance their listing to include logos, projects, and web links by visiting **www.reedregistry.com**.

Reed First Source and Buildcore
Leading Product Information Solutions for Design Professionals

Reed First Source and Buildcore are leading information solutions that allow design professionals to search, select, and specify building products throughout the design and construction cycle.

Covering both U.S. and Canadian markets, FirstSource and BuildCore provide access to over 11,000 commercial building manufacturers, all classified by MasterFormat™ 2004 categories. In addition, our specialists can create and publish SPEC-DATA 10-part format and MANU-SPEC three-part specifications for building product manufacturers.

Learn more at **www.reedfirstsource.com**.

Footing Excavation Price Sheet	QUAN.	UNIT	LABOR HOURS	COST EACH		
				MAT.	INST.	TOTAL
Clear and grub, medium brush, 30' from building, 24' x 38'	.190	Acre	9.120		575	575
26' x 46'	.210	Acre	10.080		635	635
26' x 60'	.240	Acre	11.520		725	725
30' x 66'	.260	Acre	12.480		790	790
Light trees, to 6" dia. cut & chip, 24' x 38'	.190	Acre	9.120		575	575
26' x 46'	.210	Acre	10.080		635	635
26' x 60'	.240	Acre	11.520		725	725
30' x 66'	.260	Acre	12.480		790	790
Medium trees, to 10" dia. cut & chip, 24' x 38'	.190	Acre	13.029		815	815
26' x 46'	.210	Acre	14.400		905	905
26' x 60'	.240	Acre	16.457		1,025	1,025
30' x 66'	.260	Acre	17.829		1,125	1,125
Excavation, footing, 24' x 38', 2' deep	68.000	C.Y.	.906		115	115
4' deep	174.000	C.Y.	2.319		294	294
8' deep	384.000	C.Y.	5.119		645	645
26' x 46', 2' deep	79.000	C.Y.	1.053		134	134
4' deep	201.000	C.Y.	2.679		340	340
8' deep	404.000	C.Y.	5.385		685	685
26' x 60', 2' deep	94.000	C.Y.	1.253		159	159
4' deep	240.000	C.Y.	3.199		405	405
8' deep	483.000	C.Y.	6.438		815	815
30' x 66', 2' deep	105.000	C.Y.	1.400		178	178
4' deep	268.000	C.Y.	3.572		455	455
8' deep	539.000	C.Y.	7.185		910	910
Backfill, 24' x 38', 2" lifts, no compaction	34.000	C.Y.	.227		43.50	43.50
Compaction, air tamped, add	34.000	C.Y.	2.267		375	375
4" lifts, no compaction	87.000	C.Y.	.580		112	112
Compaction, air tamped, add	87.000	C.Y.	5.800		960	960
8" lifts, no compaction	192.000	C.Y.	1.281		246	246
Compaction, air tamped, add	192.000	C.Y.	12.801		2,125	2,125
26' x 46', 2" lifts, no compaction	40.000	C.Y.	.267		51	51
Compaction, air tamped, add	40.000	C.Y.	2.667		440	440
4" lifts, no compaction	100.000	C.Y.	.667		128	128
Compaction, air tamped, add	100.000	C.Y.	6.667		1,100	1,100
8" lifts, no compaction	202.000	C.Y.	1.347		259	259
Compaction, air tamped, add	202.000	C.Y.	13.467		2,225	2,225
26' x 60', 2" lifts, no compaction	47.000	C.Y.	.313		60	60
Compaction, air tamped, add	47.000	C.Y.	3.133		520	520
4" lifts, no compaction	120.000	C.Y.	.800		154	154
Compaction, air tamped, add	120.000	C.Y.	8.000		1,325	1,325
8" lifts, no compaction	242.000	C.Y.	1.614		310	310
Compaction, air tamped, add	242.000	C.Y.	16.134		2,675	2,675
30' x 66', 2" lifts, no compaction	53.000	C.Y.	.354		68	68
Compaction, air tamped, add	53.000	C.Y.	3.534		585	585
4" lifts, no compaction	134.000	C.Y.	.894		171	171
Compaction, air tamped, add	134.000	C.Y.	8.934		1,475	1,475
8" lifts, no compaction	269.000	C.Y.	1.794		345	345
Compaction, air tamped, add	269.000	C.Y.	17.934		2,975	2,975
Rough grade, 30' from building, 24' x 38'	87.000	C.Y.	.580		112	112
26' x 46'	100.000	C.Y.	.667		128	128
26' x 60'	120.000	C.Y.	.800		154	154
30' x 66'	134.000	C.Y.	.894		171	171

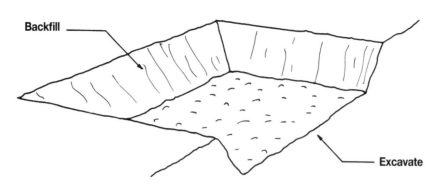

Backfill

Excavate

System Description	QUAN.	UNIT	LABOR HOURS	COST EACH		
				MAT.	INST.	TOTAL
BUILDING, 24' X 38', 8' DEEP						
Medium clearing	.190	Acre	2.027		228.95	228.95
Excavate, track loader, 1-1/2 C.Y. bucket	550.000	C.Y.	7.860		742.50	742.50
Backfill, dozer, 8" lifts, no compaction	180.000	C.Y.	1.201		230.40	230.40
Rough grade, dozer, 30' from building	280.000	C.Y.	1.868		358.40	358.40
TOTAL		Ea.	12.956		1,560.25	1,560.25
BUILDING, 26' X 46', 8' DEEP						
Medium clearing	.210	Acre	2.240		253.05	253.05
Excavate, track loader, 1-1/2 C.Y. bucket	672.000	C.Y.	9.603		907.20	907.20
Backfill, dozer, 8" lifts, no compaction	220.000	C.Y.	1.467		281.60	281.60
Rough grade, dozer, 30' from building	340.000	C.Y.	2.268		435.20	435.20
TOTAL		Ea.	15.578		1,877.05	1,877.05
BUILDING, 26' X 60', 8' DEEP						
Medium clearing	.240	Acre	2.560		289.20	289.20
Excavate, track loader, 1-1/2 C.Y. bucket	829.000	C.Y.	11.846		1,119.15	1,119.15
Backfill, dozer, 8" lifts, no compaction	270.000	C.Y.	1.801		345.60	345.60
Rough grade, dozer, 30' from building	420.000	C.Y.	2.801		537.60	537.60
TOTAL		Ea.	19.008		2,291.55	2,291.55
BUILDING, 30' X 66', 8' DEEP						
Medium clearing	.260	Acre	2.773		313.30	313.30
Excavate, track loader, 1-1/2 C.Y. bucket	990.000	C.Y.	14.147		1,336.50	1,336.50
Backfill dozer, 8" lifts, no compaction	320.000	C.Y.	2.134		409.60	409.60
Rough grade, dozer, 30' from building	500.000	C.Y.	3.335		640	640
TOTAL		Ea.	22.389		2,699.40	2,699.40

The costs in this system are on a cost each basis.
Quantities are based on 1'-0" clearance beyond footing projection.

Description	QUAN.	UNIT	LABOR HOURS	COST EACH		
				MAT.	INST.	TOTAL

Foundation Excavation Price Sheet	QUAN.	UNIT	LABOR HOURS	COST EACH		
				MAT.	INST.	TOTAL
Clear & grub, medium brush, 30' from building, 24' x 38'	.190	Acre	2.027		229	229
26' x 46'	.210	Acre	2.240		253	253
26' x 60'	.240	Acre	2.560		289	289
30' x 66'	.260	Acre	2.773		315	315
Light trees, to 6" dia. cut & chip, 24' x 38'	.190	Acre	9.120		575	575
26' x 46'	.210	Acre	10.080		635	635
26' x 60'	.240	Acre	11.520		725	725
30' x 66'	.260	Acre	12.480		790	790
Medium trees, to 10" dia. cut & chip, 24' x 38'	.190	Acre	13.029		815	815
26' x 46'	.210	Acre	14.400		905	905
26' x 60'	.240	Acre	16.457		1,025	1,025
30' x 66'	.260	Acre	17.829		1,125	1,125
Excavation, basement, 24' x 38', 2' deep	98.000	C.Y.	1.400		132	132
4' deep	220.000	C.Y.	3.144		297	297
8' deep	550.000	C.Y.	7.860		745	745
26' x 46', 2' deep	123.000	C.Y.	1.758		166	166
4' deep	274.000	C.Y.	3.915		370	370
8' deep	672.000	C.Y.	9.603		905	905
26' x 60', 2' deep	157.000	C.Y.	2.244		212	212
4' deep	345.000	C.Y.	4.930		465	465
8' deep	829.000	C.Y.	11.846		1,125	1,125
30' x 66', 2' deep	192.000	C.Y.	2.744		259	259
4' deep	419.000	C.Y.	5.988		565	565
8' deep	990.000	C.Y.	14.147		1,350	1,350
Backfill, 24' x 38', 2" lifts, no compaction	32.000	C.Y.	.213		41	41
Compaction, air tamped, add	32.000	C.Y.	2.133		355	355
4" lifts, no compaction	72.000	C.Y.	.480		92	92
Compaction, air tamped, add	72.000	C.Y.	4.800		795	795
8" lifts, no compaction	180.000	C.Y.	1.201		230	230
Compaction, air tamped, add	180.000	C.Y.	12.001		1,975	1,975
26' x 46', 2" lifts, no compaction	40.000	C.Y.	.267		51	51
Compaction, air tamped, add	40.000	C.Y.	2.667		440	440
4" lifts, no compaction	90.000	C.Y.	.600		115	115
Compaction, air tamped, add	90.000	C.Y.	6.000		995	995
8" lifts, no compaction	220.000	C.Y.	1.467		282	282
Compacton, air tamped, add	220.000	C.Y.	14.667		2,425	2,425
26' x 60', 2" lifts, no compaction	50.000	C.Y.	.334		64	64
Compaction, air tamped, add	50.000	C.Y.	3.334		555	555
4" lifts, no compaction	110.000	C.Y.	.734		141	141
Compaction, air tamped, add	110.000	C.Y.	7.334		1,225	1,225
8" lifts, no compaction	270.000	C.Y.	1.801		345	345
Compaction, air tamped, add	270.000	C.Y.	18.001		3,000	3,000
30' x 66', 2" lifts, no compaction	60.000	C.Y.	.400		77	77
Compaction, air tamped, add	60.000	C.Y.	4.000		665	665
4" lifts, no compaction	130.000	C.Y.	.867		166	166
Compaction, air tamped, add	130.000	C.Y.	8.667		1,425	1,425
8" lifts, no compaction	320.000	C.Y.	2.134		410	410
Compaction, air tamped, add	320.000	C.Y.	21.334		3,550	3,550
Rough grade, 30' from building, 24' x 38'	280.000	C.Y.	1.868		360	360
26' x 46'	340.000	C.Y.	2.268		435	435
26' x 60'	420.000	C.Y.	2.801		535	535
30' x 66'	500.000	C.Y.	3.335		640	640

Backfill · Bedding · Sewer Pipe · Excavation

System Description	QUAN.	UNIT	LABOR HOURS	COST PER L.F.		
				MAT.	INST.	TOTAL
2′ DEEP						
Excavation, backhoe	.296	C.Y.	.032		1.86	1.86
Alternate pricing method, 4″ deep	.111	C.Y.	.044	2.66	1.71	4.37
Utility, sewer, 6″ cast iron	1.000	L.F.	.283	17.63	12.43	30.06
Compaction in 12″ layers, hand tamp, add to above	.185	C.Y.	.044		1.45	1.45
TOTAL		L.F.	.403	20.29	17.45	37.74
4′ DEEP						
Excavation, backhoe	.889	C.Y.	.095		5.59	5.59
Alternate pricing method, 4″ deep	.111	C.Y.	.044	2.66	1.71	4.37
Utility, sewer, 6″ cast iron	1.000	L.F.	.283	17.63	12.43	30.06
Compaction in 12″ layers, hand tamp, add to above	.778	C.Y.	.183		6.11	6.11
TOTAL		L.F.	.605	20.29	25.84	46.13
6′ DEEP						
Excavation, backhoe	1.770	C.Y.	.189		11.13	11.13
Alternate pricing method, 4″ deep	.111	C.Y.	.044	2.66	1.71	4.37
Utility, sewer, 6″ cast iron	1.000	L.F.	.283	17.63	12.43	30.06
Compaction in 12″ layers, hand tamp, add to above	1.660	C.Y.	.391		13.03	13.03
TOTAL		L.F.	.907	20.29	38.30	58.59
8′ DEEP						
Excavation, backhoe	2.960	C.Y.	.316		18.62	18.62
Alternate pricing method, 4″ deep	.111	C.Y.	.044	2.66	1.71	4.37
Utility, sewer, 6″ cast iron	1.000	L.F.	.283	17.63	12.43	30.06
Compaction in 12″ layers, hand tamp, add to above	2.850	C.Y.	.671		22.37	22.37
TOTAL		L.F.	1.314	20.29	55.13	75.42

The costs in this system are based on a cost per linear foot of trench,
and based on 2′ wide at bottom of trench up to 6′ deep.

Description	QUAN.	UNIT	LABOR HOURS	COST PER L.F.		
				MAT.	INST.	TOTAL

Utility Trenching Price Sheet	QUAN.	UNIT	LABOR HOURS	MAT.	INST.	TOTAL
Excavation, bottom of trench 2' wide, 2' deep	.296	C.Y.	.032		1.86	1.86
4' deep	.889	C.Y.	.095		5.60	5.60
6' deep	1.770	C.Y.	.142		8.90	8.90
8' deep	2.960	C.Y.	.105		16.35	16.35
Bedding, sand, bottom of trench 2' wide, no compaction, pipe, 2" diameter	.070	C.Y.	.028	1.68	1.07	2.75
4" diameter	.084	C.Y.	.034	2.02	1.29	3.31
6" diameter	.105	C.Y.	.042	2.52	1.61	4.13
8" diameter	.122	C.Y.	.049	2.93	1.88	4.81
Compacted, pipe, 2" diameter	.074	C.Y.	.030	1.78	1.14	2.92
4" diameter	.092	C.Y.	.037	2.21	1.42	3.63
6" diameter	.111	C.Y.	.044	2.66	1.71	4.37
8" diameter	.129	C.Y.	.052	3.10	1.98	5.08
3/4" stone, bottom of trench 2' wide, pipe, 4" diameter	.082	C.Y.	.033	1.97	1.26	3.23
6" diameter	.099	C.Y.	.040	2.38	1.53	3.91
3/8" stone, bottom of trench 2' wide, pipe, 4" diameter	.084	C.Y.	.034	2.02	1.29	3.31
6" diameter	.102	C.Y.	.041	2.45	1.57	4.02
Utilities, drainage & sewerage, corrugated plastic, 6" diameter	1.000	L.F.	.069	2.51	2.36	4.87
8" diameter	1.000	L.F.	.072	5.40	2.47	7.87
Bituminous fiber, 4" diameter	1.000	L.F.	.064	1.36	2.21	3.57
6" diameter	1.000	L.F.	.069	2.51	2.36	4.87
8" diameter	1.000	L.F.	.072	5.40	2.47	7.87
Concrete, non-reinforced, 6" diameter	1.000	L.F.	.181	5.55	7.65	13.20
8" diameter	1.000	L.F.	.214	6.10	9	15.10
PVC, SDR 35, 4" diameter	1.000	L.F.	.064	1.36	2.21	3.57
6" diameter	1.000	L.F.	.069	2.51	2.36	4.87
8" diameter	1.000	L.F.	.072	5.40	2.47	7.87
Vitrified clay, 4" diameter	1.000	L.F.	.091	1.87	3.12	4.99
6" diameter	1.000	L.F.	.120	3.12	4.14	7.26
8" diameter	1.000	L.F.	.140	4.43	5.75	10.18
Gas & service, polyethylene, 1-1/4" diameter	1.000	L.F.	.059	2.38	2.37	4.75
Steel sched.40, 1" diameter	1.000	L.F.	.107	7.20	5.35	12.55
2" diameter	1.000	L.F.	.114	11.35	5.70	17.05
Sub-drainage, PVC, perforated, 3" diameter	1.000	L.F.	.064	1.36	2.21	3.57
4" diameter	1.000	L.F.	.064	1.36	2.21	3.57
5" diameter	1.000	L.F.	.069	2.51	2.36	4.87
6" diameter	1.000	L.F.	.069	2.51	2.36	4.87
Porous wall concrete, 4" diameter	1.000	L.F.	.072	3.32	2.47	5.79
Vitrified clay, perforated, 4" diameter	1.000	L.F.	.120	3.32	5.05	8.37
6" diameter	1.000	L.F.	.152	5.50	6.40	11.90
Water service, copper, type K, 3/4"	1.000	L.F.	.083	4.31	4.24	8.55
1" diameter	1.000	L.F.	.093	5.70	4.74	10.44
PVC, 3/4"	1.000	L.F.	.121	1.06	6.10	7.16
1" diameter	1.000	L.F.	.134	1.31	6.80	8.11
Backfill, bottom of trench 2' wide no compact, 2' deep, pipe, 2" diameter	.226	L.F.	.053		1.77	1.77
4" diameter	.212	L.F.	.050		1.66	1.66
6" diameter	.185	L.F.	.044		1.45	1.45
4' deep, pipe, 2" diameter	.819	C.Y.	.193		6.45	6.45
4" diameter	.805	C.Y.	.189		6.30	6.30
6" diameter	.778	C.Y.	.183		6.10	6.10
6' deep, pipe, 2" diameter	1.700	C.Y.	.400		13.35	13.35
4" diameter	1.690	C.Y.	.398		13.25	13.25
6" diameter	1.660	C.Y.	.391		13.05	13.05
8' deep, pipe, 2" diameter	2.890	C.Y.	.680		22.50	22.50
4" diameter	2.870	C.Y.	.675		22.50	22.50
6" diameter	2.850	C.Y.	.671		22.50	22.50

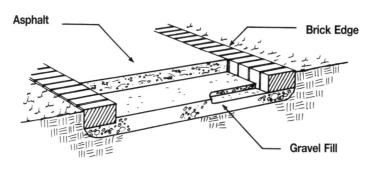

Asphalt

Brick Edge

Gravel Fill

System Description	QUAN.	UNIT	LABOR HOURS	COST PER S.F.		
				MAT.	INST.	TOTAL
ASPHALT SIDEWALK SYSTEM, 3′ WIDE WALK						
Gravel fill, 4″ deep	1.000	S.F.	.001	.42	.05	.47
Compact fill	.012	C.Y.			.01	.01
Handgrade	1.000	S.F.	.004		.14	.14
Walking surface, bituminous paving, 2″ thick	1.000	S.F.	.007	.67	.28	.95
Edging, brick, laid on edge	.670	L.F.	.079	2.28	3.22	5.50
TOTAL		S.F.	.091	3.37	3.70	7.07
CONCRETE SIDEWALK SYSTEM, 3′ WIDE WALK						
Gravel fill, 4″ deep	1.000	S.F.	.001	.42	.05	.47
Compact fill	.012	C.Y.			.01	.01
Handgrade	1.000	S.F.	.004		.14	.14
Walking surface, concrete, 4″ thick	1.000	S.F.	.040	1.83	1.60	3.43
Edging, brick, laid on edge	.670	L.F.	.079	2.28	3.22	5.50
TOTAL		S.F.	.124	4.53	5.02	9.55
PAVERS, BRICK SIDEWALK SYSTEM, 3′ WIDE WALK						
Sand base fill, 4″ deep	1.000	S.F.	.001	.53	.07	.60
Compact fill	.012	C.Y.			.01	.01
Handgrade	1.000	S.F.	.004		.14	.14
Walking surface, brick pavers	1.000	S.F.	.160	3.09	6.50	9.59
Edging, redwood, untreated, 1″ x 4″	.670	L.F.	.032	2.40	1.46	3.86
TOTAL		S.F.	.197	6.02	8.18	14.20

The costs in this system are based on a cost per square foot of sidewalk area. Concrete used is 3000 p.s.i.

Description	QUAN.	UNIT	LABOR HOURS	COST PER S.F.		
				MAT.	INST.	TOTAL

Sidewalk Price Sheet	QUAN.	UNIT	LABOR HOURS	COST PER S.F.		
				MAT.	INST.	TOTAL
Base, crushed stone, 3" deep	1.000	S.F.	.001	.55	.08	.63
6" deep	1.000	S.F.	.001	1.11	.08	1.19
9" deep	1.000	S.F.	.002	1.62	.12	1.74
12" deep	1.000	S.F.	.002	2.37	.14	2.51
Bank run gravel, 6" deep	1.000	S.F.	.001	.62	.07	.69
9" deep	1.000	S.F.	.001	.90	.08	.98
12" deep	1.000	S.F.	.001	1.24	.10	1.34
Compact base, 3" deep	.009	C.Y.	.001		.01	.01
6" deep	.019	C.Y.	.001		.02	.02
9" deep	.028	C.Y.	.001		.03	.03
Handgrade	1.000	S.F.	.004		.14	.14
Surface, brick, pavers dry joints, laid flat, running bond	1.000	S.F.	.160	3.09	6.50	9.59
Basket weave	1.000	S.F.	.168	3.41	6.85	10.26
Herringbone	1.000	S.F.	.174	3.41	7.05	10.46
Laid on edge, running bond	1.000	S.F.	.229	2.97	9.25	12.22
Mortar jts. laid flat, running bond	1.000	S.F.	.192	3.71	7.80	11.51
Basket weave	1.000	S.F.	.202	4.09	8.20	12.29
Herringbone	1.000	S.F.	.209	4.09	8.45	12.54
Laid on edge, running bond	1.000	S.F.	.274	3.56	11.10	14.66
Bituminous paving, 1-1/2" thick	1.000	S.F.	.006	.50	.22	.72
2" thick	1.000	S.F.	.007	.67	.28	.95
2-1/2" thick	1.000	S.F.	.008	.85	.31	1.16
Sand finish, 3/4" thick	1.000	S.F.	.001	.29	.10	.39
1" thick	1.000	S.F.	.001	.36	.12	.48
Concrete, reinforced, broom finish, 4" thick	1.000	S.F.	.040	1.83	1.60	3.43
5" thick	1.000	S.F.	.044	2.44	1.76	4.20
6" thick	1.000	S.F.	.047	2.85	1.88	4.73
Crushed stone, white marble, 3" thick	1.000	S.F.	.009	.23	.31	.54
Bluestone, 3" thick	1.000	S.F.	.009	.25	.31	.56
Flagging, bluestone, 1"	1.000	S.F.	.198	6.55	8	14.55
1-1/2"	1.000	S.F.	.188	11.90	7.65	19.55
Slate, natural cleft, 3/4"	1.000	S.F.	.174	7.30	7.05	14.35
Random rect., 1/2"	1.000	S.F.	.152	15.80	6.20	22
Granite blocks	1.000	S.F.	.174	8.85	7.05	15.90
Edging, corrugated aluminum, 4", 3' wide walk	.666	L.F.	.008	.48	.37	.85
4' wide walk	.500	L.F.	.006	.36	.28	.64
6", 3' wide walk	.666	L.F.	.010	.59	.44	1.03
4' wide walk	.500	L.F.	.007	.45	.33	.78
Redwood-cedar-cypress, 1" x 4", 3' wide walk	.666	L.F.	.021	1.20	.97	2.17
4' wide walk	.500	L.F.	.016	.90	.73	1.63
2" x 4", 3' wide walk	.666	L.F.	.032	2.40	1.46	3.86
4' wide walk	.500	L.F.	.024	1.80	1.10	2.90
Brick, dry joints, 3' wide walk	.666	L.F.	.079	2.28	3.22	5.50
4' wide walk	.500	L.F.	.059	1.71	2.40	4.11
Mortar joints, 3' wide walk	.666	L.F.	.095	2.74	3.86	6.60
4' wide walk	.500	L.F.	.071	2.05	2.88	4.93

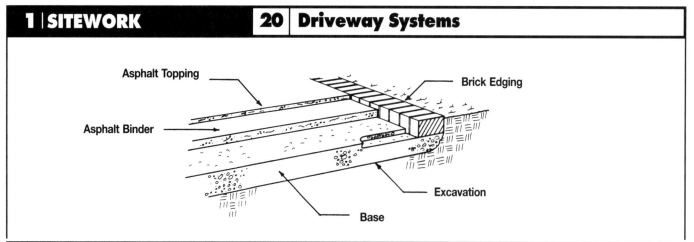

System Description	QUAN.	UNIT	LABOR HOURS	COST PER S.F.		
				MAT.	INST.	TOTAL
ASPHALT DRIVEWAY TO 10' WIDE						
Excavation, driveway to 10' wide, 6" deep	.019	C.Y.			.03	.03
Base, 6" crushed stone	1.000	S.F.	.001	1.11	.08	1.19
Handgrade base	1.000	S.F.	.004		.14	.14
2" thick base	1.000	S.F.	.002	.67	.16	.83
1" topping	1.000	S.F.	.001	.36	.12	.48
Edging, brick pavers	.200	L.F.	.024	.68	.96	1.64
TOTAL		S.F.	.032	2.82	1.49	4.31
CONCRETE DRIVEWAY TO 10' WIDE						
Excavation, driveway to 10' wide, 6" deep	.019	C.Y.			.03	.03
Base, 6" crushed stone	1.000	S.F.	.001	1.11	.08	1.19
Handgrade base	1.000	S.F.	.004		.14	.14
Surface, concrete, 4" thick	1.000	S.F.	.040	1.83	1.60	3.43
Edging, brick pavers	.200	L.F.	.024	.68	.96	1.64
TOTAL		S.F.	.069	3.62	2.81	6.43
PAVERS, BRICK DRIVEWAY TO 10' WIDE						
Excavation, driveway to 10' wide, 6" deep	.019	C.Y.			.03	.03
Base, 6" sand	1.000	S.F.	.001	.85	.10	.95
Handgrade base	1.000	S.F.	.004		.14	.14
Surface, pavers, brick laid flat, running bond	1.000	S.F.	.160	3.09	6.50	9.59
Edging, redwood, untreated, 2" x 4"	.200	L.F.	.010	.72	.44	1.16
TOTAL		S.F.	.175	4.66	7.21	11.87

Description	QUAN.	UNIT	LABOR HOURS	COST PER S.F.		
				MAT.	INST.	TOTAL

Driveway Price Sheet	QUAN.	UNIT	LABOR HOURS	COST PER S.F.		
				MAT.	INST.	TOTAL
Excavation, by machine, 10′ wide, 6″ deep	.019	C.Y.	.001		.03	.03
12″ deep	.037	C.Y.	.001		.07	.07
18″ deep	.055	C.Y.	.001		.10	.10
20′ wide, 6″ deep	.019	C.Y.	.001		.03	.03
12″ deep	.037	C.Y.	.001		.07	.07
18″ deep	.055	C.Y.	.001		.10	.10
Base, crushed stone, 10′ wide, 3″ deep	1.000	S.F.	.001	.56	.04	.60
6″ deep	1.000	S.F.	.001	1.11	.08	1.19
9″ deep	1.000	S.F.	.002	1.62	.12	1.74
20′ wide, 3″ deep	1.000	S.F.	.001	.56	.04	.60
6″ deep	1.000	S.F.	.001	1.11	.08	1.19
9″ deep	1.000	S.F.	.002	1.62	.12	1.74
Bank run gravel, 10′ wide, 3″ deep	1.000	S.F.	.001	.31	.04	.35
6″ deep	1.000	S.F.	.001	.62	.07	.69
9″ deep	1.000	S.F.	.001	.90	.08	.98
20′ wide, 3″ deep	1.000	S.F.	.001	.31	.04	.35
6″ deep	1.000	S.F.	.001	.62	.07	.69
9″ deep	1.000	S.F.	.001	.90	.08	.98
Handgrade, 10′ wide	1.000	S.F.	.004		.14	.14
20′ wide	1.000	S.F.	.004		.14	.14
Surface, asphalt, 10′ wide, 3/4″ topping, 1″ base	1.000	S.F.	.002	.81	.21	1.02
2″ base	1.000	S.F.	.003	.96	.26	1.22
1″ topping, 1″ base	1.000	S.F.	.002	.88	.23	1.11
2″ base	1.000	S.F.	.003	1.03	.28	1.31
20′ wide, 3/4″ topping, 1″ base	1.000	S.F.	.002	.81	.21	1.02
2″ base	1.000	S.F.	.003	.96	.26	1.22
1″ topping, 1″ base	1.000	S.F.	.002	.88	.23	1.11
2″ base	1.000	S.F.	.003	1.03	.28	1.31
Concrete, 10′ wide, 4″ thick	1.000	S.F.	.040	1.83	1.60	3.43
6″ thick	1.000	S.F.	.047	2.85	1.88	4.73
20′ wide, 4″ thick	1.000	S.F.	.040	1.83	1.60	3.43
6″ thick	1.000	S.F.	.047	2.85	1.88	4.73
Paver, brick 10′ wide dry joints, running bond, laid flat	1.000	S.F.	.160	3.09	6.50	9.59
Laid on edge	1.000	S.F.	.229	2.97	9.25	12.22
Mortar joints, laid flat	1.000	S.F.	.192	3.71	7.80	11.51
Laid on edge	1.000	S.F.	.274	3.56	11.10	14.66
20′ wide, running bond, dry jts., laid flat	1.000	S.F.	.160	3.09	6.50	9.59
Laid on edge	1.000	S.F.	.229	2.97	9.25	12.22
Mortar joints, laid flat	1.000	S.F.	.192	3.71	7.80	11.51
Laid on edge	1.000	S.F.	.274	3.56	11.10	14.66
Crushed stone, 10′ wide, white marble, 3″	1.000	S.F.	.009	.23	.31	.54
Bluestone, 3″	1.000	S.F.	.009	.25	.31	.56
20′ wide, white marble, 3″	1.000	S.F.	.009	.23	.31	.54
Bluestone, 3″	1.000	S.F.	.009	.25	.31	.56
Soil cement, 10′ wide	1.000	S.F.	.007	.36	.80	1.16
20′ wide	1.000	S.F.	.007	.36	.80	1.16
Granite blocks, 10′ wide	1.000	S.F.	.174	8.85	7.05	15.90
20′ wide	1.000	S.F.	.174	8.85	7.05	15.90
Asphalt block, solid 1-1/4″ thick	1.000	S.F.	.119	7.35	4.80	12.15
Solid 3″ thick	1.000	S.F.	.123	10.25	4.99	15.24
Edging, brick, 10′ wide	.200	L.F.	.024	.68	.96	1.64
20′ wide	.100	L.F.	.012	.34	.48	.82
Redwood, untreated 2″ x 4″, 10′ wide	.200	L.F.	.010	.72	.44	1.16
20′ wide	.100	L.F.	.005	.36	.22	.58
Granite, 4 1/2″ x 12″ straight, 10′ wide	.200	L.F.	.032	1.23	1.84	3.07
20′ wide	.100	L.F.	.016	.62	.92	1.54
Finishes, asphalt sealer, 10′ wide	1.000	S.F.	.023	.85	.79	1.64
20′ wide	1.000	S.F.	.023	.85	.79	1.64
Concrete, exposed aggregate 10′ wide	1.000	S.F.	.013	.23	.53	.76
20′ wide	1.000	S.F.	.013	.23	.53	.76

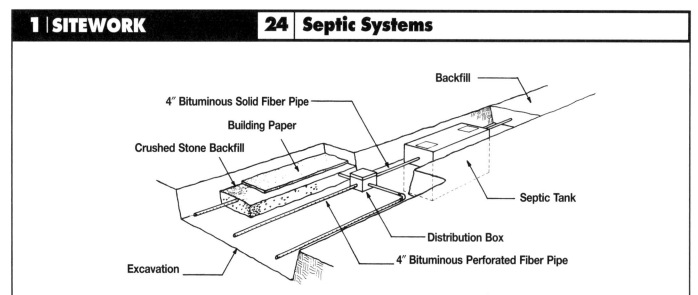

Labels on diagram:
- Backfill
- 4" Bituminous Solid Fiber Pipe
- Building Paper
- Crushed Stone Backfill
- Septic Tank
- Distribution Box
- 4" Bituminous Perforated Fiber Pipe
- Excavation

System Description	QUAN.	UNIT	LABOR HOURS	COST EACH		
				MAT.	INST.	TOTAL
SEPTIC SYSTEM WITH 1000 S.F. LEACHING FIELD, 1000 GALLON TANK						
Tank, 1000 gallon, concrete	1.000	Ea.	3.500	740	144.80	884.80
Distribution box, concrete	1.000	Ea.	1.000	136	33.50	169.50
4" PVC pipe	25.000	L.F.	1.600	34	55.25	89.25
Tank and field excavation	119.000	C.Y.	13.130		1,021.02	1,021.02
Crushed stone backfill	76.000	C.Y.	12.160	2,052	603.44	2,655.44
Backfill with excavated material	36.000	C.Y.	.240		46.08	46.08
Building paper	125.000	S.Y.	2.430	56.25	112.50	168.75
4" PVC perforated pipe	145.000	L.F.	9.280	197.20	320.45	517.65
4" pipe fittings	2.000	Ea.	1.939	22.80	88	110.80
TOTAL		Ea.	45.279	3,238.25	2,425.04	5,663.29
SEPTIC SYSTEM WITH 2 LEACHING PITS, 1000 GALLON TANK						
Tank, 1000 gallon, concrete	1.000	Ea.	3.500	740	144.80	884.80
Distribution box, concrete	1.000	Ea.	1.000	136	33.50	169.50
4" PVC pipe	75.000	L.F.	4.800	102	165.75	267.75
Excavation for tank only	20.000	C.Y.	2.207		171.60	171.60
Crushed stone backfill	10.000	C.Y.	1.600	270	79.40	349.40
Backfill with excavated material	55.000	C.Y.	.367		70.40	70.40
Pits, 6' diameter, including excavation and stone backfill	2.000	Ea.		2,250		2,250
TOTAL		Ea.	13.474	3,498	665.45	4,163.45

The costs in this system include all necessary piping and excavation.

Description	QUAN.	UNIT	LABOR HOURS	COST EACH		
				MAT.	INST.	TOTAL

Septic Systems Price Sheet	QUAN.	UNIT	LABOR HOURS	COST EACH		
				MAT.	INST.	TOTAL
Tank, precast concrete, 1000 gallon	1.000	Ea.	3.500	740	145	885
2000 gallon	1.000	Ea.	5.600	2,300	232	2,532
Distribution box, concrete, 5 outlets	1.000	Ea.	1.000	136	33.50	169.50
12 outlets	1.000	Ea.	2.000	505	66.50	571.50
4″ pipe, PVC, solid	25.000	L.F.	1.600	34	55.50	89.50
Tank and field excavation, 1000 S.F. field	119.000	C.Y.	6.565		1,025	1,025
2000 S.F. field	190.000	C.Y.	10.482		1,625	1,625
Tank excavation only, 1000 gallon tank	20.000	C.Y.	1.103		172	172
2000 gallon tank	32.000	C.Y.	1.765		274	274
Backfill, crushed stone 1000 S.F. field	76.000	C.Y.	12.160	2,050	605	2,655
2000 S.F. field	140.000	C.Y.	22.400	3,775	1,125	4,900
Backfill with excavated material, 1000 S.F. field	36.000	C.Y.	.240		46.50	46.50
2000 S.F. field	60.000	C.Y.	.400		77	77
6′ diameter pits	55.000	C.Y.	.367		70.50	70.50
3′ diameter pits	42.000	C.Y.	.280		53.50	53.50
Building paper, 1000 S.F. field	125.000	S.Y.	2.376	55	110	165
2000 S.F. field	250.000	S.Y.	4.860	113	225	338
4″ pipe, PVC, perforated, 1000 S.F. field	145.000	L.F.	9.280	197	320	517
2000 S.F. field	265.000	L.F.	16.960	360	585	945
Pipe fittings, bituminous fiber, 1000 S.F. field	2.000	Ea.	1.939	23	88	111
2000 S.F. field	4.000	Ea.	3.879	45.50	176	221.50
Leaching pit, including excavation and stone backfill, 3′ diameter	1.000	Ea.		845		845
6′ diameter	1.000	Ea.		1,125		1,125

System Description	QUAN.	UNIT	LABOR HOURS	COST PER UNIT		
				MAT.	INST.	TOTAL
Chain link fence						
Galv.9ga. wire, 1-5/8"post 10'O.C., 1-3/8"top rail, 2"corner post, 3'hi	1.000	L.F.	.130	7.85	4.47	12.32
4' high	1.000	L.F.	.141	11.70	4.87	16.57
6' high	1.000	L.F.	.209	13.20	7.20	20.40
Add for gate 3' wide 1-3/8" frame 3' high	1.000	Ea.	2.000	70.50	69	139.50
4' high	1.000	Ea.	2.400	87	82.50	169.50
6' high	1.000	Ea.	2.400	157	82.50	239.50
Add for gate 4' wide 1-3/8" frame 3' high	1.000	Ea.	2.667	82	92	174
4' high	1.000	Ea.	2.667	107	92	199
6' high	1.000	Ea.	3.000	198	103	301
Alum.9ga. wire, 1-5/8"post, 10'O.C., 1-3/8"top rail, 2"corner post,3'hi	1.000	L.F.	.130	9.60	4.47	14.07
4' high	1.000	L.F.	.141	10.95	4.87	15.82
6' high	1.000	L.F.	.209	14.05	7.20	21.25
Add for gate 3' wide 1-3/8" frame 3' high	1.000	Ea.	2.000	93.50	69	162.50
4' high	1.000	Ea.	2.400	128	82.50	210.50
6' high	1.000	Ea.	2.400	192	82.50	274.50
Add for gate 4' wide 1-3/8" frame 3' high	1.000	Ea.	2.400	128	82.50	210.50
4' high	1.000	Ea.	2.667	170	92	262
6' high	1.000	Ea.	3.000	266	103	369
Vinyl 9ga. wire, 1-5/8"post 10'O.C., 1-3/8"top rail, 2"corner post,3'hi	1.000	L.F.	.130	8.50	4.47	12.97
4' high	1.000	L.F.	.141	13.95	4.87	18.82
6' high	1.000	L.F.	.209	15.95	7.20	23.15
Add for gate 3' wide 1-3/8" frame 3' high	1.000	Ea.	2.000	104	69	173
4' high	1.000	Ea.	2.400	136	82.50	218.50
6' high	1.000	Ea.	2.400	209	82.50	291.50
Add for gate 4' wide 1-3/8" frame 3' high	1.000	Ea.	2.400	142	82.50	224.50
4' high	1.000	Ea.	2.667	188	92	280
6' high	1.000	Ea.	3.000	272	103	375
Tennis court, chain link fence, 10' high						
Galv.11ga.wire, 2"post 10'O.C., 1-3/8"top rail, 2-1/2"corner post	1.000	L.F.	.253	21	8.70	29.70
Add for gate 3' wide 1-3/8" frame	1.000	Ea.	2.400	261	82.50	343.50
Alum.11ga.wire, 2"post 10'O.C., 1-3/8"top rail, 2-1/2"corner post	1.000	L.F.	.253	30	8.70	38.70
Add for gate 3' wide 1-3/8" frame	1.000	Ea.	2.400	340	82.50	422.50
Vinyl 11ga.wire,2"post 10' O.C.,1-3/8"top rail,2-1/2"corner post	1.000	L.F.	.253	25	8.70	33.70
Add for gate 3' wide 1-3/8" frame	1.000	Ea.	2.400	375	82.50	457.50
Railings, commercial						
Aluminum balcony rail, 1-1/2" posts with pickets	1.000	L.F.	.164	58.50	10.10	68.60
With expanded metal panels	1.000	L.F.	.164	75	10.10	85.10
With porcelain enamel panel inserts	1.000	L.F.	.164	67	10.10	77.10
Mild steel, ornamental rounded top rail	1.000	L.F.	.164	65.50	10.10	75.60
As above, but pitch down stairs	1.000	L.F.	.183	71	11.25	82.25
Steel pipe, welded, 1-1/2" round, painted	1.000	L.F.	.160	24.50	9.85	34.35
Galvanized	1.000	L.F.	.160	35	9.85	44.85
Residential, stock units, mild steel, deluxe	1.000	L.F.	.102	14.95	6.25	21.20
Economy	1.000	L.F.	.102	11.20	6.25	17.45

System Description	QUAN.	UNIT	LABOR HOURS	COST PER UNIT		
				MAT.	INST.	TOTAL
Basketweave, 3/8"x4" boards, 2"x4" stringers on spreaders, 4"x4" posts						
No. 1 cedar, 6' high	1.000	L.F.	.150	9.75	6.40	16.15
Treated pine, 6' high	1.000	L.F.	.160	11.85	6.80	18.65
Board fence, 1"x4" boards, 2"x4" rails, 4"x4" posts						
Preservative treated, 2 rail, 3' high	1.000	L.F.	.166	7.25	7	14.25
4' high	1.000	L.F.	.178	7.95	7.55	15.50
3 rail, 5' high	1.000	L.F.	.185	8.95	7.80	16.75
6' high	1.000	L.F.	.192	10.25	8.15	18.40
Western cedar, No. 1, 2 rail, 3' high	1.000	L.F.	.166	7.90	7	14.90
3 rail, 4' high	1.000	L.F.	.178	9.35	7.55	16.90
5' high	1.000	L.F.	.185	10.80	7.80	18.60
6' high	1.000	L.F.	.192	11.85	8.15	20
No. 1 cedar, 2 rail, 3' high	1.000	L.F.	.166	11.85	7	18.85
4' high	1.000	L.F.	.178	13.50	7.55	21.05
3 rail, 5' high	1.000	L.F.	.185	15.60	7.80	23.40
6' high	1.000	L.F.	.192	17.40	8.15	25.55
Shadow box, 1"x6" boards, 2"x4" rails, 4"x4" posts						
Fir, pine or spruce, treated, 3 rail, 6' high	1.000	L.F.	.160	13.30	6.80	20.10
No. 1 cedar, 3 rail, 4' high	1.000	L.F.	.185	16.35	7.80	24.15
6' high	1.000	L.F.	.192	20	8.15	28.15
Open rail, split rails, No. 1 cedar, 2 rail, 3' high	1.000	L.F.	.150	6.55	6.40	12.95
3 rail, 4' high	1.000	L.F.	.160	8.85	6.80	15.65
No. 2 cedar, 2 rail, 3' high	1.000	L.F.	.150	5.10	6.40	11.50
3 rail, 4' high	1.000	L.F.	.160	5.80	6.80	12.60
Open rail, rustic rails, No. 1 cedar, 2 rail, 3' high	1.000	L.F.	.150	4.09	6.40	10.49
3 rail, 4' high	1.000	L.F.	.160	5.50	6.80	12.30
No. 2 cedar, 2 rail, 3' high	1.000	L.F.	.150	3.93	6.40	10.33
3 rail, 4' high	1.000	L.F.	.160	4.15	6.80	10.95
Rustic picket, molded pine pickets, 2 rail, 3' high	1.000	L.F.	.171	5.80	7.25	13.05
3 rail, 4' high	1.000	L.F.	.197	6.65	8.35	15
No. 1 cedar, 2 rail, 3' high	1.000	L.F.	.171	7.90	7.25	15.15
3 rail, 4' high	1.000	L.F.	.197	9.10	8.35	17.45
Picket fence, fir, pine or spruce, preserved, treated						
2 rail, 3' high	1.000	L.F.	.171	5.05	7.25	12.30
3 rail, 4' high	1.000	L.F.	.185	5.95	7.80	13.75
Western cedar, 2 rail, 3' high	1.000	L.F.	.171	6.30	7.25	13.55
3 rail, 4' high	1.000	L.F.	.185	6.45	7.80	14.25
No. 1 cedar, 2 rail, 3' high	1.000	L.F.	.171	12.60	7.25	19.85
3 rail, 4' high	1.000	L.F.	.185	14.70	7.80	22.50
Stockade, No. 1 cedar, 3-1/4" rails, 6' high	1.000	L.F.	.150	11.90	6.40	18.30
8' high	1.000	L.F.	.155	15.40	6.55	21.95
No. 2 cedar, treated rails, 6' high	1.000	L.F.	.150	11.90	6.40	18.30
Treated pine, treated rails, 6' high	1.000	L.F.	.150	11.65	6.40	18.05
Gates, No. 2 cedar, picket, 3'-6" wide 4' high	1.000	Ea.	2.667	63	114	177
No. 2 cedar, rustic round, 3' wide, 3' high	1.000	Ea.	2.667	80.50	114	194.50
No. 2 cedar, stockade screen, 3'-6" wide, 6' high	1.000	Ea.	3.000	70	128	198
General, wood, 3'-6" wide, 4' high	1.000	Ea.	2.400	61	102	163
6' high	1.000	Ea.	3.000	76.50	128	204.50

Division 2
Foundations

System Description	QUAN.	UNIT	LABOR HOURS	COST PER L.F.		
				MAT.	INST.	TOTAL
8″ THICK BY 18″ WIDE FOOTING						
Concrete, 3000 psi	.040	C.Y.		4.40		4.40
Place concrete, direct chute	.040	C.Y.	.016		.58	.58
Forms, footing, 4 uses	1.330	SFCA	.103	.93	4.06	4.99
Reinforcing, 1/2″ diameter bars, 2 each	1.380	Lb.	.011	.73	.54	1.27
Keyway, 2″ x 4″, beveled, 4 uses	1.000	L.F.	.015	.21	.68	.89
Dowels, 1/2″ diameter bars, 2′ long, 6′ O.C.	.166	Ea.	.006	.13	.28	.41
TOTAL		L.F.	.151	6.40	6.14	12.54
12″ THICK BY 24″ WIDE FOOTING						
Concrete, 3000 psi	.070	C.Y.		7.70		7.70
Place concrete, direct chute	.070	C.Y.	.028		1.02	1.02
Forms, footing, 4 uses	2.000	SFCA	.155	1.40	6.10	7.50
Reinforcing, 1/2″ diameter bars, 2 each	1.380	Lb.	.011	.73	.54	1.27
Keyway, 2″ x 4″, beveled, 4 uses	1.000	L.F.	.015	.21	.68	.89
Dowels, 1/2″ diameter bars, 2′ long, 6′ O.C.	.166	Ea.	.006	.13	.28	.41
TOTAL		L.F.	.215	10.17	8.62	18.79
12″ THICK BY 36″ WIDE FOOTING						
Concrete, 3000 psi	.110	C.Y.		12.10		12.10
Place concrete, direct chute	.110	C.Y.	.044		1.60	1.60
Forms, footing, 4 uses	2.000	SFCA	.155	1.40	6.10	7.50
Reinforcing, 1/2″ diameter bars, 2 each	1.380	Lb.	.011	.73	.54	1.27
Keyway, 2″ x 4″, beveled, 4 uses	1.000	L.F.	.015	.21	.68	.89
Dowels, 1/2″ diameter bars, 2′ long, 6′ O.C.	.166	Ea.	.006	.13	.28	.41
TOTAL		L.F.	.231	14.57	9.20	23.77

The footing costs in this system are on a cost per linear foot basis.

Description	QUAN.	UNIT	LABOR HOURS	COST PER S.F.		
				MAT.	INST.	TOTAL

Footing Price Sheet	QUAN.	UNIT	LABOR HOURS	COST PER L.F.		
				MAT.	INST.	TOTAL
Concrete, 8" thick by 18" wide footing						
2000 psi concrete	.040	C.Y.		4.28		4.28
2500 psi concrete	.040	C.Y.		4.32		4.32
3000 psi concrete	.040	C.Y.		4.40		4.40
3500 psi concrete	.040	C.Y.		4.52		4.52
4000 psi concrete	.040	C.Y.		4.68		4.68
12" thick by 24" wide footing						
2000 psi concrete	.070	C.Y.		7.50		7.50
2500 psi concrete	.070	C.Y.		7.55		7.55
3000 psi concrete	.070	C.Y.		7.70		7.70
3500 psi concrete	.070	C.Y.		7.90		7.90
4000 psi concrete	.070	C.Y.		8.20		8.20
12" thick by 36" wide footing						
2000 psi concrete	.110	C.Y.		11.75		11.75
2500 psi concrete	.110	C.Y.		11.90		11.90
3000 psi concrete	.110	C.Y.		12.10		12.10
3500 psi concrete	.110	C.Y.		12.45		12.45
4000 psi concrete	.110	C.Y.		12.85		12.85
Place concrete, 8" thick by 18" wide footing, direct chute	.040	C.Y.	.016		.58	.58
Pumped concrete	.040	C.Y.	.017		.85	.85
Crane & bucket	.040	C.Y.	.032		1.76	1.76
12" thick by 24" wide footing, direct chute	.070	C.Y.	.028		1.02	1.02
Pumped concrete	.070	C.Y.	.030		1.49	1.49
Crane & bucket	.070	C.Y.	.056		3.09	3.09
12" thick by 36" wide footing, direct chute	.110	C.Y.	.044		1.60	1.60
Pumped concrete	.110	C.Y.	.047		2.34	2.34
Crane & bucket	.110	C.Y.	.088		4.85	4.85
Forms, 8" thick footing, 1 use	1.330	SFCA	.140	.48	5.50	5.98
4 uses	1.330	SFCA	.103	.93	4.06	4.99
12" thick footing, 1 use	2.000	SFCA	.211	.72	8.25	8.97
4 uses	2.000	SFCA	.155	1.40	6.10	7.50
Reinforcing, 3/8" diameter bar, 1 each	.400	Lb.	.003	.21	.16	.37
2 each	.800	Lb.	.006	.42	.31	.73
3 each	1.200	Lb.	.009	.64	.47	1.11
1/2" diameter bar, 1 each	.700	Lb.	.005	.37	.27	.64
2 each	1.380	Lb.	.011	.73	.54	1.27
3 each	2.100	Lb.	.016	1.11	.82	1.93
5/8" diameter bar, 1 each	1.040	Lb.	.008	.55	.41	.96
2 each	2.080	Lb.	.016	1.10	.81	1.91
Keyway, beveled, 2" x 4", 1 use	1.000	L.F.	.030	.42	1.36	1.78
2 uses	1.000	L.F.	.023	.32	1.02	1.34
2" x 6", 1 use	1.000	L.F.	.032	.60	1.44	2.04
2 uses	1.000	L.F.	.024	.45	1.08	1.53
Dowels, 2 feet long, 6' O.C., 3/8" bar	.166	Ea.	.005	.07	.26	.33
1/2" bar	.166	Ea.	.006	.13	.28	.41
5/8" bar	.166	Ea.	.006	.20	.31	.51
3/4" bar	.166	Ea.	.006	.20	.31	.51

System Description	QUAN.	UNIT	LABOR HOURS	COST PER S.F.		
				MAT.	INST.	TOTAL
8″ WALL, GROUTED, FULL HEIGHT						
Concrete block, 8″ x 16″ x 8″	1.000	S.F.	.094	2.87	3.91	6.78
Masonry reinforcing, every second course	.750	L.F.	.002	.17	.09	.26
Parging, plastering with portland cement plaster, 1 coat	1.000	S.F.	.014	.25	.61	.86
Dampproofing, bituminous coating, 1 coat	1.000	S.F.	.012	.14	.50	.64
Insulation, 1″ rigid polystyrene	1.000	S.F.	.010	.56	.45	1.01
Grout, solid, pumped	1.000	S.F.	.059	1.24	2.38	3.62
Anchor bolts, 1/2″ diameter, 8″ long, 4′ O.C.	.060	Ea.	.002	.05	.11	.16
Sill plate, 2″ x 4″, treated	.250	L.F.	.007	.16	.33	.49
TOTAL		S.F.	.200	5.44	8.38	13.82
12″ WALL, GROUTED, FULL HEIGHT						
Concrete block, 8″ x 16″ x 12″	1.000	S.F.	.160	4.01	6.50	10.51
Masonry reinforcing, every second course	.750	L.F.	.003	.19	.14	.33
Parging, plastering with portland cement plaster, 1 coat	1.000	S.F.	.014	.25	.61	.86
Dampproofing, bituminous coating, 1 coat	1.000	S.F.	.012	.14	.50	.64
Insulation, 1″ rigid polystyrene	1.000	S.F.	.010	.56	.45	1.01
Grout, solid, pumped	1.000	S.F.	.063	2.03	2.54	4.57
Anchor bolts, 1/2″ diameter, 8″ long, 4′ O.C.	.060	Ea.	.002	.05	.11	.16
Sill plate, 2″ x 4″, treated	.250	L.F.	.007	.16	.33	.49
TOTAL		S.F.	.271	7.39	11.18	18.57

The costs in this system are based on a square foot of wall. Do not subtract for window or door openings.

Description	QUAN.	UNIT	LABOR HOURS	COST PER S.F.		
				MAT.	INST.	TOTAL

Block Wall Systems	QUAN.	UNIT	LABOR HOURS	COST PER S.F.		
				MAT.	INST.	TOTAL
Concrete, block, 8" x 16" x, 6" thick	1.000	S.F.	.089	2.67	3.65	6.32
8" thick	1.000	S.F.	.093	2.87	3.91	6.78
10" thick	1.000	S.F.	.095	3.74	4.75	8.49
12" thick	1.000	S.F.	.122	4.01	6.50	10.51
Solid block, 8" x 16" x, 6" thick	1.000	S.F.	.091	2.67	3.77	6.44
8" thick	1.000	S.F.	.096	3.95	4	7.95
10" thick	1.000	S.F.	.096	3.95	4	7.95
12" thick	1.000	S.F.	.126	5.90	5.55	11.45
Masonry reinforcing, wire strips, to 8" wide, every course	1.500	L.F.	.004	.33	.18	.51
Every 2nd course	.750	L.F.	.002	.17	.09	.26
Every 3rd course	.500	L.F.	.001	.11	.06	.17
Every 4th course	.400	L.F.	.001	.09	.05	.14
Wire strips to 12" wide, every course	1.500	L.F.	.006	.38	.27	.65
Every 2nd course	.750	L.F.	.003	.19	.14	.33
Every 3rd course	.500	L.F.	.002	.13	.09	.22
Every 4th course	.400	L.F.	.002	.10	.07	.17
Parging, plastering with portland cement plaster, 1 coat	1.000	S.F.	.014	.25	.61	.86
2 coats	1.000	S.F.	.022	.39	.93	1.32
Dampproofing, bituminous, brushed on, 1 coat	1.000	S.F.	.012	.14	.50	.64
2 coats	1.000	S.F.	.016	.28	.67	.95
Sprayed on, 1 coat	1.000	S.F.	.010	.14	.40	.54
2 coats	1.000	S.F.	.016	.27	.67	.94
Troweled on, 1/16" thick	1.000	S.F.	.016	.30	.67	.97
1/8" thick	1.000	S.F.	.020	.54	.84	1.38
1/2" thick	1.000	S.F.	.023	1.75	.96	2.71
Insulation, rigid, fiberglass, 1.5#/C.F., unfaced						
1-1/2" thick R 6.2	1.000	S.F.	.008	.70	.36	1.06
2" thick R 8.5	1.000	S.F.	.008	.76	.36	1.12
3" thick R 13	1.000	S.F.	.010	.88	.45	1.33
Foamglass, 1-1/2" thick R 2.64	1.000	S.F.	.010	1.46	.45	1.91
2" thick R 5.26	1.000	S.F.	.011	3.51	.50	4.01
Perlite, 1" thick R 2.77	1.000	S.F.	.010	.33	.45	.78
2" thick R 5.55	1.000	S.F.	.011	.66	.50	1.16
Polystyrene, extruded, 1" thick R 5.4	1.000	S.F.	.010	.56	.45	1.01
2" thick R 10.8	1.000	S.F.	.011	1.54	.50	2.04
Molded 1" thick R 3.85	1.000	S.F.	.010	.26	.45	.71
2" thick R 7.7	1.000	S.F.	.011	.86	.50	1.36
Grout, concrete block cores, 6" thick	1.000	S.F.	.044	.93	1.79	2.72
8" thick	1.000	S.F.	.059	1.24	2.38	3.62
10" thick	1.000	S.F.	.061	1.63	2.46	4.09
12" thick	1.000	S.F.	.063	2.03	2.54	4.57
Anchor bolts, 2' on center, 1/2" diameter, 8" long	.120	Ea.	.005	.10	.22	.32
12" long	.120	Ea.	.005	.19	.23	.42
3/4" diameter, 8" long	.120	Ea.	.006	.22	.27	.49
12" long	.120	Ea.	.006	.28	.29	.57
4' on center, 1/2" diameter, 8" long	.060	Ea.	.002	.05	.11	.16
12" long	.060	Ea.	.003	.09	.12	.21
3/4" diameter, 8" long	.060	Ea.	.003	.11	.14	.25
12" long	.060	Ea.	.003	.14	.15	.29
Sill plates, treated, 2" x 4"	.250	L.F.	.007	.16	.33	.49
4" x 4"	.250	L.F.	.007	.41	.31	.72

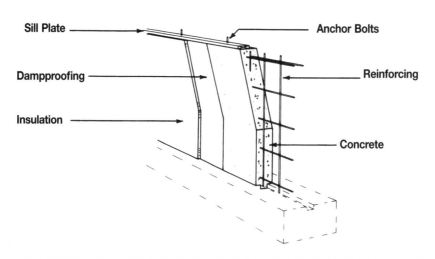

System Description	QUAN.	UNIT	LABOR HOURS	COST PER S.F.		
				MAT.	INST.	TOTAL
8″ THICK, POURED CONCRETE WALL						
Concrete, 8″ thick , 3000 psi	.025	C.Y.		2.75		2.75
Forms, prefabricated plywood, 4 uses per month	2.000	SFCA	.076	1.54	3.06	4.60
Reinforcing, light	.670	Lb.	.004	.36	.18	.54
Placing concrete, direct chute	.025	C.Y.	.013		.49	.49
Dampproofing, brushed on, 2 coats	1.000	S.F.	.016	.28	.67	.95
Rigid insulation, 1″ polystyrene	1.000	S.F.	.010	.56	.45	1.01
Anchor bolts, 1/2″ diameter, 12″ long, 4′ O.C.	.060	Ea.	.003	.09	.12	.21
Sill plates, 2″ x 4″, treated	.250	L.F.	.007	.16	.33	.49
TOTAL		S.F.	.129	5.74	5.30	11.04
12″ THICK, POURED CONCRETE WALL						
Concrete, 12″ thick, 3000 psi	.040	C.Y.		4.40		4.40
Forms, prefabricated plywood, 4 uses per month	2.000	SFCA	.076	1.54	3.06	4.60
Reinforcing, light	1.000	Lb.	.005	.53	.27	.80
Placing concrete, direct chute	.040	C.Y.	.019		.70	.70
Dampproofing, brushed on, 2 coats	1.000	S.F.	.016	.28	.67	.95
Rigid insulation, 1″ polystyrene	1.000	S.F.	.010	.56	.45	1.01
Anchor bolts, 1/2″ diameter, 12″ long, 4′ O.C.	.060	Ea.	.003	.09	.12	.21
Sill plates, 2″ x 4″ treated	.250	L.F.	.007	.16	.33	.49
TOTAL		S.F.	.136	7.56	5.60	13.16

The costs in this system are based on sq. ft. of wall. Do not subtract
for window and door openings. The costs assume a 4′ high wall.

Description	QUAN.	UNIT	LABOR HOURS	COST PER S.F.		
				MAT.	INST.	TOTAL

Concrete Wall Price Sheet	QUAN.	UNIT	LABOR HOURS	COST PER S.F.		
				MAT.	INST.	TOTAL
Formwork, prefabricated plywood, 1 use per month	2.000	SFCA	.081	4.64	3.26	7.90
4 uses per month	2.000	SFCA	.076	1.54	3.06	4.60
Job built forms, 1 use per month	2.000	SFCA	.320	5.95	10.40	16.35
4 uses per month	2.000	SFCA	.221	2.20	7.60	9.80
Reinforcing, 8" wall, light reinforcing	.670	Lb.	.004	.36	.18	.54
Heavy reinforcing	1.500	Lb.	.008	.80	.41	1.21
10" wall, light reinforcing	.850	Lb.	.005	.45	.23	.68
Heavy reinforcing	2.000	Lb.	.011	1.06	.54	1.60
12" wall light reinforcing	1.000	Lb.	.005	.53	.27	.80
Heavy reinforcing	2.250	Lb.	.012	1.19	.61	1.80
Placing concrete, 8" wall, direct chute	.025	C.Y.	.013		.49	.49
Pumped concrete	.025	C.Y.	.016		.79	.79
Crane & bucket	.025	C.Y.	.023		1.24	1.24
10" wall, direct chute	.030	C.Y.	.016		.58	.58
Pumped concrete	.030	C.Y.	.019		.95	.95
Crane & bucket	.030	C.Y.	.027		1.48	1.48
12" wall, direct chute	.040	C.Y.	.019		.70	.70
Pumped concrete	.040	C.Y.	.023		1.15	1.15
Crane & bucket	.040	C.Y.	.032		1.76	1.76
Dampproofing, bituminous, brushed on, 1 coat	1.000	S.F.	.012	.14	.50	.64
2 coats	1.000	S.F.	.016	.28	.67	.95
Sprayed on, 1 coat	1.000	S.F.	.010	.14	.40	.54
2 coats	1.000	S.F.	.016	.27	.67	.94
Troweled on, 1/16" thick	1.000	S.F.	.016	.30	.67	.97
1/8" thick	1.000	S.F.	.020	.54	.84	1.38
1/2" thick	1.000	S.F.	.023	1.75	.96	2.71
Insulation rigid, fiberglass, 1.5#/C.F., unfaced						
1-1/2" thick, R 6.2	1.000	S.F.	.008	.70	.36	1.06
2" thick, R 8.3	1.000	S.F.	.008	.76	.36	1.12
3" thick, R 12.4	1.000	S.F.	.010	.88	.45	1.33
Foamglass, 1-1/2" thick R 2.64	1.000	S.F.	.010	1.46	.45	1.91
2" thick R 5.26	1.000	S.F.	.011	3.51	.50	4.01
Perlite, 1" thick R 2.77	1.000	S.F.	.010	.33	.45	.78
2" thick R 5.55	1.000	S.F.	.011	.66	.50	1.16
Polystyrene, extruded, 1" thick R 5.40	1.000	S.F.	.010	.56	.45	1.01
2" thick R 10.8	1.000	S.F.	.011	1.54	.50	2.04
Molded, 1" thick R 3.85	1.000	S.F.	.010	.26	.45	.71
2" thick R 7.70	1.000	S.F.	.011	.86	.50	1.36
Anchor bolts, 2' on center, 1/2" diameter, 8" long	.120	Ea.	.005	.10	.22	.32
12" long	.120	Ea.	.005	.19	.23	.42
3/4" diameter, 8" long	.120	Ea.	.006	.22	.27	.49
12" long	.120	Ea.	.006	.28	.29	.57
Sill plates, treated lumber, 2" x 4"	.250	L.F.	.007	.16	.33	.49
4" x 4"	.250	L.F.	.007	.41	.31	.72

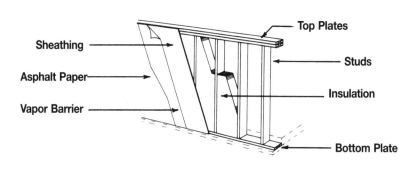

Sheathing —

Asphalt Paper —

Vapor Barrier —

Top Plates

Studs

Insulation

Bottom Plate

System Description	QUAN.	UNIT	LABOR HOURS	COST PER S.F.		
				MAT.	INST.	TOTAL
2" X 4" STUDS, 16" O.C., WALL						
Studs, 2" x 4", 16" O.C., treated	1.000	L.F.	.015	.65	.66	1.31
Plates, double top plate, single bottom plate, treated, 2" x 4"	.750	L.F.	.011	.49	.50	.99
Sheathing, 1/2", exterior grade, CDX, treated	1.000	S.F.	.014	.99	.64	1.63
Asphalt paper, 15# roll	1.100	S.F.	.002	.06	.11	.17
Vapor barrier, 4 mil polyethylene	1.000	S.F.	.002	.05	.10	.15
Insulation, batts, fiberglass, 3-1/2" thick, R 13	1.000	S.F.	.006	.41	.27	.68
TOTAL		S.F.	.050	2.65	2.28	4.93
2" X 6" STUDS, 16" O.C., WALL						
Studs, 2" x 6", 16" O.C., treated	1.000	L.F.	.016	.88	.72	1.60
Plates, double top plate, single bottom plate, treated, 2" x 6"	.750	L.F.	.012	.66	.54	1.20
Sheathing, 5/8" exterior grade, CDX, treated	1.000	S.F.	.015	1.51	.69	2.20
Asphalt paper, 15# roll	1.100	S.F.	.002	.06	.11	.17
Vapor barrier, 4 mil polyethylene	1.000	S.F.	.002	.05	.10	.15
Insulation, batts, fiberglass, 6" thick, R 19	1.000	S.F.	.006	.47	.27	.74
TOTAL		S.F.	.053	3.63	2.43	6.06
2" X 8" STUDS, 16" O.C., WALL						
Studs, 2" x 8", 16" O.C. treated	1.000	L.F.	.018	1.16	.80	1.96
Plates, double top plate, single bottom plate, treated, 2" x 8"	.750	L.F.	.013	.87	.60	1.47
Sheathing, 3/4" exterior grade, CDX, treated	1.000	S.F.	.016	1.72	.74	2.46
Asphalt paper, 15# roll	1.100	S.F.	.002	.06	.11	.17
Vapor barrier, 4 mil polyethylene	1.000	S.F.	.002	.05	.10	.15
Insulation, batts, fiberglass, 9" thick, R 30	1.000	S.F.	.006	.88	.27	1.15
TOTAL		S.F.	.057	4.74	2.62	7.36

The costs in this system are based on a sq. ft. of wall area. Do not subtract for window or door openings. The costs assume a 4' high wall.

Description	QUAN.	UNIT	LABOR HOURS	COST PER S.F.		
				MAT.	INST.	TOTAL

Wood Wall Foundation Price Sheet	QUAN.	UNIT	LABOR HOURS	COST PER S.F.		
				MAT.	INST.	TOTAL
Studs, treated, 2″ x 4″, 12″ O.C.	1.250	L.F.	.018	.81	.83	1.64
16″ O.C.	1.000	L.F.	.015	.65	.66	1.31
2″ x 6″, 12″ O.C.	1.250	L.F.	.020	1.10	.90	2
16″ O.C.	1.000	L.F.	.016	.88	.72	1.60
2″ x 8″, 12″ O.C.	1.250	L.F.	.022	1.45	1	2.45
16″ O.C.	1.000	L.F.	.018	1.16	.80	1.96
Plates, treated double top single bottom, 2″ x 4″	.750	L.F.	.011	.49	.50	.99
2″ x 6″	.750	L.F.	.012	.66	.54	1.20
2″ x 8″	.750	L.F.	.013	.87	.60	1.47
Sheathing, treated exterior grade CDX, 1/2″ thick	1.000	S.F.	.014	.99	.64	1.63
5/8″ thick	1.000	S.F.	.015	1.51	.69	2.20
3/4″ thick	1.000	S.F.	.016	1.72	.74	2.46
Asphalt paper, 15# roll	1.100	S.F.	.002	.06	.11	.17
Vapor barrier, polyethylene, 4 mil	1.000	S.F.	.002	.03	.10	.13
10 mil	1.000	S.F.	.002	.06	.10	.16
Insulation, rigid, fiberglass, 1.5#/C.F., unfaced	1.000	S.F.	.008	.48	.36	.84
1-1/2″ thick, R 6.2	1.000	S.F.	.008	.70	.36	1.06
2″ thick, R 8.3	1.000	S.F.	.008	.76	.36	1.12
3″ thick, R 12.4	1.000	S.F.	.010	.90	.46	1.36
Foamglass 1 1/2″ thick, R 2.64	1.000	S.F.	.010	1.46	.45	1.91
2″ thick, R 5.26	1.000	S.F.	.011	3.51	.50	4.01
Perlite 1″ thick, R 2.77	1.000	S.F.	.010	.33	.45	.78
2″ thick, R 5.55	1.000	S.F.	.011	.66	.50	1.16
Polystyrene, extruded, 1″ thick, R 5.40	1.000	S.F.	.010	.56	.45	1.01
2″ thick, R 10.8	1.000	S.F.	.011	1.54	.50	2.04
Molded 1″ thick, R 3.85	1.000	S.F.	.010	.26	.45	.71
2″ thick, R 7.7	1.000	S.F.	.011	.86	.50	1.36
Non rigid, batts, fiberglass, paper backed, 3-1/2″ thick roll, R 11	1.000	S.F.	.005	.41	.27	.68
6″, R 19	1.000	S.F.	.006	.47	.27	.74
9″, R 30	1.000	S.F.	.006	.88	.27	1.15
12″, R 38	1.000	S.F.	.006	1.10	.27	1.37
Mineral fiber, paper backed, 3-1/2″, R 13	1.000	S.F.	.005	.42	.23	.65
6″, R 19	1.000	S.F.	.005	.56	.23	.79
10″, R 30	1.000	S.F.	.006	.83	.27	1.10

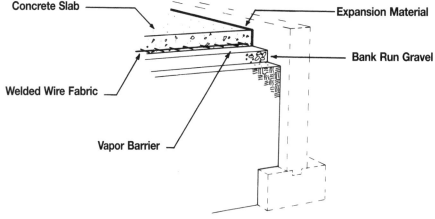

Concrete Slab — Expansion Material

Welded Wire Fabric — Bank Run Gravel

Vapor Barrier

System Description	QUAN.	UNIT	LABOR HOURS	COST PER S.F.		
				MAT.	INST.	TOTAL
4″ THICK SLAB						
Concrete, 4″ thick, 3000 psi concrete	.012	C.Y.		1.32		1.32
Place concrete, direct chute	.012	C.Y.	.005		.19	.19
Bank run gravel, 4″ deep	1.000	S.F.	.001	.47	.05	.52
Polyethylene vapor barrier, .006″ thick	1.000	S.F.	.002	.05	.10	.15
Edge forms, expansion material	.100	L.F.	.005	.04	.21	.25
WELDED WIRE FABRIC, 6 x 6, 10/10 (W1.4/W1.4)	1.100	S.F.	.005	.17	.25	.42
Steel trowel finish	1.000	S.F.	.014		.57	.57
TOTAL		S.F.	.032	2.05	1.37	3.42
6″ THICK SLAB						
Concrete, 6″ thick, 3000 psi concrete	.019	C.Y.		2.09		2.09
Place concrete, direct chute	.019	C.Y.	.008		.30	.30
Bank run gravel, 4″ deep	1.000	S.F.	.001	.47	.05	.52
Polyethylene vapor barrier, .006″ thick	1.000	S.F.	.002	.05	.10	.15
Edge forms, expansion material	.100	L.F.	.005	.04	.21	.25
WELDED WIRE FABRIC, 6 x 6, 10/10 (W1.4/W1.4)	1.100	S.F.	.005	.17	.25	.42
Steel trowel finish	1.000	S.F.	.014		.57	.57
TOTAL		S.F.	.035	2.82	1.48	4.30

The slab costs in this section are based on a cost per square foot of floor area.

Description	QUAN.	UNIT	LABOR HOURS	COST PER S.F.		
				MAT.	INST.	TOTAL

Floor Slab Price Sheet	QUAN.	UNIT	LABOR HOURS	COST PER S.F.		
				MAT.	INST.	TOTAL
Concrete, 4" thick slab, 2000 psi concrete	.012	C.Y.		1.28		1.28
2500 psi concrete	.012	C.Y.		1.30		1.30
3000 psi concrete	.012	C.Y.		1.32		1.32
3500 psi concrete	.012	C.Y.		1.36		1.36
4000 psi concrete	.012	C.Y.		1.40		1.40
4500 psi concrete	.012	C.Y.		1.44		1.44
5" thick slab, 2000 psi concrete	.015	C.Y.		1.61		1.61
2500 psi concrete	.015	C.Y.		1.62		1.62
3000 psi concrete	.015	C.Y.		1.65		1.65
3500 psi concrete	.015	C.Y.		1.70		1.70
4000 psi concrete	.015	C.Y.		1.76		1.76
4500 psi concrete	.015	C.Y.		1.80		1.80
6" thick slab, 2000 psi concrete	.019	C.Y.		2.03		2.03
2500 psi concrete	.019	C.Y.		2.05		2.05
3000 psi concrete	.019	C.Y.		2.09		2.09
3500 psi concrete	.019	C.Y.		2.15		2.15
4000 psi concrete	.019	C.Y.		2.22		2.22
4500 psi concrete	.019	C.Y.		2.28		2.28
Place concrete, 4" slab, direct chute	.012	C.Y.	.005		.19	.19
Pumped concrete	.012	C.Y.	.006		.29	.29
Crane & bucket	.012	C.Y.	.008		.43	.43
5" slab, direct chute	.015	C.Y.	.007		.24	.24
Pumped concrete	.015	C.Y.	.007		.37	.37
Crane & bucket	.015	C.Y.	.010		.54	.54
6" slab, direct chute	.019	C.Y.	.008		.30	.30
Pumped concrete	.019	C.Y.	.009		.47	.47
Crane & bucket	.019	C.Y.	.012		.69	.69
Gravel, bank run, 4" deep	1.000	S.F.	.001	.47	.05	.52
6" deep	1.000	S.F.	.001	.62	.07	.69
9" deep	1.000	S.F.	.001	.90	.08	.98
12" deep	1.000	S.F.	.001	1.24	.10	1.34
3/4" crushed stone, 3" deep	1.000	S.F.	.001	.56	.04	.60
6" deep	1.000	S.F.	.001	1.11	.08	1.19
9" deep	1.000	S.F.	.002	1.62	.12	1.74
12" deep	1.000	S.F.	.002	2.37	.14	2.51
Vapor barrier polyethylene, .004" thick	1.000	S.F.	.002	.03	.10	.13
.006" thick	1.000	S.F.	.002	.05	.10	.15
Edge forms, expansion material, 4" thick slab	.100	L.F.	.004	.02	.14	.16
6" thick slab	.100	L.F.	.005	.04	.21	.25
Welded wire fabric 6 x 6, 10/10 (W1.4/W1.4)	1.100	S.F.	.005	.17	.25	.42
6 x 6, 6/6 (W2.9/W2.9)	1.100	S.F.	.006	.24	.31	.55
4 x 4, 10/10 (W1.4/W1.4)	1.100	S.F.	.006	.24	.29	.53
Finish concrete, screed finish	1.000	S.F.	.009		.19	.19
Float finish	1.000	S.F.	.011		.23	.23
Steel trowel, for resilient floor	1.000	S.F.	.013		.74	.74
For finished floor	1.000	S.F.	.015		.57	.57

Division 3
Framing

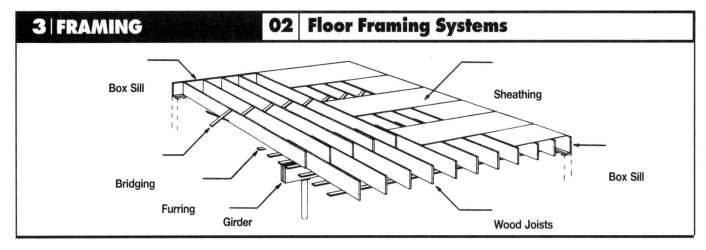

System Description	QUAN.	UNIT	LABOR HOURS	COST PER S.F.		
				MAT.	INST.	TOTAL
2″ X 8″, 16″ O.C.						
Wood joists, 2″ x 8″, 16″ O.C.	1.000	L.F.	.015	.83	.66	1.49
Bridging, 1″ x 3″, 6′ O.C.	.080	Pr.	.005	.02	.22	.24
Box sills, 2″ x 8″	.150	L.F.	.002	.12	.10	.22
Concrete filled steel column, 4″ diameter	.125	L.F.	.002	.13	.11	.24
Girder, built up from three 2″ x 8″	.125	L.F.	.013	.31	.60	.91
Sheathing, plywood, subfloor, 5/8″ CDX	1.000	S.F.	.012	.75	.54	1.29
Furring, 1″ x 3″, 16″ O.C.	1.000	L.F.	.023	.19	1.03	1.22
TOTAL		S.F.	.072	2.35	3.26	5.61
2″ X 10″, 16″ O.C.						
Wood joists, 2″ x 10″, 16″ OC	1.000	L.F.	.018	1.13	.80	1.93
Bridging, 1″ x 3″, 6′ OC	.080	Pr.	.005	.02	.22	.24
Box sills, 2″ x 10″	.150	L.F.	.003	.17	.12	.29
Girder, built up from three 2″ x 10″	.125	L.F.	.002	.13	.11	.24
Girder, built up from three 2″ x 10″	.125	L.F.	.014	.42	.64	1.06
Sheathing, plywood, subfloor, 5/8″ CDX	1.000	S.F.	.012	.75	.54	1.29
Furring, 1″ x 3″,16″ OC	1.000	L.F.	.023	.19	1.03	1.22
TOTAL		S.F.	.077	2.81	3.46	6.27
2″ X 12″, 16″ O.C.						
Wood joists, 2″ x 12″, 16″ O.C.	1.000	L.F.	.018	1.37	.83	2.20
Bridging, 1″ x 3″, 6′ O.C.	.080	Pr.	.005	.02	.22	.24
Box sills, 2″ x 12″	.150	L.F.	.003	.21	.12	.33
Concrete filled steel column, 4″ diameter	.125	L.F.	.002	.13	.11	.24
Girder, built up from three 2″ x 12″	.125	L.F.	.015	.51	.68	1.19
Sheathing, plywood, subfloor, 5/8″ CDX	1.000	S.F.	.012	.75	.54	1.29
Furring, 1″ x 3″, 16″ O.C.	1.000	L.F.	.023	.19	1.03	1.22
TOTAL		S.F.	.078	3.18	3.53	6.71

Floor costs on this page are given on a cost per square foot basis.

Description	QUAN.	UNIT	LABOR HOURS	COST PER S.F.		
				MAT.	INST.	TOTAL

Floor Framing Price Sheet (Wood)	QUAN.	UNIT	LABOR HOURS	COST PER S.F.		
				MAT.	INST.	TOTAL
Joists, #2 or better, pine, 2″ x 4″, 12″ O.C.	1.250	L.F.	.016	.49	.73	1.22
16″ O.C.	1.000	L.F.	.013	.39	.58	.97
2″ x 6″, 12″ O.C.	1.250	L.F.	.016	.75	.73	1.48
16″ O.C.	1.000	L.F.	.013	.60	.58	1.18
2″ x 8″, 12″ O.C.	1.250	L.F.	.018	1.04	.83	1.87
16″ O.C.	1.000	L.F.	.015	.83	.66	1.49
2″ x 10″, 12″ O.C.	1.250	L.F.	.022	1.41	1	2.41
16″ O.C.	1.000	L.F.	.018	1.13	.80	1.93
2″x 12″, 12″ O.C.	1.250	L.F.	.023	1.71	1.04	2.75
16″ O.C.	1.000	L.F.	.018	1.37	.83	2.20
Bridging, wood 1″ x 3″, joists 12″ O.C.	.100	Pr.	.006	.03	.28	.31
16″ O.C.	.080	Pr.	.005	.02	.22	.24
Metal, galvanized, joists 12″ O.C.	.100	Pr.	.006	.14	.28	.42
16″ O.C.	.080	Pr.	.005	.11	.22	.33
Compression type, joists 12″ O.C.	.100	Pr.	.004	.17	.18	.35
16″ O.C.	.080	Pr.	.003	.13	.14	.27
Box sills, #2 or better pine, 2″ x 4″	.150	L.F.	.002	.06	.09	.15
2″ x 6″	.150	L.F.	.002	.09	.09	.18
2″ x 8″	.150	L.F.	.002	.12	.10	.22
2″ x 10″	.150	L.F.	.003	.17	.12	.29
2″ x 12″	.150	L.F.	.003	.21	.12	.33
Girders, including lally columns, 3 pieces spiked together, 2″ x 8″	.125	L.F.	.015	.44	.71	1.15
2″ x 10″	.125	L.F.	.016	.55	.75	1.30
2″ x 12″	.125	L.F.	.017	.64	.79	1.43
Solid girders, 3″ x 8″	.040	L.F.	.004	.24	.18	.42
3″ x 10″	.040	L.F.	.004	.27	.19	.46
3″ x 12″	.040	L.F.	.004	.30	.20	.50
4″ x 8″	.040	L.F.	.004	.33	.20	.53
4″ x 10″	.040	L.F.	.004	.38	.21	.59
4″ x 12″	.040	L.F.	.004	.43	.22	.65
Steel girders, bolted & including fabrication, wide flange shapes						
12″ deep, 14#/l.f.	.040	L.F.	.003	.88	.25	1.13
10″ deep, 15#/l.f.	.040	L.F.	.003	.88	.25	1.13
8″ deep, 10#/l.f.	.040	L.F.	.003	.58	.25	.83
6″ deep, 9#/l.f.	.040	L.F.	.003	.52	.25	.77
5″ deep, 16#/l.f.	.040	L.F.	.003	.88	.25	1.13
Sheathing, plywood exterior grade CDX, 1/2″ thick	1.000	S.F.	.011	.57	.52	1.09
5/8″ thick	1.000	S.F.	.012	.75	.54	1.29
3/4″ thick	1.000	S.F.	.013	.96	.58	1.54
Boards, 1″ x 8″ laid regular	1.000	S.F.	.016	1.50	.72	2.22
Laid diagonal	1.000	S.F.	.019	1.50	.85	2.35
1″ x 10″ laid regular	1.000	S.F.	.015	1.82	.66	2.48
Laid diagonal	1.000	S.F.	.018	1.82	.80	2.62
Furring, 1″ x 3″, 12″ O.C.	1.250	L.F.	.029	.24	1.29	1.53
16″ O.C.	1.000	L.F.	.023	.19	1.03	1.22
24″ O.C.	.750	L.F.	.017	.14	.77	.91

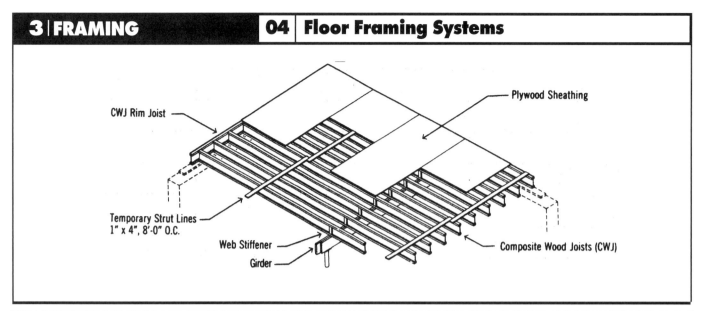

System Description	QUAN.	UNIT	LABOR HOURS	COST PER S.F.		
				MAT.	INST.	TOTAL
9-1/2″ COMPOSITE WOOD JOISTS, 16″ O.C.						
CWJ, 9-1/2″, 16″ O.C., 15′ span	1.000	L.F.	.018	2.23	.81	3.04
Temp. strut line, 1″ x 4″, 8′ O.C.	.160	L.F.	.003	.07	.14	.21
CWJ rim joist, 9-1/2″	.150	L.F.	.003	.33	.12	.45
Concrete filled steel column, 4″ diameter	.125	L.F.	.002	.13	.11	.24
Girder, built up from three 2″ x 8″	.125	L.F.	.013	.31	.60	.91
Sheathing, plywood, subfloor, 5/8″ CDX	1.000	S.F.	.012	.75	.54	1.29
TOTAL		S.F.	.051	3.82	2.32	6.14
11-1/2″ COMPOSITE WOOD JOISTS, 16″ O.C.						
CWJ, 11-1/2″, 16″ O.C., 18′ span	1.000	L.F.	.018	2.38	.82	3.20
Temp. strut line, 1″ x 4″, 8′ O.C.	.160	L.F.	.003	.07	.14	.21
CWJ rim joist, 11-1/2″	.150	L.F.	.003	.36	.12	.48
Concrete filled steel column, 4″ diameter	.125	L.F.	.002	.13	.11	.24
Girder, built up from three 2″ x 10″	.125	L.F.	.014	.42	.64	1.06
Sheathing, plywood, subfloor, 5/8″ CDX	1.000	S.F.	.012	.75	.54	1.29
TOTAL		S.F.	.052	4.11	2.37	6.48
14″ COMPOSITE WOOD JOISTS, 16″ O.C.						
CWJ, 14″, 16″ O.C., 22′ span	1.000	L.F.	.020	2.83	.88	3.71
Temp. strut line, 1″ x 4″, 8′ O.C.	.160	L.F.	.003	.07	.14	.21
CWJ rim joist, 14″	.150	L.F.	.003	.42	.13	.55
Concrete filled steel column, 4″ diameter	.600	L.F.	.002	.13	.11	.24
Girder, built up from three 2″ x 12″	.600	L.F.	.015	.51	.68	1.19
Sheathing, plywood, subfloor, 5/8″ CDX	1.000	S.F.	.012	.75	.54	1.29
TOTAL		S.F.	.055	4.71	2.48	7.19

Floor costs on this page are given on a cost per square foot basis.

Description	QUAN.	UNIT	LABOR HOURS	COST PER S.F.		
				MAT.	INST.	TOTAL

Floor Framing Price Sheet (Wood)

	QUAN.	UNIT	LABOR HOURS	COST PER S.F.		
				MAT.	INST.	TOTAL
Composite wood joist 9-1/2" deep, 12" O.C.	1.250	L.F.	.022	2.78	1.01	3.79
16" O.C.	1.000	L.F.	.018	2.23	.81	3.04
11-1/2" deep, 12" O.C.	1.250	L.F.	.023	2.97	1.03	4
16" O.C.	1.000	L.F.	.018	2.38	.82	3.20
14" deep, 12" O.C.	1.250	L.F.	.024	3.53	1.10	4.63
16" O.C.	1.000	L.F.	.020	2.83	.88	3.71
16 " deep, 12" O.C.	1.250	L.F.	.026	3.91	1.16	5.07
16" O.C.	1.000	L.F.	.021	3.13	.93	4.06
CWJ rim joist, 9-1/2"	.150	L.F.	.003	.33	.12	.45
11-1/2"	.150	L.F.	.003	.36	.12	.48
14"	.150	L.F.	.003	.42	.13	.55
16"	.150	L.F.	.003	.47	.14	.61
Girders, including lally columns, 3 pieces spiked together, 2" x 8"	.125	L.F.	.015	.44	.71	1.15
2" x 10"	.125	L.F.	.016	.55	.75	1.30
2" x 12"	.125	L.F.	.017	.64	.79	1.43
Solid girders, 3" x 8"	.040	L.F.	.004	.24	.18	.42
3" x 10"	.040	L.F.	.004	.27	.19	.46
3" x 12"	.040	L.F.	.004	.30	.20	.50
4" x 8"	.040	L.F.	.004	.33	.20	.53
4" x 10"	.040	L.F.	.004	.38	.21	.59
4" x 12"	.040	L.F.	.004	.43	.22	.65
Steel girders, bolted & including fabrication, wide flange shapes						
12" deep, 14#/l.f.	.040	L.F.	.061	20	5.55	25.55
10" deep, 15#/l.f.	.040	L.F.	.067	22	6.05	28.05
8" deep, 10#/l.f.	.040	L.F.	.067	14.50	6.05	20.55
6" deep, 9#/l.f.	.040	L.F.	.067	13.05	6.05	19.10
5" deep, 16#/l.f.	.040	L.F.	.064	21.50	5.85	27.35
Sheathing, plywood exterior grade CDX, 1/2" thick	1.000	S.F.	.011	.57	.52	1.09
5/8" thick	1.000	S.F.	.012	.75	.54	1.29
3/4" thick	1.000	S.F.	.013	.96	.58	1.54
Boards, 1" x 8" laid regular	1.000	S.F.	.016	1.50	.72	2.22
Laid diagonal	1.000	S.F.	.019	1.50	.85	2.35
1" x 10" laid regular	1.000	S.F.	.015	1.82	.66	2.48
Laid diagonal	1.000	S.F.	.018	1.82	.80	2.62
Furring, 1" x 3", 12" O.C.	1.250	L.F.	.029	.24	1.29	1.53
16" O.C.	1.000	L.F.	.023	.19	1.03	1.22
24" O.C.	.750	L.F.	.017	.14	.77	.91

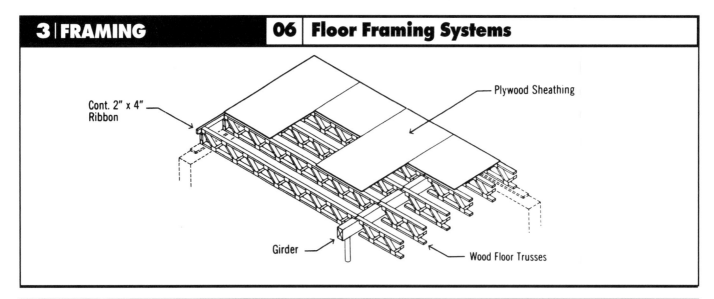

Cont. 2" x 4" Ribbon

Plywood Sheathing

Girder

Wood Floor Trusses

System Description	QUAN.	UNIT	LABOR HOURS	COST PER S.F.		
				MAT.	INST.	TOTAL
12″ OPEN WEB JOISTS, 16″ O.C.						
OWJ 12″, 16″ O.C., 21′ span	1.000	L.F.	.018	2.58	.82	3.40
Continuous ribbing, 2″ x 4″	.150	L.F.	.002	.06	.09	.15
Concrete filled steel column, 4″ diameter	.125	L.F.	.002	.13	.11	.24
Girder, built up from three 2″ x 8″	.125	L.F.	.013	.31	.60	.91
Sheathing, plywood, subfloor, 5/8″ CDX	1.000	S.F.	.012	.75	.54	1.29
Furring, 1″ x 3″, 16″ O.C.	1.000	L.F.	.023	.19	1.03	1.22
TOTAL		S.F.	.070	4.02	3.19	7.21
14″ OPEN WEB WOOD JOISTS, 16″ O.C.						
OWJ 14″, 16″ O.C., 22′ span	1.000	L.F.	.020	2.90	.88	3.78
Continuous ribbing, 2″ x 4″	.150	L.F.	.002	.06	.09	.15
Concrete filled steel column, 4″ diameter	.125	L.F.	.002	.13	.11	.24
Girder, built up from three 2″ x 10″	.125	L.F.	.014	.42	.64	1.06
Sheathing, plywood, subfloor, 5/8″ CDX	1.000	S.F.	.012	.75	.54	1.29
Furring, 1″ x 3″,16″ O.C.	1.000	L.F.	.023	.19	1.03	1.22
TOTAL		S.F.	.073	4.45	3.29	7.74
16″ OPEN WEB WOOD JOISTS, 16″ O.C.						
OWJ 16″, 16″ O.C., 24′ span	1.000	L.F.	.021	3.03	.93	3.96
Continuous ribbing, 2″ x 4″	.150	L.F.	.002	.06	.09	.15
Concrete filled steel column, 4″ diameter	.125	L.F.	.002	.13	.11	.24
Girder, built up from three 2″ x 12″	.125	L.F.	.015	.51	.68	1.19
Sheathing, plywood, subfloor, 5/8″ CDX	1.000	S.F.	.012	.75	.54	1.29
Furring, 1″ x 3″, 16″ O.C.	1.000	L.F.	.023	.19	1.03	1.22
TOTAL		S.F.	.075	4.67	3.38	8.05

Floor costs on this page are given on a cost per square foot basis.

Description	QUAN.	UNIT	LABOR HOURS	COST PER S.F.		
				MAT.	INST.	TOTAL

Floor Framing Price Sheet (Wood)	QUAN.	UNIT	LABOR HOURS	COST PER S.F.		
				MAT.	INST.	TOTAL
Open web joists, 12" deep, 12" O.C.	1.250	L.F.	.023	3.22	1.03	4.25
16" O.C.	1.000	L.F.	.018	2.58	.82	3.40
14" deep, 12" O.C.	1.250	L.F.	.024	3.63	1.10	4.73
16" O.C.	1.000	L.F.	.020	2.90	.88	3.78
16 " deep, 12" O.C.	1.250	L.F.	.026	3.78	1.16	4.94
16" O.C.	1.000	L.F.	.021	3.03	.93	3.96
18" deep, 12" O.C.	1.250	L.F.	.027	2.88	1.22	4.10
16" O.C.	1.000	L.F.	.022	2.30	.98	3.28
Continuous ribbing, 2" x 4"	.150	L.F.	.002	.06	.09	.15
2" x 6"	.150	L.F.	.002	.09	.09	.18
2" x 8"	.150	L.F.	.002	.12	.10	.22
2" x 10"	.150	L.F.	.003	.17	.12	.29
2" x 12"	.150	L.F.	.003	.21	.12	.33
Girders, including lally columns, 3 pieces spiked together, 2" x 8"	.125	L.F.	.015	.44	.71	1.15
2" x 10"	.125	L.F.	.016	.55	.75	1.30
2" x 12"	.125	L.F.	.017	.64	.79	1.43
Solid girders, 3" x 8"	.040	L.F.	.004	.24	.18	.42
3" x 10"	.040	L.F.	.004	.27	.19	.46
3" x 12"	.040	L.F.	.004	.30	.20	.50
4" x 8"	.040	L.F.	.004	.33	.20	.53
4" x 10"	.040	L.F.	.004	.38	.21	.59
4" x 12"	.040	L.F.	.004	.43	.22	.65
Steel girders, bolted & including fabrication, wide flange shapes						
12" deep, 14#/l.f.	.040	L.F.	.061	20	5.55	25.55
10" deep, 15#/l.f.	.040	L.F.	.067	22	6.05	28.05
8" deep, 10#/l.f.	.040	L.F.	.067	14.50	6.05	20.55
6" deep, 9#/l.f.	.040	L.F.	.067	13.05	6.05	19.10
5" deep, 16#/l.f.	.040	L.F.	.064	21.50	5.85	27.35
Sheathing, plywood exterior grade CDX, 1/2" thick	1.000	S.F.	.011	.57	.52	1.09
5/8" thick	1.000	S.F.	.012	.75	.54	1.29
3/4" thick	1.000	S.F.	.013	.96	.58	1.54
Boards, 1" x 8" laid regular	1.000	S.F.	.016	1.50	.72	2.22
Laid diagonal	1.000	S.F.	.019	1.50	.85	2.35
1" x 10" laid regular	1.000	S.F.	.015	1.82	.66	2.48
Laid diagonal	1.000	S.F.	.018	1.82	.80	2.62
Furring, 1" x 3", 12" O.C.	1.250	L.F.	.029	.24	1.29	1.53
16" O.C.	1.000	L.F.	.023	.19	1.03	1.22
24" O.C.	.750	L.F.	.017	.14	.77	.91

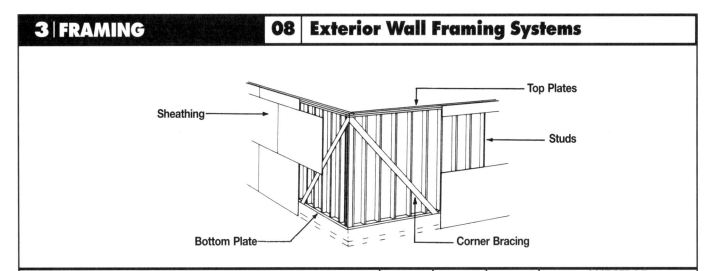

System Description	QUAN.	UNIT	LABOR HOURS	COST PER S.F.		
				MAT.	INST.	TOTAL
2″ X 4″, 16″ O.C.						
2″ x 4″ studs, 16″ O.C.	1.000	L.F.	.015	.39	.66	1.05
Plates, 2″ x 4″, double top, single bottom	.375	L.F.	.005	.15	.25	.40
Corner bracing, let-in, 1″ x 6″	.063	L.F.	.003	.04	.15	.19
Sheathing, 1/2″ plywood, CDX	1.000	S.F.	.011	.57	.52	1.09
TOTAL		S.F.	.034	1.15	1.58	2.73
2″ X 4″, 24″ O.C.						
2″ x 4″ studs, 24″ O.C.	.750	L.F.	.011	.29	.50	.79
Plates, 2″ x 4″, double top, single bottom	.375	L.F.	.005	.15	.25	.40
Corner bracing, let-in, 1″ x 6″	.063	L.F.	.002	.04	.10	.14
Sheathing, 1/2″ plywood, CDX	1.000	S.F.	.011	.57	.52	1.09
TOTAL		S.F.	.029	1.05	1.37	2.42
2″ X 6″, 16″ O.C.						
2″ x 6″ studs, 16″ O.C.	1.000	L.F.	.016	.60	.72	1.32
Plates, 2″ x 6″, double top, single bottom	.375	L.F.	.006	.23	.27	.50
Corner bracing, let-in, 1″ x 6″	.063	L.F.	.003	.04	.15	.19
Sheathing, 1/2″ plywood, CDX	1.000	S.F.	.014	.57	.64	1.21
TOTAL		S.F.	.039	1.44	1.78	3.22
2″ X 6″, 24″ O.C.						
2″ x 6″ studs, 24″ O.C.	.750	L.F.	.012	.45	.54	.99
Plates, 2″ x 6″, double top, single bottom	.375	L.F.	.006	.23	.27	.50
Corner bracing, let-in, 1″ x 6″	.063	L.F.	.002	.04	.10	.14
Sheathing, 1/2″ plywood, CDX	1.000	S.F.	.011	.57	.52	1.09
TOTAL		S.F.	.031	1.29	1.43	2.72

The wall costs on this page are given in cost per square foot of wall.
For window and door openings see below.

Description	QUAN.	UNIT	LABOR HOURS	COST PER S.F.		
				MAT.	INST.	TOTAL

Exterior Wall Framing Price Sheet	QUAN.	UNIT	LABOR HOURS	COST PER S.F.		
				MAT.	INST.	TOTAL
Studs, #2 or better, 2" x 4", 12" O.C.	1.250	L.F.	.018	.49	.83	1.32
16" O.C.	1.000	L.F.	.015	.39	.66	1.05
24" O.C.	.750	L.F.	.011	.29	.50	.79
32" O.C.	.600	L.F.	.009	.23	.40	.63
2" x 6", 12" O.C.	1.250	L.F.	.020	.75	.90	1.65
16" O.C.	1.000	L.F.	.016	.60	.72	1.32
24" O.C.	.750	L.F.	.012	.45	.54	.99
32" O.C.	.600	L.F.	.010	.36	.43	.79
2" x 8", 12" O.C.	1.250	L.F.	.025	1.28	1.13	2.41
16" O.C.	1.000	L.F.	.020	1.02	.90	1.92
24" O.C.	.750	L.F.	.015	.77	.68	1.45
32" O.C.	.600	L.F.	.012	.61	.54	1.15
Plates, #2 or better, double top, single bottom, 2" x 4"	.375	L.F.	.005	.15	.25	.40
2" x 6"	.375	L.F.	.006	.23	.27	.50
2" x 8"	.375	L.F.	.008	.38	.34	.72
Corner bracing, let-in 1" x 6" boards, studs, 12" O.C.	.070	L.F.	.004	.05	.17	.22
16" O.C.	.063	L.F.	.003	.04	.15	.19
24" O.C.	.063	L.F.	.002	.04	.10	.14
32" O.C.	.057	L.F.	.002	.04	.09	.13
Let-in steel ("T" shape), studs, 12" O.C.	.070	L.F.	.001	.04	.04	.08
16" O.C.	.063	L.F.	.001	.04	.04	.08
24" O.C.	.063	L.F.	.001	.04	.04	.08
32" O.C.	.057	L.F.	.001	.03	.03	.06
Sheathing, plywood CDX, 3/8" thick	1.000	S.F.	.010	.51	.47	.98
1/2" thick	1.000	S.F.	.011	.57	.52	1.09
5/8" thick	1.000	S.F.	.012	.75	.56	1.31
3/4" thick	1.000	S.F.	.013	.96	.60	1.56
Boards, 1" x 6", laid regular	1.000	S.F.	.025	1.50	1.11	2.61
Laid diagonal	1.000	S.F.	.027	1.50	1.24	2.74
1" x 8", laid regular	1.000	S.F.	.021	1.50	.95	2.45
Laid diagonal	1.000	S.F.	.025	1.50	1.11	2.61
Wood fiber, regular, no vapor barrier, 1/2" thick	1.000	S.F.	.013	.61	.60	1.21
5/8" thick	1.000	S.F.	.013	.79	.60	1.39
Asphalt impregnated 25/32" thick	1.000	S.F.	.013	.31	.60	.91
1/2" thick	1.000	S.F.	.013	.20	.60	.80
Polystyrene, regular, 3/4" thick	1.000	S.F.	.010	.56	.45	1.01
2" thick	1.000	S.F.	.011	1.54	.50	2.04
Fiberglass, foil faced, 1" thick	1.000	S.F.	.008	1.01	.36	1.37
2" thick	1.000	S.F.	.009	1.88	.41	2.29

Window & Door Openings	QUAN.	UNIT	LABOR HOURS	COST EACH		
				MAT.	INST.	TOTAL
The following costs are to be added to the total costs of the wall for each opening. Do not subtract the area of the openings.						
Headers, 2" x 6" double, 2' long	4.000	L.F.	.178	2.40	8.05	10.45
3' long	6.000	L.F.	.267	3.60	12.05	15.65
4' long	8.000	L.F.	.356	4.80	16.10	20.90
5' long	10.000	L.F.	.444	6	20	26
2" x 8" double, 4' long	8.000	L.F.	.376	6.65	17.05	23.70
5' long	10.000	L.F.	.471	8.30	21.50	29.80
6' long	12.000	L.F.	.565	9.95	25.50	35.45
8' long	16.000	L.F.	.753	13.30	34	47.30
2" x 10" double, 4' long	8.000	L.F.	.400	9.05	18.10	27.15
6' long	12.000	L.F.	.600	13.55	27	40.55
8' long	16.000	L.F.	.800	18.10	36	54.10
10' long	20.000	L.F.	1.000	22.50	45	67.50
2" x 12" double, 8' long	16.000	L.F.	.853	22	38.50	60.50
12' long	24.000	L.F.	1.280	33	58	91

System Description	QUAN.	UNIT	LABOR HOURS	COST PER S.F.		
				MAT.	INST.	TOTAL
2″ X 6″ RAFTERS, 16″ O.C., 4/12 PITCH						
Rafters, 2″ x 6″, 16″ O.C., 4/12 pitch	1.170	L.F.	.019	.70	.84	1.54
Ceiling joists, 2″ x 4″, 16″ O.C.	1.000	L.F.	.013	.39	.58	.97
Ridge board, 2″ x 6″	.050	L.F.	.002	.03	.07	.10
Fascia board, 2″ x 6″	.100	L.F.	.005	.06	.24	.30
Rafter tie, 1″ x 4″, 4′ O.C.	.060	L.F.	.001	.03	.05	.08
Soffit nailer (outrigger), 2″ x 4″, 24″ O.C.	.170	L.F.	.004	.07	.20	.27
Sheathing, exterior, plywood, CDX, 1/2″ thick	1.170	S.F.	.013	.67	.61	1.28
Furring strips, 1″ x 3″, 16″ O.C.	1.000	L.F.	.023	.19	1.03	1.22
TOTAL		S.F.	.080	2.14	3.62	5.76
2″ X 8″ RAFTERS, 16″ O.C., 4/12 PITCH						
Rafters, 2″ x 8″, 16″ O.C., 4/12 pitch	1.170	L.F.	.020	.97	.89	1.86
Ceiling joists, 2″ x 6″, 16″ O.C.	1.000	L.F.	.013	.60	.58	1.18
Ridge board, 2″ x 8″	.050	L.F.	.002	.04	.08	.12
Fascia board, 2″ x 8″	.100	L.F.	.007	.08	.32	.40
Rafter tie, 1″ x 4″, 4′ O.C.	.060	L.F.	.001	.03	.05	.08
Soffit nailer (outrigger), 2″ x 4″, 24″ O.C.	.170	L.F.	.004	.07	.20	.27
Sheathing, exterior, plywood, CDX, 1/2″ thick	1.170	S.F.	.013	.67	.61	1.28
Furring strips, 1″ x 3″, 16″ O.C.	1.000	L.F.	.023	.19	1.03	1.22
TOTAL		S.F.	.083	2.65	3.76	6.41

The cost of this system is based on the square foot of plan area.
All quantities have been adjusted accordingly.

Description	QUAN.	UNIT	LABOR HOURS	COST PER S.F.		
				MAT.	INST.	TOTAL

Gable End Roof Framing Price Sheet	QUAN.	UNIT	LABOR HOURS	COST PER S.F.		
				MAT.	INST.	TOTAL
Rafters, #2 or better, 16" O.C., 2" x 6", 4/12 pitch	1.170	L.F.	.019	.70	.84	1.54
8/12 pitch	1.330	L.F.	.027	.80	1.20	2
2" x 8", 4/12 pitch	1.170	L.F.	.020	.97	.89	1.86
8/12 pitch	1.330	L.F.	.028	1.10	1.28	2.38
2" x 10", 4/12 pitch	1.170	L.F.	.030	1.32	1.35	2.67
8/12 pitch	1.330	L.F.	.043	1.50	1.94	3.44
24" O.C., 2" x 6", 4/12 pitch	.940	L.F.	.015	.56	.68	1.24
8/12 pitch	1.060	L.F.	.021	.64	.95	1.59
2" x 8", 4/12 pitch	.940	L.F.	.016	.78	.71	1.49
8/12 pitch	1.060	L.F.	.023	.88	1.02	1.90
2" x 10", 4/12 pitch	.940	L.F.	.024	1.06	1.08	2.14
8/12 pitch	1.060	L.F.	.034	1.20	1.55	2.75
Ceiling joist, #2 or better, 2" x 4", 16" O.C.	1.000	L.F.	.013	.39	.58	.97
24" O.C.	.750	L.F.	.010	.29	.44	.73
2" x 6", 16" O.C.	1.000	L.F.	.013	.60	.58	1.18
24" O.C.	.750	L.F.	.010	.45	.44	.89
2" x 8", 16" O.C.	1.000	L.F.	.015	.83	.66	1.49
24" O.C.	.750	L.F.	.011	.62	.50	1.12
2" x 10", 16" O.C.	1.000	L.F.	.018	1.13	.80	1.93
24" O.C.	.750	L.F.	.013	.85	.60	1.45
Ridge board, #2 or better, 1" x 6"	.050	L.F.	.001	.03	.06	.09
1" x 8"	.050	L.F.	.001	.05	.07	.12
1" x 10"	.050	L.F.	.002	.07	.07	.14
2" x 6"	.050	L.F.	.002	.03	.07	.10
2" x 8"	.050	L.F.	.002	.04	.08	.12
2" x 10"	.050	L.F.	.002	.06	.09	.15
Fascia board, #2 or better, 1" x 6"	.100	L.F.	.004	.05	.18	.23
1" x 8"	.100	L.F.	.005	.05	.21	.26
1" x 10"	.100	L.F.	.005	.06	.23	.29
2" x 6"	.100	L.F.	.006	.07	.26	.33
2" x 8"	.100	L.F.	.007	.08	.32	.40
2" x 10"	.100	L.F.	.004	.23	.16	.39
Rafter tie, #2 or better, 4' O.C., 1" x 4"	.060	L.F.	.001	.03	.05	.08
1" x 6"	.060	L.F.	.001	.03	.06	.09
2" x 4"	.060	L.F.	.002	.03	.07	.10
2" x 6"	.060	L.F.	.002	.04	.09	.13
Soffit nailer (outrigger), 2" x 4", 16" O.C.	.220	L.F.	.006	.09	.26	.35
24" O.C.	.170	L.F.	.004	.07	.20	.27
2" x 6", 16" O.C.	.220	L.F.	.006	.10	.29	.39
24" O.C.	.170	L.F.	.005	.08	.23	.31
Sheathing, plywood CDX, 4/12 pitch, 3/8" thick.	1.170	S.F.	.012	.60	.55	1.15
1/2" thick	1.170	S.F.	.013	.67	.61	1.28
5/8" thick	1.170	S.F.	.014	.88	.66	1.54
8/12 pitch, 3/8"	1.330	S.F.	.014	.68	.63	1.31
1/2" thick	1.330	S.F.	.015	.76	.69	1.45
5/8" thick	1.330	S.F.	.016	1	.74	1.74
Boards, 4/12 pitch roof, 1" x 6"	1.170	S.F.	.026	1.76	1.17	2.93
1" x 8"	1.170	S.F.	.021	1.76	.97	2.73
8/12 pitch roof, 1" x 6"	1.330	S.F.	.029	2	1.33	3.33
1" x 8"	1.330	S.F.	.024	2	1.10	3.10
Furring, 1" x 3", 12" O.C.	1.200	L.F.	.027	.23	1.24	1.47
16" O.C.	1.000	L.F.	.023	.19	1.03	1.22
24" O.C.	.800	L.F.	.018	.15	.82	.97

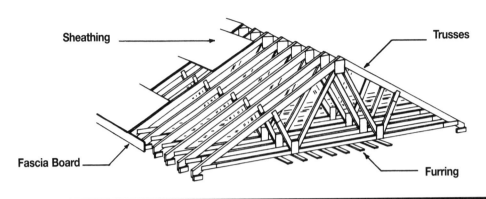

Sheathing · Trusses · Fascia Board · Furring

System Description	QUAN.	UNIT	LABOR HOURS	COST PER S.F.		
				MAT.	INST.	TOTAL
TRUSS, 16″ O.C., 4/12 PITCH, 1′ OVERHANG, 26′ SPAN						
Truss, 40# loading, 16″ O.C., 4/12 pitch, 26′ span	.030	Ea.	.021	2.88	1.30	4.18
Fascia board, 2″ x 6″	.100	L.F.	.005	.06	.24	.30
Sheathing, exterior, plywood, CDX, 1/2″ thick	1.170	S.F.	.013	.67	.61	1.28
Furring, 1″ x 3″, 16″ O.C.	1.000	L.F.	.023	.19	1.03	1.22
TOTAL		S.F.	.062	3.80	3.18	6.98
TRUSS, 16″ O.C., 8/12 PITCH, 1′ OVERHANG, 26′ SPAN						
Truss, 40# loading, 16″ O.C., 8/12 pitch, 26′ span	.030	Ea.	.023	3.33	1.44	4.77
Fascia board, 2″ x 6″	.100	L.F.	.005	.06	.24	.30
Sheathing, exterior, plywood, CDX, 1/2″ thick	1.330	S.F.	.015	.76	.69	1.45
Furring, 1″ x 3″, 16″ O.C.	1.000	L.F.	.023	.19	1.03	1.22
TOTAL		S.F.	.066	4.34	3.40	7.74
TRUSS, 24″ O.C., 4/12 PITCH, 1′ OVERHANG, 26′ SPAN						
Truss, 40# loading, 24″ O.C., 4/12 pitch, 26′ span	.020	Ea.	.014	1.92	.87	2.79
Fascia board, 2″ x 6″	.100	L.F.	.005	.06	.24	.30
Sheathing, exterior, plywood, CDX, 1/2″ thick	1.170	S.F.	.013	.67	.61	1.28
Furring, 1″ x 3″, 16″ O.C.	1.000	L.F.	.023	.19	1.03	1.22
TOTAL		S.F.	.055	2.84	2.75	5.59
TRUSS, 24″ O.C., 8/12 PITCH, 1′ OVERHANG, 26′ SPAN						
Truss, 40# loading, 24″ O.C., 8/12 pitch, 26′ span	.020	Ea.	.015	2.22	.95	3.17
Fascia board, 2″ x 6″	.100	L.F.	.005	.06	.24	.30
Sheathing, exterior, plywood, CDX, 1/2″ thick	1.330	S.F.	.015	.76	.69	1.45
Furring, 1″ x 3″, 16″ O.C.	1.000	L.F.	.023	.19	1.03	1.22
TOTAL		S.F.	.058	3.23	2.91	6.14

The cost of this system is based on the square foot of plan area.
A one foot overhang is included.

Description	QUAN.	UNIT	LABOR HOURS	COST PER S.F.		
				MAT.	INST.	TOTAL

Truss Roof Framing Price Sheet	QUAN.	UNIT	LABOR HOURS	COST PER S.F.		
				MAT.	INST.	TOTAL
Truss, 40# loading, including 1' overhang, 4/12 pitch, 24' span, 16" O.C.	.033	Ea.	.022	3.05	1.35	4.40
24" O.C.	.022	Ea.	.015	2.04	.90	2.94
26' span, 16" O.C.	.030	Ea.	.021	2.88	1.30	4.18
24" O.C.	.020	Ea.	.014	1.92	.87	2.79
28' span, 16" O.C.	.027	Ea.	.020	2.30	1.25	3.55
24" O.C.	.019	Ea.	.014	1.62	.88	2.50
32' span, 16" O.C.	.024	Ea.	.019	2.95	1.18	4.13
24" O.C.	.016	Ea.	.013	1.97	.79	2.76
36' span, 16" O.C.	.022	Ea.	.019	3.59	1.18	4.77
24" O.C.	.015	Ea.	.013	2.45	.81	3.26
8/12 pitch, 24' span, 16" O.C.	.033	Ea.	.024	3.53	1.48	5.01
24" O.C.	.022	Ea.	.016	2.35	.99	3.34
26' span, 16" O.C.	.030	Ea.	.023	3.33	1.44	4.77
24" O.C.	.020	Ea.	.015	2.22	.95	3.17
28' span, 16" O.C.	.027	Ea.	.022	3.32	1.36	4.68
24" O.C.	.019	Ea.	.016	2.34	.97	3.31
32' span, 16" O.C.	.024	Ea.	.021	3.53	1.31	4.84
24" O.C.	.016	Ea.	.014	2.35	.88	3.23
36' span, 16" O.C.	.022	Ea.	.021	4.03	1.32	5.35
24" O.C.	.015	Ea.	.015	2.75	.90	3.65
Fascia board, #2 or better, 1" x 6"	.100	L.F.	.004	.05	.18	.23
1" x 8"	.100	L.F.	.005	.05	.21	.26
1" x 10"	.100	L.F.	.005	.06	.23	.29
2" x 6"	.100	L.F.	.006	.07	.26	.33
2" x 8"	.100	L.F.	.007	.08	.32	.40
2" x 10"	.100	L.F.	.009	.11	.40	.51
Sheathing, plywood CDX, 4/12 pitch, 3/8" thick	1.170	S.F.	.012	.60	.55	1.15
1/2" thick	1.170	S.F.	.013	.67	.61	1.28
5/8" thick	1.170	S.F.	.014	.88	.66	1.54
8/12 pitch, 3/8" thick	1.330	S.F.	.014	.68	.63	1.31
1/2" thick	1.330	S.F.	.015	.76	.69	1.45
5/8" thick	1.330	S.F.	.016	1	.74	1.74
Boards, 4/12 pitch, 1" x 6"	1.170	S.F.	.026	1.76	1.17	2.93
1" x 8"	1.170	S.F.	.021	1.76	.97	2.73
8/12 pitch, 1" x 6"	1.330	S.F.	.029	2	1.33	3.33
1" x 8"	1.330	S.F.	.024	2	1.10	3.10
Furring, 1" x 3", 12" O.C.	1.200	L.F.	.027	.23	1.24	1.47
16" O.C.	1.000	L.F.	.023	.19	1.03	1.22
24" O.C.	.800	L.F.	.018	.15	.82	.97

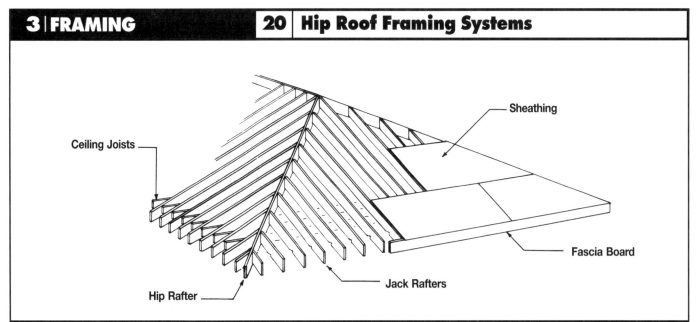

Ceiling Joists — Sheathing — Fascia Board — Jack Rafters — Hip Rafter

System Description	QUAN.	UNIT	LABOR HOURS	COST PER S.F.		
				MAT.	INST.	TOTAL
2″ X 6″, 16″ O.C., 4/12 PITCH						
Hip rafters, 2″ x 8″, 4/12 pitch	.160	L.F.	.004	.13	.16	.29
Jack rafters, 2″ x 6″, 16″ O.C., 4/12 pitch	1.430	L.F.	.038	.86	1.73	2.59
Ceiling joists, 2″ x 6″, 16″ O.C.	1.000	L.F.	.013	.60	.58	1.18
Fascia board, 2″ x 8″	.220	L.F.	.016	.18	.71	.89
Soffit nailer (outrigger), 2″ x 4″, 24″ O.C.	.220	L.F.	.006	.09	.26	.35
Sheathing, 1/2″ exterior plywood, CDX	1.570	S.F.	.018	.89	.82	1.71
Furring strips, 1″ x 3″, 16″ O.C.	1.000	L.F.	.023	.19	1.03	1.22
TOTAL		S.F.	.118	2.94	5.29	8.23
2″ X 8″, 16″ O.C., 4/12 PITCH						
Hip rafters, 2″ x 10″, 4/12 pitch	.160	L.F.	.004	.18	.20	.38
Jack rafters, 2″ x 8″, 16″ O.C., 4/12 pitch	1.430	L.F.	.047	1.19	2.12	3.31
Ceiling joists, 2″ x 6″, 16″ O.C.	1.000	L.F.	.013	.60	.58	1.18
Fascia board, 2″ x 8″	.220	L.F.	.012	.14	.55	.69
Soffit nailer (outrigger), 2″ x 4″, 24″ O.C.	.220	L.F.	.006	.09	.26	.35
Sheathing, 1/2″ exterior plywood, CDX	1.570	S.F.	.018	.89	.82	1.71
Furring strips, 1″ x 3″, 16″ O.C.	1.000	L.F.	.023	.19	1.03	1.22
TOTAL		S.F.	.123	3.28	5.56	8.84

The cost of this system is based on S.F. of plan area. Measurement is area under the hip roof only. See gable roof system for added costs.

Description	QUAN.	UNIT	LABOR HOURS	COST PER S.F.		
				MAT.	INST.	TOTAL

Hip Roof Framing Price Sheet	QUAN.	UNIT	LABOR HOURS	COST PER S.F.		
				MAT.	INST.	TOTAL
Hip rafters, #2 or better, 2" x 6", 4/12 pitch	.160	L.F.	.003	.10	.15	.25
8/12 pitch	.210	L.F.	.006	.13	.26	.39
2" x 8", 4/12 pitch	.160	L.F.	.004	.13	.16	.29
8/12 pitch	.210	L.F.	.006	.17	.28	.45
2" x 10", 4/12 pitch	.160	L.F.	.004	.18	.20	.38
8/12 pitch roof	.210	L.F.	.008	.24	.34	.58
Jack rafters, #2 or better, 16" O.C., 2" x 6", 4/12 pitch	1.430	L.F.	.038	.86	1.73	2.59
8/12 pitch	1.800	L.F.	.061	1.08	2.74	3.82
2" x 8", 4/12 pitch	1.430	L.F.	.047	1.19	2.12	3.31
8/12 pitch	1.800	L.F.	.075	1.49	3.38	4.87
2" x 10", 4/12 pitch	1.430	L.F.	.051	1.62	2.30	3.92
8/12 pitch	1.800	L.F.	.082	2.03	3.73	5.76
24" O.C., 2" x 6", 4/12 pitch	1.150	L.F.	.031	.69	1.39	2.08
8/12 pitch	1.440	L.F.	.048	.86	2.19	3.05
2" x 8", 4/12 pitch	1.150	L.F.	.038	.95	1.70	2.65
8/12 pitch	1.440	L.F.	.060	1.20	2.71	3.91
2" x 10", 4/12 pitch	1.150	L.F.	.041	1.30	1.85	3.15
8/12 pitch	1.440	L.F.	.066	1.63	2.98	4.61
Ceiling joists, #2 or better, 2" x 4", 16" O.C.	1.000	L.F.	.013	.39	.58	.97
24" O.C.	.750	L.F.	.010	.29	.44	.73
2" x 6", 16" O.C.	1.000	L.F.	.013	.60	.58	1.18
24" O.C.	.750	L.F.	.010	.45	.44	.89
2" x 8", 16" O.C.	1.000	L.F.	.015	.83	.66	1.49
24" O.C.	.750	L.F.	.011	.62	.50	1.12
2" x 10", 16" O.C.	1.000	L.F.	.018	1.13	.80	1.93
24" O.C.	.750	L.F.	.013	.85	.60	1.45
Fascia board, #2 or better, 1" x 6"	.220	L.F.	.009	.10	.39	.49
1" x 8"	.220	L.F.	.010	.12	.45	.57
1" x 10"	.220	L.F.	.011	.13	.51	.64
2" x 6"	.220	L.F.	.013	.15	.56	.71
2" x 8"	.220	L.F.	.016	.18	.71	.89
2" x 10"	.220	L.F.	.020	.25	.88	1.13
Soffit nailer (outrigger), 2" x 4", 16" O.C.	.280	L.F.	.007	.11	.33	.44
24" O.C.	.220	L.F.	.006	.09	.26	.35
2" x 8", 16" O.C.	.280	L.F.	.007	.17	.30	.47
24" O.C.	.220	L.F.	.005	.14	.25	.39
Sheathing, plywood CDX, 4/12 pitch, 3/8" thick	1.570	S.F.	.016	.80	.74	1.54
1/2" thick	1.570	S.F.	.018	.89	.82	1.71
5/8" thick	1.570	S.F.	.019	1.18	.88	2.06
8/12 pitch, 3/8" thick	1.900	S.F.	.020	.97	.89	1.86
1/2" thick	1.900	S.F.	.022	1.08	.99	2.07
5/8" thick	1.900	S.F.	.023	1.43	1.06	2.49
Boards, 4/12 pitch, 1" x 6" boards	1.450	S.F.	.032	2.18	1.45	3.63
1" x 8" boards	1.450	S.F.	.027	2.18	1.20	3.38
8/12 pitch, 1" x 6" boards	1.750	S.F.	.039	2.63	1.75	4.38
1" x 8" boards	1.750	S.F.	.032	2.63	1.45	4.08
Furring, 1" x 3", 12" O.C.	1.200	L.F.	.027	.23	1.24	1.47
16" O.C.	1.000	L.F.	.023	.19	1.03	1.22
24" O.C.	.800	L.F.	.018	.15	.82	.97

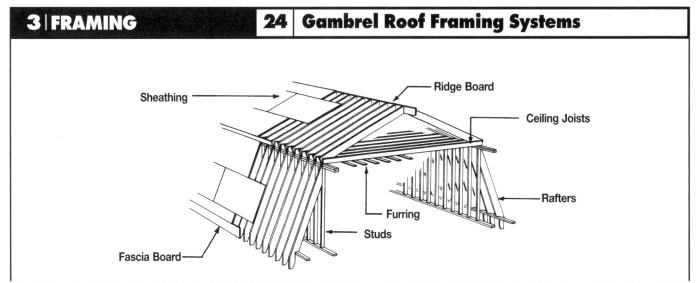

System Description	QUAN.	UNIT	LABOR HOURS	COST PER S.F.		
				MAT.	INST.	TOTAL
2″ X 6″ RAFTERS, 16″ O.C.						
Roof rafters, 2″ x 6″, 16″ O.C.	1.430	L.F.	.029	.86	1.29	2.15
Ceiling joists, 2″ x 6″, 16″ O.C.	.710	L.F.	.009	.43	.41	.84
Stud wall, 2″ x 4″, 16″ O.C., including plates	.790	L.F.	.012	.31	.56	.87
Furring strips, 1″ x 3″, 16″ O.C.	.710	L.F.	.016	.13	.73	.86
Ridge board, 2″ x 8″	.050	L.F.	.002	.04	.08	.12
Fascia board, 2″ x 6″	.100	L.F.	.006	.07	.26	.33
Sheathing, exterior grade plywood, 1/2″ thick	1.450	S.F.	.017	.83	.75	1.58
TOTAL		S.F.	.091	2.67	4.08	6.75
2″ X 8″ RAFTERS, 16″ O.C.						
Roof rafters, 2″ x 8″, 16″ O.C.	1.430	L.F.	.031	1.19	1.37	2.56
Ceiling joists, 2″ x 6″, 16″ O.C.	.710	L.F.	.009	.43	.41	.84
Stud wall, 2″ x 4″, 16″ O.C., including plates	.790	L.F.	.012	.31	.56	.87
Furring strips, 1″ x 3″, 16″ O.C.	.710	L.F.	.016	.13	.73	.86
Ridge board, 2″ x 8″	.050	L.F.	.002	.04	.08	.12
Fascia board, 2″ x 8″	.100	L.F.	.007	.08	.32	.40
Sheathing, exterior grade plywood, 1/2″ thick	1.450	S.F.	.017	.83	.75	1.58
TOTAL		S.F.	.094	3.01	4.22	7.23

The cost of this system is based on the square foot of plan area on the first floor.

Description	QUAN.	UNIT	LABOR HOURS	COST PER S.F.		
				MAT.	INST.	TOTAL

Gambrel Roof Framing Price Sheet

	QUAN.	UNIT	LABOR HOURS	COST PER S.F. MAT.	COST PER S.F. INST.	COST PER S.F. TOTAL
Roof rafters, #2 or better, 2″ x 6″, 16″ O.C.	1.430	L.F.	.029	.86	1.29	2.15
24″ O.C.	1.140	L.F.	.023	.68	1.03	1.71
2″ x 8″, 16″ O.C.	1.430	L.F.	.031	1.19	1.37	2.56
24″ O.C.	1.140	L.F.	.024	.95	1.09	2.04
2″ x 10″, 16″ O.C.	1.430	L.F.	.046	1.62	2.09	3.71
24″ O.C.	1.140	L.F.	.037	1.29	1.66	2.95
Ceiling joist, #2 or better, 2″ x 4″, 16″ O.C.	.710	L.F.	.009	.28	.41	.69
24″ O.C.	.570	L.F.	.007	.22	.33	.55
2″ x 6″, 16″ O.C.	.710	L.F.	.009	.43	.41	.84
24″ O.C.	.570	L.F.	.007	.34	.33	.67
2″ x 8″, 16″ O.C.	.710	L.F.	.010	.59	.47	1.06
24″ O.C.	.570	L.F.	.008	.47	.38	.85
Stud wall, #2 or better, 2″ x 4″, 16″ O.C.	.790	L.F.	.012	.31	.56	.87
24″ O.C.	.630	L.F.	.010	.25	.45	.70
2″ x 6″, 16″ O.C.	.790	L.F.	.014	.47	.64	1.11
24″ O.C.	.630	L.F.	.011	.38	.51	.89
Furring, 1″ x 3″, 16″ O.C.	.710	L.F.	.016	.13	.73	.86
24″ O.C.	.590	L.F.	.013	.11	.61	.72
Ridge board, #2 or better, 1″ x 6″	.050	L.F.	.001	.03	.06	.09
1″ x 8″	.050	L.F.	.001	.05	.07	.12
1″ x 10″	.050	L.F.	.002	.07	.07	.14
2″ x 6″	.050	L.F.	.002	.03	.07	.10
2″ x 8″	.050	L.F.	.002	.04	.08	.12
2″ x 10″	.050	L.F.	.002	.06	.09	.15
Fascia board, #2 or better, 1″ x 6″	.100	L.F.	.004	.05	.18	.23
1″ x 8″	.100	L.F.	.005	.05	.21	.26
1″ x 10″	.100	L.F.	.005	.06	.23	.29
2″ x 6″	.100	L.F.	.006	.07	.26	.33
2″ x 8″	.100	L.F.	.007	.08	.32	.40
2″ x 10″	.100	L.F.	.009	.11	.40	.51
Sheathing, plywood, exterior grade CDX, 3/8″ thick	1.450	S.F.	.015	.74	.68	1.42
1/2″ thick	1.450	S.F.	.017	.83	.75	1.58
5/8″ thick	1.450	S.F.	.018	1.09	.81	1.90
3/4″ thick	1.450	S.F.	.019	1.39	.87	2.26
Boards, 1″ x 6″, laid regular	1.450	S.F.	.032	2.18	1.45	3.63
Laid diagonal	1.450	S.F.	.036	2.18	1.61	3.79
1″ x 8″, laid regular	1.450	S.F.	.027	2.18	1.20	3.38
Laid diagonal	1.450	S.F.	.032	2.18	1.45	3.63

System Description	QUAN.	UNIT	LABOR HOURS	COST PER S.F.		
				MAT.	INST.	TOTAL
2″ X 6″ RAFTERS, 16″ O.C.						
Roof rafters, 2″ x 6″, 16″ O.C.	1.210	L.F.	.033	.73	1.49	2.22
Rafter plates, 2″ x 6″, double top, single bottom	.364	L.F.	.010	.22	.45	.67
Ceiling joists, 2″ x 4″, 16″ O.C.	.920	L.F.	.012	.36	.53	.89
Hip rafter, 2″ x 6″	.070	L.F.	.002	.04	.10	.14
Jack rafter, 2″ x 6″, 16″ O.C.	1.000	L.F.	.039	.60	1.76	2.36
Ridge board, 2″ x 6″	.018	L.F.	.001	.01	.03	.04
Sheathing, exterior grade plywood, 1/2″ thick	2.210	S.F.	.025	1.26	1.15	2.41
Furring strips, 1″ x 3″, 16″ O.C.	.920	L.F.	.021	.17	.95	1.12
TOTAL		S.F.	.143	3.39	6.46	9.85
2″ X 8″ RAFTERS, 16″ O.C.						
Roof rafters, 2″ x 8″, 16″ O.C.	1.210	L.F.	.036	1	1.62	2.62
Rafter plates, 2″ x 8″, double top, single bottom	.364	L.F.	.011	.30	.49	.79
Ceiling joists, 2″ x 6″, 16″ O.C.	.920	L.F.	.012	.55	.53	1.08
Hip rafter, 2″ x 8″	.070	L.F.	.002	.06	.11	.17
Jack rafter, 2″ x 8″, 16″ O.C.	1.000	L.F.	.048	.83	2.16	2.99
Ridge board, 2″ x 8″	.018	L.F.	.001	.01	.03	.04
Sheathing, exterior grade plywood, 1/2″ thick	2.210	S.F.	.025	1.26	1.15	2.41
Furring strips, 1″ x 3″, 16″ O.C.	.920	L.F.	.021	.17	.95	1.12
TOTAL		S.F.	.156	4.18	7.04	11.22

The cost of this system is based on the square foot of plan area.

Description	QUAN.	UNIT	LABOR HOURS	COST PER S.F.		
				MAT.	INST.	TOTAL

Mansard Roof Framing Price Sheet	QUAN.	UNIT	LABOR HOURS	COST PER S.F. MAT.	COST PER S.F. INST.	COST PER S.F. TOTAL
Roof rafters, #2 or better, 2" x 6", 16" O.C.	1.210	L.F.	.033	.73	1.49	2.22
24" O.C.	.970	L.F.	.026	.58	1.19	1.77
2" x 8", 16" O.C.	1.210	L.F.	.036	1	1.62	2.62
24" O.C.	.970	L.F.	.029	.81	1.30	2.11
2" x 10", 16" O.C.	1.210	L.F.	.046	1.37	2.06	3.43
24" O.C.	.970	L.F.	.037	1.10	1.65	2.75
Rafter plates, #2 or better double top single bottom, 2" x 6"	.364	L.F.	.010	.22	.45	.67
2" x 8"	.364	L.F.	.011	.30	.49	.79
2" x 10"	.364	L.F.	.014	.41	.62	1.03
Ceiling joist, #2 or better, 2" x 4", 16" O.C.	.920	L.F.	.012	.36	.53	.89
24" O.C.	.740	L.F.	.009	.29	.43	.72
2" x 6", 16" O.C.	.920	L.F.	.012	.55	.53	1.08
24" O.C.	.740	L.F.	.009	.44	.43	.87
2" x 8", 16" O.C.	.920	L.F.	.013	.76	.61	1.37
24" O.C.	.740	L.F.	.011	.61	.49	1.10
Hip rafter, #2 or better, 2" x 6"	.070	L.F.	.002	.04	.10	.14
2" x 8"	.070	L.F.	.002	.06	.11	.17
2" x 10"	.070	L.F.	.003	.08	.13	.21
Jack rafter, #2 or better, 2" x 6", 16" O.C.	1.000	L.F.	.039	.60	1.76	2.36
24" O.C.	.800	L.F.	.031	.48	1.41	1.89
2" x 8", 16" O.C.	1.000	L.F.	.048	.83	2.16	2.99
24" O.C.	.800	L.F.	.038	.66	1.73	2.39
Ridge board, #2 or better, 1" x 6"	.018	L.F.	.001	.01	.02	.03
1" x 8"	.018	L.F.	.001	.02	.02	.04
1" x 10"	.018	L.F.	.001	.03	.03	.06
2" x 6"	.018	L.F.	.001	.01	.03	.04
2" x 8"	.018	L.F.	.001	.01	.03	.04
2" x 10"	.018	L.F.	.001	.02	.03	.05
Sheathing, plywood exterior grade CDX, 3/8" thick	2.210	S.F.	.023	1.13	1.04	2.17
1/2" thick	2.210	S.F.	.025	1.26	1.15	2.41
5/8" thick	2.210	S.F.	.027	1.66	1.24	2.90
3/4" thick	2.210	S.F.	.029	2.12	1.33	3.45
Boards, 1" x 6", laid regular	2.210	S.F.	.049	3.32	2.21	5.53
Laid diagonal	2.210	S.F.	.054	3.32	2.45	5.77
1" x 8", laid regular	2.210	S.F.	.040	3.32	1.83	5.15
Laid diagonal	2.210	S.F.	.049	3.32	2.21	5.53
Furring, 1" x 3", 12" O.C.	1.150	L.F.	.026	.22	1.18	1.40
24" O.C.	.740	L.F.	.017	.14	.76	.90

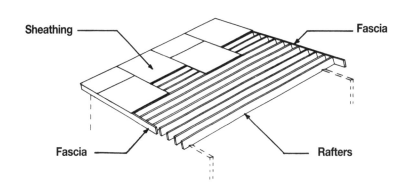

System Description	QUAN.	UNIT	LABOR HOURS	COST PER S.F.		
				MAT.	INST.	TOTAL
2" X 6",16" O.C., 4/12 PITCH						
Rafters, 2" x 6", 16" O.C., 4/12 pitch	1.170	L.F.	.019	.70	.84	1.54
Fascia, 2" x 6"	.100	L.F.	.006	.07	.26	.33
Bridging, 1" x 3", 6' O.C.	.080	Pr.	.005	.02	.22	.24
Sheathing, exterior grade plywood, 1/2" thick	1.230	S.F.	.014	.70	.64	1.34
TOTAL		S.F.	.044	1.49	1.96	3.45
2" X 6", 24" O.C., 4/12 PITCH						
Rafters, 2" x 6", 24" O.C., 4/12 pitch	.940	L.F.	.015	.56	.68	1.24
Fascia, 2" x 6"	.100	L.F.	.006	.07	.26	.33
Bridging, 1" x 3", 6' O.C.	.060	Pr.	.004	.02	.17	.19
Sheathing, exterior grade plywood, 1/2" thick	1.230	S.F.	.014	.70	.64	1.34
TOTAL		S.F.	.039	1.35	1.75	3.10
2" X 8", 16" O.C., 4/12 PITCH						
Rafters, 2" x 8", 16" O.C., 4/12 pitch	1.170	L.F.	.020	.97	.89	1.86
Fascia, 2" x 8"	.100	L.F.	.007	.08	.32	.40
Bridging, 1" x 3", 6' O.C.	.080	Pr.	.005	.02	.22	.24
Sheathing, exterior grade plywood, 1/2" thick	1.230	S.F.	.014	.70	.64	1.34
TOTAL		S.F.	.046	1.77	2.07	3.84
2" X 8", 24" O.C., 4/12 PITCH						
Rafters, 2" x 8", 24" O.C., 4/12 pitch	.940	L.F.	.016	.78	.71	1.49
Fascia, 2" x 8"	.100	L.F.	.007	.08	.32	.40
Bridging, 1" x 3", 6' O.C.	.060	Pr.	.004	.02	.17	.19
Sheathing, exterior grade plywood, 1/2" thick	1.230	S.F.	.014	.70	.64	1.34
TOTAL		S.F.	.041	1.58	1.84	3.42

The cost of this system is based on the square foot of plan area.
A 1' overhang is assumed. No ceiling joists or furring are included.

Description	QUAN.	UNIT	LABOR HOURS	COST PER S.F.		
				MAT.	INST.	TOTAL

Shed/Flat Roof Framing Price Sheet	QUAN.	UNIT	LABOR HOURS	COST PER S.F.		
				MAT.	INST.	TOTAL
Rafters, #2 or better, 16" O.C., 2" x 4", 0 - 4/12 pitch	1.170	L.F.	.014	.52	.63	1.15
5/12 - 8/12 pitch	1.330	L.F.	.020	.60	.90	1.50
2" x 6", 0 - 4/12 pitch	1.170	L.F.	.019	.70	.84	1.54
5/12 - 8/12 pitch	1.330	L.F.	.027	.80	1.20	2
2" x 8", 0 - 4/12 pitch	1.170	L.F.	.020	.97	.89	1.86
5/12 - 8/12 pitch	1.330	L.F.	.028	1.10	1.28	2.38
2" x 10", 0 - 4/12 pitch	1.170	L.F.	.030	1.32	1.35	2.67
5/12 - 8/12 pitch	1.330	L.F.	.043	1.50	1.94	3.44
24" O.C., 2" x 4", 0 - 4/12 pitch	.940	L.F.	.011	.43	.51	.94
5/12 - 8/12 pitch	1.060	L.F.	.021	.64	.95	1.59
2" x 6", 0 - 4/12 pitch	.940	L.F.	.015	.56	.68	1.24
5/12 - 8/12 pitch	1.060	L.F.	.021	.64	.95	1.59
2" x 8", 0 - 4/12 pitch	.940	L.F.	.016	.78	.71	1.49
5/12 - 8/12 pitch	1.060	L.F.	.023	.88	1.02	1.90
2" x 10", 0 - 4/12 pitch	.940	L.F.	.024	1.06	1.08	2.14
5/12 - 8/12 pitch	1.060	L.F.	.034	1.20	1.55	2.75
Fascia, #2 or better,, 1" x 4"	.100	L.F.	.003	.03	.13	.16
1" x 6"	.100	L.F.	.004	.05	.18	.23
1" x 8"	.100	L.F.	.005	.05	.21	.26
1" x 10"	.100	L.F.	.005	.06	.23	.29
2" x 4"	.100	L.F.	.005	.06	.22	.28
2" x 6"	.100	L.F.	.006	.07	.26	.33
2" x 8"	.100	L.F.	.007	.08	.32	.40
2" x 10"	.100	L.F.	.009	.11	.40	.51
Bridging, wood 6' O.C., 1" x 3", rafters, 16" O.C.	.080	Pr.	.005	.02	.22	.24
24" O.C.	.060	Pr.	.004	.02	.17	.19
Metal, galvanized, rafters, 16" O.C.	.080	Pr.	.005	.11	.22	.33
24" O.C.	.060	Pr.	.003	.10	.15	.25
Compression type, rafters, 16" O.C.	.080	Pr.	.003	.13	.14	.27
24" O.C.	.060	Pr.	.002	.10	.11	.21
Sheathing, plywood, exterior grade, 3/8" thick, flat 0 - 4/12 pitch	1.230	S.F.	.013	.63	.58	1.21
5/12 - 8/12 pitch	1.330	S.F.	.014	.68	.63	1.31
1/2" thick, flat 0 - 4/12 pitch	1.230	S.F.	.014	.70	.64	1.34
5/12 - 8/12 pitch	1.330	S.F.	.015	.76	.69	1.45
5/8" thick, flat 0 - 4/12 pitch	1.230	S.F.	.015	.92	.69	1.61
5/12 - 8/12 pitch	1.330	S.F.	.016	1	.74	1.74
3/4" thick, flat 0 - 4/12 pitch	1.230	S.F.	.016	1.18	.74	1.92
5/12 - 8/12 pitch	1.330	S.F.	.018	1.28	.80	2.08
Boards, 1" x 6", laid regular, flat 0 - 4/12 pitch	1.230	S.F.	.027	1.85	1.23	3.08
5/12 - 8/12 pitch	1.330	S.F.	.041	2	1.85	3.85
Laid diagonal, flat 0 - 4/12 pitch	1.230	S.F.	.030	1.85	1.37	3.22
5/12 - 8/12 pitch	1.330	S.F.	.044	2	2.01	4.01
1" x 8", laid regular, flat 0 - 4/12 pitch	1.230	S.F.	.022	1.85	1.02	2.87
5/12 - 8/12 pitch	1.330	S.F.	.034	2	1.52	3.52
Laid diagonal, flat 0 - 4/12 pitch	1.230	S.F.	.027	1.85	1.23	3.08
5/12 - 8/12 pitch	1.330	S.F.	.044	2	2.01	4.01

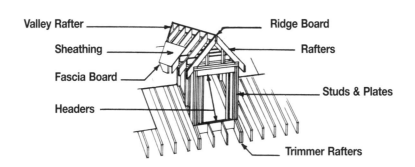

Valley Rafter — ... — Ridge Board
Sheathing — ... — Rafters
Fascia Board — ...
Headers — ... — Studs & Plates
... — Trimmer Rafters

System Description	QUAN.	UNIT	LABOR HOURS	COST PER S.F.		
				MAT.	INST.	TOTAL
2″ X 6″, 16″ O.C.						
Dormer rafter, 2″ x 6″, 16″ O.C.	1.330	L.F.	.036	.80	1.64	2.44
Ridge board, 2″ x 6″	.280	L.F.	.009	.17	.41	.58
Trimmer rafters, 2″ x 6″	.880	L.F.	.014	.53	.63	1.16
Wall studs & plates, 2″ x 4″, 16″ O.C.	3.160	L.F.	.056	1.23	2.53	3.76
Fascia, 2″ x 6″	.220	L.F.	.012	.14	.55	.69
Valley rafter, 2″ x 6″, 16″ O.C.	.280	L.F.	.009	.17	.40	.57
Cripple rafter, 2″ x 6″, 16″ O.C.	.560	L.F.	.022	.34	.99	1.33
Headers, 2″ x 6″, doubled	.670	L.F.	.030	.40	1.35	1.75
Ceiling joist, 2″ x 4″, 16″ O.C.	1.000	L.F.	.013	.39	.58	.97
Sheathing, exterior grade plywood, 1/2″ thick	3.610	S.F.	.041	2.06	1.88	3.94
TOTAL		S.F.	.242	6.23	10.96	17.19
2″ X 8″, 16″ O.C.						
Dormer rafter, 2″ x 8″, 16″ O.C.	1.330	L.F.	.039	1.10	1.78	2.88
Ridge board, 2″ x 8″	.280	L.F.	.010	.23	.45	.68
Trimmer rafter, 2″ x 8″	.880	L.F.	.015	.73	.67	1.40
Wall studs & plates, 2″ x 4″, 16″ O.C.	3.160	L.F.	.056	1.23	2.53	3.76
Fascia, 2″ x 8″	.220	L.F.	.016	.18	.71	.89
Valley rafter, 2″ x 8″, 16″ O.C.	.280	L.F.	.010	.23	.43	.66
Cripple rafter, 2″ x 8″, 16″ O.C.	.560	L.F.	.027	.46	1.21	1.67
Headers, 2″ x 8″, doubled	.670	L.F.	.032	.56	1.43	1.99
Ceiling joist, 2″ x 4″, 16″ O.C.	1.000	L.F.	.013	.39	.58	.97
Sheathing,, exterior grade plywood, 1/2″ thick	3.610	S.F.	.041	2.06	1.88	3.94
TOTAL		S.F.	.259	7.17	11.67	18.84

The cost in this system is based on the square foot of plan area.
The measurement being the plan area of the dormer only.

Description	QUAN.	UNIT	LABOR HOURS	COST PER S.F.		
				MAT.	INST.	TOTAL

Gable Dormer Framing Price Sheet	QUAN.	UNIT	LABOR HOURS	COST PER S.F.		
				MAT.	INST.	TOTAL
Dormer rafters, #2 or better, 2" x 4", 16" O.C.	1.330	L.F.	.029	.64	1.31	1.95
24" O.C.	1.060	L.F.	.023	.51	1.05	1.56
2" x 6", 16" O.C.	1.330	L.F.	.036	.80	1.64	2.44
24" O.C.	1.060	L.F.	.029	.64	1.30	1.94
2" x 8", 16" O.C.	1.330	L.F.	.039	1.10	1.78	2.88
24" O.C.	1.060	L.F.	.031	.88	1.42	2.30
Ridge board, #2 or better, 1" x 4"	.280	L.F.	.006	.15	.27	.42
1" x 6"	.280	L.F.	.007	.19	.34	.53
1" x 8"	.280	L.F.	.008	.26	.37	.63
2" x 4"	.280	L.F.	.007	.13	.32	.45
2" x 6"	.280	L.F.	.009	.17	.41	.58
2" x 8"	.280	L.F.	.010	.23	.45	.68
Trimmer rafters, #2 or better, 2" x 4"	.880	L.F.	.011	.42	.51	.93
2" x 6"	.880	L.F.	.014	.53	.63	1.16
2" x 8"	.880	L.F.	.015	.73	.67	1.40
2" x 10"	.880	L.F.	.022	.99	1.01	2
Wall studs & plates, #2 or better, 2" x 4" studs, 16" O.C.	3.160	L.F.	.056	1.23	2.53	3.76
24" O.C.	2.800	L.F.	.050	1.09	2.24	3.33
2" x 6" studs, 16" O.C.	3.160	L.F.	.063	1.90	2.84	4.74
24" O.C.	2.800	L.F.	.056	1.68	2.52	4.20
Fascia, #2 or better, 1" x 4"	.220	L.F.	.006	.07	.29	.36
1" x 6"	.220	L.F.	.008	.09	.35	.44
1" x 8"	.220	L.F.	.009	.11	.41	.52
2" x 4"	.220	L.F.	.011	.12	.48	.60
2" x 6"	.220	L.F.	.014	.16	.61	.77
2" x 8"	.220	L.F.	.016	.18	.71	.89
Valley rafter, #2 or better, 2" x 4"	.280	L.F.	.007	.13	.32	.45
2" x 6"	.280	L.F.	.009	.17	.40	.57
2" x 8"	.280	L.F.	.010	.23	.43	.66
2" x 10"	.280	L.F.	.012	.32	.53	.85
Cripple rafter, #2 or better, 2" x 4", 16" O.C.	.560	L.F.	.018	.27	.79	1.06
24" O.C.	.450	L.F.	.014	.22	.63	.85
2" x 6", 16" O.C.	.560	L.F.	.022	.34	.99	1.33
24" O.C.	.450	L.F.	.018	.27	.79	1.06
2" x 8", 16" O.C.	.560	L.F.	.027	.46	1.21	1.67
24" O.C.	.450	L.F.	.021	.37	.97	1.34
Headers, #2 or better double header, 2" x 4"	.670	L.F.	.024	.32	1.09	1.41
2" x 6"	.670	L.F.	.030	.40	1.35	1.75
2" x 8"	.670	L.F.	.032	.56	1.43	1.99
2" x 10"	.670	L.F.	.034	.76	1.51	2.27
Ceiling joist, #2 or better, 2" x 4", 16" O.C.	1.000	L.F.	.013	.39	.58	.97
24" O.C.	.800	L.F.	.010	.31	.46	.77
2" x 6", 16" O.C.	1.000	L.F.	.013	.60	.58	1.18
24" O.C.	.800	L.F.	.010	.48	.46	.94
Sheathing, plywood exterior grade, 3/8" thick	3.610	S.F.	.038	1.84	1.70	3.54
1/2" thick	3.610	S.F.	.041	2.06	1.88	3.94
5/8" thick	3.610	S.F.	.044	2.71	2.02	4.73
3/4" thick	3.610	S.F.	.048	3.47	2.17	5.64
Boards, 1" x 6", laid regular	3.610	S.F.	.089	5.40	4.01	9.41
Laid diagonal	3.610	S.F.	.099	5.40	4.48	9.88
1" x 8", laid regular	3.610	S.F.	.076	5.40	3.43	8.83
Laid diagonal	3.610	S.F.	.089	5.40	4.01	9.41

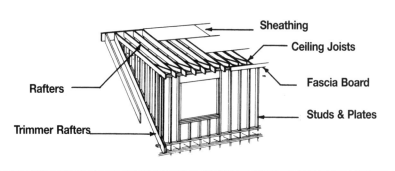

System Description	QUAN.	UNIT	LABOR HOURS	COST PER S.F.		
				MAT.	INST.	TOTAL
2″ X 6″ RAFTERS, 16″ O.C.						
Dormer rafter, 2″ x 6″, 16″ O.C.	1.080	L.F.	.029	.65	1.33	1.98
Trimmer rafter, 2″ x 6″	.400	L.F.	.006	.24	.29	.53
Studs & plates, 2″ x 4″, 16″ O.C.	2.750	L.F.	.049	1.07	2.20	3.27
Fascia, 2″ x 6″	.250	L.F.	.014	.16	.61	.77
Ceiling joist, 2″ x 4″, 16″ O.C.	1.000	L.F.	.013	.39	.58	.97
Sheathing, exterior grade plywood, CDX, 1/2″ thick	2.940	S.F.	.034	1.68	1.53	3.21
TOTAL		S.F.	.145	4.19	6.54	10.73
2″ X 8″ RAFTERS, 16″ O.C.						
Dormer rafter, 2″ x 8″, 16″ O.C.	1.080	L.F.	.032	.90	1.45	2.35
Trimmer rafter, 2″ x 8″	.400	L.F.	.007	.33	.30	.63
Studs & plates, 2″ x 4″, 16″ O.C.	2.750	L.F.	.049	1.07	2.20	3.27
Fascia, 2″ x 8″	.250	L.F.	.018	.21	.80	1.01
Ceiling joist, 2″ x 6″, 16″ O.C.	1.000	L.F.	.013	.60	.58	1.18
Sheathing, exterior grade plywood, CDX, 1/2″ thick	2.940	S.F.	.034	1.68	1.53	3.21
TOTAL		S.F.	.153	4.79	6.86	11.65
2″ X 10″ RAFTERS, 16″ O.C.						
Dormer rafter, 2″ x 10″, 16″ O.C.	1.080	L.F.	.041	1.22	1.84	3.06
Trimmer rafter, 2″ x 10″	.400	L.F.	.010	.45	.46	.91
Studs & plates, 2″ x 4″, 16″ O.C.	2.750	L.F.	.049	1.07	2.20	3.27
Fascia, 2″ x 10″	.250	L.F.	.022	.28	1.01	1.29
Ceiling joist, 2″ x 6″, 16″ O.C.	1.000	L.F.	.013	.60	.58	1.18
Sheathing, exterior grade plywood, CDX, 1/2″ thick	2.940	S.F.	.034	1.68	1.53	3.21
TOTAL		S.F.	.169	5.30	7.62	12.92

The cost in this system is based on the square foot of plan area.
The measurement is the plan area of the dormer only.

Description	QUAN.	UNIT	LABOR HOURS	COST PER S.F.		
				MAT.	INST.	TOTAL

Shed Dormer Framing Price Sheet	QUAN.	UNIT	LABOR HOURS	COST PER S.F.		
				MAT.	INST.	TOTAL
Dormer rafters, #2 or better, 2" x 4", 16" O.C.	1.080	L.F.	.023	.52	1.06	1.58
24" O.C.	.860	L.F.	.019	.41	.85	1.26
2" x 6", 16" O.C.	1.080	L.F.	.029	.65	1.33	1.98
24" O.C.	.860	L.F.	.023	.52	1.06	1.58
2" x 8", 16" O.C.	1.080	L.F.	.032	.90	1.45	2.35
24" O.C.	.860	L.F.	.025	.71	1.15	1.86
2" x 10", 16" O.C.	1.080	L.F.	.041	1.22	1.84	3.06
24" O.C.	.860	L.F.	.032	.97	1.46	2.43
Trimmer rafter, #2 or better, 2" x 4"	.400	L.F.	.005	.19	.23	.42
2" x 6"	.400	L.F.	.006	.24	.29	.53
2" x 8"	.400	L.F.	.007	.33	.30	.63
2" x 10"	.400	L.F.	.010	.45	.46	.91
Studs & plates, #2 or better, 2" x 4", 16" O.C.	2.750	L.F.	.049	1.07	2.20	3.27
24" O.C.	2.200	L.F.	.039	.86	1.76	2.62
2" x 6", 16" O.C.	2.750	L.F.	.055	1.65	2.48	4.13
24" O.C.	2.200	L.F.	.044	1.32	1.98	3.30
Fascia, #2 or better, 1" x 4"	.250	L.F.	.006	.07	.29	.36
1" x 6"	.250	L.F.	.008	.09	.35	.44
1" x 8"	.250	L.F.	.009	.11	.41	.52
2" x 4"	.250	L.F.	.011	.12	.48	.60
2" x 6"	.250	L.F.	.014	.16	.61	.77
2" x 8"	.250	L.F.	.018	.21	.80	1.01
Ceiling joist, #2 or better, 2" x 4", 16" O.C.	1.000	L.F.	.013	.39	.58	.97
24" O.C.	.800	L.F.	.010	.31	.46	.77
2" x 6", 16" O.C.	1.000	L.F.	.013	.60	.58	1.18
24" O.C.	.800	L.F.	.010	.48	.46	.94
2" x 8", 16" O.C.	1.000	L.F.	.015	.83	.66	1.49
24" O.C.	.800	L.F.	.012	.66	.53	1.19
Sheathing, plywood exterior grade, 3/8" thick	2.940	S.F.	.031	1.50	1.38	2.88
1/2" thick	2.940	S.F.	.034	1.68	1.53	3.21
5/8" thick	2.940	S.F.	.036	2.21	1.65	3.86
3/4" thick	2.940	S.F.	.039	2.82	1.76	4.58
Boards, 1" x 6", laid regular	2.940	S.F.	.072	4.41	3.26	7.67
Laid diagonal	2.940	S.F.	.080	4.41	3.65	8.06
1" x 8", laid regular	2.940	S.F.	.062	4.41	2.79	7.20
Laid diagonal	2.940	S.F.	.072	4.41	3.26	7.67

Window Openings	QUAN.	UNIT	LABOR HOURS	COST EACH		
				MAT.	INST.	TOTAL
The following are to be added to the total cost of the dormers for window openings. Do not subtract window area from the stud wall quantities.						
Headers, 2" x 6" doubled, 2' long	4.000	L.F.	.178	2.40	8.05	10.45
3' long	6.000	L.F.	.267	3.60	12.05	15.65
4' long	8.000	L.F.	.356	4.80	16.10	20.90
5' long	10.000	L.F.	.444	6	20	26
2" x 8" doubled, 4' long	8.000	L.F.	.376	6.65	17.05	23.70
5' long	10.000	L.F.	.471	8.30	21.50	29.80
6' long	12.000	L.F.	.565	9.95	25.50	35.45
8' long	16.000	L.F.	.753	13.30	34	47.30
2" x 10" doubled, 4' long	8.000	L.F.	.400	9.05	18.10	27.15
6' long	12.000	L.F.	.600	13.55	27	40.55
8' long	16.000	L.F.	.800	18.10	36	54.10
10' long	20.000	L.F.	1.000	22.50	45	67.50

System Description		QUAN.	UNIT	LABOR HOURS	COST PER S.F.		
					MAT.	INST.	TOTAL
2″ X 4″, 16″ O.C.							
2″ x 4″ studs, #2 or better, 16″ O.C.		1.000	L.F.	.015	.39	.66	1.05
Plates, double top, single bottom		.375	L.F.	.005	.15	.25	.40
Cross bracing, let-in, 1″ x 6″		.080	L.F.	.004	.06	.19	.25
	TOTAL		S.F.	.024	.60	1.10	1.70
2″ X 4″, 24″ O.C.							
2″ x 4″ studs, #2 or better, 24″ O.C.		.800	L.F.	.012	.31	.53	.84
Plates, double top, single bottom		.375	L.F.	.005	.15	.25	.40
Cross bracing, let-in, 1″ x 6″		.080	L.F.	.003	.06	.13	.19
	TOTAL		S.F.	.020	.52	.91	1.43
2″ X 6″, 16″ O.C.							
2″ x 6″ studs, #2 or better, 16″ O.C.		1.000	L.F.	.016	.60	.72	1.32
Plates, double top, single bottom		.375	L.F.	.006	.23	.27	.50
Cross bracing, let-in, 1″ x 6″		.080	L.F.	.004	.06	.19	.25
	TOTAL		S.F.	.026	.89	1.18	2.07
2″ X 6″, 24″ O.C.							
2″ x 6″ studs, #2 or better, 24″ O.C.		.800	L.F.	.013	.48	.58	1.06
Plates, double top, single bottom		.375	L.F.	.006	.23	.27	.50
Cross bracing, let-in, 1″ x 6″		.080	L.F.	.003	.06	.13	.19
	TOTAL		S.F.	.022	.77	.98	1.75

The costs in this system are based on a square foot of wall area. Do not subtract for door or window openings.

Description	QUAN.	UNIT	LABOR HOURS	COST PER S.F.		
				MAT.	INST.	TOTAL

Partition Framing Price Sheet	QUAN.	UNIT	LABOR HOURS	COST PER S.F.		
				MAT.	INST.	TOTAL
Wood studs, #2 or better, 2" x 4", 12" O.C.	1.250	L.F.	.018	.49	.83	1.32
16" O.C.	1.000	L.F.	.015	.39	.66	1.05
24" O.C.	.800	L.F.	.012	.31	.53	.84
32" O.C.	.650	L.F.	.009	.25	.43	.68
2" x 6", 12" O.C.	1.250	L.F.	.020	.75	.90	1.65
16" O.C.	1.000	L.F.	.016	.60	.72	1.32
24" O.C.	.800	L.F.	.013	.48	.58	1.06
32" O.C.	.650	L.F.	.010	.39	.47	.86
Plates, #2 or better double top single bottom, 2" x 4"	.375	L.F.	.005	.15	.25	.40
2" x 6"	.375	L.F.	.006	.23	.27	.50
2" x 8"	.375	L.F.	.005	.31	.25	.56
Cross bracing, let-in, 1" x 6" boards studs, 12" O.C.	.080	L.F.	.005	.07	.24	.31
16" O.C.	.080	L.F.	.004	.06	.19	.25
24" O.C.	.080	L.F.	.003	.06	.13	.19
32" O.C.	.080	L.F.	.002	.04	.10	.14
Let-in steel (T shaped) studs, 12" O.C.	.080	L.F.	.001	.06	.06	.12
16" O.C.	.080	L.F.	.001	.05	.05	.10
24" O.C.	.080	L.F.	.001	.05	.05	.10
32" O.C.	.080	L.F.	.001	.04	.04	.08
Steel straps studs, 12" O.C.	.080	L.F.	.001	.07	.05	.12
16" O.C.	.080	L.F.	.001	.07	.05	.12
24" O.C.	.080	L.F.	.001	.07	.05	.12
32" O.C.	.080	L.F.	.001	.07	.04	.11
Metal studs, load bearing 24" O.C., 20 ga. galv., 2-1/2" wide	1.000	S.F.	.015	.72	.68	1.40
3-5/8" wide	1.000	S.F.	.015	.86	.69	1.55
4" wide	1.000	S.F.	.016	.90	.70	1.60
6" wide	1.000	S.F.	.016	1.15	.72	1.87
16 ga., 2-1/2" wide	1.000	S.F.	.017	.84	.77	1.61
3-5/8" wide	1.000	S.F.	.017	1	.79	1.79
4" wide	1.000	S.F.	.018	1.06	.81	1.87
6" wide	1.000	S.F.	.018	1.33	.82	2.15
Non-load bearing 24" O.C., 25 ga. galv., 1-5/8" wide	1.000	S.F.	.011	.21	.48	.69
2-1/2" wide	1.000	S.F.	.011	.26	.48	.74
3-5/8" wide	1.000	S.F.	.011	.29	.49	.78
4" wide	1.000	S.F.	.011	.32	.49	.81
6" wide	1.000	S.F.	.011	.44	.50	.94
20 ga., 2-1/2" wide	1.000	S.F.	.013	.37	.60	.97
3-5/8" wide	1.000	S.F.	.014	.42	.61	1.03
4" wide	1.000	S.F.	.014	.50	.61	1.11
6" wide	1.000	S.F.	.014	.58	.62	1.20

Window & Door Openings	QUAN.	UNIT	LABOR HOURS	COST EACH		
				MAT.	INST.	TOTAL
The following costs are to be added to the total costs of the walls.						
Do not subtract openings from total wall area.						
Headers, 2" x 6" double, 2' long	4.000	L.F.	.178	2.40	8.05	10.45
3' long	6.000	L.F.	.267	3.60	12.05	15.65
4' long	8.000	L.F.	.356	4.80	16.10	20.90
5' long	10.000	L.F.	.444	6	20	26
2" x 8" double, 4' long	8.000	L.F.	.376	6.65	17.05	23.70
5' long	10.000	L.F.	.471	8.30	21.50	29.80
6' long	12.000	L.F.	.565	9.95	25.50	35.45
8' long	16.000	L.F.	.753	13.30	34	47.30
2" x 10" double, 4' long	8.000	L.F.	.400	9.05	18.10	27.15
6' long	12.000	L.F.	.600	13.55	27	40.55
8' long	16.000	L.F.	.800	18.10	36	54.10
10' long	20.000	L.F.	1.000	22.50	45	67.50
2" x 12" double, 8' long	16.000	L.F.	.853	22	38.50	60.50
12' long	24.000	L.F.	1.280	33	58	91

Division 4
Exterior Walls

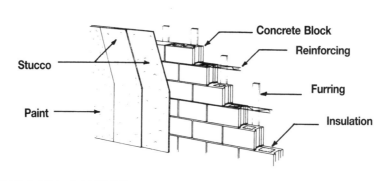

Concrete Block

Reinforcing

Stucco

Furring

Paint

Insulation

System Description	QUAN.	UNIT	LABOR HOURS	COST PER S.F.		
				MAT.	INST.	TOTAL
6″ THICK CONCRETE BLOCK WALL						
6″ thick concrete block, 6″ x 8″ x 16″	1.000	S.F.	.100	2.09	4.15	6.24
Masonry reinforcing, truss strips every other course	.625	L.F.	.002	.14	.08	.22
Furring, 1″ x 3″, 16″ O.C.	1.000	L.F.	.016	.19	.73	.92
Masonry insulation, poured vermiculite	1.000	S.F.	.013	.63	.60	1.23
Stucco, 2 coats	1.000	S.F.	.069	.20	2.89	3.09
Masonry paint, 2 coats	1.000	S.F.	.016	.21	.63	.84
TOTAL		S.F.	.216	3.46	9.08	12.54
8″ THICK CONCRETE BLOCK WALL						
8″ thick concrete block, 8″ x 8″ x 16″	1.000	S.F.	.107	2.28	4.43	6.71
Masonry reinforcing, truss strips every other course	.625	L.F.	.002	.14	.08	.22
Furring, 1″ x 3″, 16″ O.C.	1.000	L.F.	.016	.19	.73	.92
Masonry insulation, poured vermiculite	1.000	S.F.	.018	.83	.80	1.63
Stucco, 2 coats	1.000	S.F.	.069	.20	2.89	3.09
Masonry paint, 2 coats	1.000	S.F.	.016	.21	.63	.84
TOTAL		S.F.	.228	3.85	9.56	13.41
12″ THICK CONCRETE BLOCK WALL						
12″ thick concrete block, 12″ x 8″ x 16″	1.000	S.F.	.141	3.39	5.70	9.09
Masonry reinforcing, truss strips every other course	.625	L.F.	.003	.16	.11	.27
Furring, 1″ x 3″, 16″ O.C.	1.000	L.F.	.016	.19	.73	.92
Masonry insulation, poured vermiculite	1.000	S.F.	.026	1.23	1.18	2.41
Stucco, 2 coats	1.000	S.F.	.069	.20	2.89	3.09
Masonry paint, 2 coats	1.000	S.F.	.016	.21	.63	.84
TOTAL		S.F.	.271	5.38	11.24	16.62

Costs for this system are based on a square foot of wall area. Do not subtract for window openings.

Description	QUAN.	UNIT	LABOR HOURS	COST PER S.F.		
				MAT.	INST.	TOTAL

Masonry Block Price Sheet	QUAN.	UNIT	LABOR HOURS	COST PER S.F.		
				MAT.	INST.	TOTAL
Block concrete, 8" x 16" regular, 4" thick	1.000	S.F.	.093	1.44	3.86	5.30
6" thick	1.000	S.F.	.100	2.09	4.15	6.24
8" thick	1.000	S.F.	.107	2.28	4.43	6.71
10" thick	1.000	S.F.	.111	3.13	4.61	7.74
12" thick	1.000	S.F.	.141	3.39	5.70	9.09
Solid block, 4" thick	1.000	S.F.	.096	1.96	4	5.96
6" thick	1.000	S.F.	.104	2.09	4.31	6.40
8" thick	1.000	S.F.	.111	3.36	4.61	7.97
10" thick	1.000	S.F.	.133	4.77	5.40	10.17
12" thick	1.000	S.F.	.148	5.30	6	11.30
Lightweight, 4" thick	1.000	S.F.	.093	1.44	3.86	5.30
6" thick	1.000	S.F.	.100	2.09	4.15	6.24
8" thick	1.000	S.F.	.107	2.28	4.43	6.71
10" thick	1.000	S.F.	.111	3.13	4.61	7.74
12" thick	1.000	S.F.	.141	3.39	5.70	9.09
Split rib profile, 4" thick	1.000	S.F.	.116	3.20	4.81	8.01
6" thick	1.000	S.F.	.123	3.71	5.10	8.81
8" thick	1.000	S.F.	.131	4.25	5.55	9.80
10" thick	1.000	S.F.	.157	4.59	6.35	10.94
12" thick	1.000	S.F.	.175	5.10	7.05	12.15
Masonry reinforcing, wire truss strips, every course, 8" block	1.375	L.F.	.004	.30	.17	.47
12" block	1.375	L.F.	.006	.34	.25	.59
Every other course, 8" block	.625	L.F.	.002	.14	.08	.22
12" block	.625	L.F.	.003	.16	.11	.27
Furring, wood, 1" x 3", 12" O.C.	1.250	L.F.	.020	.24	.91	1.15
16" O.C.	1.000	L.F.	.016	.19	.73	.92
24" O.C.	.800	L.F.	.013	.15	.58	.73
32" O.C.	.640	L.F.	.010	.12	.47	.59
Steel, 3/4" channels, 12" O.C.	1.250	L.F.	.034	.30	1.34	1.64
16" O.C.	1.000	L.F.	.030	.27	1.19	1.46
24" O.C.	.800	L.F.	.023	.18	.90	1.08
32" O.C.	.640	L.F.	.018	.14	.72	.86
Masonry insulation, vermiculite or perlite poured 4" thick	1.000	S.F.	.009	.41	.39	.80
6" thick	1.000	S.F.	.013	.62	.60	1.22
8" thick	1.000	S.F.	.018	.83	.80	1.63
10" thick	1.000	S.F.	.021	1.01	.96	1.97
12" thick	1.000	S.F.	.026	1.23	1.18	2.41
Block inserts polystyrene, 6" thick	1.000	S.F.		1.99		1.99
8" thick	1.000	S.F.		1.99		1.99
10" thick	1.000	S.F.		2.34		2.34
12" thick	1.000	S.F.		2.46		2.46
Stucco, 1 coat	1.000	S.F.	.057	.17	2.38	2.55
2 coats	1.000	S.F.	.069	.20	2.89	3.09
3 coats	1.000	S.F.	.081	.24	3.40	3.64
Painting, 1 coat	1.000	S.F.	.011	.13	.44	.57
2 coats	1.000	S.F.	.016	.21	.63	.84
Primer & 1 coat	1.000	S.F.	.013	.21	.51	.72
2 coats	1.000	S.F.	.018	.29	.72	1.01
Lath, metal lath expanded 2.5 lb/S.Y., painted	1.000	S.F.	.010	.37	.41	.78
Galvanized	1.000	S.F.	.012	.41	.45	.86

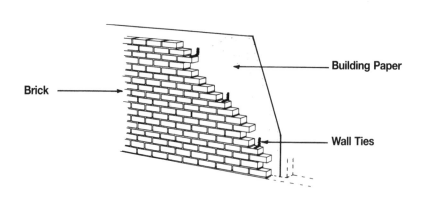

Brick

Building Paper

Wall Ties

System Description	QUAN.	UNIT	LABOR HOURS	COST PER S.F.		
				MAT.	INST.	TOTAL
SELECT COMMON BRICK						
Brick, select common, running bond	1.000	S.F.	.174	6	7.20	13.20
Wall ties, 7/8″ x 7″, 22 gauge	1.000	Ea.	.008	.07	.35	.42
Building paper, spunbonded polypropylene	1.100	S.F.	.002	.15	.10	.25
Trim, pine, painted	.125	L.F.	.004	.09	.18	.27
TOTAL		S.F.	.188	6.31	7.83	14.14
RED FACED COMMON BRICK						
Brick, common, red faced, running bond	1.000	S.F.	.182	6	7.55	13.55
Wall ties, 7/8″ x 7″, 22 gauge	1.000	Ea.	.008	.07	.35	.42
Building paper, spundbonded polypropylene	1.100	S.F.	.002	.15	.10	.25
Trim, pine, painted	.125	L.F.	.004	.09	.18	.27
TOTAL		S.F.	.196	6.31	8.18	14.49
BUFF OR GREY FACE BRICK						
Brick, buff or grey	1.000	S.F.	.182	6.35	7.55	13.90
Wall ties, 7/8″ x 7″, 22 gauge	1.000	Ea.	.008	.07	.35	.42
Building paper, spundbonded polypropylene	1.100	S.F.	.002	.15	.10	.25
Trim, pine, painted	.125	L.F.	.004	.09	.18	.27
TOTAL		S.F.	.196	6.66	8.18	14.84
STONE WORK, ROUGH STONE, AVERAGE						
Field stone veneer	1.000	S.F.	.223	7.37	9.28	16.65
Wall ties, 7/8″ x 7″, 22 gauge	1.000	Ea.	.008	.07	.35	.42
Building paper, spundbonded polypropylene	1.000	S.F.	.002	.15	.10	.25
Trim, pine, painted	.125	L.F.	.004	.09	.18	.27
TOTAL		S.F.	.237	7.68	9.91	17.59

The costs in this system are based on a square foot of wall area. Do not subtract area for window & door openings.

Description	QUAN.	UNIT	LABOR HOURS	COST PER S.F.		
				MAT.	INST.	TOTAL

Brick/Stone Veneer Price Sheet	QUAN.	UNIT	LABOR HOURS	COST PER S.F.		
				MAT.	INST.	TOTAL
Brick						
Select common, running bond	1.000	S.F.	.174	6	7.20	13.20
Red faced, running bond	1.000	S.F.	.182	6	7.55	13.55
Buff or grey faced, running bond	1.000	S.F.	.182	6.35	7.55	13.90
Header every 6th course	1.000	S.F.	.216	7	9	16
English bond	1.000	S.F.	.286	8.95	11.85	20.80
Flemish bond	1.000	S.F.	.195	6.35	8.10	14.45
Common bond	1.000	S.F.	.267	8	11.05	19.05
Stack bond	1.000	S.F.	.182	6.35	7.55	13.90
Jumbo, running bond	1.000	S.F.	.092	4.99	3.82	8.81
Norman, running bond	1.000	S.F.	.125	6.40	5.20	11.60
Norwegian, running bond	1.000	S.F.	.107	4.01	4.43	8.44
Economy, running bond	1.000	S.F.	.129	4.53	5.35	9.88
Engineer, running bond	1.000	S.F.	.154	3.70	6.40	10.10
Roman, running bond	1.000	S.F.	.160	6.30	6.65	12.95
Utility, running bond	1.000	S.F.	.089	3.97	3.69	7.66
Glazed, running bond	1.000	S.F.	.190	10.95	7.90	18.85
Stone work, rough stone, average	1.000	S.F.	.179	7.35	9.30	16.65
Maximum	1.000	S.F.	.267	11	13.85	24.85
Wall ties, galvanized, corrugated 7/8" x 7", 22 gauge	1.000	Ea.	.008	.07	.35	.42
16 gauge	1.000	Ea.	.008	.25	.35	.60
Cavity wall, every 3rd course 6" long Z type, 1/4" diameter	1.330	L.F.	.010	.52	.45	.97
3/16" diameter	1.330	L.F.	.010	.26	.45	.71
8" long, Z type, 1/4" diameter	1.330	L.F.	.010	.62	.45	1.07
3/16" diameter	1.330	L.F.	.010	.29	.45	.74
Building paper, aluminum and kraft laminated foil, 1 side	1.000	S.F.	.002	.06	.10	.16
2 sides	1.000	S.F.	.002	.09	.10	.19
#15 asphalt paper	1.100	S.F.	.002	.06	.11	.17
Polyethylene, .002" thick	1.000	S.F.	.002	.01	.10	.11
.004" thick	1.000	S.F.	.002	.03	.10	.13
.006" thick	1.000	S.F.	.002	.05	.10	.15
.010" thick	1.000	S.F.	.002	.06	.10	.16
Trim, 1" x 4", cedar	.125	L.F.	.005	.22	.23	.45
Fir	.125	L.F.	.005	.10	.23	.33
Redwood	.125	L.F.	.005	.22	.23	.45
White pine	.125	L.F.	.005	.10	.23	.33

Trim

Building Paper

Beveled Cedar Siding

System Description	QUAN.	UNIT	LABOR HOURS	COST PER S.F.		
				MAT.	INST.	TOTAL
1/2″ X 6″ BEVELED CEDAR SIDING, ″A″ GRADE						
1/2″ x 6″ beveled cedar siding	1.000	S.F.	.027	3.63	1.23	4.86
Building wrap, spunbonded polypropylene	1.100	S.F.	.002	.15	.10	.25
Trim, cedar	.125	L.F.	.005	.22	.23	.45
Paint, primer & 2 coats	1.000	S.F.	.017	.20	.68	.88
TOTAL		S.F.	.051	4.20	2.24	6.44
1/2″ X 8″ BEVELED CEDAR SIDING, ″A″ GRADE						
1/2″ x 8″ beveled cedar siding	1.000	S.F.	.024	4.36	1.10	5.46
Building wrap, spunbonded polypropylene	1.100	S.F.	.002	.15	.10	.25
Trim, cedar	.125	L.F.	.005	.22	.23	.45
Paint, primer & 2 coats	1.000	S.F.	.017	.20	.68	.88
TOTAL		S.F.	.048	4.93	2.11	7.04
1″ X 4″ TONGUE & GROOVE, REDWOOD, VERTICAL GRAIN						
Redwood, clear, vertical grain, 1″ x 10″	1.000	S.F.	.020	5.46	.88	6.34
Building wrap, spunbonded polypropylene	1.100	S.F.	.002	.15	.10	.25
Trim, redwood	.125	L.F.	.005	.22	.23	.45
Sealer, 1 coat, stain, 1 coat	1.000	S.F.	.013	.13	.52	.65
TOTAL		S.F.	.040	5.96	1.73	7.69
1″ X 6″ TONGUE & GROOVE, REDWOOD, VERTICAL GRAIN						
Redwood, clear, vertical grain, 1″ x 10″	1.000	S.F.	.020	5.61	.91	6.52
Building wrap, spunbonded polypropylene	1.100	S.F.	.002	.15	.10	.25
Trim, redwood	.125	L.F.	.005	.22	.23	.45
Sealer, 1 coat, stain, 1 coat	1.000	S.F.	.013	.13	.52	.65
TOTAL		S.F.	.040	6.11	1.76	7.87

The costs in this system are based on a square foot of wall area.
Do not subtract area for door or window openings.

Description	QUAN.	UNIT	LABOR HOURS	COST PER S.F.		
				MAT.	INST.	TOTAL

Wood Siding Price Sheet	QUAN.	UNIT	LABOR HOURS	COST PER S.F.		
				MAT.	INST.	TOTAL
Siding, beveled cedar, "A" grade, 1/2" x 6"	1.000	S.F.	.028	3.63	1.23	4.86
1/2" x 8"	1.000	S.F.	.023	4.36	1.10	5.46
"B" grade, 1/2" x 6"	1.000	S.F.	.032	4.03	1.37	5.40
1/2" x 8"	1.000	S.F.	.029	4.84	1.22	6.06
Clear grade, 1/2" x 6"	1.000	S.F.	.028	4.54	1.54	6.08
1/2" x 8"	1.000	S.F.	.023	5.45	1.38	6.83
Redwood, clear vertical grain, 1/2" x 6"	1.000	S.F.	.036	3.25	1.23	4.48
1/2" x 8"	1.000	S.F.	.032	2.62	1.10	3.72
Clear all heart vertical grain, 1/2" x 6"	1.000	S.F.	.028	3.61	1.37	4.98
1/2" x 8"	1.000	S.F.	.023	2.91	1.22	4.13
Siding board & batten, cedar, "B" grade, 1" x 10"	1.000	S.F.	.031	1.21	.86	2.07
1" x 12"	1.000	S.F.	.031	1.21	.86	2.07
Redwood, clear vertical grain, 1" x 6"	1.000	S.F.	.043	3.11	1.23	4.34
1" x 8"	1.000	S.F.	.018	2.95	1.10	4.05
White pine, #2 & better, 1" x 10"	1.000	S.F.	.029	1.21	1.10	2.31
1" x 12"	1.000	S.F.	.029	1.21	1.10	2.31
Siding vertical, tongue & groove, cedar "B" grade, 1" x 4"	1.000	S.F.	.033	2	.88	2.88
1" x 6"	1.000	S.F.	.024	2.06	.91	2.97
1" x 8"	1.000	S.F.	.024	2.12	.93	3.05
1" x 10"	1.000	S.F.	.021	2.18	.96	3.14
"A" grade, 1" x 4"	1.000	S.F.	.033	1.83	.81	2.64
1" x 6"	1.000	S.F.	.024	1.88	.83	2.71
1" x 8"	1.000	S.F.	.024	1.93	.85	2.78
1" x 10"	1.000	S.F.	.021	1.98	.87	2.85
Clear vertical grain, 1" x 4"	1.000	S.F.	.033	1.69	.74	2.43
1" x 6"	1.000	S.F.	.024	1.73	.76	2.49
1" x 8"	1.000	S.F.	.024	1.77	.78	2.55
1" x 10"	1.000	S.F.	.021	1.82	.80	2.62
Redwood, clear vertical grain, 1" x 4"	1.000	S.F.	.033	5.45	.88	6.33
1" x 6"	1.000	S.F.	.024	5.60	.91	6.51
1" x 8"	1.000	S.F.	.024	5.80	.93	6.73
1" x 10"	1.000	S.F.	.021	5.95	.96	6.91
Clear all heart vertical grain, 1" x 4"	1.000	S.F.	.033	5	.81	5.81
1" x 6"	1.000	S.F.	.024	5.15	.83	5.98
1" x 8"	1.000	S.F.	.024	5.25	.85	6.10
1" x 10"	1.000	S.F.	.021	5.40	.87	6.27
White pine, 1" x 10"	1.000	S.F.	.024	2.08	.96	3.04
Siding plywood, texture 1-11 cedar, 3/8" thick	1.000	S.F.	.024	1.33	1.07	2.40
5/8" thick	1.000	S.F.	.024	2.70	1.07	3.77
Redwood, 3/8" thick	1.000	S.F.	.024	1.33	1.07	2.40
5/8" thick	1.000	S.F.	.024	2.13	1.07	3.20
Fir, 3/8" thick	1.000	S.F.	.024	.85	1.07	1.92
5/8" thick	1.000	S.F.	.024	1.24	1.07	2.31
Southern yellow pine, 3/8" thick	1.000	S.F.	.024	.85	1.07	1.92
5/8" thick	1.000	S.F.	.024	1.33	1.07	2.40
Paper, #15 asphalt felt	1.100	S.F.	.002	.06	.11	.17
Trim, cedar	.125	L.F.	.005	.22	.23	.45
Fir	.125	L.F.	.005	.10	.23	.33
Redwood	.125	L.F.	.005	.22	.23	.45
White pine	.125	L.F.	.005	.10	.23	.33
Painting, primer, & 1 coat	1.000	S.F.	.013	.13	.52	.65
2 coats	1.000	S.F.	.017	.20	.68	.88
Stain, sealer, & 1 coat	1.000	S.F.	.017	.11	.68	.79
2 coats	1.000	S.F.	.019	.17	.74	.91

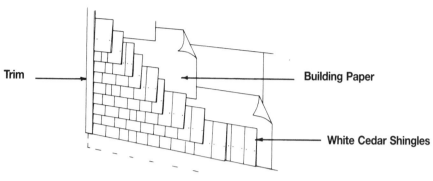

Trim → White Cedar Shingles

Building Paper

System Description	QUAN.	UNIT	LABOR HOURS	COST PER S.F.		
				MAT.	INST.	TOTAL
WHITE CEDAR SHINGLES, 5″ EXPOSURE						
White cedar shingles, 16″ long, grade "A", 5″ exposure	1.000	S.F.	.033	1.96	1.51	3.47
Building wrap, spunbonded polypropylene	1.100	S.F.	.002	.15	.10	.25
Trim, cedar	.125	S.F.	.005	.22	.23	.45
Paint, primer & 1 coat	1.000	S.F.	.017	.11	.68	.79
TOTAL		S.F.	.057	2.44	2.52	4.96
RESQUARED & REBUTTED PERFECTIONS, 5-1/2″ EXPOSURE						
Resquared & rebutted perfections, 5-1/2″ exposure	1.000	S.F.	.027	3.55	1.21	4.76
Building wrap, spunbonded polypropylene	1.100	S.F.	.002	.15	.10	.25
Trim, cedar	.125	S.F.	.005	.22	.23	.45
Stain, sealer & 1 coat	1.000	S.F.	.017	.11	.68	.79
TOTAL		S.F.	.051	4.03	2.22	6.25
HAND-SPLIT SHAKES, 8-1/2″ EXPOSURE						
Hand-split red cedar shakes, 18″ long, 8-1/2″ exposure	1.000	S.F.	.040	2.11	1.81	3.92
Building wrap, spunbonded polypropylene	1.100	S.F.	.002	.15	.10	.25
Trim, cedar	.125	S.F.	.005	.22	.23	.45
Stain, sealer & 1 coat	1.000	S.F.	.017	.11	.68	.79
TOTAL		S.F.	.064	2.59	2.82	5.41

The costs in this system are based on a square foot of wall area.
Do not subtract area for door or window openings.

Description	QUAN.	UNIT	LABOR HOURS	COST PER S.F.		
				MAT.	INST.	TOTAL

Shingle Siding Price Sheet	QUAN.	UNIT	LABOR HOURS	COST PER S.F.		
				MAT.	INST.	TOTAL
Shingles wood, white cedar 16" long, "A" grade, 5" exposure	1.000	S.F.	.033	1.96	1.51	3.47
7" exposure	1.000	S.F.	.030	1.76	1.36	3.12
8-1/2" exposure	1.000	S.F.	.032	1.12	1.45	2.57
10" exposure	1.000	S.F.	.028	.98	1.27	2.25
"B" grade, 5" exposure	1.000	S.F.	.040	1.65	1.81	3.46
7" exposure	1.000	S.F.	.028	1.16	1.27	2.43
8-1/2" exposure	1.000	S.F.	.024	.99	1.09	2.08
10" exposure	1.000	S.F.	.020	.83	.91	1.74
Fire retardant, "A" grade, 5" exposure	1.000	S.F.	.033	2.42	1.51	3.93
7" exposure	1.000	S.F.	.028	1.48	1.27	2.75
8-1/2" exposure	1.000	S.F.	.032	1.94	1.45	3.39
10" exposure	1.000	S.F.	.025	1.51	1.13	2.64
Fire retardant, 5" exposure	1.000	S.F.	.029	3.39	1.31	4.70
7" exposure	1.000	S.F.	.036	2.61	1.61	4.22
8-1/2" exposure	1.000	S.F.	.032	2.35	1.45	3.80
10" exposure	1.000	S.F.	.025	1.83	1.13	2.96
Resquared & rebutted, 5-1/2" exposure	1.000	S.F.	.027	3.55	1.21	4.76
7" exposure	1.000	S.F.	.024	3.20	1.09	4.29
8-1/2" exposure	1.000	S.F.	.021	2.84	.97	3.81
10" exposure	1.000	S.F.	.019	2.49	.85	3.34
Fire retardant, 5" exposure	1.000	S.F.	.027	4.01	1.21	5.22
7" exposure	1.000	S.F.	.024	3.61	1.09	4.70
8-1/2" exposure	1.000	S.F.	.021	3.21	.97	4.18
10" exposure	1.000	S.F.	.023	2.14	1.04	3.18
Hand-split, red cedar, 24" long, 7" exposure	1.000	S.F.	.045	3.51	2.03	5.54
8-1/2" exposure	1.000	S.F.	.038	3.01	1.74	4.75
10" exposure	1.000	S.F.	.032	2.51	1.45	3.96
12" exposure	1.000	S.F.	.026	2.01	1.16	3.17
Fire retardant, 7" exposure	1.000	S.F.	.045	4.15	2.03	6.18
8-1/2" exposure	1.000	S.F.	.038	3.56	1.74	5.30
10" exposure	1.000	S.F.	.032	2.97	1.45	4.42
12" exposure	1.000	S.F.	.026	2.38	1.16	3.54
18" long, 5" exposure	1.000	S.F.	.068	3.59	3.08	6.67
7" exposure	1.000	S.F.	.048	2.53	2.17	4.70
8-1/2" exposure	1.000	S.F.	.040	2.11	1.81	3.92
10" exposure	1.000	S.F.	.036	1.90	1.63	3.53
Fire retardant, 5" exposure	1.000	S.F.	.068	4.37	3.08	7.45
7" exposure	1.000	S.F.	.048	3.08	2.17	5.25
8-1/2" exposure	1.000	S.F.	.040	2.57	1.81	4.38
10" exposure	1.000	S.F.	.036	2.31	1.63	3.94
Paper, #15 asphalt felt	1.100	S.F.	.002	.05	.10	.15
Trim, cedar	.125	S.F.	.005	.22	.23	.45
Fir	.125	S.F.	.005	.10	.23	.33
Redwood	.125	S.F.	.005	.22	.23	.45
White pine	.125	S.F.	.005	.10	.23	.33
Painting, primer, & 1 coat	1.000	S.F.	.013	.13	.52	.65
2 coats	1.000	S.F.	.017	.20	.68	.88
Staining, sealer, & 1 coat	1.000	S.F.	.017	.11	.68	.79
2 coats	1.000	S.F.	.019	.17	.74	.91

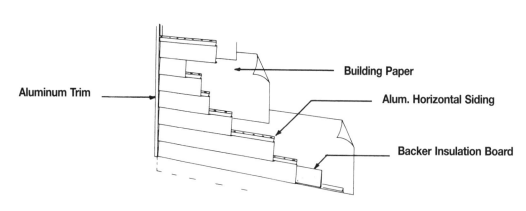

Aluminum Trim

Building Paper

Alum. Horizontal Siding

Backer Insulation Board

System Description	QUAN.	UNIT	LABOR HOURS	COST PER S.F.		
				MAT.	INST.	TOTAL
ALUMINUM CLAPBOARD SIDING, 8″ WIDE, WHITE						
Aluminum horizontal siding, 8″ clapboard	1.000	S.F.	.031	1.89	1.40	3.29
Backer, insulation board	1.000	S.F.	.008	.70	.36	1.06
Trim, aluminum	.600	L.F.	.016	.89	.71	1.60
Building wrap, spunbonded polypropylene	1.100	S.F.	.002	.15	.10	.25
TOTAL		S.F.	.057	3.63	2.57	6.20
ALUMINUM VERTICAL BOARD & BATTEN, WHITE						
Aluminum vertical board & batten	1.000	S.F.	.027	2.08	1.23	3.31
Backer insulation board	1.000	S.F.	.008	.70	.36	1.06
Trim, aluminum	.600	L.F.	.016	.89	.71	1.60
Building wrap, spunbonded polypropylene	1.100	S.F.	.002	.15	.10	.25
TOTAL		S.F.	.053	3.82	2.40	6.22
VINYL CLAPBOARD SIDING, 8″ WIDE, WHITE						
Vinyl siding, clabboard profile, smooth texture, .042 thick, single 8	1.000		.032	.91	1.46	2.37
Backer, insulation board	1.000	S.F.	.008	.70	.36	1.06
Vinyl siding, access., outside corner, woodgrain, 4″ face, 3/4″ pocket	1.000		.023	1.60	1.03	2.63
Building wrap, spunbonded polypropylene	1.100	S.F.	.002	.15	.10	.25
TOTAL		S.F.	.065	3.36	2.95	6.31
VINYL VERTICAL BOARD & BATTEN, WHITE						
Vinyl siding, vertical pattern, .046 thick, double 5	1.000	S.F.	.029	1.06	1.31	2.37
Backer, insulation board	1.000	S.F.	.008	.70	.36	1.06
Vinyl siding, access., outside corner, woodgrain, 4″ face, 3/4″ pocket	.600	L.F.	.014	.96	.62	1.58
Building wrap, spunbonded polypropylene	1.100	S.F.	.002	.15	.10	.25
TOTAL		S.F.	.053	2.87	2.39	5.26

The costs in this system are on a square foot of wall basis.
Do not subtract openings from wall area.

Description	QUAN.	UNIT	LABOR HOURS	COST PER S.F.		
				MAT.	INST.	TOTAL

Metal & Plastic Siding Price Sheet	QUAN.	UNIT	LABOR HOURS	COST PER S.F.		
				MAT.	INST.	TOTAL
Siding, aluminum, .024" thick, smooth, 8" wide, white	1.000	S.F.	.031	1.89	1.40	3.29
Color	1.000	S.F.	.031	2.01	1.40	3.41
Double 4" pattern, 8" wide, white	1.000	S.F.	.031	1.35	1.40	2.75
Color	1.000	S.F.	.031	1.47	1.40	2.87
Double 5" pattern, 10" wide, white	1.000	S.F.	.029	1.39	1.31	2.70
Color	1.000	S.F.	.029	1.51	1.31	2.82
Embossed, single, 8" wide, white	1.000	S.F.	.031	1.89	1.40	3.29
Color	1.000	S.F.	.031	2.01	1.40	3.41
Double 4" pattern, 8" wide, white	1.000	S.F.	.031	2	1.40	3.40
Color	1.000	S.F.	.031	2.12	1.40	3.52
Double 5" pattern, 10" wide, white	1.000	S.F.	.029	2	1.31	3.31
Color	1.000	S.F.	.029	2.12	1.31	3.43
Alum siding with insulation board, smooth, 8" wide, white	1.000	S.F.	.031	1.77	1.40	3.17
Color	1.000	S.F.	.031	1.89	1.40	3.29
Double 4" pattern, 8" wide, white	1.000	S.F.	.031	1.75	1.40	3.15
Color	1.000	S.F.	.031	1.87	1.40	3.27
Double 5" pattern, 10" wide, white	1.000	S.F.	.029	1.75	1.31	3.06
Color	1.000	S.F.	.029	1.87	1.31	3.18
Embossed, single, 8" wide, white	1.000	S.F.	.031	2.05	1.40	3.45
Color	1.000	S.F.	.031	2.17	1.40	3.57
Double 4" pattern, 8" wide, white	1.000	S.F.	.031	2.08	1.40	3.48
Color	1.000	S.F.	.031	2.20	1.40	3.60
Double 5" pattern, 10" wide, white	1.000	S.F.	.029	2.08	1.31	3.39
Color	1.000	S.F.	.029	2.20	1.31	3.51
Aluminum, shake finish, 10" wide, white	1.000	S.F.	.029	2.20	1.31	3.51
Color	1.000	S.F.	.029	2.32	1.31	3.63
Aluminum, vertical, 12" wide, white	1.000	S.F.	.027	2.08	1.23	3.31
Color	1.000	S.F.	.027	2.20	1.23	3.43
Vinyl siding, 8" wide, smooth, white	1.000	S.F.	.032	.91	1.46	2.37
Color	1.000	S.F.	.032	1.09	1.46	2.55
10" wide, Dutch lap, smooth, white	1.000	S.F.	.029	.88	1.31	2.19
Color	1.000	S.F.	.029	1.06	1.31	2.37
Double 4" pattern, 8" wide, white	1.000	S.F.	.032	.72	1.46	2.18
Color	1.000	S.F.	.032	.90	1.46	2.36
Double 5" pattern, 10" wide, white	1.000	S.F.	.029	.72	1.31	2.03
Color	1.000	S.F.	.029	.90	1.31	2.21
Embossed, single, 8" wide, white	1.000	S.F.	.032	.92	1.46	2.38
Color	1.000	S.F.	.032	1.10	1.46	2.56
10" wide, white	1.000	S.F.	.029	1.11	1.31	2.42
Color	1.000	S.F.	.029	1.29	1.31	2.60
Double 4" pattern, 8" wide, white	1.000	S.F.	.032	.88	1.46	2.34
Color	1.000	S.F.	.032	1.06	1.46	2.52
Double 5" pattern, 10" wide, white	1.000	S.F.	.029	.88	1.31	2.19
Color	1.000	S.F.	.029	1.06	1.31	2.37
Vinyl, shake finish, 10" wide, white	1.000	S.F.	.029	2.10	1.81	3.91
Color	1.000	S.F.	.029	2.28	1.81	4.09
Vinyl, vertical, double 5" pattern, 10" wide, white	1.000	S.F.	.029	1.06	1.31	2.37
Color	1.000	S.F.	.029	1.24	1.31	2.55
Backer board, installed in siding panels 8" or 10" wide	1.000	S.F.	.008	.70	.36	1.06
4' x 8' sheets, polystyrene, 3/4" thick	1.000	S.F.	.010	.56	.45	1.01
4' x 8' fiberboard, plain	1.000	S.F.	.008	.70	.36	1.06
Trim, aluminum, white	.600	L.F.	.016	.89	.71	1.60
Color	.600	L.F.	.016	.95	.71	1.66
Vinyl, white	.600	L.F.	.014	.96	.62	1.58
Color	.600	L.F.	.014	1.17	.62	1.79
Paper, #15 asphalt felt	1.100	S.F.	.002	.06	.11	.17
Kraft paper, plain	1.100	S.F.	.002	.07	.11	.18
Foil backed	1.100	S.F.	.002	.10	.11	.21

Description	QUAN.	UNIT	LABOR HOURS	COST PER S.F.		
				MAT.	INST.	TOTAL
Poured insulation, cellulose fiber, R3.8 per inch (1" thick)	1.000	S.F.	.003	.06	.15	.21
Fiberglass , R4.0 per inch (1" thick)	1.000	S.F.	.003	.05	.15	.20
Mineral wool, R3.0 per inch (1" thick)	1.000	S.F.	.003	.04	.15	.19
Polystyrene, R4.0 per inch (1" thick)	1.000	S.F.	.003	.28	.15	.43
Vermiculite, R2.7 per inch (1" thick)	1.000	S.F.	.003	.16	.15	.31
Perlite, R2.7 per inch (1" thick)	1.000	S.F.	.003	.16	.15	.31
Reflective insulation, aluminum foil reinforced with scrim	1.000	S.F.	.004	.15	.19	.34
Reinforced with woven polyolefin	1.000	S.F.	.004	.19	.19	.38
With single bubble air space, R8.8	1.000	S.F.	.005	.28	.24	.52
With double bubble air space, R9.8	1.000	S.F.	.005	.29	.24	.53
Rigid insulation, fiberglass, unfaced,						
1-1/2" thick, R6.2	1.000	S.F.	.008	.70	.36	1.06
2" thick, R8.3	1.000	S.F.	.008	.76	.36	1.12
2-1/2" thick, R10.3	1.000	S.F.	.010	.88	.45	1.33
3" thick, R12.4	1.000	S.F.	.010	.88	.45	1.33
Foil faced, 1" thick, R4.3	1.000	S.F.	.008	1.01	.36	1.37
1-1/2" thick, R6.2	1.000	S.F.	.008	1.50	.36	1.86
2" thick, R8.7	1.000	S.F.	.009	1.88	.41	2.29
2-1/2" thick, R10.9	1.000	S.F.	.010	2.22	.45	2.67
3" thick, R13.0	1.000	S.F.	.010	2.41	.45	2.86
Foam glass, 1-1/2" thick R2.64	1.000	S.F.	.010	1.46	.45	1.91
2" thick R5.26	1.000	S.F.	.011	3.51	.50	4.01
Perlite, 1" thick R2.77	1.000	S.F.	.010	.33	.45	.78
2" thick R5.55	1.000	S.F.	.011	.66	.50	1.16
Polystyrene, extruded, blue, 2.2#/C.F., 3/4" thick R4	1.000	S.F.	.010	.56	.45	1.01
1-1/2" thick R8.1	1.000	S.F.	.011	1.14	.50	1.64
2" thick R10.8	1.000	S.F.	.011	1.54	.50	2.04
Molded bead board, white, 1" thick R3.85	1.000	S.F.	.010	.26	.45	.71
1-1/2" thick, R5.6	1.000	S.F.	.011	.67	.50	1.17
2" thick, R7.7	1.000	S.F.	.011	.86	.50	1.36
Non-rigid insulation, batts						
Fiberglass, kraft faced, 3-1/2" thick, R11, 11" wide	1.000	S.F.	.005	.41	.27	.68
15" wide	1.000	S.F.	.005	.41	.27	.68
23" wide	1.000	S.F.	.005	.41	.27	.68
6" thick, R19, 11" wide	1.000	S.F.	.006	.47	.27	.74
15" wide	1.000	S.F.	.006	.47	.27	.74
23" wide	1.000	S.F.	.006	.47	.27	.74
9" thick, R30, 15" wide	1.000	S.F.	.006	.88	.27	1.15
23" wide	1.000	S.F.	.006	.88	.27	1.15
12" thick, R38, 15" wide	1.000	S.F.	.006	1.10	.27	1.37
23" wide	1.000	S.F.	.006	1.10	.27	1.37
Fiberglass, foil faced, 3-1/2" thick, R11, 15" wide	1.000	S.F.	.005	.61	.27	.88
23" wide	1.000	S.F.	.005	.61	.27	.88
6" thick, R19, 15" thick	1.000	S.F.	.005	.59	.23	.82
23" wide	1.000	S.F.	.005	.59	.23	.82
9" thick, R30, 15" wide	1.000	S.F.	.006	.92	.27	1.19
23" wide	1.000	S.F.	.006	.92	.27	1.19

Insulation Systems	QUAN.	UNIT	LABOR HOURS	COST PER S.F.		
				MAT.	INST.	TOTAL
Non-rigid insulation batts						
Fiberglass unfaced, 3-1/2" thick, R11, 15" wide	1.000	S.F.	.005	.40	.23	.63
23" wide	1.000	S.F.	.005	.40	.23	.63
6" thick, R19, 15" wide	1.000	S.F.	.006	.64	.27	.91
23" wide	1.000	S.F.	.006	.64	.27	.91
9" thick, R19, 15" wide	1.000	S.F.	.007	.92	.31	1.23
23" wide	1.000	S.F.	.007	.92	.31	1.23
12" thick, R38, 15" wide	1.000	S.F.	.007	.99	.31	1.30
23" wide	1.000	S.F.	.007	.99	.31	1.30
Mineral fiber batts, 3" thick, R11	1.000	S.F.	.005	.42	.23	.65
3-1/2" thick, R13	1.000	S.F.	.005	.42	.23	.65
6" thick, R19	1.000	S.F.	.005	.56	.23	.79
6-1/2" thick, R22	1.000	S.F.	.005	.56	.23	.79
10" thick, R30	1.000	S.F.	.006	.83	.27	1.10

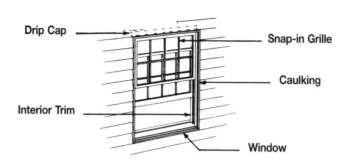

Drip Cap
Snap-in Grille
Caulking
Interior Trim
Window

System Description	QUAN.	UNIT	LABOR HOURS	COST EACH		
				MAT.	INST.	TOTAL
BUILDER'S QUALITY WOOD WINDOW 2' X 3', DOUBLE HUNG						
Window, primed, builder's quality, 2' x 3', insulating glass	1.000	Ea.	.800	229	36	265
Trim, interior casing	11.000	L.F.	.367	15.29	16.61	31.90
Paint, interior & exterior, primer & 2 coats	2.000	Face	1.778	2.38	70	72.38
Caulking	10.000	L.F.	.323	2.10	14.70	16.80
Snap-in grille	1.000	Set	.333	52.50	15.05	67.55
Drip cap, metal	2.000	L.F.	.040	.92	1.80	2.72
TOTAL		Ea.	3.641	302.19	154.16	456.35
PLASTIC CLAD WOOD WINDOW 3' X 4', DOUBLE HUNG						
Window, plastic clad, premium, 3' x 4', insulating glass	1.000	Ea.	.889	400	40	440
Trim, interior casing	15.000	L.F.	.500	20.85	22.65	43.50
Paint, interior, primer & 2 coats	1.000	Face	.889	1.19	35	36.19
Caulking	14.000	L.F.	.452	2.94	20.58	23.52
Snap-in grille	1.000	Set	.333	52.50	15.05	67.55
TOTAL		Ea.	3.063	477.48	133.28	610.76
METAL CLAD WOOD WINDOW, 3' X 5', DOUBLE HUNG						
Window, metal clad, deluxe, 3' x 5', insulating glass	1.000	Ea.	1.000	365	45	410
Trim, interior casing	17.000	L.F.	.567	23.63	25.67	49.30
Paint, interior, primer & 2 coats	1.000	Face	.889	1.19	35	36.19
Caulking	16.000	L.F.	.516	3.36	23.52	26.88
Snap-in grille	1.000	Set	.235	140	10.65	150.65
Drip cap, metal	3.000	L.F.	.060	1.38	2.70	4.08
TOTAL		Ea.	3.267	534.56	142.54	677.10

The cost of this system is on a cost per each window basis.

Description	QUAN.	UNIT	LABOR HOURS	COST EACH		
				MAT.	INST.	TOTAL

Double Hung Window Price Sheet	QUAN.	UNIT	LABOR HOURS	COST EACH		
				MAT.	INST.	TOTAL
Windows, double-hung, builder's quality, 2' x 3', single glass	1.000	Ea.	.800	202	36	238
Insulating glass	1.000	Ea.	.800	229	36	265
3' x 4', single glass	1.000	Ea.	.889	280	40	320
Insulating glass	1.000	Ea.	.889	290	40	330
4' x 4'-6", single glass	1.000	Ea.	1.000	345	45	390
Insulating glass	1.000	Ea.	1.000	375	45	420
Plastic clad premium insulating glass, 2'-6" x 3'	1.000	Ea.	.800	243	36	279
3' x 3'-6"	1.000	Ea.	.800	286	36	322
3' x 4'	1.000	Ea.	.889	400	40	440
3' x 4'-6"	1.000	Ea.	.889	380	40	420
3' x 5'	1.000	Ea.	1.000	345	45	390
3'-6" x 6'	1.000	Ea.	1.000	405	45	450
Metal clad deluxe insulating glass, 2'-6" x 3'	1.000	Ea.	.800	267	36	303
3' x 3'-6"	1.000	Ea.	.800	305	36	341
3' x 4'	1.000	Ea.	.889	320	40	360
3' x 4'-6"	1.000	Ea.	.889	335	40	375
3' x 5'	1.000	Ea.	1.000	365	45	410
3'-6" x 6'	1.000	Ea.	1.000	445	45	490
Trim, interior casing, window 2' x 3'	11.000	L.F.	.367	15.30	16.60	31.90
2'-6" x 3'	12.000	L.F.	.400	16.70	18.10	34.80
3' x 3'-6"	14.000	L.F.	.467	19.45	21	40.45
3' x 4'	15.000	L.F.	.500	21	22.50	43.50
3' x 4'-6"	16.000	L.F.	.533	22	24	46
3' x 5'	17.000	L.F.	.567	23.50	25.50	49
3'-6" x 6'	20.000	L.F.	.667	28	30	58
4' x 4'-6"	18.000	L.F.	.600	25	27	52
Paint or stain, interior or exterior, 2' x 3' window, 1 coat	1.000	Face	.444	.41	17.50	17.91
2 coats	1.000	Face	.727	.81	28.50	29.31
Primer & 1 coat	1.000	Face	.727	.78	28.50	29.28
Primer & 2 coats	1.000	Face	.889	1.19	35	36.19
3' x 4' window, 1 coat	1.000	Face	.667	.90	26	26.90
2 coats	1.000	Face	.667	.98	26	26.98
Primer & 1 coat	1.000	Face	.727	1.21	28.50	29.71
Primer & 2 coats	1.000	Face	.889	1.19	35	36.19
4' x 4'-6" window, 1 coat	1.000	Face	.667	.90	26	26.90
2 coats	1.000	Face	.667	.98	26	26.98
Primer & 1 coat	1.000	Face	.727	1.21	28.50	29.71
Primer & 2 coats	1.000	Face	.889	1.19	35	36.19
Caulking, window, 2' x 3'	10.000	L.F.	.323	2.10	14.70	16.80
2'-6" x 3'	11.000	L.F.	.355	2.31	16.15	18.46
3' x 3'-6"	13.000	L.F.	.419	2.73	19.10	21.83
3' x 4'	14.000	L.F.	.452	2.94	20.50	23.44
3' x 4'-6"	15.000	L.F.	.484	3.15	22	25.15
3' x 5'	16.000	L.F.	.516	3.36	23.50	26.86
3'-6" x 6'	19.000	L.F.	.613	3.99	28	31.99
4' x 4'-6"	17.000	L.F.	.548	3.57	25	28.57
Grilles, glass size to, 16" x 24" per sash	1.000	Set	.333	52.50	15.05	67.55
32" x 32" per sash	1.000	Set	.235	140	10.65	150.65
Drip cap, aluminum, 2' long	2.000	L.F.	.040	.92	1.80	2.72
3' long	3.000	L.F.	.060	1.38	2.70	4.08
4' long	4.000	L.F.	.080	1.84	3.60	5.44
Wood, 2' long	2.000	L.F.	.067	2.78	3.02	5.80
3' long	3.000	L.F.	.100	4.17	4.53	8.70
4' long	4.000	L.F.	.133	5.55	6.05	11.60

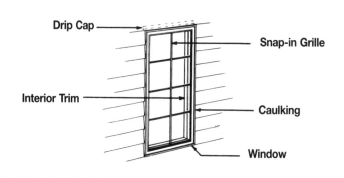

Drip Cap

Snap-in Grille

Interior Trim

Caulking

Window

System Description	QUAN.	UNIT	LABOR HOURS	COST EACH		
				MAT.	INST.	TOTAL
BUILDER'S QUALITY WINDOW, WOOD, 2′ BY 3′, CASEMENT						
Window, primed, builder's quality, 2′ x 3′, insulating glass	1.000	Ea.	.800	310	36	346
Trim, interior casing	11.000	L.F.	.367	15.29	16.61	31.90
Paint, interior & exterior, primer & 2 coats	2.000	Face	1.778	2.38	70	72.38
Caulking	10.000	L.F.	.323	2.10	14.70	16.80
Snap-in grille	1.000	Ea.	.267	30	12.05	42.05
Drip cap, metal	2.000	L.F.	.040	.92	1.80	2.72
TOTAL		Ea.	3.575	360.69	151.16	511.85
PLASTIC CLAD WOOD WINDOW, 2′ X 4′, CASEMENT						
Window, plastic clad, premium, 2′ x 4′, insulating glass	1.000	Ea.	.889	345	40	385
Trim, interior casing	13.000	L.F.	.433	18.07	19.63	37.70
Paint, interior, primer & 2 coats	1.000	Ea.	.889	1.19	35	36.19
Caulking	12.000	L.F.	.387	2.52	17.64	20.16
Snap-in grille	1.000	Ea.	.267	30	12.05	42.05
TOTAL		Ea.	2.865	396.78	124.32	521.10
METAL CLAD WOOD WINDOW, 2′ X 5′, CASEMENT						
Window, metal clad, deluxe, 2′ x 5′, insulating glass	1.000	Ea.	1.000	315	45	360
Trim, interior casing	15.000	L.F.	.500	20.85	22.65	43.50
Paint, interior, primer & 2 coats	1.000	Ea.	.889	1.19	35	36.19
Caulking	14.000	L.F.	.452	2.94	20.58	23.52
Snap-in grille	1.000	Ea.	.250	43	11.30	54.30
Drip cap, metal	12.000	L.F.	.040	.92	1.80	2.72
TOTAL		Ea.	3.131	383.90	136.33	520.23

The cost of this system is on a cost per each window basis.

Description	QUAN.	UNIT	LABOR HOURS	COST EACH		
				MAT.	INST.	TOTAL

Casement Window Price Sheet	QUAN.	UNIT	LABOR HOURS	COST EACH		
				MAT.	INST.	TOTAL
Window, casement, builders quality, 2' x 3', single glass	1.000	Ea.	.800	299	36	335
Insulating glass	1.000	Ea.	.800	310	36	346
2' x 4'-6", single glass	1.000	Ea.	.727	870	33	903
Insulating glass	1.000	Ea.	.727	720	33	753
2' x 6', single glass	1.000	Ea.	.889	445	45	490
Insulating glass	1.000	Ea.	.889	1,125	40	1,165
Plastic clad premium insulating glass, 2' x 3'	1.000	Ea.	.800	264	36	300
2' x 4'	1.000	Ea.	.889	425	40	465
2' x 5'	1.000	Ea.	1.000	575	45	620
2' x 6'	1.000	Ea.	1.000	445	45	490
Metal clad deluxe insulating glass, 2' x 3'	1.000	Ea.	.800	231	36	267
2' x 4'	1.000	Ea.	.889	278	40	318
2' x 5'	1.000	Ea.	1.000	315	45	360
2' x 6'	1.000	Ea.	1.000	365	45	410
Trim, interior casing, window 2' x 3'	11.000	L.F.	.367	15.30	16.60	31.90
2' x 4'	13.000	L.F.	.433	18.05	19.65	37.70
2' x 4'-6"	14.000	L.F.	.467	19.45	21	40.45
2' x 5'	15.000	L.F.	.500	21	22.50	43.50
2' x 6'	17.000	L.F.	.567	23.50	25.50	49
Paint or stain, interior or exterior, 2' x 3' window, 1 coat	1.000	Face	.444	.41	17.50	17.91
2 coats	1.000	Face	.727	.81	28.50	29.31
Primer & 1 coat	1.000	Face	.727	.78	28.50	29.28
Primer & 2 coats	1.000	Face	.889	1.19	35	36.19
2' x 4' window, 1 coat	1.000	Face	.444	.41	17.50	17.91
2 coats	1.000	Face	.727	.81	28.50	29.31
Primer & 1 coat	1.000	Face	.727	.78	28.50	29.28
Primer & 2 coats	1.000	Face	.889	1.19	35	36.19
2' x 6' window, 1 coat	1.000	Face	.667	.90	26	26.90
2 coats	1.000	Face	.667	.98	26	26.98
Primer & 1 coat	1.000	Face	.727	1.21	28.50	29.71
Primer & 2 coats	1.000	Face	.889	1.19	35	36.19
Caulking, window, 2' x 3'	10.000	L.F.	.323	2.10	14.70	16.80
2' x 4'	12.000	L.F.	.387	2.52	17.65	20.17
2' x 4'-6"	13.000	L.F.	.419	2.73	19.10	21.83
2' x 5'	14.000	L.F.	.452	2.94	20.50	23.44
2' x 6'	16.000	L.F.	.516	3.36	23.50	26.86
Grilles, glass size, to 20" x 36"	1.000	Ea.	.267	30	12.05	42.05
To 20" x 56"	1.000	Ea.	.250	43	11.30	54.30
Drip cap, metal, 2' long	2.000	L.F.	.040	.92	1.80	2.72
Wood, 2' long	2.000	L.F.	.067	2.78	3.02	5.80

Drip Cap

Interior Trim

Snap-in Grille

Caulking

Window

System Description	QUAN.	UNIT	LABOR HOURS	COST EACH		
				MAT.	INST.	TOTAL
BUILDER'S QUALITY WINDOW, WOOD, 34" X 22", AWNING						
Window, builder quality, 34" x 22", insulating glass	1.000	Ea.	.800	277	36	313
Trim, interior casing	10.500	L.F.	.350	14.60	15.86	30.46
Paint, interior & exterior, primer & 2 coats	2.000	Face	1.778	2.38	70	72.38
Caulking	9.500	L.F.	.306	2	13.97	15.97
Snap-in grille	1.000	Ea.	.267	24.50	12.05	36.55
Drip cap, metal	3.000	L.F.	.060	1.38	2.70	4.08
TOTAL		Ea.	3.561	321.86	150.58	472.44
PLASTIC CLAD WOOD WINDOW, 40" X 28", AWNING						
Window, plastic clad, premium, 40" x 28", insulating glass	1.000	Ea.	.889	360	40	400
Trim interior casing	13.500	L.F.	.450	18.77	20.39	39.16
Paint, interior, primer & 2 coats	1.000	Face	.889	1.19	35	36.19
Caulking	12.500	L.F.	.403	2.63	18.38	21.01
Snap-in grille	1.000	Ea.	.267	24.50	12.05	36.55
TOTAL		Ea.	2.898	407.09	125.82	532.91
METAL CLAD WOOD WINDOW, 48" X 36", AWNING						
Window, metal clad, deluxe, 48" x 36", insulating glass	1.000	Ea.	1.000	385	45	430
Trim, interior casing	15.000	L.F.	.500	20.85	22.65	43.50
Paint, interior, primer & 2 coats	1.000	Face	.889	1.19	35	36.19
Caulking	14.000	L.F.	.452	2.94	20.58	23.52
Snap-in grille	1.000	Ea.	.250	35.50	11.30	46.80
Drip cap, metal	4.000	L.F.	.080	1.84	3.60	5.44
TOTAL		Ea.	3.171	447.32	138.13	585.45

The cost of this system is on a cost per each window basis.

Description	QUAN.	UNIT	LABOR HOURS	COST EACH		
				MAT.	INST.	TOTAL

Awning Window Price Sheet	QUAN.	UNIT	LABOR HOURS	COST EACH		
				MAT.	INST.	TOTAL
Windows, awning, builder's quality, 34" x 22", insulated glass	1.000	Ea.	.800	262	36	298
Low E glass	1.000	Ea.	.800	277	36	313
40" x 28", insulated glass	1.000	Ea.	.889	330	40	370
Low E glass	1.000	Ea.	.889	350	40	390
48" x 36", insulated glass	1.000	Ea.	1.000	485	45	530
Low E glass	1.000	Ea.	1.000	510	45	555
Plastic clad premium insulating glass, 34" x 22"	1.000	Ea.	.800	279	36	315
40" x 22"	1.000	Ea.	.800	305	36	341
36" x 28"	1.000	Ea.	.889	325	40	365
36" x 36"	1.000	Ea.	.889	360	40	400
48" x 28"	1.000	Ea.	1.000	390	45	435
60" x 36"	1.000	Ea.	1.000	560	45	605
Metal clad deluxe insulating glass, 34" x 22"	1.000	Ea.	.800	260	36	296
40" x 22"	1.000	Ea.	.800	305	36	341
36" x 25"	1.000	Ea.	.889	285	40	325
40" x 30"	1.000	Ea.	.889	355	40	395
48" x 28"	1.000	Ea.	1.000	365	45	410
60" x 36"	1.000	Ea.	1.000	385	45	430
Trim, interior casing window, 34" x 22"	10.500	L.F.	.350	14.60	15.85	30.45
40" x 22"	11.500	L.F.	.383	16	17.35	33.35
36" x 28"	12.500	L.F.	.417	17.40	18.90	36.30
40" x 28"	13.500	L.F.	.450	18.75	20.50	39.25
48" x 28"	14.500	L.F.	.483	20	22	42
48" x 36"	15.000	L.F.	.500	21	22.50	43.50
Paint or stain, interior or exterior, 34" x 22", 1 coat	1.000	Face	.444	.41	17.50	17.91
2 coats	1.000	Face	.727	.81	28.50	29.31
Primer & 1 coat	1.000	Face	.727	.78	28.50	29.28
Primer & 2 coats	1.000	Face	.889	1.19	35	36.19
36" x 28", 1 coat	1.000	Face	.444	.41	17.50	17.91
2 coats	1.000	Face	.727	.81	28.50	29.31
Primer & 1 coat	1.000	Face	.727	.78	28.50	29.28
Primer & 2 coats	1.000	Face	.889	1.19	35	36.19
48" x 36", 1 coat	1.000	Face	.667	.90	26	26.90
2 coats	1.000	Face	.667	.98	26	26.98
Primer & 1 coat	1.000	Face	.727	1.21	28.50	29.71
Primer & 2 coats	1.000	Face	.889	1.19	35	36.19
Caulking, window, 34" x 22"	9.500	L.F.	.306	2	13.95	15.95
40" x 22"	10.500	L.F.	.339	2.21	15.45	17.66
36" x 28"	11.500	L.F.	.371	2.42	16.90	19.32
40" x 28"	12.500	L.F.	.403	2.63	18.40	21.03
48" x 28"	13.500	L.F.	.436	2.84	19.85	22.69
48" x 36"	14.000	L.F.	.452	2.94	20.50	23.44
Grilles, glass size, to 28" by 16"	1.000	Ea.	.267	24.50	12.05	36.55
To 44" by 24"	1.000	Ea.	.250	35.50	11.30	46.80
Drip cap, aluminum, 3' long	3.000	L.F.	.060	1.38	2.70	4.08
3'-6" long	3.500	L.F.	.070	1.61	3.15	4.76
4' long	4.000	L.F.	.080	1.84	3.60	5.44
Wood, 3' long	3.000	L.F.	.100	4.17	4.53	8.70
3'-6" long	3.500	L.F.	.117	4.87	5.30	10.17
4' long	4.000	L.F.	.133	5.55	6.05	11.60

System Description	QUAN.	UNIT	LABOR HOURS	COST EACH		
				MAT.	INST.	TOTAL
BUILDER'S QUALITY WOOD WINDOW, 3′ X 2′, SLIDING						
Window, primed, builder's quality, 3′ x 2′, insul. glass	1.000	Ea.	.800	288	36	324
Trim, interior casing	11.000	L.F.	.367	15.29	16.61	31.90
Paint, interior & exterior, primer & 2 coats	2.000	Face	1.778	2.38	70	72.38
Caulking	10.000	L.F.	.323	2.10	14.70	16.80
Snap-in grille	1.000	Set	.333	27.50	15.05	42.55
Drip cap, metal	3.000	L.F.	.060	1.38	2.70	4.08
TOTAL		Ea.	3.661	336.65	155.06	491.71
PLASTIC CLAD WOOD WINDOW, 4′ X 3′-6″, SLIDING						
Window, plastic clad, premium, 4′ x 3′-6″, insulating glass	1.000	Ea.	.889	730	40	770
Trim, interior casing	16.000	L.F.	.533	22.24	24.16	46.40
Paint, interior, primer & 2 coats	1.000	Face	.889	1.19	35	36.19
Caulking	17.000	L.F.	.548	3.57	24.99	28.56
Snap-in grille	1.000	Set	.333	27.50	15.05	42.55
TOTAL		Ea.	3.192	784.50	139.20	923.70
METAL CLAD WOOD WINDOW, 6′ X 5′, SLIDING						
Window, metal clad, deluxe, 6′ x 5′, insulating glass	1.000	Ea.	1.000	750	45	795
Trim, interior casing	23.000	L.F.	.767	31.97	34.73	66.70
Paint, interior, primer & 2 coats	1.000	Face	.889	1.19	35	36.19
Caulking	22.000	L.F.	.710	4.62	32.34	36.96
Snap-in grille	1.000	Set	.364	43	16.45	59.45
Drip cap, metal	6.000	L.F.	.120	2.76	5.40	8.16
TOTAL		Ea.	3.850	833.54	168.92	1,002.46

The cost of this system is on a cost per each window basis.

Description	QUAN.	UNIT	LABOR HOURS	COST EACH		
				MAT.	INST.	TOTAL

Sliding Window Price Sheet

Sliding Window Price Sheet	QUAN.	UNIT	LABOR HOURS	COST EACH		
				MAT.	INST.	TOTAL
Windows, sliding, builder's quality, 3' x 3', single glass	1.000	Ea.	.800	264	36	300
Insulating glass	1.000	Ea.	.800	288	36	324
4' x 3'-6", single glass	1.000	Ea.	.889	310	40	350
Insulating glass	1.000	Ea.	.889	330	40	370
6' x 5', single glass	1.000	Ea.	1.000	455	45	500
Insulating glass	1.000	Ea.	1.000	500	45	545
Plastic clad premium insulating glass, 3' x 3'	1.000	Ea.	.800	625	36	661
4' x 3'-6"	1.000	Ea.	.889	730	40	770
5' x 4'	1.000	Ea.	.889	935	40	975
6' x 5'	1.000	Ea.	1.000	1,175	45	1,220
Metal clad deluxe insulating glass, 3' x 3'	1.000	Ea.	.800	340	36	376
4' x 3'-6"	1.000	Ea.	.889	415	40	455
5' x 4'	1.000	Ea.	.889	500	40	540
6' x 5'	1.000	Ea.	1.000	750	45	795
Trim, interior casing, window 3' x 2'	11.000	L.F.	.367	15.30	16.60	31.90
3' x 3'	13.000	L.F.	.433	18.05	19.65	37.70
4' x 3'-6"	16.000	L.F.	.533	22	24	46
5' x 4'	19.000	L.F.	.633	26.50	28.50	55
6' x 5'	23.000	L.F.	.767	32	34.50	66.50
Paint or stain, interior or exterior, 3' x 2' window, 1 coat	1.000	Face	.444	.41	17.50	17.91
2 coats	1.000	Face	.727	.81	28.50	29.31
Primer & 1 coat	1.000	Face	.727	.78	28.50	29.28
Primer & 2 coats	1.000	Face	.889	1.19	35	36.19
4' x 3'-6" window, 1 coat	1.000	Face	.667	.90	26	26.90
2 coats	1.000	Face	.667	.98	26	26.98
Primer & 1 coat	1.000	Face	.727	1.21	28.50	29.71
Primer & 2 coats	1.000	Face	.889	1.19	35	36.19
6' x 5' window, 1 coat	1.000	Face	.889	2.30	35	37.30
2 coats	1.000	Face	1.333	4.20	52.50	56.70
Primer & 1 coat	1.000	Face	1.333	4.15	52.50	56.65
Primer & 2 coats	1.000	Face	1.600	6.35	63	69.35
Caulking, window, 3' x 2'	10.000	L.F.	.323	2.10	14.70	16.80
3' x 3'	12.000	L.F.	.387	2.52	17.65	20.17
4' x 3'-6"	15.000	L.F.	.484	3.15	22	25.15
5' x 4'	18.000	L.F.	.581	3.78	26.50	30.28
6' x 5'	22.000	L.F.	.710	4.62	32.50	37.12
Grilles, glass size, to 14" x 36"	1.000	Set	.333	27.50	15.05	42.55
To 36" x 36"	1.000	Set	.364	43	16.45	59.45
Drip cap, aluminum, 3' long	3.000	L.F.	.060	1.38	2.70	4.08
4' long	4.000	L.F.	.080	1.84	3.60	5.44
5' long	5.000	L.F.	.100	2.30	4.50	6.80
6' long	6.000	L.F.	.120	2.76	5.40	8.16
Wood, 3' long	3.000	L.F.	.100	4.17	4.53	8.70
4' long	4.000	L.F.	.133	5.55	6.05	11.60
5' long	5.000	L.F.	.167	6.95	7.55	14.50
6' long	6.000	L.F.	.200	8.35	9.05	17.40

System Description	QUAN.	UNIT	LABOR HOURS	COST EACH		
				MAT.	INST.	TOTAL
AWNING TYPE BOW WINDOW, BUILDER'S QUALITY, 8′ X 5′						
Window, primed, builder's quality, 8′ x 5′, insulating glass	1.000	Ea.	1.600	1,400	72.50	1,472.50
Trim, interior casing	27.000	L.F.	.900	37.53	40.77	78.30
Paint, interior & exterior, primer & 1 coat	2.000	Face	3.200	12.70	126	138.70
Drip cap, vinyl	1.000	Ea.	.533	82.50	24	106.50
Caulking	26.000	L.F.	.839	5.46	38.22	43.68
Snap-in grilles	1.000	Set	1.067	120	48.20	168.20
TOTAL		Ea.	8.139	1,658.19	349.69	2,007.88
CASEMENT TYPE BOW WINDOW, PLASTIC CLAD, 10′ X 6′						
Window, plastic clad, premium, 10′ x 6′, insulating glass	1.000	Ea.	2.286	2,125	103	2,228
Trim, interior casing	33.000	L.F.	1.100	45.87	49.83	95.70
Paint, interior, primer & 1 coat	1.000	Face	1.778	2.38	70	72.38
Drip cap, vinyl	1.000	Ea.	.615	90	28	118
Caulking	32.000	L.F.	1.032	6.72	47.04	53.76
Snap-in grilles	1.000	Set	1.333	150	60.25	210.25
TOTAL		Ea.	8.144	2,419.97	358.12	2,778.09
DOUBLE HUNG TYPE, METAL CLAD, 9′ X 5′						
Window, metal clad, deluxe, 9′ x 5′, insulating glass	1.000	Ea.	2.667	1,425	121	1,546
Trim, interior casing	29.000	L.F.	.967	40.31	43.79	84.10
Paint, interior, primer & 1 coat	1.000	Face	1.778	2.38	70	72.38
Drip cap, vinyl	1.000	Set	.615	90	28	118
Caulking	28.000	L.F.	.903	5.88	41.16	47.04
Snap-in grilles	1.000	Set	1.067	120	48.20	168.20
TOTAL		Ea.	7.997	1,683.57	352.15	2,035.72

The cost of this system is on a cost per each window basis.

Description	QUAN.	UNIT	LABOR HOURS	COST EACH		
				MAT.	INST.	TOTAL

Bow/Bay Window Price Sheet	QUAN.	UNIT	LABOR HOURS	COST EACH		
				MAT.	INST.	TOTAL
Windows, bow awning type, builder's quality, 8' x 5', insulating glass	1.000	Ea.	1.600	1,650	72.50	1,722.50
Low E glass	1.000	Ea.	1.600	1,400	72.50	1,472.50
12' x 6', insulating glass	1.000	Ea.	2.667	1,475	121	1,596
Low E glass	1.000	Ea.	2.667	1,600	121	1,721
Plastic clad premium insulating glass, 6' x 4'	1.000	Ea.	1.600	1,975	72.50	2,047.50
9' x 4'	1.000	Ea.	2.000	1,600	90.50	1,690.50
10' x 5'	1.000	Ea.	2.286	2,600	103	2,703
12' x 6'	1.000	Ea.	2.667	3,300	121	3,421
Metal clad deluxe insulating glass, 6' x 4'	1.000	Ea.	1.600	945	72.50	1,017.50
9' x 4'	1.000	Ea.	2.000	1,325	90.50	1,415.50
10' x 5'	1.000	Ea.	2.286	1,825	103	1,928
12' x 6'	1.000	Ea.	2.667	2,550	121	2,671
Bow casement type, builder's quality, 8' x 5', single glass	1.000	Ea.	1.600	1,875	72.50	1,947.50
Insulating glass	1.000	Ea.	1.600	2,275	72.50	2,347.50
12' x 6', single glass	1.000	Ea.	2.667	2,325	121	2,446
Insulating glass	1.000	Ea.	2.667	2,375	121	2,496
Plastic clad premium insulating glass, 8' x 5'	1.000	Ea.	1.600	1,425	72.50	1,497.50
10' x 5'	1.000	Ea.	2.000	2,025	90.50	2,115.50
10' x 6'	1.000	Ea.	2.286	2,125	103	2,228
12' x 6'	1.000	Ea.	2.667	2,525	121	2,646
Metal clad deluxe insulating glass, 8' x 5'	1.000	Ea.	1.600	1,650	72.50	1,722.50
10' x 5'	1.000	Ea.	2.000	1,775	90.50	1,865.50
10' x 6'	1.000	Ea.	2.286	2,100	103	2,203
12' x 6'	1.000	Ea.	2.667	2,900	121	3,021
Bow, double hung type, builder's quality, 8' x 4', single glass	1.000	Ea.	1.600	1,325	72.50	1,397.50
Insulating glass	1.000	Ea.	1.600	1,425	72.50	1,497.50
9' x 5', single glass	1.000	Ea.	2.667	1,425	121	1,546
Insulating glass	1.000	Ea.	2.667	1,500	121	1,621
Plastic clad premium insulating glass, 7' x 4'	1.000	Ea.	1.600	1,350	72.50	1,422.50
8' x 4'	1.000	Ea.	2.000	1,400	90.50	1,490.50
8' x 5'	1.000	Ea.	2.286	1,450	103	1,553
9' x 5'	1.000	Ea.	2.667	1,500	121	1,621
Metal clad deluxe insulating glass, 7' x 4'	1.000	Ea.	1.600	1,250	72.50	1,322.50
8' x 4'	1.000	Ea.	2.000	1,300	90.50	1,390.50
8' x 5'	1.000	Ea.	2.286	1,350	103	1,453
9' x 5'	1.000	Ea.	2.667	1,425	121	1,546
Trim, interior casing, window 7' x 4'	1.000	Ea.	.767	32	34.50	66.50
8' x 5'	1.000	Ea.	.900	37.50	41	78.50
10' x 6'	1.000	Ea.	1.100	46	50	96
12' x 6'	1.000	Ea.	1.233	51.50	56	107.50
Paint or stain, interior, or exterior, 7' x 4' window, 1 coat	1.000	Face	.889	2.30	35	37.30
Primer & 1 coat	1.000	Face	1.333	4.15	52.50	56.65
8' x 5' window, 1 coat	1.000	Face	.889	2.30	35	37.30
Primer & 1 coat	1.000	Face	1.333	4.15	52.50	56.65
10' x 6' window, 1 coat	1.000	Face	1.333	1.80	52	53.80
Primer & 1 coat	1.000	Face	1.778	2.38	70	72.38
12' x 6' window, 1 coat	1.000	Face	1.778	4.60	70	74.60
Primer & 1 coat	1.000	Face	2.667	8.30	105	113.30
Drip cap, vinyl moulded window, 7' long	1.000	Ea.	.533	72	21	93
8' long	1.000	Ea.	.533	82.50	24	106.50
Caulking, window, 7' x 4'	1.000	Ea.	.710	4.62	32.50	37.12
8' x 5'	1.000	Ea.	.839	5.45	38	43.45
10' x 6'	1.000	Ea.	1.032	6.70	47	53.70
12' x 6'	1.000	Ea.	1.161	7.55	53	60.55
Grilles, window, 7' x 4'	1.000	Set	.800	90	36	126
8' x 5'	1.000	Set	1.067	120	48	168
10' x 6'	1.000	Set	1.333	150	60.50	210.50
12' x 6'	1.000	Set	1.600	180	72.50	252.50

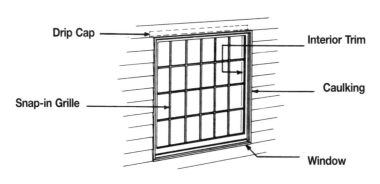

Drip Cap — Interior Trim
Caulking
Snap-in Grille — Window

System Description	QUAN.	UNIT	LABOR HOURS	COST EACH		
				MAT.	INST.	TOTAL
BUILDER'S QUALITY PICTURE WINDOW, 4′ X 4′						
Window, primed, builder's quality, 4′ x 4′, insulating glass	1.000	Ea.	1.333	510	60.50	570.50
Trim, interior casing	17.000	L.F.	.567	23.63	25.67	49.30
Paint, interior & exterior, primer & 2 coats	2.000	Face	1.778	2.38	70	72.38
Caulking	16.000	L.F.	.516	3.36	23.52	26.88
Snap-in grille	1.000	Ea.	.267	160	12.05	172.05
Drip cap, metal	4.000	L.F.	.080	1.84	3.60	5.44
TOTAL		Ea.	4.541	701.21	195.34	896.55
PLASTIC CLAD WOOD WINDOW, 4′-6″ X 6′-6″						
Window, plastic clad, prem., 4′-6″ x 6′-6″, insul. glass	1.000	Ea.	1.455	1,000	66	1,066
Trim, interior casing	23.000	L.F.	.767	31.97	34.73	66.70
Paint, interior, primer & 2 coats	1.000	Face	.889	1.19	35	36.19
Caulking	22.000	L.F.	.710	4.62	32.34	36.96
Snap-in grille	1.000	Ea.	.267	160	12.05	172.05
TOTAL		Ea.	4.088	1,197.78	180.12	1,377.90
METAL CLAD WOOD WINDOW, 6′-6″ X 6′-6″						
Window, metal clad, deluxe, 6′-6″ x 6′-6″, insulating glass	1.000	Ea.	1.600	690	72.50	762.50
Trim interior casing	27.000	L.F.	.900	37.53	40.77	78.30
Paint, interior, primer & 2 coats	1.000	Face	1.600	6.35	63	69.35
Caulking	26.000	L.F.	.839	5.46	38.22	43.68
Snap-in grille	1.000	Ea.	.267	160	12.05	172.05
Drip cap, metal	6.500	L.F.	.130	2.99	5.85	8.84
TOTAL		Ea.	5.336	902.33	232.39	1,134.72

The cost of this system is on a cost per each window basis.

Description	QUAN.	UNIT	LABOR HOURS	COST EACH		
				MAT.	INST.	TOTAL

Fixed Window Price Sheet	QUAN.	UNIT	LABOR HOURS	COST EACH		
				MAT.	INST.	TOTAL
Window-picture, builder's quality, 4' x 4', single glass	1.000	Ea.	1.333	465	60.50	525.50
Insulating glass	1.000	Ea.	1.333	510	60.50	570.50
4' x 4'-6", single glass	1.000	Ea.	1.455	485	66	551
Insulating glass	1.000	Ea.	1.455	505	66	571
5' x 4', single glass	1.000	Ea.	1.455	565	66	631
Insulating glass	1.000	Ea.	1.455	590	66	656
6' x 4'-6", single glass	1.000	Ea.	1.600	615	72.50	687.50
Insulating glass	1.000	Ea.	1.600	635	72.50	707.50
Plastic clad premium insulating glass, 4' x 4'	1.000	Ea.	1.333	530	60.50	590.50
4'-6" x 6'-6"	1.000	Ea.	1.455	1,000	66	1,066
5'-6" x 6'-6"	1.000	Ea.	1.600	1,100	72.50	1,172.50
6'-6" x 6'-6"	1.000	Ea.	1.600	1,125	72.50	1,197.50
Metal clad deluxe insulating glass, 4' x 4'	1.000	Ea.	1.333	370	60.50	430.50
4'-6" x 6'-6"	1.000	Ea.	1.455	545	66	611
5'-6" x 6'-6"	1.000	Ea.	1.600	600	72.50	672.50
6'-6" x 6'-6"	1.000	Ea.	1.600	690	72.50	762.50
Trim, interior casing, window 4' x 4'	17.000	L.F.	.567	23.50	25.50	49
4'-6" x 4'-6"	19.000	L.F.	.633	26.50	28.50	55
5'-0" x 4'-0"	19.000	L.F.	.633	26.50	28.50	55
4'-6" x 6'-6"	23.000	L.F.	.767	32	34.50	66.50
5'-6" x 6'-6"	25.000	L.F.	.833	35	38	73
6'-6" x 6'-6"	27.000	L.F.	.900	37.50	41	78.50
Paint or stain, interior or exterior, 4' x 4' window, 1 coat	1.000	Face	.667	.90	26	26.90
2 coats	1.000	Face	.667	.98	26	26.98
Primer & 1 coat	1.000	Face	.727	1.21	28.50	29.71
Primer & 2 coats	1.000	Face	.889	1.19	35	36.19
4'-6" x 6'-6" window, 1 coat	1.000	Face	.667	.90	26	26.90
2 coats	1.000	Face	.667	.98	26	26.98
Primer & 1 coat	1.000	Face	.727	1.21	28.50	29.71
Primer & 2 coats	1.000	Face	.889	1.19	35	36.19
6'-6" x 6'-6" window, 1 coat	1.000	Face	.889	2.30	35	37.30
2 coats	1.000	Face	1.333	4.20	52.50	56.70
Primer & 1 coat	1.000	Face	1.333	4.15	52.50	56.65
Primer & 2 coats	1.000	Face	1.600	6.35	63	69.35
Caulking, window, 4' x 4'	1.000	Ea.	.516	3.36	23.50	26.86
4'-6" x 4'-6"	1.000	Ea.	.581	3.78	26.50	30.28
5'-0" x 4'-0"	1.000	Ea.	.581	3.78	26.50	30.28
4'-6" x 6'-6"	1.000	Ea.	.710	4.62	32.50	37.12
5'-6" x 6'-6"	1.000	Ea.	.774	5.05	35.50	40.55
6'-6" x 6'-6"	1.000	Ea.	.839	5.45	38	43.45
Grilles, glass size, to 48" x 48"	1.000	Ea.	.267	160	12.05	172.05
To 60" x 68"	1.000	Ea.	.286	120	12.90	132.90
Drip cap, aluminum, 4' long	4.000	L.F.	.080	1.84	3.60	5.44
4'-6" long	4.500	L.F.	.090	2.07	4.05	6.12
5' long	5.000	L.F.	.100	2.30	4.50	6.80
6' long	6.000	L.F.	.120	2.76	5.40	8.16
Wood, 4' long	4.000	L.F.	.133	5.55	6.05	11.60
4'-6" long	4.500	L.F.	.150	6.25	6.80	13.05
5' long	5.000	L.F.	.167	6.95	7.55	14.50
6' long	6.000	L.F.	.200	8.35	9.05	17.40

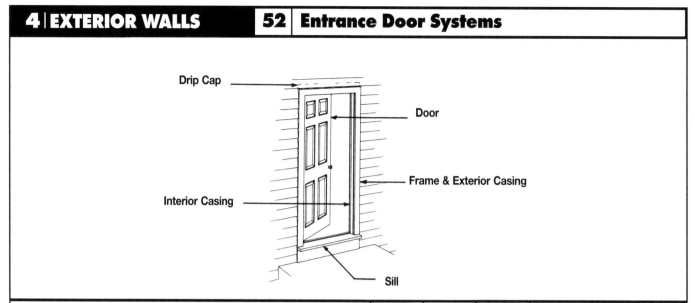

System Description	QUAN.	UNIT	LABOR HOURS	COST EACH		
				MAT.	INST.	TOTAL
COLONIAL, 6 PANEL, 3′ X 6′-8″, WOOD						
Door, 3′ x 6′-8″ x 1-3/4″ thick, pine, 6 panel colonial	1.000	Ea.	1.067	445	48	493
Frame, 5-13/16″ deep, incl. exterior casing & drip cap	17.000	L.F.	.725	205.70	32.81	238.51
Interior casing, 2-1/2″ wide	18.000	L.F.	.600	25.02	27.18	52.20
Sill, 8/4 x 8″ deep	3.000	L.F.	.480	61.50	21.75	83.25
Butt hinges, brass, 4-1/2″ x 4-1/2″	1.500	Pr.		22.58		22.58
Lockset	1.000	Ea.	.571	38	26	64
Weatherstripping, metal, spring type, bronze	1.000	Set	1.053	20.50	47.50	68
Paint, interior & exterior, primer & 2 coats	2.000	Face	1.778	12.50	70	82.50
TOTAL		Ea.	6.274	830.80	273.24	1,104.04
SOLID CORE BIRCH, FLUSH, 3′ X 6′-8″						
Door, 3′-0″ x 6′-8″, 1-3/4″ thick, birch, flush solid core	1.000	Ea.	1.067	114	48	162
Frame, 5-13/16″ deep, incl. exterior casing & drip cap	17.000	L.F.	.725	205.70	32.81	238.51
Interior casing, 2-1/2″ wide	18.000	L.F.	.600	25.02	27.18	52.20
Sill, 8/4 x 8″ deep	3.000	L.F.	.480	61.50	21.75	83.25
Butt hinges, brass, 4-1/2″ x 4-1/2″	1.500	Pr.		22.58		22.58
Lockset	1.000	Ea.	.571	38	26	64
Weatherstripping, metal, spring type, bronze	1.000	Set	1.053	20.50	47.50	68
Paint, Interior & exterior, primer & 2 coats	2.000	Face	1.778	11.70	70	81.70
TOTAL		Ea.	6.274	499	273.24	772.24

These systems are on a cost per each door basis.

Description	QUAN.	UNIT	LABOR HOURS	COST EACH		
				MAT.	INST.	TOTAL

Entrance Door Price Sheet	QUAN.	UNIT	LABOR HOURS	COST EACH		
				MAT.	INST.	TOTAL
Door exterior wood 1-3/4" thick, pine, dutch door, 2'-8" x 6'-8" minimum	1.000	Ea.	1.333	750	60.50	810.50
Maximum	1.000	Ea.	1.600	795	72.50	867.50
3'-0" x 6'-8", minimum	1.000	Ea.	1.333	765	60.50	825.50
Maximum	1.000	Ea.	1.600	840	72.50	912.50
Colonial, 6 panel, 2'-8" x 6'-8"	1.000	Ea.	1.000	425	45	470
3'-0" x 6'-8"	1.000	Ea.	1.067	445	48	493
8 panel, 2'-6" x 6'-8"	1.000	Ea.	1.000	625	45	670
3'-0" x 6'-8"	1.000	Ea.	1.067	605	48	653
Flush, birch, solid core, 2'-8" x 6'-8"	1.000	Ea.	1.000	109	45	154
3'-0" x 6'-8"	1.000	Ea.	1.067	114	48	162
Porch door, 2'-8" x 6'-8"	1.000	Ea.	1.000	570	45	615
3'-0" x 6'-8"	1.000	Ea.	1.067	430	48	478
Hand carved mahogany, 2'-8" x 6'-8"	1.000	Ea.	1.067	550	48	598
3'-0" x 6'-8"	1.000	Ea.	1.067	615	48	663
Rosewood, 2'-8" x 6'-8"	1.000	Ea.	1.067	825	48	873
3'-0" x 6-8"	1.000	Ea.	1.067	845	48	893
Door, metal clad wood 1-3/8" thick raised panel, 2'-8" x 6'-8"	1.000	Ea.	1.067	300	42.50	342.50
3'-0" x 6'-8"	1.000	Ea.	1.067	271	48	319
Deluxe metal door, 3'-0" x 6'-8"	1.000	Ea.	1.231	271	48	319
3'-0" x 6'-8"	1.000	Ea.	1.231	271	48	319
Frame, pine, including exterior trim & drip cap, 5/4, x 4-9/16" deep	17.000	L.F.	.725	101	33	134
5-13/16" deep	17.000	L.F.	.725	206	33	239
6-9/16" deep	17.000	L.F.	.725	156	33	189
Safety glass lites, add	1.000	Ea.		72		72
Interior casing, 2'-8" x 6'-8" door	18.000	L.F.	.600	25	27	52
3'-0" x 6'-8" door	19.000	L.F.	.633	26.50	28.50	55
Sill, oak, 8/4 x 8" deep	3.000	L.F.	.480	61.50	22	83.50
8/4 x 10" deep	3.000	L.F.	.533	70.50	24	94.50
Butt hinges, steel plated, 4-1/2" x 4-1/2", plain	1.500	Pr.		22.50		22.50
Ball bearing	1.500	Pr.		49.50		49.50
Bronze, 4-1/2" x 4-1/2", plain	1.500	Pr.		25.50		25.50
Ball bearing	1.500	Pr.		52.50		52.50
Lockset, minimum	1.000	Ea.	.571	38	26	64
Maximum	1.000	Ea.	1.000	160	45	205
Weatherstripping, metal, interlocking, zinc	1.000	Set	2.667	15.80	121	136.80
Bronze	1.000	Set	2.667	25	121	146
Spring type, bronze	1.000	Set	1.053	20.50	47.50	68
Rubber, minimum	1.000	Set	1.053	5.10	47.50	52.60
Maximum	1.000	Set	1.143	5.85	51.50	57.35
Felt minimum	1.000	Set	.571	2.37	26	28.37
Maximum	1.000	Set	.615	2.59	28	30.59
Paint or stain, flush door, interior or exterior, 1 coat	2.000	Face	.941	4.48	37	41.48
2 coats	2.000	Face	1.455	8.95	57	65.95
Primer & 1 coat	2.000	Face	1.455	7.50	57	64.50
Primer & 2 coats	2.000	Face	1.778	11.70	70	81.70
Paneled door, interior & exterior, 1 coat	2.000	Face	1.143	4.78	45	49.78
2 coats	2.000	Face	2.000	9.60	79	88.60
Primer & 1 coat	2.000	Face	1.455	8.05	57	65.05
Primer & 2 coats	2.000	Face	1.778	12.50	70	82.50

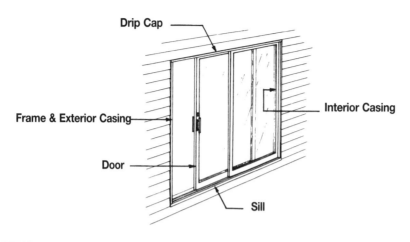

System Description	QUAN.	UNIT	LABOR HOURS	COST EACH		
				MAT.	INST.	TOTAL
WOOD SLIDING DOOR, 8′ WIDE, PREMIUM						
Wood, tempered insul. glass, 8′ wide, premium	1.000	Ea.	5.333	1,500	241	1,741
Interior casing	22.000	L.F.	.733	30.58	33.22	63.80
Exterior casing	22.000	L.F.	.733	30.58	33.22	63.80
Sill, oak, 8/4 x 8″ deep	8.000	L.F.	1.280	164	58	222
Drip cap	8.000	L.F.	.160	3.68	7.20	10.88
Paint, interior & exterior, primer & 2 coats	2.000	Face	2.816	17.60	110.88	128.48
TOTAL		Ea.	11.055	1,746.44	483.52	2,229.96
ALUMINUM SLIDING DOOR, 8′ WIDE, PREMIUM						
Aluminum, tempered insul. glass, 8′ wide, premium	1.000	Ea.	5.333	1,725	241	1,966
Interior casing	22.000	L.F.	.733	30.58	33.22	63.80
Exterior casing	22.000	L.F.	.733	30.58	33.22	63.80
Sill, oak, 8/4 x 8″ deep	8.000	L.F.	1.280	164	58	222
Drip cap	8.000	L.F.	.160	3.68	7.20	10.88
Paint, interior & exterior, primer & 2 coats	2.000	Face	2.816	17.60	110.88	128.48
TOTAL		Ea.	11.055	1,971.44	483.52	2,454.96

The cost of this system is on a cost per each door basis.

Description	QUAN.	UNIT	LABOR HOURS	COST EACH		
				MAT.	INST.	TOTAL

Sliding Door Price Sheet	QUAN.	UNIT	LABOR HOURS	MAT.	INST.	TOTAL
Sliding door, wood, 5/8" thick, tempered insul. glass, 6' wide, premium	1.000	Ea.	4.000	1,300	181	1,481
Economy	1.000	Ea.	4.000	880	181	1,061
8'wide, wood premium	1.000	Ea.	5.333	1,500	241	1,741
Economy	1.000	Ea.	5.333	1,025	241	1,266
12' wide, wood premium	1.000	Ea.	6.400	3,175	289	3,464
Economy	1.000	Ea.	6.400	2,325	289	2,614
Aluminum, 5/8" thick, tempered insul. glass, 6'wide, premium	1.000	Ea.	4.000	1,550	181	1,731
Economy	1.000	Ea.	4.000	850	181	1,031
8'wide, premium	1.000	Ea.	5.333	1,725	241	1,966
Economy	1.000	Ea.	5.333	1,450	241	1,691
12' wide, premium	1.000	Ea.	6.400	2,800	289	3,089
Economy	1.000	Ea.	6.400	1,700	289	1,989
Interior casing, 6' wide door	20.000	L.F.	.667	28	30	58
8' wide door	22.000	L.F.	.733	30.50	33	63.50
12' wide door	26.000	L.F.	.867	36	39.50	75.50
Exterior casing, 6' wide door	20.000	L.F.	.667	28	30	58
8' wide door	22.000	L.F.	.733	30.50	33	63.50
12' wide door	26.000	L.F.	.867	36	39.50	75.50
Sill, oak, 8/4 x 8" deep, 6' wide door	6.000	L.F.	.960	123	43.50	166.50
8' wide door	8.000	L.F.	1.280	164	58	222
12' wide door	12.000	L.F.	1.920	246	87	333
8/4 x 10" deep, 6' wide door	6.000	L.F.	1.067	141	48.50	189.50
8' wide door	8.000	L.F.	1.422	188	64.50	252.50
12' wide door	12.000	L.F.	2.133	282	96.50	378.50
Drip cap, 6' wide door	6.000	L.F.	.120	2.76	5.40	8.16
8' wide door	8.000	L.F.	.160	3.68	7.20	10.88
12' wide door	12.000	L.F.	.240	5.50	10.80	16.30
Paint or stain, interior & exterior, 6' wide door, 1 coat	2.000	Face	1.600	6.40	63	69.40
2 coats	2.000	Face	1.600	6.40	63	69.40
Primer & 1 coat	2.000	Face	1.778	10.40	69.50	79.90
Primer & 2 coats	2.000	Face	2.560	16	101	117
8' wide door, 1 coat	2.000	Face	1.760	7.05	69.50	76.55
2 coats	2.000	Face	1.760	7.05	69.50	76.55
Primer & 1 coat	2.000	Face	1.955	11.45	76.50	87.95
Primer & 2 coats	2.000	Face	2.816	17.60	111	128.60
12' wide door, 1 coat	2.000	Face	2.080	8.30	82	90.30
2 coats	2.000	Face	2.080	8.30	82	90.30
Primer & 1 coat	2.000	Face	2.311	13.50	90.50	104
Primer & 2 coats	2.000	Face	3.328	21	131	152
Aluminum door, trim only, interior & exterior, 6' door, 1 coat	2.000	Face	.800	3.20	31.50	34.70
2 coats	2.000	Face	.800	3.20	31.50	34.70
Primer & 1 coat	2.000	Face	.889	5.20	35	40.20
Primer & 2 coats	2.000	Face	1.280	8	50.50	58.50
8' wide door, 1 coat	2.000	Face	.880	3.52	35	38.52
2 coats	2.000	Face	.880	3.52	35	38.52
Primer & 1 coat	2.000	Face	.978	5.70	38.50	44.20
Primer & 2 coats	2.000	Face	1.408	8.80	55.50	64.30
12' wide door, 1 coat	2.000	Face	1.040	4.16	41	45.16
2 coats	2.000	Face	1.040	4.16	41	45.16
Primer & 1 coat	2.000	Face	1.155	6.75	45	51.75
Primer & 2 coats	2.000	Face	1.664	10.40	65.50	75.90

System Description	QUAN.	UNIT	LABOR HOURS	COST EACH		
				MAT.	INST.	TOTAL
OVERHEAD, SECTIONAL GARAGE DOOR, 9' X 7'						
Wood, overhead sectional door, std., incl. hardware, 9' x 7'	1.000	Ea.	2.000	595	90.50	685.50
Jamb & header blocking, 2" x 6"	25.000	L.F.	.901	15	40.75	55.75
Exterior trim	25.000	L.F.	.833	34.75	37.75	72.50
Paint, interior & exterior, primer & 2 coats	2.000	Face	3.556	25	140	165
Weatherstripping, molding type	1.000	Set	.767	31.97	34.73	66.70
Drip cap	9.000	L.F.	.180	4.14	8.10	12.24
TOTAL		Ea.	8.237	705.86	351.83	1,057.69
OVERHEAD, SECTIONAL GARAGE DOOR, 16' X 7'						
Wood, overhead sectional, std., incl. hardware, 16' x 7'	1.000	Ea.	2.667	1,200	121	1,321
Jamb & header blocking, 2" x 6"	30.000	L.F.	1.081	18	48.90	66.90
Exterior trim	30.000	L.F.	1.000	41.70	45.30	87
Paint, interior & exterior, primer & 2 coats	2.000	Face	5.333	37.50	210	247.50
Weatherstripping, molding type	1.000	Set	1.000	41.70	45.30	87
Drip cap	16.000	L.F.	.320	7.36	14.40	21.76
TOTAL		Ea.	11.401	1,346.26	484.90	1,831.16
OVERHEAD, SWING-UP TYPE, GARAGE DOOR, 16' X 7'						
Wood, overhead, swing-up, std., incl. hardware, 16' x 7'	1.000	Ea.	2.667	790	121	911
Jamb & header blocking, 2" x 6"	30.000	L.F.	1.081	18	48.90	66.90
Exterior trim	30.000	L.F.	1.000	41.70	45.30	87
Paint, interior & exterior, primer & 2 coats	2.000	Face	5.333	37.50	210	247.50
Weatherstripping, molding type	1.000	Set	1.000	41.70	45.30	87
Drip cap	16.000	L.F.	.320	7.36	14.40	21.76
TOTAL		Ea.	11.401	936.26	484.90	1,421.16

This system is on a cost per each door basis.

Description	QUAN.	UNIT	LABOR HOURS	COST EACH		
				MAT.	INST.	TOTAL

Resi Garage Door Price Sheet	QUAN.	UNIT	LABOR HOURS	COST EACH		
				MAT.	INST.	TOTAL
Overhead, sectional, including hardware, fiberglass, 9' x 7', standard	1.000	Ea.	3.030	710	137	847
Deluxe	1.000	Ea.	3.030	905	137	1,042
16' x 7', standard	1.000	Ea.	2.667	1,300	121	1,421
Deluxe	1.000	Ea.	2.667	1,625	121	1,746
Hardboard, 9' x 7', standard	1.000	Ea.	2.000	480	90.50	570.50
Deluxe	1.000	Ea.	2.000	645	90.50	735.50
16' x 7', standard	1.000	Ea.	2.667	945	121	1,066
Deluxe	1.000	Ea.	2.667	1,100	121	1,221
Metal, 9' x 7', standard	1.000	Ea.	3.030	560	137	697
Deluxe	1.000	Ea.	2.000	755	90.50	845.50
16' x 7', standard	1.000	Ea.	5.333	710	241	951
Deluxe	1.000	Ea.	2.667	1,150	121	1,271
Wood, 9' x 7', standard	1.000	Ea.	2.000	595	90.50	685.50
Deluxe	1.000	Ea.	2.000	1,700	90.50	1,790.50
16' x 7', standard	1.000	Ea.	2.667	1,200	121	1,321
Deluxe	1.000	Ea.	2.667	2,500	121	2,621
Overhead swing-up type including hardware, fiberglass, 9' x 7', standard	1.000	Ea.	2.000	825	90.50	915.50
Deluxe	1.000	Ea.	2.000	870	90.50	960.50
16' x 7', standard	1.000	Ea.	2.667	1,050	121	1,171
Deluxe	1.000	Ea.	2.667	1,075	121	1,196
Hardboard, 9' x 7', standard	1.000	Ea.	2.000	380	90.50	470.50
Deluxe	1.000	Ea.	2.000	500	90.50	590.50
16' x 7', standard	1.000	Ea.	2.667	530	121	651
Deluxe	1.000	Ea.	2.667	785	121	906
Metal, 9' x 7', standard	1.000	Ea.	2.000	415	90.50	505.50
Deluxe	1.000	Ea.	2.000	735	90.50	825.50
16' x 7', standard	1.000	Ea.	2.667	650	121	771
Deluxe	1.000	Ea.	2.667	1,050	121	1,171
Wood, 9' x 7', standard	1.000	Ea.	2.000	455	90.50	545.50
Deluxe	1.000	Ea.	2.000	800	90.50	890.50
16' x 7', standard	1.000	Ea.	2.667	790	121	911
Deluxe	1.000	Ea.	2.667	1,100	121	1,221
Jamb & header blocking, 2" x 6", 9' x 7' door	25.000	L.F.	.901	15	41	56
16' x 7' door	30.000	L.F.	1.081	18	49	67
2" x 8", 9' x 7' door	25.000	L.F.	1.000	21	45.50	66.50
16' x 7' door	30.000	L.F.	1.200	25	54.50	79.50
Exterior trim, 9' x 7' door	25.000	L.F.	.833	35	38	73
16' x 7' door	30.000	L.F.	1.000	41.50	45.50	87
Paint or stain, interior & exterior, 9' x 7' door, 1 coat	1.000	Face	2.286	9.55	90	99.55
2 coats	1.000	Face	4.000	19.15	158	177.15
Primer & 1 coat	1.000	Face	2.909	16.10	114	130.10
Primer & 2 coats	1.000	Face	3.556	25	140	165
16' x 7' door, 1 coat	1.000	Face	3.429	14.35	135	149.35
2 coats	1.000	Face	6.000	28.50	237	265.50
Primer & 1 coat	1.000	Face	4.364	24	171	195
Primer & 2 coats	1.000	Face	5.333	37.50	210	247.50
Weatherstripping, molding type, 9' x 7' door	1.000	Set	.767	32	34.50	66.50
16' x 7' door	1.000	Set	1.000	41.50	45.50	87
Drip cap, 9' door	9.000	L.F.	.180	4.14	8.10	12.24
16' door	16.000	L.F.	.320	7.35	14.40	21.75
Garage door opener, economy	1.000	Ea.	1.000	345	45	390
Deluxe, including remote control	1.000	Ea.	1.000	500	45	545

System Description	QUAN.	UNIT	LABOR HOURS	COST EACH		
				MAT.	INST.	TOTAL
SINGLE HUNG, 2′ X 3′ OPENING						
Window, 2′ x 3′ opening, insulating glass	1.000	Ea.	1.600	249	89.50	338.50
Blocking, 1″ x 3″ furring strip nailers	10.000	L.F.	.146	1.90	6.60	8.50
Drywall, 1/2″ thick, standard	5.000	S.F.	.040	1.40	1.80	3.20
Corner bead, 1″ x 1″, galvanized steel	8.000	L.F.	.160	1.04	7.20	8.24
Finish drywall, tape and finish corners inside and outside	16.000	L.F.	.269	1.60	12.16	13.76
Sill, slate	2.000	L.F.	.400	24	16.20	40.20
TOTAL		Ea.	2.615	278.94	133.46	412.40
SLIDING, 3′ X 2′ OPENING						
Window, 3′ x 2′ opening, enameled, insulating glass	1.000	Ea.	1.600	233	89.50	322.50
Blocking, 1″ x 3″ furring strip nailers	10.000	L.F.	.146	1.90	6.60	8.50
Drywall, 1/2″ thick, standard	5.000	S.F.	.040	1.40	1.80	3.20
Corner bead, 1″ x 1″, galvanized steel	7.000	L.F.	.140	.91	6.30	7.21
Finish drywall, tape and finish corners inside and outside	14.000	L.F.	.236	1.40	10.64	12.04
Sill, slate	3.000	L.F.	.600	36	24.30	60.30
TOTAL		Ea.	2.762	274.61	139.14	413.75
AWNING, 3′-1″ X 3′-2″						
Window, 3′-1″ x 3′-2″ opening, enameled, insul. glass	1.000	Ea.	1.600	269	89.50	358.50
Blocking, 1″ x 3″ furring strip, nailers	12.500	L.F.	.182	2.38	8.25	10.63
Drywall, 1/2″ thick, standard	4.500	S.F.	.036	1.26	1.62	2.88
Corner bead, 1″ x 1″, galvanized steel	9.250	L.F.	.185	1.20	8.33	9.53
Finish drywall, tape and finish corners, inside and outside	18.500	L.F.	.312	1.85	14.06	15.91
Sill, slate	3.250	L.F.	.650	39	26.33	65.33
TOTAL		Ea.	2.965	314.69	148.09	462.78

Description	QUAN.	UNIT	LABOR HOURS	COST PER S.F.		
				MAT.	INST.	TOTAL

Aluminum Window Price Sheet	QUAN.	UNIT	LABOR HOURS	COST EACH		
				MAT.	INST.	TOTAL
Window, aluminum, awning, 3'-1" x 3'-2", standard glass	1.000	Ea.	1.600	345	89.50	434.50
Insulating glass	1.000	Ea.	1.600	269	89.50	358.50
4'-5" x 5'-3", standard glass	1.000	Ea.	2.000	390	112	502
Insulating glass	1.000	Ea.	2.000	405	112	517
Casement, 3'-1" x 3'-2", standard glass	1.000	Ea.	1.600	360	89.50	449.50
Insulating glass	1.000	Ea.	1.600	460	89.50	549.50
Single hung, 2' x 3', standard glass	1.000	Ea.	1.600	206	89.50	295.50
Insulating glass	1.000	Ea.	1.600	249	89.50	338.50
2'-8" x 6'-8", standard glass	1.000	Ea.	2.000	360	112	472
Insulating glass	1.000	Ea.	2.000	465	112	577
3'-4" x 5'-0", standard glass	1.000	Ea.	1.778	297	99.50	396.50
Insulating glass	1.000	Ea.	1.778	330	99.50	429.50
Sliding, 3' x 2', standard glass	1.000	Ea.	1.600	217	89.50	306.50
Insulating glass	1.000	Ea.	1.600	233	89.50	322.50
5' x 3', standard glass	1.000	Ea.	1.778	330	99.50	429.50
Insulating glass	1.000	Ea.	1.778	385	99.50	484.50
8' x 4', standard glass	1.000	Ea.	2.667	350	149	499
Insulating glass	1.000	Ea.	2.667	565	149	714
Blocking, 1" x 3" furring, opening 3' x 2'	10.000	L.F.	.146	1.90	6.60	8.50
3' x 3'	12.500	L.F.	.182	2.38	8.25	10.63
3' x 5'	16.000	L.F.	.233	3.04	10.55	13.59
4' x 4'	16.000	L.F.	.233	3.04	10.55	13.59
4' x 5'	18.000	L.F.	.262	3.42	11.90	15.32
4' x 6'	20.000	L.F.	.291	3.80	13.20	17
4' x 8'	24.000	L.F.	.349	4.56	15.85	20.41
6'-8" x 2'-8"	19.000	L.F.	.276	3.61	12.55	16.16
Drywall, 1/2" thick, standard, opening 3' x 2'	5.000	S.F.	.040	1.40	1.80	3.20
3' x 3'	6.000	S.F.	.048	1.68	2.16	3.84
3' x 5'	8.000	S.F.	.064	2.24	2.88	5.12
4' x 4'	8.000	S.F.	.064	2.24	2.88	5.12
4' x 5'	9.000	S.F.	.072	2.52	3.24	5.76
4' x 6'	10.000	S.F.	.080	2.80	3.60	6.40
4' x 8'	12.000	S.F.	.096	3.36	4.32	7.68
6'-8" x 2'	9.500	S.F.	.076	2.66	3.42	6.08
Corner bead, 1" x 1", galvanized steel, opening 3' x 2'	7.000	L.F.	.140	.91	6.30	7.21
3' x 3'	9.000	L.F.	.180	1.17	8.10	9.27
3' x 5'	11.000	L.F.	.220	1.43	9.90	11.33
4' x 4'	12.000	L.F.	.240	1.56	10.80	12.36
4' x 5'	13.000	L.F.	.260	1.69	11.70	13.39
4' x 6'	14.000	L.F.	.280	1.82	12.60	14.42
4' x 8'	16.000	L.F.	.320	2.08	14.40	16.48
6'-8" x 2'	15.000	L.F.	.300	1.95	13.50	15.45
Tape and finish corners, inside and outside, opening 3' x 2'	14.000	L.F.	.204	1.40	10.65	12.05
3' x 3'	18.000	L.F.	.262	1.80	13.70	15.50
3' x 5'	22.000	L.F.	.320	2.20	16.70	18.90
4' x 4'	24.000	L.F.	.349	2.40	18.25	20.65
4' x 5'	26.000	L.F.	.378	2.60	19.75	22.35
4' x 6'	28.000	L.F.	.407	2.80	21.50	24.30
4' x 8'	32.000	L.F.	.466	3.20	24.50	27.70
6'-8" x 2'	30.000	L.F.	.437	3	23	26
Sill, slate, 2' long	2.000	L.F.	.400	24	16.20	40.20
3' long	3.000	L.F.	.600	36	24.50	60.50
4' long	4.000	L.F.	.800	48	32.50	80.50
Wood, 1-5/8" x 6-1/4", 2' long	2.000	L.F.	.128	14	5.80	19.80
3' long	3.000	L.F.	.192	21	8.65	29.65
4' long	4.000	L.F.	.256	28	11.55	39.55

Aluminum Window

Aluminum Door

System Description	QUAN.	UNIT	LABOR HOURS	COST EACH		
				MAT.	INST.	TOTAL
Storm door, aluminum, combination, storm & screen, anodized, 2'-6" x 6'-8"	1.000	Ea.	1.067	185	48	233
2'-8" x 6'-8"	1.000	Ea.	1.143	213	51.50	264.50
3'-0" x 6'-8"	1.000	Ea.	1.143	213	51.50	264.50
Mill finish, 2'-6" x 6'-8"	1.000	Ea.	1.067	246	48	294
2'-8" x 6'-8"	1.000	Ea.	1.143	246	51.50	297.50
3'-0" x 6'-8"	1.000	Ea.	1.143	266	51.50	317.50
Painted, 2'-6" x 6'-8"	1.000	Ea.	1.067	294	48	342
2'-8" x 6'-8"	1.000	Ea.	1.143	251	51.50	302.50
3'-0" x 6'-8"	1.000	Ea.	1.143	289	51.50	340.50
Wood, combination, storm & screen, crossbuck, 2'-6" x 6'-9"	1.000	Ea.	1.455	360	66	426
2'-8" x 6'-9"	1.000	Ea.	1.600	305	72.50	377.50
3'-0" x 6'-9"	1.000	Ea.	1.778	310	80.50	390.50
Full lite, 2'-6" x 6'-9"	1.000	Ea.	1.455	325	66	391
2'-8" x 6'-9"	1.000	Ea.	1.600	325	72.50	397.50
3'-0" x 6'-9"	1.000	Ea.	1.778	335	80.50	415.50
Windows, aluminum, combination storm & screen, basement, 1'-10" x 1'-0"	1.000	Ea.	.533	33.50	24	57.50
2'-9" x 1'-6"	1.000	Ea.	.533	36.50	24	60.50
3'-4" x 2'-0"	1.000	Ea.	.533	44	24	68
Double hung, anodized, 2'-0" x 3'-5"	1.000	Ea.	.533	87	24	111
2'-6" x 5'-0"	1.000	Ea.	.571	116	26	142
4'-0" x 6'-0"	1.000	Ea.	.640	247	29	276
Painted, 2'-0" x 3'-5"	1.000	Ea.	.533	104	24	128
2'-6" x 5'-0"	1.000	Ea.	.571	166	26	192
4'-0" x 6'-0"	1.000	Ea.	.640	298	29	327
Fixed window, anodized, 4'-6" x 4'-6"	1.000	Ea.	.640	133	29	162
5'-8" x 4'-6"	1.000	Ea.	.800	151	36	187
Painted, 4'-6" x 4'-6"	1.000	Ea.	.640	133	29	162
5'-8" x 4'-6"	1.000	Ea.	.800	151	36	187

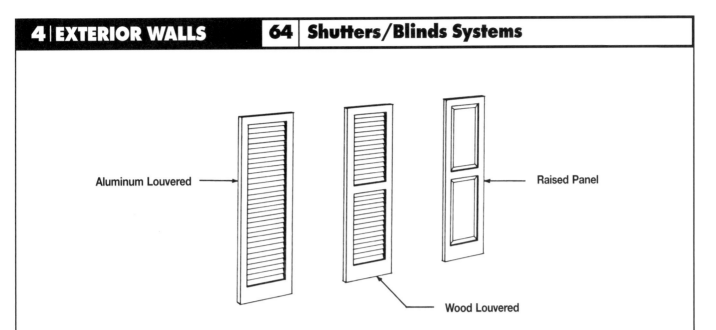

Aluminum Louvered

Raised Panel

Wood Louvered

System Description	QUAN.	UNIT	LABOR HOURS	COST PER PAIR		
				MAT.	INST.	TOTAL
Shutters, exterior blinds, aluminum, louvered, 1'-4" wide, 3"-0" long	1.000	Set	.800	53	36	89
4'-0" long	1.000	Set	.800	63.50	36	99.50
5'-4" long	1.000	Set	.800	84	36	120
6'-8" long	1.000	Set	.889	107	40	147
Wood, louvered, 1'-2" wide, 3'-3" long	1.000	Set	.800	101	36	137
4'-7" long	1.000	Set	.800	137	36	173
5'-3" long	1.000	Set	.800	155	36	191
1'-6" wide, 3'-3" long	1.000	Set	.800	107	36	143
4'-7" long	1.000	Set	.800	151	36	187
Polystyrene, louvered, 1'-2" wide, 3'-3" long	1.000	Set	.800	30.50	36	66.50
4'-7" long	1.000	Set	.800	37.50	36	73.50
5'-3" long	1.000	Set	.800	43	36	79
6'-8" long	1.000	Set	.889	51	40	91
Vinyl, louvered, 1'-2" wide, 4'-7" long	1.000	Set	.720	34	32.50	66.50
1'-4" x 6'-8" long	1.000	Set	.889	52.50	40	92.50

Division 5
Roofing

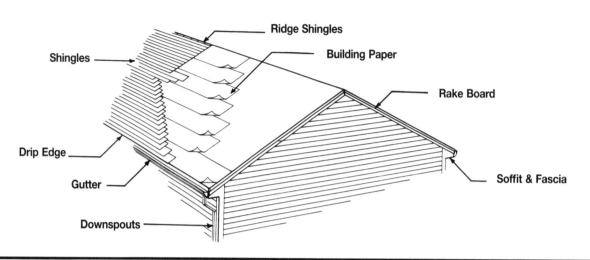

System Description	QUAN.	UNIT	LABOR HOURS	COST PER S.F.		
				MAT.	INST.	TOTAL
ASPHALT, ROOF SHINGLES, CLASS A						
Shingles, inorganic class A, 210-235 lb./sq., 4/12 pitch	1.160	S.F.	.017	.56	.73	1.29
Drip edge, metal, 5″ wide	.150	L.F.	.003	.09	.14	.23
Building paper, #15 felt	1.300	S.F.	.002	.06	.08	.14
Ridge shingles, asphalt	.042	L.F.	.001	.07	.04	.11
Soffit & fascia, white painted aluminum, 1′ overhang	.083	L.F.	.012	.27	.54	.81
Rake trim, 1″ x 6″	.040	L.F.	.002	.05	.07	.12
Rake trim, prime and paint	.040	L.F.	.002	.01	.07	.08
Gutter, seamless, aluminum painted	.083	L.F.	.006	.17	.28	.45
Downspouts, aluminum painted	.035	L.F.	.002	.06	.08	.14
TOTAL		S.F.	.047	1.34	2.03	3.37
WOOD, CEDAR SHINGLES NO. 1 PERFECTIONS, 18″ LONG						
Shingles, wood, cedar, No. 1 perfections, 4/12 pitch	1.160	S.F.	.035	3.52	1.57	5.09
Drip edge, metal, 5″ wide	.150	L.F.	.003	.09	.14	.23
Building paper, #15 felt	1.300	S.F.	.002	.06	.08	.14
Ridge shingles, cedar	.042	L.F.	.001	.17	.05	.22
Soffit & fascia, white painted aluminum, 1′ overhang	.083	L.F.	.012	.27	.54	.81
Rake trim, 1″ x 6″	.040	L.F.	.002	.05	.07	.12
Rake trim, prime and paint	.040	L.F.	.002	.01	.07	.08
Gutter, seamless, aluminum, painted	.083	L.F.	.006	.17	.28	.45
Downspouts, aluminum, painted	.035	L.F.	.002	.06	.08	.14
TOTAL		S.F.	.065	4.40	2.88	7.28

The prices in these systems are based on a square foot of plan area.
All quantities have been adjusted accordingly.

Description	QUAN.	UNIT	LABOR HOURS	COST PER S.F.		
				MAT.	INST.	TOTAL

Gable End Roofing Price Sheet	QUAN.	UNIT	LABOR HOURS	COST PER S.F.		
				MAT.	INST.	TOTAL
Shingles, asphalt, inorganic, class A, 210-235 lb./sq., 4/12 pitch	1.160	S.F.	.017	.56	.73	1.29
8/12 pitch	1.330	S.F.	.019	.61	.79	1.40
Laminated, multi-layered, 240-260 lb./sq., 4/12 pitch	1.160	S.F.	.021	.71	.89	1.60
8/12 pitch	1.330	S.F.	.023	.77	.97	1.74
Premium laminated, multi-layered, 260-300 lb./sq., 4/12 pitch	1.160	S.F.	.027	.92	1.15	2.07
8/12 pitch	1.330	S.F.	.030	.99	1.25	2.24
Clay tile, Spanish tile, red, 4/12 pitch	1.160	S.F.	.053	4.14	2.23	6.37
8/12 pitch	1.330	S.F.	.058	4.49	2.42	6.91
Mission tile, red, 4/12 pitch	1.160	S.F.	.083	9.80	3.49	13.29
8/12 pitch	1.330	S.F.	.090	10.60	3.78	14.38
French tile, red, 4/12 pitch	1.160	S.F.	.071	8.90	2.98	11.88
8/12 pitch	1.330	S.F.	.077	9.60	3.22	12.82
Slate, Buckingham, Virginia, black, 4/12 pitch	1.160	S.F.	.055	5.40	2.30	7.70
8/12 pitch	1.330	S.F.	.059	5.85	2.50	8.35
Vermont, black or grey, 4/12 pitch	1.160	S.F.	.055	6.05	2.30	8.35
8/12 pitch	1.330	S.F.	.059	6.55	2.50	9.05
Wood, No. 1 red cedar, 5X, 16" long, 5" exposure, 4/12 pitch	1.160	S.F.	.038	3.05	1.74	4.79
8/12 pitch	1.330	S.F.	.042	3.30	1.89	5.19
Fire retardant, 4/12 pitch	1.160	S.F.	.038	3.60	1.74	5.34
8/12 pitch	1.330	S.F.	.042	3.90	1.89	5.79
18" long, No.1 perfections, 5" exposure, 4/12 pitch	1.160	S.F.	.035	3.52	1.57	5.09
8/12 pitch	1.330	S.F.	.038	3.81	1.70	5.51
Fire retardant, 4/12 pitch	1.160	S.F.	.035	4.07	1.57	5.64
8/12 pitch	1.330	S.F.	.038	4.41	1.70	6.11
Resquared & rebutted, 18" long, 6" exposure, 4/12 pitch	1.160	S.F.	.032	4.26	1.45	5.71
8/12 pitch	1.330	S.F.	.035	4.62	1.57	6.19
Fire retardant, 4/12 pitch	1.160	S.F.	.032	4.81	1.45	6.26
8/12 pitch	1.330	S.F.	.035	5.20	1.57	6.77
Wood shakes hand split, 24" long, 10" exposure, 4/12 pitch	1.160	S.F.	.038	3.01	1.74	4.75
8/12 pitch	1.330	S.F.	.042	3.26	1.89	5.15
Fire retardant, 4/12 pitch	1.160	S.F.	.038	3.56	1.74	5.30
8/12 pitch	1.330	S.F.	.042	3.86	1.89	5.75
18" long, 8" exposure, 4/12 pitch	1.160	S.F.	.048	2.53	2.17	4.70
8/12 pitch	1.330	S.F.	.052	2.74	2.35	5.09
Fire retardant, 4/12 pitch	1.160	S.F.	.048	3.08	2.17	5.25
8/12 pitch	1.330	S.F.	.052	3.34	2.35	5.69
Drip edge, metal, 5" wide	.150	L.F.	.003	.09	.14	.23
8" wide	.150	L.F.	.003	.10	.14	.24
Building paper, #15 asphalt felt	1.300	S.F.	.002	.06	.08	.14
Ridge shingles, asphalt	.042	L.F.	.001	.07	.04	.11
Clay	.042	L.F.	.002	.50	.07	.57
Slate	.042	L.F.	.002	.43	.07	.50
Wood, shingles	.042	L.F.	.001	.17	.05	.22
Shakes	.042	L.F.	.001	.17	.05	.22
Soffit & fascia, aluminum, vented, 1' overhang	.083	L.F.	.012	.27	.54	.81
2' overhang	.083	L.F.	.013	.41	.60	1.01
Vinyl, vented, 1' overhang	.083	L.F.	.011	.24	.50	.74
2' overhang	.083	L.F.	.012	.33	.54	.87
Wood, board fascia, plywood soffit, 1' overhang	.083	L.F.	.004	.02	.14	.16
2' overhang	.083	L.F.	.006	.03	.22	.25
Rake trim, painted, 1" x 6"	.040	L.F.	.004	.06	.14	.20
1" x 8"	.040	L.F.	.004	.10	.16	.26
Gutter, 5" box, aluminum, seamless, painted	.083	L.F.	.006	.17	.28	.45
Vinyl	.083	L.F.	.006	.11	.27	.38
Downspout, 2" x 3", aluminum, one story house	.035	L.F.	.001	.06	.07	.13
Two story house	.060	L.F.	.003	.11	.13	.24
Vinyl, one story house	.035	L.F.	.002	.06	.08	.14
Two story house	.060	L.F.	.003	.11	.13	.24

System Description	QUAN.	UNIT	LABOR HOURS	COST PER S.F.		
				MAT.	INST.	TOTAL
ASPHALT, ROOF SHINGLES, CLASS A						
Shingles, inorganic, class A, 210-235 lb./sq. 4/12 pitch	1.570	S.F.	.023	.75	.98	1.73
Drip edge, metal, 5" wide	.122	L.F.	.002	.07	.11	.18
Building paper, #15 asphalt felt	1.800	S.F.	.002	.08	.10	.18
Ridge shingles, asphalt	.075	L.F.	.002	.12	.08	.20
Soffit & fascia, white painted aluminum, 1' overhang	.120	L.F.	.017	.39	.79	1.18
Gutter, seamless, aluminum, painted	.120	L.F.	.008	.24	.40	.64
Downspouts, aluminum, painted	.035	L.F.	.002	.06	.08	.14
TOTAL		S.F.	.056	1.71	2.54	4.25
WOOD, CEDAR SHINGLES, NO. 1 PERFECTIONS, 18" LONG						
Shingles, red cedar, No. 1 perfections, 5" exp., 4/12 pitch	1.570	S.F.	.047	4.69	2.10	6.79
Drip edge, metal, 5" wide	.122	L.F.	.002	.07	.11	.18
Building paper, #15 asphalt felt	1.800	S.F.	.002	.08	.10	.18
Ridge shingles, wood, cedar	.075	L.F.	.002	.30	.10	.40
Soffit & fascia, white painted aluminum, 1' overhang	.120	L.F.	.017	.39	.79	1.18
Gutter, seamless, aluminum, painted	.120	L.F.	.008	.24	.40	.64
Downspouts, aluminum, painted	.035	L.F.	.002	.06	.08	.14
TOTAL		S.F.	.080	5.83	3.68	9.51

The prices in these systems are based on a square foot of plan area.
All quantities have been adjusted accordingly.

Description	QUAN.	UNIT	LABOR HOURS	COST PER S.F.		
				MAT.	INST.	TOTAL

Hip Roof - Roofing Price Sheet	QUAN.	UNIT	LABOR HOURS	COST PER S.F.		
				MAT.	INST.	TOTAL
Shingles, asphalt, inorganic, class A, 210-235 lb./sq., 4/12 pitch	1.570	S.F.	.023	.75	.98	1.73
8/12 pitch	1.850	S.F.	.028	.89	1.16	2.05
Laminated, multi-layered, 240-260 lb./sq., 4/12 pitch	1.570	S.F.	.028	.94	1.19	2.13
8/12 pitch	1.850	S.F.	.034	1.12	1.42	2.54
Prem. laminated, multi-layered, 260-300 lb./sq., 4/12 pitch	1.570	S.F.	.037	1.22	1.54	2.76
8/12 pitch	1.850	S.F.	.043	1.45	1.82	3.27
Clay tile, Spanish tile, red, 4/12 pitch	1.570	S.F.	.071	5.50	2.98	8.48
8/12 pitch	1.850	S.F.	.084	6.55	3.53	10.08
Mission tile, red, 4/12 pitch	1.570	S.F.	.111	13.05	4.66	17.71
8/12 pitch	1.850	S.F.	.132	15.50	5.55	21.05
French tile, red, 4/12 pitch	1.570	S.F.	.095	11.85	3.97	15.82
8/12 pitch	1.850	S.F.	.113	14.05	4.71	18.76
Slate, Buckingham, Virginia, black, 4/12 pitch	1.570	S.F.	.073	7.20	3.07	10.27
8/12 pitch	1.850	S.F.	.087	8.55	3.65	12.20
Vermont, black or grey, 4/12 pitch	1.570	S.F.	.073	8.10	3.07	11.17
8/12 pitch	1.850	S.F.	.087	9.60	3.65	13.25
Wood, red cedar, No.1 5X, 16" long, 5" exposure, 4/12 pitch	1.570	S.F.	.051	4.06	2.32	6.38
8/12 pitch	1.850	S.F.	.061	4.83	2.76	7.59
Fire retardant, 4/12 pitch	1.570	S.F.	.051	4.80	2.32	7.12
8/12 pitch	1.850	S.F.	.061	5.70	2.76	8.46
18" long, No.1 perfections, 5" exposure, 4/12 pitch	1.570	S.F.	.047	4.69	2.10	6.79
8/12 pitch	1.850	S.F.	.055	5.55	2.49	8.04
Fire retardant, 4/12 pitch	1.570	S.F.	.047	5.45	2.10	7.55
8/12 pitch	1.850	S.F.	.055	6.45	2.49	8.94
Resquared & rebutted, 18" long, 6" exposure, 4/12 pitch	1.570	S.F.	.043	5.70	1.94	7.64
8/12 pitch	1.850	S.F.	.051	6.75	2.30	9.05
Fire retardant, 4/12 pitch	1.570	S.F.	.043	6.40	1.94	8.34
8/12 pitch	1.850	S.F.	.051	7.60	2.30	9.90
Wood shakes hand split, 24" long, 10" exposure, 4/12 pitch	1.570	S.F.	.051	4.02	2.32	6.34
8/12 pitch	1.850	S.F.	.061	4.77	2.76	7.53
Fire retardant, 4/12 pitch	1.570	S.F.	.051	4.76	2.32	7.08
8/12 pitch	1.850	S.F.	.061	5.65	2.76	8.41
18" long, 8" exposure, 4/12 pitch	1.570	S.F.	.064	3.38	2.90	6.28
8/12 pitch	1.850	S.F.	.076	4.01	3.44	7.45
Fire retardant, 4/12 pitch	1.570	S.F.	.064	4.12	2.90	7.02
8/12 pitch	1.850	S.F.	.076	4.88	3.44	8.32
Drip edge, metal, 5" wide	.122	L.F.	.002	.07	.11	.18
8" wide	.122	L.F.	.002	.08	.11	.19
Building paper, #15 asphalt felt	1.800	S.F.	.002	.08	.10	.18
Ridge shingles, asphalt	.075	L.F.	.002	.12	.08	.20
Clay	.075	L.F.	.003	.89	.13	1.02
Slate	.075	L.F.	.003	.77	.13	.90
Wood, shingles	.075	L.F.	.002	.30	.10	.40
Shakes	.075	L.F.	.002	.30	.10	.40
Soffit & fascia, aluminum, vented, 1' overhang	.120	L.F.	.017	.39	.79	1.18
2' overhang	.120	L.F.	.019	.59	.87	1.46
Vinyl, vented, 1' overhang	.120	L.F.	.016	.35	.73	1.08
2' overhang	.120	L.F.	.017	.48	.79	1.27
Wood, board fascia, plywood soffit, 1' overhang	.120	L.F.	.004	.02	.14	.16
2' overhang	.120	L.F.	.006	.03	.22	.25
Gutter, 5" box, aluminum, seamless, painted	.120	L.F.	.008	.24	.40	.64
Vinyl	.120	L.F.	.009	.16	.39	.55
Downspout, 2" x 3", aluminum, one story house	.035	L.F.	.002	.06	.08	.14
Two story house	.060	L.F.	.003	.11	.13	.24
Vinyl, one story house	.035	L.F.	.001	.06	.07	.13
Two story house	.060	L.F.	.003	.11	.13	.24

Labels: Shingles, Ridge Shingles, Building Paper, Rake Boards, Soffit, Drip Edge

System Description	QUAN.	UNIT	LABOR HOURS	COST PER S.F.		
				MAT.	INST.	TOTAL
ASPHALT, ROOF SHINGLES, CLASS A						
Shingles, asphalt, inorganic, class A, 210-235 lb./sq.	1.450	S.F.	.022	.71	.92	1.63
Drip edge, metal, 5″ wide	.146	L.F.	.003	.08	.13	.21
Building paper, #15 asphalt felt	1.500	S.F.	.002	.07	.09	.16
Ridge shingles, asphalt	.042	L.F.	.001	.07	.04	.11
Soffit & fascia, painted aluminum, 1′ overhang	.083	L.F.	.012	.27	.54	.81
Rake trim, 1″ x 6″	.063	L.F.	.003	.07	.11	.18
Rake trim, prime and paint	.063	L.F.	.003	.02	.11	.13
Gutter, seamless, alumunum, painted	.083	L.F.	.006	.17	.28	.45
Downspouts, aluminum, painted	.042	L.F.	.002	.08	.09	.17
TOTAL		S.F.	.054	1.54	2.31	3.85
WOOD, CEDAR SHINGLES, NO. 1 PERFECTIONS, 18″ LONG						
Shingles, wood, red cedar, No. 1 perfections, 5″ exposure	1.450	S.F.	.044	4.40	1.97	6.37
Drip edge, metal, 5″ wide	.146	L.F.	.003	.08	.13	.21
Building paper, #15 asphalt felt	1.500	S.F.	.002	.07	.09	.16
Ridge shingles, wood	.042	L.F.	.001	.17	.05	.22
Soffit & fascia, white painted aluminum, 1′ overhang	.083	L.F.	.012	.27	.54	.81
Rake trim, 1″ x 6″	.063	L.F.	.003	.07	.11	.18
Rake trim, prime and paint	.063	L.F.	.001	.02	.05	.07
Gutter, seamless, aluminum, painted	.083	L.F.	.006	.17	.28	.45
Downspouts, aluminum, painted	.042	L.F.	.002	.08	.09	.17
TOTAL		S.F.	.074	5.33	3.31	8.64

The prices in this system are based on a square foot of plan area.
All quantities have been adjusted accordingly.

Description	QUAN.	UNIT	LABOR HOURS	COST PER S.F.		
				MAT.	INST.	TOTAL

MeansCostWorks.com:
- ## Online Construction Cost Estimator
- ## Online Square Foot Estimator

Estimates that are Efficient, Customized, and Online!

- **Create Customized Estimates based on your specific building needs in a 24/7 secure online environment.**

- **Our Online Construction Cost Estimator gives you access to the entire RSMeans unit cost, assemblies and repair & remodeling databases!**

- **The Online Square Foot Estimator offers design professionals an extensive library of RSMeans commercial building models and systems all in one easy-to-use conceptual estimating package !**

Cost Data Page

Lines 1 - 31 of 31

	Line Number	Description	Unit	Crew	Daily Output	Labor Hours	Bare Material	Bare Labor	Bare Equip	Bare Total	Total O&P
	042313000000	Vertical Glass U...								30.65	38.50
	042313100010	GLASS BLOCK	S.F.	D8	115.00	0.348	18.70	11.95		19.15	24.50
	042313100100	Plain, 4" thick, U...	S.F.	D8	160.00	0.250	10.60	8.55		43.55	51.50
	042313100150	8" x 8"	S.F.	D8	160.00	0.250	35.00	8.55		42.55	50.50
	042313100160	end block	S.F.	D8	160.00	0.250	34.00	8.55		24.30	30.50
	042313100170	90 deg ...	S.F.	D8	160.00	0.250	15.75	8.55		21.40	27.00
	042313100180	45 deg ...	S.F.	D8	175.00	0.229	13.55	7.85		17.10	22.50
	042313100200	12" x 12"	S.F.	D8	160.00	0.250	8.55	8.55		18.65	24.00
	042313100210	4" x 8"	S.F.	D8	160.00	0.250	10.10	8.55			
	042313100220	6" x 8"									

Estimate

Page 1 of 1   View: Basic

	Quanti... Line Number	Description	Unit	Extended Total	Extended Total O&P	Labor Type	Notes
	200813131300...	Doors, commercial, steel, flush,...	Ea.	$ 5,770.00	$ 6,700.00	Standard ...	
	150611100202...	Miscellaneous wood blocking, to...	M...	$ 32,775.00	$ 47,625.00	Standard ...	
	12612191004...	Oil filled transformer pad mount...	Ea.	$ 22,805.00	$ 26,000.00	Standard ...	
	52721231011...	Network hub, dual speed, 24 po...	Ea.	$ 15,625.00	$ 20,250.00	Standard ...	
	2500951231011...	Suspended Acoustic Ceiling Tile...	S.F.	$ 235.00	$ 312.50	Standard ...	
	1650968161029...	Carpet, commercial grades, dir...	S.Y.	$ 4,286.70	$ 5,032.50	Standard ...	
	272651134009...	High pressure sodium fixture, in...	Ea.	$ 17,739.00	$ 20,790.00	Standard ...	
	7,0000991032005...	Paint Preparation, sanding & put...	S.F.	$ 280.00	$ 420.00	Standard ...	
				$ 99,515.70	$ 127,130.00		

RSMeans

Gambrel Roofing Price Sheet

Gambrel Roofing Price Sheet	QUAN.	UNIT	LABOR HOURS	COST PER S.F.		
				MAT.	INST.	TOTAL
Shingles, asphalt, standard, inorganic, class A, 210-235 lb./sq.	1.450	S.F.	.022	.71	.92	1.63
Laminated, multi-layered, 240-260 lb./sq.	1.450	S.F.	.027	.89	1.12	2.01
Premium laminated, multi-layered, 260-300 lb./sq.	1.450	S.F.	.034	1.15	1.44	2.59
Slate, Buckingham, Virginia, black	1.450	S.F.	.069	6.75	2.88	9.63
Vermont, black or grey	1.450	S.F.	.069	7.60	2.88	10.48
Wood, red cedar, No.1 5X, 16" long, 5" exposure, plain	1.450	S.F.	.048	3.81	2.18	5.99
Fire retardant	1.450	S.F.	.048	4.50	2.18	6.68
18" long, No.1 perfections, 6" exposure, plain	1.450	S.F.	.044	4.40	1.97	6.37
Fire retardant	1.450	S.F.	.044	5.10	1.97	7.07
Resquared & rebutted, 18" long, 6" exposure, plain	1.450	S.F.	.040	5.35	1.82	7.17
Fire retardant	1.450	S.F.	.040	6	1.82	7.82
Shakes, hand split, 24" long, 10" exposure, plain	1.450	S.F.	.048	3.77	2.18	5.95
Fire retardant	1.450	S.F.	.048	4.46	2.18	6.64
18" long, 8" exposure, plain	1.450	S.F.	.060	3.17	2.72	5.89
Fire retardant	1.450	S.F.	.060	3.86	2.72	6.58
Drip edge, metal, 5" wide	.146	L.F.	.003	.08	.13	.21
8" wide	.146	L.F.	.003	.10	.13	.23
Building paper, #15 asphalt felt	1.500	S.F.	.002	.07	.09	.16
Ridge shingles, asphalt	.042	L.F.	.001	.07	.04	.11
Slate	.042	L.F.	.002	.43	.07	.50
Wood, shingles	.042	L.F.	.001	.17	.05	.22
Shakes	.042	L.F.	.001	.17	.05	.22
Soffit & fascia, aluminum, vented, 1' overhang	.083	L.F.	.012	.27	.54	.81
2' overhang	.083	L.F.	.013	.41	.60	1.01
Vinyl vented, 1' overhang	.083	L.F.	.011	.24	.50	.74
2' overhang	.083	L.F.	.012	.33	.54	.87
Wood board fascia, plywood soffit, 1' overhang	.083	L.F.	.004	.02	.14	.16
2' overhang	.083	L.F.	.006	.03	.22	.25
Rake trim, painted, 1" x 6"	.063	L.F.	.006	.09	.22	.31
1" x 8"	.063	L.F.	.007	.12	.29	.41
Gutter, 5" box, aluminum, seamless, painted	.083	L.F.	.006	.17	.28	.45
Vinyl	.083	L.F.	.006	.11	.27	.38
Downspout 2" x 3", aluminum, one story house	.042	L.F.	.002	.07	.09	.16
Two story house	.070	L.F.	.003	.12	.15	.27
Vinyl, one story house	.042	L.F.	.002	.07	.09	.16
Two story house	.070	L.F.	.003	.12	.15	.27

System Description	QUAN.	UNIT	LABOR HOURS	COST PER S.F.		
				MAT.	INST.	TOTAL
ASPHALT, ROOF SHINGLES, CLASS A						
Shingles, standard inorganic class A 210-235 lb./sq.	2.210	S.F.	.032	1.03	1.34	2.37
Drip edge, metal, 5″ wide	.122	L.F.	.002	.07	.11	.18
Building paper, #15 asphalt felt	2.300	S.F.	.003	.10	.13	.23
Ridge shingles, asphalt	.090	L.F.	.002	.15	.09	.24
Soffit & fascia, white painted aluminum, 1′ overhang	.122	L.F.	.018	.40	.80	1.20
Gutter, seamless, aluminum, painted	.122	L.F.	.008	.25	.41	.66
Downspouts, aluminum, painted	.042	L.F.	.002	.08	.09	.17
TOTAL		S.F.	.067	2.08	2.97	5.05
WOOD, CEDAR SHINGLES, NO. 1 PERFECTIONS, 18″ LONG						
Shingles, wood, red cedar, No. 1 perfections, 5″ exposure	2.210	S.F.	.064	6.45	2.88	9.33
Drip edge, metal, 5″ wide	.122	L.F.	.002	.07	.11	.18
Building paper, #15 asphalt felt	2.300	S.F.	.003	.10	.13	.23
Ridge shingles, wood	.090	L.F.	.003	.36	.12	.48
Soffit & fascia, white painted aluminum, 1′ overhang	.122	L.F.	.018	.40	.80	1.20
Gutter, seamless, aluminum, painted	.122	L.F.	.008	.25	.41	.66
Downspouts, aluminum, painted	.042	L.F.	.002	.08	.09	.17
TOTAL		S.F.	.100	7.71	4.54	12.25

The prices in these systems are based on a square foot of plan area.
All quantities have been adjusted accordingly.

Description	QUAN.	UNIT	LABOR HOURS	COST PER S.F.		
				MAT.	INST.	TOTAL

Mansard Roofing Price Sheet	QUAN.	UNIT	LABOR HOURS	COST PER S.F.		
				MAT.	INST.	TOTAL
Shingles, asphalt, standard, inorganic, class A, 210-235 lb./sq.	2.210	S.F.	.032	1.03	1.34	2.37
Laminated, multi-layered, 240-260 lb./sq.	2.210	S.F.	.039	1.30	1.64	2.94
Premium laminated, multi-layered, 260-300 lb./sq.	2.210	S.F.	.050	1.68	2.11	3.79
Slate Buckingham, Virginia, black	2.210	S.F.	.101	9.90	4.22	14.12
Vermont, black or grey	2.210	S.F.	.101	11.10	4.22	15.32
Wood, red cedar, No.1 5X, 16" long, 5" exposure, plain	2.210	S.F.	.070	5.60	3.19	8.79
Fire retardant	2.210	S.F.	.070	6.60	3.19	9.79
18" long, No.1 perfections 6" exposure, plain	2.210	S.F.	.064	6.45	2.88	9.33
Fire retardant	2.210	S.F.	.064	7.45	2.88	10.33
Fire retardant	2.210	S.F.	.059	8.80	2.66	11.46
Shakes, hand split, 24" long 10" exposure, plain	2.210	S.F.	.070	5.50	3.19	8.69
Fire retardant	2.210	S.F.	.070	6.55	3.19	9.74
18" long, 8" exposure, plain	2.210	S.F.	.088	4.64	3.98	8.62
Fire retardant	2.210	S.F.	.088	5.65	3.98	9.63
Drip edge, metal, 5" wide	.122	S.F.	.002	.07	.11	.18
8" wide	.122	S.F.	.002	.08	.11	.19
Building paper, #15 asphalt felt	2.300	S.F.	.003	.10	.13	.23
Ridge shingles, asphalt	.090	L.F.	.002	.15	.09	.24
Slate	.090	L.F.	.004	.92	.15	1.07
Wood, shingles	.090	L.F.	.003	.36	.12	.48
Shakes	.090	L.F.	.003	.36	.12	.48
Soffit & fascia, aluminum vented, 1' overhang	.122	L.F.	.018	.40	.80	1.20
2' overhang	.122	L.F.	.020	.60	.88	1.48
Vinyl vented, 1' overhang	.122	L.F.	.016	.36	.74	1.10
2' overhang	.122	L.F.	.018	.49	.80	1.29
Wood board fascia, plywood soffit, 1' overhang	.122	L.F.	.013	.31	.55	.86
2' overhang	.122	L.F.	.019	.43	.84	1.27
Gutter, 5" box, aluminum, seamless, painted	.122	L.F.	.008	.25	.41	.66
Vinyl	.122	L.F.	.009	.16	.40	.56
Downspout 2" x 3", aluminum, one story house	.042	L.F.	.002	.07	.09	.16
Two story house	.070	L.F.	.003	.12	.15	.27
Vinyl, one story house	.042	L.F.	.002	.07	.09	.16
Two story house	.070	L.F.	.003	.12	.15	.27

System Description	QUAN.	UNIT	LABOR HOURS	COST PER S.F.		
				MAT.	INST.	TOTAL
ASPHALT, ROOF SHINGLES, CLASS A						
Shingles, inorganic class A 210-235 lb./sq. 4/12 pitch	1.230	S.F.	.019	.61	.79	1.40
Drip edge, metal, 5" wide	.100	L.F.	.002	.06	.09	.15
Building paper, #15 asphalt felt	1.300	S.F.	.002	.06	.08	.14
Soffit & fascia, white painted aluminum, 1' overhang	.080	L.F.	.012	.26	.52	.78
Rake trim, 1" x 6"	.043	L.F.	.002	.05	.08	.13
Rake trim, prime and paint	.043	L.F.	.002	.01	.07	.08
Gutter, seamless, aluminum, painted	.040	L.F.	.003	.08	.13	.21
Downspouts, painted aluminum	.020	L.F.	.001	.04	.04	.08
TOTAL		S.F.	.043	1.17	1.80	2.97
WOOD, CEDAR SHINGLES, NO. 1 PERFECTIONS, 18" LONG						
Shingles, red cedar, No. 1 perfections, 5" exp., 4/12 pitch	1.230	S.F.	.035	3.52	1.57	5.09
Drip edge, metal, 5" wide	.100	L.F.	.002	.06	.09	.15
Building paper, #15 asphalt felt	1.300	S.F.	.002	.06	.08	.14
Soffit & fascia, white painted aluminum, 1' overhang	.080	L.F.	.012	.26	.52	.78
Rake trim, 1" x 6"	.043	L.F.	.002	.05	.08	.13
Rake trim, prime and paint	.043	L.F.	.001	.01	.03	.04
Gutter, seamless, aluminum, painted	.040	L.F.	.003	.08	.13	.21
Downspouts, painted aluminum	.020	L.F.	.001	.04	.04	.08
TOTAL		S.F.	.058	4.08	2.54	6.62

The prices in these systems are based on a square foot of plan area.
All quantities have been adjusted accordingly.

Description	QUAN.	UNIT	LABOR HOURS	COST PER S.F.		
				MAT.	INST.	TOTAL

Shed Roofing Price Sheet	QUAN.	UNIT	LABOR HOURS	COST PER S.F.		
				MAT.	INST.	TOTAL
Shingles, asphalt, inorganic, class A, 210-235 lb./sq., 4/12 pitch	1.230	S.F.	.017	.56	.73	1.29
8/12 pitch	1.330	S.F.	.019	.61	.79	1.40
Laminated, multi-layered, 240-260 lb./sq. 4/12 pitch	1.230	S.F.	.021	.71	.89	1.60
8/12 pitch	1.330	S.F.	.023	.77	.97	1.74
Premium laminated, multi-layered, 260-300 lb./sq. 4/12 pitch	1.230	S.F.	.027	.92	1.15	2.07
8/12 pitch	1.330	S.F.	.030	.99	1.25	2.24
Clay tile, Spanish tile, red, 4/12 pitch	1.230	S.F.	.053	4.14	2.23	6.37
8/12 pitch	1.330	S.F.	.058	4.49	2.42	6.91
Mission tile, red, 4/12 pitch	1.230	S.F.	.083	9.80	3.49	13.29
8/12 pitch	1.330	S.F.	.090	10.60	3.78	14.38
French tile, red, 4/12 pitch	1.230	S.F.	.071	8.90	2.98	11.88
8/12 pitch	1.330	S.F.	.077	9.60	3.22	12.82
Slate, Buckingham, Virginia, black, 4/12 pitch	1.230	S.F.	.055	5.40	2.30	7.70
8/12 pitch	1.330	S.F.	.059	5.85	2.50	8.35
Vermont, black or grey, 4/12 pitch	1.230	S.F.	.055	6.05	2.30	8.35
8/12 pitch	1.330	S.F.	.059	6.55	2.50	9.05
Wood, red cedar, No.1 5X, 16" long, 5" exposure, 4/12 pitch	1.230	S.F.	.038	3.05	1.74	4.79
8/12 pitch	1.330	S.F.	.042	3.30	1.89	5.19
Fire retardant, 4/12 pitch	1.230	S.F.	.038	3.60	1.74	5.34
8/12 pitch	1.330	S.F.	.042	3.90	1.89	5.79
18" long, 6" exposure, 4/12 pitch	1.230	S.F.	.035	3.52	1.57	5.09
8/12 pitch	1.330	S.F.	.038	3.81	1.70	5.51
Fire retardant, 4/12 pitch	1.230	S.F.	.035	4.07	1.57	5.64
8/12 pitch	1.330	S.F.	.038	4.41	1.70	6.11
Resquared & rebutted, 18" long, 6" exposure, 4/12 pitch	1.230	S.F.	.032	4.26	1.45	5.71
8/12 pitch	1.330	S.F.	.035	4.62	1.57	6.19
Fire retardant, 4/12 pitch	1.230	S.F.	.032	4.81	1.45	6.26
8/12 pitch	1.330	S.F.	.035	5.20	1.57	6.77
Wood shakes, hand split, 24" long, 10" exposure, 4/12 pitch	1.230	S.F.	.038	3.01	1.74	4.75
8/12 pitch	1.330	S.F.	.042	3.26	1.89	5.15
Fire retardant, 4/12 pitch	1.230	S.F.	.038	3.56	1.74	5.30
8/12 pitch	1.330	S.F.	.042	3.86	1.89	5.75
18" long, 8" exposure, 4/12 pitch	1.230	S.F.	.048	2.53	2.17	4.70
8/12 pitch	1.330	S.F.	.052	2.74	2.35	5.09
Fire retardant, 4/12 pitch	1.230	S.F.	.048	3.08	2.17	5.25
8/12 pitch	1.330	S.F.	.052	3.34	2.35	5.69
Drip edge, metal, 5" wide	.100	L.F.	.002	.06	.09	.15
8" wide	.100	L.F.	.002	.07	.09	.16
Building paper, #15 asphalt felt	1.300	S.F.	.002	.06	.08	.14
Soffit & fascia, aluminum vented, 1' overhang	.080	L.F.	.012	.26	.52	.78
2' overhang	.080	L.F.	.013	.40	.58	.98
Vinyl vented, 1' overhang	.080	L.F.	.011	.24	.48	.72
2' overhang	.080	L.F.	.012	.32	.52	.84
Wood board fascia, plywood soffit, 1' overhang	.080	L.F.	.010	.22	.41	.63
2' overhang	.080	L.F.	.014	.30	.62	.92
Rake, trim, painted, 1" x 6"	.043	L.F.	.004	.06	.15	.21
1" x 8"	.043	L.F.	.004	.06	.15	.21
Gutter, 5" box, aluminum, seamless, painted	.040	L.F.	.003	.08	.13	.21
Vinyl	.040	L.F.	.003	.05	.13	.18
Downspout 2" x 3", aluminum, one story house	.020	L.F.	.001	.04	.04	.08
Two story house	.020	L.F.	.001	.06	.07	.13
Vinyl, one story house	.020	L.F.	.001	.04	.04	.08
Two story house	.020	L.F.	.001	.06	.07	.13

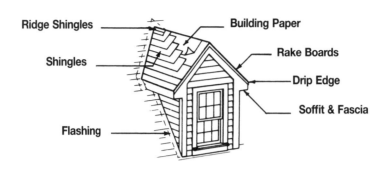

Ridge Shingles — Building Paper — Shingles — Rake Boards — Drip Edge — Soffit & Fascia — Flashing

System Description	QUAN.	UNIT	LABOR HOURS	COST PER S.F.		
				MAT.	INST.	TOTAL
ASPHALT, ROOF SHINGLES, CLASS A						
Shingles, standard inorganic class A 210-235 lb./sq	1.400	S.F.	.020	.66	.85	1.51
Drip edge, metal, 5″ wide	.220	L.F.	.004	.13	.20	.33
Building paper, #15 asphalt felt	1.500	S.F.	.002	.07	.09	.16
Ridge shingles, asphalt	.280	L.F.	.007	.46	.29	.75
Soffit & fascia, aluminum, vented	.220	L.F.	.032	.72	1.44	2.16
Flashing, aluminum, mill finish, .013″ thick	1.500	S.F.	.083	.78	3.47	4.25
TOTAL		S.F.	.148	2.82	6.34	9.16
WOOD, CEDAR, NO. 1 PERFECTIONS						
Shingles, red cedar, No.1 perfections, 18″ long, 5″ exp.	1.400	S.F.	.041	4.10	1.83	5.93
Drip edge, metal, 5″ wide	.220	L.F.	.004	.13	.20	.33
Building paper, #15 asphalt felt	1.500	S.F.	.002	.07	.09	.16
Ridge shingles, wood	.280	L.F.	.008	1.11	.36	1.47
Soffit & fascia, aluminum, vented	.220	L.F.	.032	.72	1.44	2.16
Flashing, aluminum, mill finish, .013″ thick	1.500	S.F.	.083	.78	3.47	4.25
TOTAL		S.F.	.170	6.91	7.39	14.30
SLATE, BUCKINGHAM, BLACK						
Shingles, Buckingham, Virginia, black	1.400	S.F.	.064	6.30	2.69	8.99
Drip edge, metal, 5″ wide	.220	L.F.	.004	.13	.20	.33
Building paper, #15 asphalt felt	1.500	S.F.	.002	.07	.09	.16
Ridge shingles, slate	.280	L.F.	.011	2.86	.47	3.33
Soffit & fascia, aluminum, vented	.220	L.F.	.032	.72	1.44	2.16
Flashing, copper, 16 oz.	1.500	S.F.	.104	10.13	4.38	14.51
TOTAL		S.F.	.217	20.21	9.27	29.48

The prices in these systems are based on a square foot of plan area under the dormer roof.

Description	QUAN.	UNIT	LABOR HOURS	COST PER S.F.		
				MAT.	INST.	TOTAL

Gable Dormer Roofing Price Sheet	QUAN.	UNIT	LABOR HOURS	COST PER S.F.		
				MAT.	INST.	TOTAL
Shingles, asphalt, standard, inorganic, class A, 210-235 lb./sq.	1.400	S.F.	.020	.66	.85	1.51
Laminated, multi-layered, 240-260 lb./sq.	1.400	S.F.	.025	.83	1.04	1.87
Premium laminated, multi-layered, 260-300 lb./sq.	1.400	S.F.	.032	1.07	1.34	2.41
Clay tile, Spanish tile, red	1.400	S.F.	.062	4.83	2.60	7.43
Mission tile, red	1.400	S.F.	.097	11.40	4.07	15.47
French tile, red	1.400	S.F.	.083	10.35	3.47	13.82
Slate Buckingham, Virginia, black	1.400	S.F.	.064	6.30	2.69	8.99
Vermont, black or grey	1.400	S.F.	.064	7.05	2.69	9.74
Wood, red cedar, No.1 5X, 16" long, 5" exposure	1.400	S.F.	.045	3.56	2.03	5.59
Fire retardant	1.400	S.F.	.045	4.20	2.03	6.23
18" long, No.1 perfections, 5" exposure	1.400	S.F.	.041	4.10	1.83	5.93
Fire retardant	1.400	S.F.	.041	4.74	1.83	6.57
Resquared & rebutted, 18" long, 5" exposure	1.400	S.F.	.037	4.97	1.69	6.66
Fire retardant	1.400	S.F.	.037	5.60	1.69	7.29
Shakes hand split, 24" long, 10" exposure	1.400	S.F.	.045	3.51	2.03	5.54
Fire retardant	1.400	S.F.	.045	4.15	2.03	6.18
18" long, 8" exposure	1.400	S.F.	.056	2.95	2.53	5.48
Fire retardant	1.400	S.F.	.056	3.59	2.53	6.12
Drip edge, metal, 5" wide	.220	L.F.	.004	.13	.20	.33
8" wide	.220	L.F.	.004	.15	.20	.35
Building paper, #15 asphalt felt	1.500	S.F.	.002	.07	.09	.16
Ridge shingles, asphalt	.280	L.F.	.007	.46	.29	.75
Clay	.280	L.F.	.011	3.30	.47	3.77
Slate	.280	L.F.	.011	2.86	.47	3.33
Wood	.280	L.F.	.008	1.11	.36	1.47
Soffit & fascia, aluminum, vented	.220	L.F.	.032	.72	1.44	2.16
Vinyl, vented	.220	L.F.	.029	.65	1.33	1.98
Wood, board fascia, plywood soffit	.220	L.F.	.026	.60	1.11	1.71
Flashing, aluminum, .013" thick	1.500	S.F.	.083	.78	3.47	4.25
.032" thick	1.500	S.F.	.083	2.13	3.47	5.60
.040" thick	1.500	S.F.	.083	3.18	3.47	6.65
.050" thick	1.500	S.F.	.083	3.62	3.47	7.09
Copper, 16 oz.	1.500	S.F.	.104	10.15	4.38	14.53
20 oz.	1.500	S.F.	.109	11.70	4.58	16.28
24 oz.	1.500	S.F.	.114	14.35	4.79	19.14
32 oz.	1.500	S.F.	.120	19.05	5.05	24.10

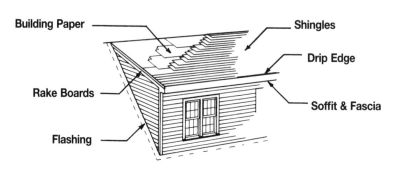

Building Paper — Shingles

Drip Edge

Rake Boards — Soffit & Fascia

Flashing

System Description	QUAN.	UNIT	LABOR HOURS	COST PER S.F.		
				MAT.	INST.	TOTAL
ASPHALT, ROOF SHINGLES, CLASS A						
Shingles, standard inorganic class A 210-235 lb./sq.	1.100	S.F.	.016	.52	.67	1.19
Drip edge, aluminum, 5″ wide	.250	L.F.	.005	.12	.23	.35
Building paper, #15 asphalt felt	1.200	S.F.	.002	.05	.07	.12
Soffit & fascia, aluminum, vented, 1′ overhang	.250	L.F.	.036	.82	1.64	2.46
Flashing, aluminum, mill finish, 0.013″ thick	.800	L.F.	.044	.42	1.85	2.27
TOTAL		S.F.	.103	1.93	4.46	6.39
WOOD, CEDAR, NO. 1 PERFECTIONS, 18″ LONG						
Shingles, wood, red cedar, #1 perfections, 5″ exposure	1.100	S.F.	.032	3.22	1.44	4.66
Drip edge, aluminum, 5″ wide	.250	L.F.	.005	.12	.23	.35
Building paper, #15 asphalt felt	1.200	S.F.	.002	.05	.07	.12
Soffit & fascia, aluminum, vented, 1′ overhang	.250	L.F.	.036	.82	1.64	2.46
Flashing, aluminum, mill finish, 0.013″ thick	.800	L.F.	.044	.42	1.85	2.27
TOTAL		S.F.	.119	4.63	5.23	9.86
SLATE, BUCKINGHAM, BLACK						
Shingles, slate, Buckingham, black	1.100	S.F.	.050	4.95	2.11	7.06
Drip edge, aluminum, 5″ wide	.250	L.F.	.005	.12	.23	.35
Building paper, #15 asphalt felt	1.200	S.F.	.002	.05	.07	.12
Soffit & fascia, aluminum, vented, 1′ overhang	.250	L.F.	.036	.82	1.64	2.46
Flashing, copper, 16 oz.	.800	L.F.	.056	5.40	2.34	7.74
TOTAL		S.F.	.149	11.34	6.39	17.73

The prices in this system are based on a square foot of plan area under the dormer roof.

Description	QUAN.	UNIT	LABOR HOURS	COST PER S.F.		
				MAT.	INST.	TOTAL

Shed Dormer Roofing Price Sheet	QUAN.	UNIT	LABOR HOURS	COST PER S.F.		
				MAT.	INST.	TOTAL
Shingles, asphalt, standard, inorganic, class A, 210-235 lb./sq.	1.100	S.F.	.016	.52	.67	1.19
Laminated, multi-layered, 240-260 lb./sq.	1.100	S.F.	.020	.65	.82	1.47
Premium laminated, multi-layered, 260-300 lb./sq.	1.100	S.F.	.025	.84	1.06	1.90
Clay tile, Spanish tile, red	1.100	S.F.	.049	3.80	2.05	5.85
Mission tile, red	1.100	S.F.	.077	8.95	3.20	12.15
French tile, red	1.100	S.F.	.065	8.15	2.73	10.88
Slate Buckingham, Virginia, black	1.100	S.F.	.050	4.95	2.11	7.06
Vermont, black or grey	1.100	S.F.	.050	5.55	2.11	7.66
Wood, red cedar, No. 1 5X, 16" long, 5" exposure	1.100	S.F.	.035	2.79	1.60	4.39
Fire retardant	1.100	S.F.	.035	3.30	1.60	4.90
18" long, No.1 perfections, 5" exposure	1.100	S.F.	.032	3.22	1.44	4.66
Fire retardant	1.100	S.F.	.032	3.73	1.44	5.17
Resquared & rebutted, 18" long, 5" exposure	1.100	S.F.	.029	3.91	1.33	5.24
Fire retardant	1.100	S.F.	.029	4.42	1.33	5.75
Shakes hand split, 24" long, 10" exposure	1.100	S.F.	.035	2.76	1.60	4.36
Fire retardant	1.100	S.F.	.035	3.27	1.60	4.87
18" long, 8" exposure	1.100	S.F.	.044	2.32	1.99	4.31
Fire retardant	1.100	S.F.	.044	2.83	1.99	4.82
Drip edge, metal, 5" wide	.250	L.F.	.005	.12	.23	.35
8" wide	.250	L.F.	.005	.17	.23	.40
Building paper, #15 asphalt felt	1.200	S.F.	.002	.05	.07	.12
Soffit & fascia, aluminum, vented	.250	L.F.	.036	.82	1.64	2.46
Vinyl, vented	.250	L.F.	.033	.74	1.51	2.25
Wood, board fascia, plywood soffit	.250	L.F.	.030	.67	1.27	1.94
Flashing, aluminum, .013" thick	.800	L.F.	.044	.42	1.85	2.27
.032" thick	.800	L.F.	.044	1.14	1.85	2.99
.040" thick	.800	L.F.	.044	1.70	1.85	3.55
.050" thick	.800	L.F.	.044	1.93	1.85	3.78
Copper, 16 oz.	.800	L.F.	.056	5.40	2.34	7.74
20 oz.	.800	L.F.	.058	6.25	2.44	8.69
24 oz.	.800	L.F.	.061	7.65	2.55	10.20
32 oz.	.800	L.F.	.064	10.15	2.68	12.83

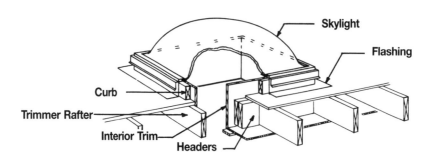

System Description	QUAN.	UNIT	LABOR HOURS	COST EACH		
				MAT.	INST.	TOTAL
SKYLIGHT, FIXED, 32″ X 32″						
Skylight, fixed bubble, insulating, 32″ x 32″	1.000	Ea.	1.422	156.44	59.38	215.82
Trimmer rafters, 2″ x 6″	28.000	L.F.	.448	16.80	20.16	36.96
Headers, 2″ x 6″	6.000	L.F.	.267	3.60	12.06	15.66
Curb, 2″ x 4″	12.000	L.F.	.154	4.68	6.96	11.64
Flashing, aluminum, .013″ thick	13.500	S.F.	.745	7.02	31.19	38.21
Trim, stock pine, 11/16″ x 2-1/2″	12.000	L.F.	.400	16.68	18.12	34.80
Trim primer coat, oil base, brushwork	12.000	L.F.	.148	.36	5.76	6.12
Trim paint, 1 coat, brushwork	12.000	L.F.	.148	.36	5.76	6.12
TOTAL		Ea.	3.732	205.94	159.39	365.33
SKYLIGHT, FIXED, 48″ X 48″						
Skylight, fixed bubble, insulating, 48″ x 48″	1.000	Ea.	1.296	320	54.24	374.24
Trimmer rafters, 2″ x 6″	28.000	L.F.	.448	16.80	20.16	36.96
Headers, 2″ x 6″	8.000	L.F.	.356	4.80	16.08	20.88
Curb, 2″ x 4″	16.000	L.F.	.205	6.24	9.28	15.52
Flashing, aluminum, .013″ thick	16.000	S.F.	.883	8.32	36.96	45.28
Trim, stock pine, 11/16″ x 2-1/2″	16.000	L.F.	.533	22.24	24.16	46.40
Trim primer coat, oil base, brushwork	16.000	L.F.	.197	.48	7.68	8.16
Trim paint, 1 coat, brushwork	16.000	L.F.	.197	.48	7.68	8.16
TOTAL		Ea.	4.115	379.36	176.24	555.60
SKYWINDOW, OPERATING, 24″ X 48″						
Skywindow, operating, thermopane glass, 24″ x 48″	1.000	Ea.	3.200	600	134	734
Trimmer rafters, 2″ x 6″	28.000	L.F.	.448	16.80	20.16	36.96
Headers, 2″ x 6″	8.000	L.F.	.267	3.60	12.06	15.66
Curb, 2″ x 4″	14.000	L.F.	.179	5.46	8.12	13.58
Flashing, aluminum, .013″ thick	14.000	S.F.	.772	7.28	32.34	39.62
Trim, stock pine, 11/16″ x 2-1/2″	14.000	L.F.	.467	19.46	21.14	40.60
Trim primer coat, oil base, brushwork	14.000	L.F.	.172	.42	6.72	7.14
Trim paint, 1 coat, brushwork	14.000	L.F.	.172	.42	6.72	7.14
TOTAL		Ea.	5.677	653.44	241.26	894.70

The prices in these systems are on a cost each basis.

Description	QUAN.	UNIT	LABOR HOURS	COST EACH		
				MAT.	INST.	TOTAL

Skylight/Skywindow Price Sheet	QUAN.	UNIT	LABOR HOURS	COST EACH		
				MAT.	INST.	TOTAL
Skylight, fixed bubble insulating, 24″ x 24″	1.000	Ea.	.800	88	33.50	121.50
32″ x 32″	1.000	Ea.	1.422	156	59.50	215.50
32″ x 48″	1.000	Ea.	.864	213	36	249
48″ x 48″	1.000	Ea.	1.296	320	54	374
Ventilating bubble insulating, 36″ x 36″	1.000	Ea.	2.667	420	112	532
52″ x 52″	1.000	Ea.	2.667	625	112	737
28″ x 52″	1.000	Ea.	3.200	490	134	624
36″ x 52″	1.000	Ea.	3.200	530	134	664
Skywindow, operating, thermopane glass, 24″ x 48″	1.000	Ea.	3.200	600	134	734
32″ x 48″	1.000	Ea.	3.556	630	149	779
Trimmer rafters, 2″ x 6″	28.000	L.F.	.448	16.80	20	36.80
2″ x 8″	28.000	L.F.	.472	23	21.50	44.50
2″ x 10″	28.000	L.F.	.711	31.50	32	63.50
Headers, 24″ window, 2″ x 6″	4.000	L.F.	.178	2.40	8.05	10.45
2″ x 8″	4.000	L.F.	.188	3.32	8.50	11.82
2″ x 10″	4.000	L.F.	.200	4.52	9.05	13.57
32″ window, 2″ x 6″	6.000	L.F.	.267	3.60	12.05	15.65
2″ x 8″	6.000	L.F.	.282	4.98	12.80	17.78
2″ x 10″	6.000	L.F.	.300	6.80	13.55	20.35
48″ window, 2″ x 6″	8.000	L.F.	.356	4.80	16.10	20.90
2″ x 8″	8.000	L.F.	.376	6.65	17.05	23.70
2″ x 10″	8.000	L.F.	.400	9.05	18.10	27.15
Curb, 2″ x 4″, skylight, 24″ x 24″	8.000	L.F.	.102	3.12	4.64	7.76
32″ x 32″	12.000	L.F.	.154	4.68	6.95	11.63
32″ x 48″	14.000	L.F.	.179	5.45	8.10	13.55
48″ x 48″	16.000	L.F.	.205	6.25	9.30	15.55
Flashing, aluminum .013″ thick, skylight, 24″ x 24″	9.000	S.F.	.497	4.68	21	25.68
32″ x 32″	13.500	S.F.	.745	7	31	38
32″ x 48″	14.000	S.F.	.772	7.30	32.50	39.80
48″ x 48″	16.000	S.F.	.883	8.30	37	45.30
Copper 16 oz., skylight, 24″ x 24″	9.000	S.F.	.626	61	26.50	87.50
32″ x 32″	13.500	S.F.	.939	91	39.50	130.50
32″ x 48″	14.000	S.F.	.974	94.50	41	135.50
48″ x 48″	16.000	S.F.	1.113	108	46.50	154.50
Trim, interior casing painted, 24″ x 24″	8.000	L.F.	.347	12.10	15.20	27.30
32″ x 32″	12.000	L.F.	.520	18.10	23	41.10
32″ x 48″	14.000	L.F.	.607	21	26.50	47.50
48″ x 48″	16.000	L.F.	.693	24	30.50	54.50

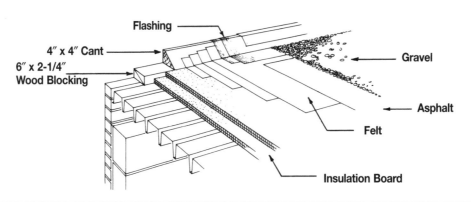

System Description	QUAN.	UNIT	LABOR HOURS	COST PER S.F.		
				MAT.	INST.	TOTAL
ASPHALT, ORGANIC, 4-PLY, INSULATED DECK						
Membrane, asphalt, 4-plies #15 felt, gravel surfacing	1.000	S.F.	.025	.96	1.21	2.17
Insulation board, 2-layers of 1-1/16″ glass fiber	2.000	S.F.	.016	2.04	.68	2.72
Wood blocking, 2″ x 6″	.040	L.F.	.004	.07	.20	.27
Treated 4″ x 4″ cant strip	.040	L.F.	.001	.07	.04	.11
Flashing, aluminum, 0.040″ thick	.050	S.F.	.003	.11	.12	.23
TOTAL		S.F.	.049	3.25	2.25	5.50
ASPHALT, INORGANIC, 3-PLY, INSULATED DECK						
Membrane, asphalt, 3-plies type IV glass felt, gravel surfacing	1.000	S.F.	.028	.90	1.33	2.23
Insulation board, 2-layers of 1-1/16″ glass fiber	2.000	S.F.	.016	2.04	.68	2.72
Wood blocking, 2″ x 6″	.040	L.F.	.004	.07	.20	.27
Treated 4″ x 4″ cant strip	.040	L.F.	.001	.07	.04	.11
Flashing, aluminum, 0.040″ thick	.050	S.F.	.003	.11	.12	.23
TOTAL		S.F.	.052	3.19	2.37	5.56
COAL TAR, ORGANIC, 4-PLY, INSULATED DECK						
Membrane, coal tar, 4-plies #15 felt, gravel surfacing	1.000	S.F.	.027	1.49	1.27	2.76
Insulation board, 2-layers of 1-1/16″ glass fiber	2.000	S.F.	.016	2.04	.68	2.72
Wood blocking, 2″ x 6″	.040	L.F.	.004	.07	.20	.27
Treated 4″ x 4″ cant strip	.040	L.F.	.001	.07	.04	.11
Flashing, aluminum, 0.040″ thick	.050	S.F.	.003	.11	.12	.23
TOTAL		S.F.	.051	3.78	2.31	6.09
COAL TAR, INORGANIC, 3-PLY, INSULATED DECK						
Membrane, coal tar, 3-plies type IV glass felt, gravel surfacing	1.000	S.F.	.029	1.22	1.40	2.62
Insulation board, 2-layers of 1-1/16″ glass fiber	2.000	S.F.	.016	2.04	.68	2.72
Wood blocking, 2″ x 6″	.040	L.F.	.004	.07	.20	.27
Treated 4″ x 4″ cant strip	.040	L.F.	.001	.07	.04	.11
Flashing, aluminum, 0.040″ thick	.050	S.F.	.003	.11	.12	.23
TOTAL		S.F.	.053	3.51	2.44	5.95

Built-Up Roofing Price Sheet	QUAN.	UNIT	LABOR HOURS	COST PER S.F.		
				MAT.	INST.	TOTAL
Membrane, asphalt, 4-plies #15 organic felt, gravel surfacing	1.000	S.F.	.025	.96	1.21	2.17
Asphalt base sheet & 3-plies #15 asphalt felt	1.000	S.F.	.025	.74	1.21	1.95
3-plies type IV glass fiber felt	1.000	S.F.	.028	.90	1.33	2.23
4-plies type IV glass fiber felt	1.000	S.F.	.028	1.10	1.33	2.43
Coal tar, 4-plies #15 organic felt, gravel surfacing	1.000	S.F.	.027			
4-plies tarred felt	1.000	S.F.	.027	1.49	1.27	2.76
3-plies type IV glass fiber felt	1.000	S.F.	.029	1.22	1.40	2.62
4-plies type IV glass fiber felt	1.000	S.F.	.027	1.69	1.27	2.96
Roll, asphalt, 1-ply #15 organic felt, 2-plies mineral surfaced	1.000	S.F.	.021	.59	.99	1.58
3-plies type IV glass fiber, 1-ply mineral surfaced	1.000	S.F.	.022	.91	1.06	1.97
Insulation boards, glass fiber, 1-1/16" thick	1.000	S.F.	.008	1.02	.34	1.36
2-1/16" thick	1.000	S.F.	.010	1.49	.42	1.91
2-7/16" thick	1.000	S.F.	.010	1.71	.42	2.13
Expanded perlite, 1" thick	1.000	S.F.	.010	.50	.42	.92
1-1/2" thick	1.000	S.F.	.010	.52	.42	.94
2" thick	1.000	S.F.	.011	.87	.48	1.35
Fiberboard, 1" thick	1.000	S.F.	.010	.46	.42	.88
1-1/2" thick	1.000	S.F.	.010	.70	.42	1.12
2" thick	1.000	S.F.	.010	.94	.42	1.36
Extruded polystyrene, 15 PSI compressive strength, 2" thick R10	1.000	S.F.	.006	.68	.27	.95
3" thick R15	1.000	S.F.	.008	1.40	.34	1.74
4" thick R20	1.000	S.F.	.008	1.80	.34	2.14
Tapered for drainage	1.000	S.F.	.005	.58	.22	.80
40 PSI compressive strength, 1" thick R5	1.000	S.F.	.005	.56	.22	.78
2" thick R10	1.000	S.F.	.006	1.06	.27	1.33
3" thick R15	1.000	S.F.	.008	1.54	.34	1.88
4" thick R20	1.000	S.F.	.008	2.07	.34	2.41
Fiberboard high density, 1/2" thick R1.3	1.000	S.F.	.008	.24	.34	.58
1" thick R2.5	1.000	S.F.	.010	.48	.42	.90
1 1/2" thick R3.8	1.000	S.F.	.010	.73	.42	1.15
Polyisocyanurate, 1 1/2" thick R10.87	1.000	S.F.	.006	.69	.27	.96
2" thick R14.29	1.000	S.F.	.007	.91	.30	1.21
3 1/2" thick R25	1.000	S.F.	.008	2.12	.34	2.46
Tapered for drainage	1.000	S.F.	.006	2.12	.24	2.36
Expanded polystyrene, 1" thick	1.000	S.F.	.005	.34	.22	.56
2" thick R10	1.000	S.F.	.006	.68	.27	.95
3" thick	1.000	S.F.	.006	1	.27	1.27
Wood blocking, treated, 6" x 2" & 4" x 4" cant	.040	L.F.	.002	.10	.11	.21
6" x 4-1/2" & 4" x 4" cant	.040	L.F.	.005	.16	.24	.40
6" x 5" & 4" x 4" cant	.040	L.F.	.007	.20	.30	.50
Flashing, aluminum, 0.019" thick	.050	S.F.	.003	.05	.12	.17
0.032" thick	.050	S.F.	.003	.07	.12	.19
0.040" thick	.050	S.F.	.003	.11	.12	.23
Copper sheets, 16 oz., under 500 lbs.	.050	S.F.	.003	.34	.15	.49
Over 500 lbs.	.050	S.F.	.003	.40	.11	.51
20 oz., under 500 lbs.	.050	S.F.	.004	.39	.15	.54
Over 500 lbs.	.050	S.F.	.003	.40	.12	.52
Stainless steel, 32 gauge	.050	S.F.	.003	.19	.11	.30
28 gauge	.050	S.F.	.003	.23	.11	.34
26 gauge	.050	S.F.	.003	.28	.11	.39
24 gauge	.050	S.F.	.003	.36	.11	.47

Division 6
Interiors

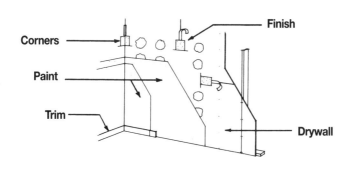

System Description	QUAN.	UNIT	LABOR HOURS	COST PER S.F.		
				MAT.	INST.	TOTAL
1/2" DRYWALL, TAPED & FINISHED						
Gypsum wallboard, 1/2" thick, standard	1.000	S.F.	.008	.28	.36	.64
Finish, taped & finished joints	1.000	S.F.	.008	.05	.36	.41
Corners, taped & finished, 32 L.F. per 12' x 12' room	.083	L.F.	.002	.01	.07	.08
Painting, primer & 2 coats	1.000	S.F.	.011	.19	.41	.60
Paint trim, to 6" wide, primer + 1 coat enamel	.125	L.F.	.001	.02	.05	.07
Trim, baseboard	.125	L.F.	.005	.33	.23	.56
TOTAL		S.F.	.035	.88	1.48	2.36
THINCOAT, SKIM-COAT, ON 1/2" BACKER DRYWALL						
Gypsum wallboard, 1/2" thick, thincoat backer	1.000	S.F.	.008	.28	.36	.64
Thincoat plaster	1.000	S.F.	.011	.09	.47	.56
Corners, taped & finished, 32 L.F. per 12' x 12' room	.083	L.F.	.002	.01	.07	.08
Painting, primer & 2 coats	1.000	S.F.	.011	.19	.41	.60
Paint trim, to 6" wide, primer + 1 coat enamel	.125	L.F.	.001	.02	.05	.07
Trim, baseboard	.125	L.F.	.005	.33	.23	.56
TOTAL		S.F.	.038	.92	1.59	2.51
5/8" DRYWALL, TAPED & FINISHED						
Gypsum wallboard, 5/8" thick, standard	1.000	S.F.	.008	.31	.36	.67
Finish, taped & finished joints	1.000	S.F.	.008	.05	.36	.41
Corners, taped & finished, 32 L.F. per 12' x 12' room	.083	L.F.	.002	.01	.07	.08
Painting, primer & 2 coats	1.000	S.F.	.011	.19	.41	.60
Trim, baseboard	.125	L.F.	.005	.33	.23	.56
Paint trim, to 6" wide, primer + 1 coat enamel	.125	L.F.	.001	.02	.05	.07
TOTAL		S.F.	.035	.91	1.48	2.39

The costs in this system are based on a square foot of wall.
Do not deduct for openings.

Description	QUAN.	UNIT	LABOR HOURS	COST PER S.F.		
				MAT.	INST.	TOTAL

Drywall & Thincoat Wall Price Sheet	QUAN.	UNIT	LABOR HOURS	COST PER S.F.		
				MAT.	INST.	TOTAL
Gypsum wallboard, 1/2" thick, standard	1.000	S.F.	.008	.28	.36	.64
Fire resistant	1.000	S.F.	.008	.29	.36	.65
Water resistant	1.000	S.F.	.008	.39	.36	.75
5/8" thick, standard	1.000	S.F.	.008	.31	.36	.67
Fire resistant	1.000	S.F.	.008	.33	.36	.69
Water resistant	1.000	S.F.	.008	.37	.36	.73
Gypsum wallboard backer for thincoat system, 1/2" thick	1.000	S.F.	.008	.28	.36	.64
5/8" thick	1.000	S.F.	.008	.31	.36	.67
Gypsum wallboard, taped & finished	1.000	S.F.	.008	.05	.36	.41
Texture spray	1.000	S.F.	.010	.06	.40	.46
Thincoat plaster, including tape	1.000	S.F.	.011	.09	.47	.56
Gypsum wallboard corners, taped & finished, 32 L.F. per 4' x 4' room	.250	L.F.	.004	.03	.19	.22
6' x 6' room	.110	L.F.	.002	.01	.08	.09
10' x 10' room	.100	L.F.	.001	.01	.08	.09
12' x 12' room	.083	L.F.	.001	.01	.06	.07
16' x 16' room	.063	L.F.	.001	.01	.05	.06
Thincoat system, 32 L.F. per 4' x 4' room	.250	L.F.	.003	.02	.12	.14
6' x 6' room	.110	L.F.	.001	.01	.05	.06
10' x 10' room	.100	L.F.	.001	.01	.04	.05
12' x 12' room	.083	L.F.	.001	.01	.04	.05
16' x 16' room	.063	L.F.	.001	.01	.03	.04
Painting, primer, & 1 coat	1.000	S.F.	.008	.12	.32	.44
& 2 coats	1.000	S.F.	.011	.19	.41	.60
Wallpaper, $7/double roll	1.000	S.F.	.013	.36	.49	.85
$17/double roll	1.000	S.F.	.015	.64	.59	1.23
$40/double roll	1.000	S.F.	.018	2.46	.72	3.18
Wallcovering, medium weight vinyl		S.F.	.017	.81	.66	1.47
Tile, ceramic adhesive thin set, 4 1/4" x 4 1/4" tiles	1.000	S.F.	.084	2.44	3.14	5.58
6" x 6" tiles	1.000	S.F.	.080	3.33	2.98	6.31
Pregrouted sheets	1.000	S.F.	.067	5.05	2.48	7.53
Trim, painted or stained, baseboard	.125	L.F.	.006	.35	.28	.63
Base shoe	.125	L.F.	.005	.18	.24	.42
Chair rail	.125	L.F.	.005	.21	.22	.43
Cornice molding	.125	L.F.	.004	.15	.19	.34
Cove base, vinyl	.125	L.F.	.003	.10	.13	.23
Paneling, not including furring or trim						
Plywood, prefinished, 1/4" thick, 4' x 8' sheets, vert. grooves						
Birch faced, minimum	1.000	S.F.	.032	.96	1.45	2.41
Average	1.000	S.F.	.038	1.45	1.72	3.17
Maximum	1.000	S.F.	.046	2.12	2.07	4.19
Mahogany, African	1.000	S.F.	.040	2.71	1.81	4.52
Philippine (lauan)	1.000	S.F.	.032	1.17	1.45	2.62
Oak or cherry, minimum	1.000	S.F.	.032	2.27	1.45	3.72
Maximum	1.000	S.F.	.040	3.48	1.81	5.29
Rosewood	1.000	S.F.	.050	4.94	2.26	7.20
Teak	1.000	S.F.	.040	3.48	1.81	5.29
Chestnut	1.000	S.F.	.043	5.15	1.93	7.08
Pecan	1.000	S.F.	.040	2.22	1.81	4.03
Walnut, minimum	1.000	S.F.	.032	2.97	1.45	4.42
Maximum	1.000	S.F.	.040	5.60	1.81	7.41

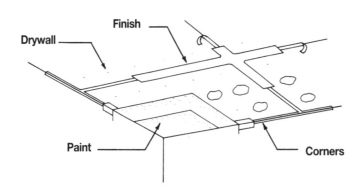

System Description	QUAN.	UNIT	LABOR HOURS	COST PER S.F.		
				MAT.	INST.	TOTAL
1/2″ SHEETROCK®, TAPED & FINISHED						
Gypsum wallboard, 1/2″ thick, standard	1.000	S.F.	.008	.28	.36	.64
Finish, taped & finished	1.000	S.F.	.008	.05	.36	.41
Corners, taped & finished, 12′ x 12′ room	.333	L.F.	.006	.03	.25	.28
Paint, primer & 2 coats	1.000	S.F.	.011	.19	.41	.60
TOTAL		S.F.	.033	.55	1.38	1.93
THINCOAT, SKIM COAT ON 1/2″ GYPSUM WALLBOARD						
Gypsum wallboard, 1/2″ thick, thincoat backer	1.000	S.F.	.008	.28	.36	.64
Thincoat plaster	1.000	S.F.	.011	.09	.47	.56
Corners, taped & finished, 12′ x 12′ room	.333	L.F.	.006	.03	.25	.28
Paint, primer & 2 coats	1.000	S.F.	.011	.19	.41	.60
TOTAL		S.F.	.036	.59	1.49	2.08
WATER-RESISTANT GYPSUM WALLBOARD, 1/2″ THICK, TAPED & FINISHED						
Gypsum wallboard, 1/2″ thick, water-resistant	1.000	S.F.	.008	.39	.36	.75
Finish, taped & finished	1.000	S.F.	.008	.05	.36	.41
Corners, taped & finished, 12′ x 12′ room	.333	L.F.	.006	.03	.25	.28
Paint, primer & 2 coats	1.000	S.F.	.011	.19	.41	.60
TOTAL		S.F.	.033	.66	1.38	2.04
5/8″ GYPSUM WALLBOARD, TAPED & FINISHED						
Gypsum wallboard, 5/8″ thick, standard	1.000	S.F.	.008	.31	.36	.67
Finish, taped & finished	1.000	S.F.	.008	.05	.36	.41
Corners, taped & finished, 12′ x 12′ room	.333	L.F.	.006	.03	.25	.28
Paint, primer & 2 coats	1.000	S.F.	.011	.19	.41	.60
TOTAL		S.F.	.033	.58	1.38	1.96

The costs in this system are based on a square foot of ceiling.

Description	QUAN.	UNIT	LABOR HOURS	COST PER S.F.		
				MAT.	INST.	TOTAL

Drywall & Thincoat Ceilings	QUAN.	UNIT	LABOR HOURS	COST PER S.F.		
				MAT.	INST.	TOTAL
Gypsum wallboard ceilings, 1/2" thick, standard	1.000	S.F.	.008	.28	.36	.64
Fire resistant	1.000	S.F.	.008	.29	.36	.65
Water resistant	1.000	S.F.	.008	.39	.36	.75
5/8" thick, standard	1.000	S.F.	.008	.31	.36	.67
Fire resistant	1.000	S.F.	.008	.33	.36	.69
Water resistant	1.000	S.F.	.008	.37	.36	.73
Gypsum wallboard backer for thincoat ceiling system, 1/2" thick	1.000	S.F.	.016	.57	.72	1.29
5/8" thick	1.000	S.F.	.016	.60	.72	1.32
Gypsum wallboard ceilings, taped & finished	1.000	S.F.	.008	.05	.36	.41
Texture spray	1.000	S.F.	.010	.06	.40	.46
Thincoat plaster	1.000	S.F.	.011	.09	.47	.56
Corners taped & finished, 4' x 4' room	1.000	L.F.	.015	.10	.76	.86
6' x 6' room	.667	L.F.	.010	.07	.51	.58
10' x 10' room	.400	L.F.	.006	.04	.30	.34
12' x 12' room	.333	L.F.	.005	.03	.25	.28
16' x 16' room	.250	L.F.	.003	.02	.14	.16
Thincoat system, 4' x 4' room	1.000	L.F.	.011	.09	.47	.56
6' x 6' room	.667	L.F.	.007	.06	.32	.38
10' x 10' room	.400	L.F.	.004	.04	.19	.23
12' x 12' room	.333	L.F.	.004	.03	.15	.18
16' x 16' room	.250	L.F.	.002	.02	.09	.11
Painting, primer & 1 coat	1.000	S.F.	.008	.12	.32	.44
& 2 coats	1.000	S.F.	.011	.19	.41	.60
Wallpaper, double roll, solid pattern, avg. workmanship	1.000	S.F.	.013	.36	.49	.85
Basic pattern, avg. workmanship	1.000	S.F.	.015	.64	.59	1.23
Basic pattern, quality workmanship	1.000	S.F.	.018	2.46	.72	3.18
Tile, ceramic adhesive thin set, 4 1/4" x 4 1/4" tiles	1.000	S.F.	.084	2.44	3.14	5.58
6" x 6" tiles	1.000	S.F.	.080	3.33	2.98	6.31
Pregrouted sheets	1.000	S.F.	.067	5.05	2.48	7.53

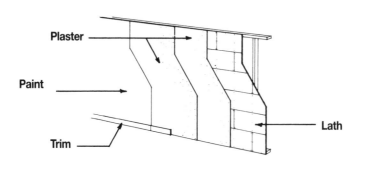

System Description	QUAN.	UNIT	LABOR HOURS	COST PER S.F.		
				MAT.	INST.	TOTAL
PLASTER ON GYPSUM LATH						
Plaster, gypsum or perlite, 2 coats	1.000	S.F.	.053	.44	2.24	2.68
Lath, 3/8″ gypsum	1.000	S.F.	.010	.61	.41	1.02
Corners, expanded metal, 32 L.F. per 12′ x 12′ room	.083	L.F.	.002	.01	.07	.08
Painting, primer & 2 coats	1.000	S.F.	.011	.19	.41	.60
Paint trim, to 6″ wide, primer + 1 coat enamel	.125	L.F.	.001	.02	.05	.07
Trim, baseboard	.125	L.F.	.005	.33	.23	.56
TOTAL		S.F.	.082	1.60	3.41	5.01
PLASTER ON METAL LATH						
Plaster, gypsum or perlite, 2 coats	1.000	S.F.	.053	.44	2.24	2.68
Lath, 2.5 Lb. diamond, metal	1.000	S.F.	.010	.37	.41	.78
Corners, expanded metal, 32 L.F. per 12′ x 12′ room	.083	L.F.	.002	.01	.07	.08
Painting, primer & 2 coats	1.000	S.F.	.011	.19	.41	.60
Paint trim, to 6″ wide, primer + 1 coat enamel	.125	L.F.	.001	.02	.05	.07
Trim, baseboard	.125	L.F.	.005	.33	.23	.56
TOTAL		S.F.	.082	1.36	3.41	4.77
STUCCO ON METAL LATH						
Stucco, 2 coats	1.000	S.F.	.041	.25	1.72	1.97
Lath, 2.5 Lb. diamond, metal	1.000	S.F.	.010	.37	.41	.78
Corners, expanded metal, 32 L.F. per 12′ x 12′ room	.083	L.F.	.002	.01	.07	.08
Painting, primer & 2 coats	1.000	S.F.	.011	.19	.41	.60
Paint trim, to 6″ wide, primer + 1 coat enamel	.125	L.F.	.001	.02	.05	.07
Trim, baseboard	.125	L.F.	.005	.33	.23	.56
TOTAL		S.F.	.070	1.17	2.89	4.06

The costs in these systems are based on a per square foot of wall area.
Do not deduct for openings.

Description	QUAN.	UNIT	LABOR HOURS	COST PER S.F.		
				MAT.	INST.	TOTAL

Plaster & Stucco Wall Price Sheet	QUAN.	UNIT	LABOR HOURS	COST PER S.F.		
				MAT.	INST.	TOTAL
Plaster, gypsum or perlite, 2 coats	1.000	S.F.	.053	.44	2.24	2.68
3 coats	1.000	S.F.	.065	.63	2.71	3.34
Lath, gypsum, standard, 3/8" thick	1.000	S.F.	.010	.61	.41	1.02
Fire resistant, 3/8" thick	1.000	S.F.	.013	.33	.50	.83
1/2" thick	1.000	S.F.	.014	.37	.54	.91
Metal, diamond, 2.5 Lb.	1.000	S.F.	.010	.37	.41	.78
3.4 Lb.	1.000	S.F.	.012	.42	.47	.89
Rib, 2.75 Lb.	1.000	S.F.	.012	.33	.47	.80
3.4 Lb.	1.000	S.F.	.013	.51	.50	1.01
Corners, expanded metal, 32 L.F. per 4' x 4' room	.250	L.F.	.005	.03	.23	.26
6' x 6' room	.110	L.F.	.002	.01	.10	.11
10' x 10' room	.100	L.F.	.002	.01	.09	.10
12' x 12' room	.083	L.F.	.002	.01	.07	.08
16' x 16' room	.063	L.F.	.001	.01	.06	.07
Painting, primer & 1 coats	1.000	S.F.	.008	.12	.32	.44
Primer & 2 coats	1.000	S.F.	.011	.19	.41	.60
Wallpaper, low price double roll	1.000	S.F.	.013	.36	.49	.85
Medium price double roll	1.000	S.F.	.015	.64	.59	1.23
High price double roll	1.000	S.F.	.018	2.46	.72	3.18
Tile, ceramic thin set, 4-1/4" x 4-1/4" tiles	1.000	S.F.	.084	2.44	3.14	5.58
6" x 6" tiles	1.000	S.F.	.080	3.33	2.98	6.31
Pregrouted sheets	1.000	S.F.	.067	5.05	2.48	7.53
Trim, painted or stained, baseboard	.125	L.F.	.006	.35	.28	.63
Base shoe	.125	L.F.	.005	.18	.24	.42
Chair rail	.125	L.F.	.005	.21	.22	.43
Cornice molding	.125	L.F.	.004	.15	.19	.34
Cove base, vinyl	.125	L.F.	.003	.10	.13	.23
Paneling not including furring or trim						
Plywood, prefinished, 1/4" thick, 4' x 8' sheets, vert. grooves						
Birch faced, minimum	1.000	S.F.	.032	.96	1.45	2.41
Average	1.000	S.F.	.038	1.45	1.72	3.17
Maximum	1.000	S.F.	.046	2.12	2.07	4.19
Mahogany, African	1.000	S.F.	.040	2.71	1.81	4.52
Philippine (lauan)	1.000	S.F.	.032	1.17	1.45	2.62
Oak or cherry, minimum	1.000	S.F.	.032	2.27	1.45	3.72
Maximum	1.000	S.F.	.040	3.48	1.81	5.29
Rosewood	1.000	S.F.	.050	4.94	2.26	7.20
Teak	1.000	S.F.	.040	3.48	1.81	5.29
Chestnut	1.000	S.F.	.043	5.15	1.93	7.08
Pecan	1.000	S.F.	.040	2.22	1.81	4.03
Walnut, minimum	1.000	S.F.	.032	2.97	1.45	4.42
Maximum	1.000	S.F.	.040	5.60	1.81	7.41

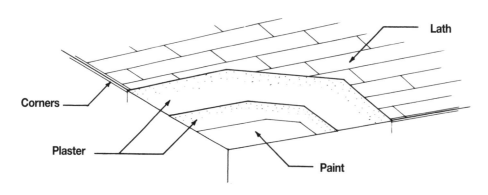

System Description	QUAN.	UNIT	LABOR HOURS	COST PER S.F.		
				MAT.	INST.	TOTAL
PLASTER ON GYPSUM LATH						
Plaster, gypsum or perlite, 2 coats	1.000	S.F.	.061	.44	2.55	2.99
Gypsum lath, plain or perforated, nailed, 3/8" thick	1.000	S.F.	.010	.61	.41	1.02
Gypsum lath, ceiling installation adder	1.000	S.F.	.004		.16	.16
Corners, expanded metal, 12' x 12' room	.330	L.F.	.007	.04	.30	.34
Painting, primer & 2 coats	1.000	S.F.	.011	.19	.41	.60
TOTAL		S.F.	.093	1.28	3.83	5.11
PLASTER ON METAL LATH						
Plaster, gypsum or perlite, 2 coats	1.000	S.F.	.061	.44	2.55	2.99
Lath, 2.5 Lb. diamond, metal	1.000	S.F.	.012	.37	.47	.84
Corners, expanded metal, 12' x 12' room	.330	L.F.	.007	.04	.30	.34
Painting, primer & 2 coats	1.000	S.F.	.011	.19	.41	.60
TOTAL		S.F.	.091	1.04	3.73	4.77
STUCCO ON GYPSUM LATH						
Stucco, 2 coats	1.000	S.F.	.041	.25	1.72	1.97
Gypsum lath, plain or perforated, nailed, 3/8" thick	1.000	S.F.	.010	.61	.41	1.02
Gypsum lath, ceiling installation adder	1.000	S.F.	.004		.16	.16
Corners, expanded metal, 12' x 12' room	.330	L.F.	.007	.04	.30	.34
Painting, primer & 2 coats	1.000	S.F.	.011	.19	.41	.60
TOTAL		S.F.	.073	1.09	3	4.09
STUCCO ON METAL LATH						
Stucco, 2 coats	1.000	S.F.	.041	.25	1.72	1.97
Lath, 2.5 Lb. diamond, metal	1.000	S.F.	.012	.37	.47	.84
Corners, expanded metal, 12' x 12' room	.330	L.F.	.007	.04	.30	.34
Painting, primer & 2 coats	1.000	S.F.	.011	.19	.41	.60
TOTAL		S.F.	.071	.85	2.90	3.75

The costs in these systems are based on a square foot of ceiling area.

Description	QUAN.	UNIT	LABOR HOURS	COST PER S.F.		
				MAT.	INST.	TOTAL

Plaster & Stucco Ceiling Price Sheet	QUAN.	UNIT	LABOR HOURS	COST PER S.F.		
				MAT.	INST.	TOTAL
Plaster, gypsum or perlite, 2 coats	1.000	S.F.	.061	.44	2.55	2.99
3 coats	1.000	S.F.	.065	.63	2.71	3.34
Lath, gypsum, standard, 3/8″ thick	1.000	S.F.	.014	.61	.57	1.18
1/2″ thick	1.000	S.F.	.015	.68	.60	1.28
Fire resistant, 3/8″ thick	1.000	S.F.	.017	.33	.66	.99
1/2″ thick	1.000	S.F.	.018	.37	.70	1.07
Metal, diamond, 2.5 Lb.	1.000	S.F.	.012	.37	.47	.84
3.4 Lb.	1.000	S.F.	.015	.42	.59	1.01
Rib, 2.75 Lb.	1.000	S.F.	.012	.33	.47	.80
3.4 Lb.	1.000	S.F.	.013	.51	.50	1.01
Corners expanded metal, 4′ x 4′ room	1.000	L.F.	.020	.13	.90	1.03
6′ x 6′ room	.667	L.F.	.013	.09	.60	.69
10′ x 10′ room	.400	L.F.	.008	.05	.36	.41
12′ x 12′ room	.333	L.F.	.007	.04	.30	.34
16′ x 16′ room	.250	L.F.	.004	.02	.17	.19
Painting, primer & 1 coat	1.000	S.F.	.008	.12	.32	.44
Primer & 2 coats	1.000	S.F.	.011	.19	.41	.60

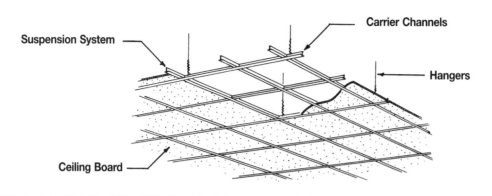

Carrier Channels

Suspension System

Hangers

Ceiling Board

System Description	QUAN.	UNIT	LABOR HOURS	COST PER S.F.		
				MAT.	INST.	TOTAL
2' X 2' GRID, FILM FACED FIBERGLASS, 5/8" THICK						
Suspension system, 2' x 2' grid, T bar	1.000	S.F.	.012	.72	.56	1.28
Ceiling board, film faced fiberglass, 5/8" thick	1.000	S.F.	.013	.67	.58	1.25
Carrier channels, 1-1/2" x 3/4"	1.000	S.F.	.017	.14	.77	.91
Hangers, #12 wire	1.000	S.F.	.002	.08	.08	.16
TOTAL		S.F.	.044	1.61	1.99	3.60
2' X 4' GRID, FILM FACED FIBERGLASS, 5/8" THICK						
Suspension system, 2' x 4' grid, T bar	1.000	S.F.	.010	.58	.45	1.03
Ceiling board, film faced fiberglass, 5/8" thick	1.000	S.F.	.013	.67	.58	1.25
Carrier channels, 1-1/2" x 3/4"	1.000	S.F.	.017	.14	.77	.91
Hangers, #12 wire	1.000	S.F.	.002	.08	.08	.16
TOTAL		S.F.	.042	1.47	1.88	3.35
2' X 2' GRID, MINERAL FIBER, REVEAL EDGE, 1" THICK						
Suspension system, 2' x 2' grid, T bar	1.000	S.F.	.012	.72	.56	1.28
Ceiling board, mineral fiber, reveal edge, 1" thick	1.000	S.F.	.013	1.47	.60	2.07
Carrier channels, 1-1/2" x 3/4"	1.000	S.F.	.017	.14	.77	.91
Hangers, #12 wire	1.000	S.F.	.002	.08	.08	.16
TOTAL		S.F.	.044	2.41	2.01	4.42
2' X 4' GRID, MINERAL FIBER, REVEAL EDGE, 1" THICK						
Suspension system, 2' x 4' grid, T bar	1.000	S.F.	.010	.58	.45	1.03
Ceiling board, mineral fiber, reveal edge, 1" thick	1.000	S.F.	.013	1.47	.60	2.07
Carrier channels, 1-1/2" x 3/4"	1.000	S.F.	.017	.14	.77	.91
Hangers, #12 wire	1.000	S.F.	.002	.08	.08	.16
TOTAL		S.F.	.042	2.27	1.90	4.17

Description	QUAN.	UNIT	LABOR HOURS	COST PER S.F.		
				MAT.	INST.	TOTAL

Suspended Ceiling Price Sheet

	QUAN.	UNIT	LABOR HOURS	COST PER S.F. MAT.	COST PER S.F. INST.	COST PER S.F. TOTAL
Suspension systems, T bar, 2' x 2' grid	1.000	S.F.	.012	.72	.56	1.28
2' x 4' grid	1.000	S.F.	.010	.58	.45	1.03
Concealed Z bar, 12" module	1.000	S.F.	.015	.68	.70	1.38
Ceiling boards, fiberglass, film faced, 2' x 2' or 2' x 4', 5/8" thick	1.000	S.F.	.013	.67	.58	1.25
3/4" thick	1.000	S.F.	.013	1.53	.60	2.13
3" thick thermal R11	1.000	S.F.	.018	1.61	.80	2.41
Glass cloth faced, 3/4" thick	1.000	S.F.	.016	1.91	.72	2.63
1" thick	1.000	S.F.	.016	2.12	.75	2.87
1-1/2" thick, nubby face	1.000	S.F.	.017	2.78	.76	3.54
Mineral fiber boards, 5/8" thick, aluminum face 2' x 2'	1.000	S.F.	.013	1.80	.60	2.40
2' x 4'	1.000	S.F.	.012	1.22	.56	1.78
Standard faced, 2' x 2' or 2' x 4'	1.000	S.F.	.012	.75	.54	1.29
Plastic coated face, 2' x 2' or 2' x 4'	1.000	S.F.	.020	1.18	.90	2.08
Fire rated, 2 hour rating, 5/8" thick	1.000	S.F.	.012	1.12	.54	1.66
Tegular edge, 2' x 2' or 2' x 4', 5/8" thick, fine textured	1.000	S.F.	.013	1.39	.77	2.16
Rough textured	1.000	S.F.	.015	1.82	.77	2.59
3/4" thick, fine textured	1.000	S.F.	.016	1.99	.80	2.79
Rough textured	1.000	S.F.	.018	2.24	.80	3.04
Luminous panels, prismatic, acrylic	1.000	S.F.	.020	2.12	.90	3.02
Polystyrene	1.000	S.F.	.020	1.09	.90	1.99
Flat or ribbed, acrylic	1.000	S.F.	.020	3.70	.90	4.60
Polystyrene	1.000	S.F.	.020	2.53	.90	3.43
Drop pan, white, acrylic	1.000	S.F.	.020	5.40	.90	6.30
Polystyrene	1.000	S.F.	.020	4.52	.90	5.42
Carrier channels, 4'-0" on center, 3/4" x 1-1/2"	1.000	S.F.	.017	.14	.77	.91
1-1/2" x 3-1/2"	1.000	S.F.	.017	.35	.77	1.12
Hangers, #12 wire	1.000	S.F.	.002	.08	.08	.16

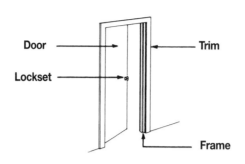

System Description	QUAN.	UNIT	LABOR HOURS	COST EACH		
				MAT.	INST.	TOTAL
LAUAN, FLUSH DOOR, HOLLOW CORE						
Door, flush, lauan, hollow core, 2'-8" wide x 6'-8" high	1.000	Ea.	.889	36	40	76
Frame, pine, 4-5/8" jamb	17.000	L.F.	.725	118.15	32.81	150.96
Trim, stock pine, 11/16" x 2-1/2"	34.000	L.F.	1.133	47.26	51.34	98.60
Paint trim, to 6" wide, primer + 1 coat enamel	34.000	L.F.	.340	4.08	13.26	17.34
Butt hinges, chrome, 3-1/2" x 3-1/2"	1.500	Pr.		40.50		40.50
Lockset, passage	1.000	Ea.	.500	17.10	22.50	39.60
Prime door & frame, oil, brushwork	2.000	Face	1.600	4.86	63	67.86
Paint door and frame, oil, 2 coats	2.000	Face	2.667	8.54	105	113.54
TOTAL		Ea.	7.854	276.49	327.91	604.40
BIRCH, FLUSH DOOR, HOLLOW CORE						
Door, flush, birch, hollow core, 2'-8" wide x 6'-8" high	1.000	Ea.	.889	51.50	40	91.50
Frame, pine, 4-5/8" jamb	17.000	L.F.	.725	118.15	32.81	150.96
Trim, stock pine, 11/16" x 2-1/2"	34.000	L.F.	1.133	47.26	51.34	98.60
Butt hinges, chrome, 3-1/2" x 3-1/2"	1.500	Pr.		40.50		40.50
Lockset, passage	1.000	Ea.	.500	17.10	22.50	39.60
Prime door & frame, oil, brushwork	2.000	Face	1.600	4.86	63	67.86
Paint door and frame, oil, 2 coats	2.000	Face	2.667	8.54	105	113.54
TOTAL		Ea.	7.514	287.91	314.65	602.56
RAISED PANEL, SOLID, PINE DOOR						
Door, pine, raised panel, 2'-8" wide x 6'-8" high	1.000	Ea.	.889	170	40	210
Frame, pine, 4-5/8" jamb	17.000	L.F.	.725	118.15	32.81	150.96
Trim, stock pine, 11/16" x 2-1/2"	34.000	L.F.	1.133	47.26	51.34	98.60
Butt hinges, bronze, 3-1/2" x 3-1/2"	1.500	Pr.		45.75		45.75
Lockset, passage	1.000	Ea.	.500	17.10	22.50	39.60
Prime door & frame, oil, brushwork	2.000		1.600	4.86	63	67.86
Paint door and frame, oil, 2 coats	2.000		2.667	8.54	105	113.54
TOTAL		Ea.	7.514	411.66	314.65	726.31

The costs in these systems are based on a cost per each door.

Description	QUAN.	UNIT	LABOR HOURS	COST EACH		
				MAT.	INST.	TOTAL

Interior Door Price Sheet	QUAN.	UNIT	LABOR HOURS	COST EACH		
				MAT.	INST.	TOTAL
Door, hollow core, lauan 1-3/8" thick, 6'-8" high x 1'-6" wide	1.000	Ea.	.889	32	40	72
2'-0" wide	1.000	Ea.	.889	30.50	40	70.50
2'-6" wide	1.000	Ea.	.889	34	40	74
2'-8" wide	1.000	Ea.	.889	36	40	76
3'-0" wide	1.000	Ea.	.941	37.50	42.50	80
Birch 1-3/8" thick, 6'-8" high x 1'-6" wide	1.000	Ea.	.889	40.50	40	80.50
2'-0" wide	1.000	Ea.	.889	44.50	40	84.50
2'-6" wide	1.000	Ea.	.889	49.50	40	89.50
2'-8" wide	1.000	Ea.	.889	51.50	40	91.50
3'-0" wide	1.000	Ea.	.941	56	42.50	98.50
Louvered pine 1-3/8" thick, 6'-8" high x 1'-6" wide	1.000	Ea.	.842	111	38	149
2'-0" wide	1.000	Ea.	.889	140	40	180
2'-6" wide	1.000	Ea.	.889	153	40	193
2'-8" wide	1.000	Ea.	.889	161	40	201
3'-0" wide	1.000	Ea.	.941	172	42.50	214.50
Paneled pine 1-3/8" thick, 6'-8" high x 1'-6" wide	1.000	Ea.	.842	121	38	159
2'-0" wide	1.000	Ea.	.889	140	40	180
2'-6" wide	1.000	Ea.	.889	157	40	197
2'-8" wide	1.000	Ea.	.889	170	40	210
3'-0" wide	1.000	Ea.	.941	179	42.50	221.50
Frame, pine, 1'-6" thru 2'-0" wide door, 3-5/8" deep	16.000	L.F.	.683	91	31	122
4-5/8" deep	16.000	L.F.	.683	111	31	142
5-5/8" deep	16.000	L.F.	.683	70	31	101
2'-6" thru 3'0" wide door, 3-5/8" deep	17.000	L.F.	.725	97	33	130
4-5/8" deep	17.000	L.F.	.725	118	33	151
5-5/8" deep	17.000	L.F.	.725	74.50	33	107.50
Trim, casing, painted, both sides, 1'-6" thru 2'-6" wide door	32.000	L.F.	1.855	46.50	79	125.50
2'-6" thru 3'-0" wide door	34.000	L.F.	1.971	49.50	84	133.50
Butt hinges 3-1/2" x 3-1/2", steel plated, chrome	1.500	Pr.		40.50		40.50
Bronze	1.500	Pr.		46		46
Locksets, passage, minimum	1.000	Ea.	.500	17.10	22.50	39.60
Maximum	1.000	Ea.	.575	19.65	26	45.65
Privacy, miniumum	1.000	Ea.	.625	21.50	28	49.50
Maximum	1.000	Ea.	.675	23	30.50	53.50
Paint 2 sides, primer & 2 cts., flush door, 1'-6" to 2'-0" wide	2.000	Face	5.547	15.50	218	233.50
2'-6" thru 3'-0" wide	2.000	Face	6.933	19.35	273	292.35
Louvered door, 1'-6" thru 2'-0" wide	2.000	Face	6.400	15.25	252	267.25
2'-6" thru 3'-0" wide	2.000	Face	8.000	19.05	315	334.05
Paneled door, 1'-6" thru 2'-0" wide	2.000	Face	6.400	15.25	252	267.25
2'-6" thru 3'-0" wide	2.000	Face	8.000	19.05	315	334.05

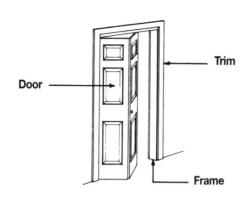

Trim

Door

Frame

System Description	QUAN.	UNIT	LABOR HOURS	COST EACH		
				MAT.	INST.	TOTAL
BI-PASSING, FLUSH, LAUAN, HOLLOW CORE, 4'-0" X 6'-8"						
Door, flush, lauan, hollow core, 4'-0" x 6'-8" opening	1.000	Ea.	1.333	186	60.50	246.50
Frame, pine, 4-5/8" jamb	18.000	L.F.	.768	125.10	34.74	159.84
Trim, stock pine, 11/16" x 2-1/2"	36.000	L.F.	1.200	50.04	54.36	104.40
Prime door & frame, oil, brushwork	2.000	Face	1.600	4.86	63	67.86
Paint door and frame, oil, 2 coats	2.000	Face	2.667	8.54	105	113.54
TOTAL		Ea.	7.568	374.54	317.60	692.14
BI-PASSING, FLUSH, BIRCH, HOLLOW CORE, 6'-0" X 6'-8"						
Door, flush, birch, hollow core, 6'-0" x 6'-8" opening	1.000	Ea.	1.600	277	72.50	349.50
Frame, pine, 4-5/8" jamb	19.000	L.F.	.811	132.05	36.67	168.72
Trim, stock pine, 11/16" x 2-1/2"	38.000	L.F.	1.267	52.82	57.38	110.20
Prime door & frame, oil, brushwork	2.000	Face	2.000	6.08	78.75	84.83
Paint door and frame, oil, 2 coats	2.000	Face	3.333	10.68	131.25	141.93
TOTAL		Ea.	9.011	478.63	376.55	855.18
BI-FOLD, PINE, PANELED, 3'-0" X 6'-8"						
Door, pine, paneled, 3'-0" x 6'-8" opening	1.000	Ea.	1.231	180	55.50	235.50
Frame, pine, 4-5/8" jamb	17.000	L.F.	.725	118.15	32.81	150.96
Trim, stock pine, 11/16" x 2-1/2"	34.000	L.F.	1.133	47.26	51.34	98.60
Prime door & frame, oil, brushwork	2.000	Face	1.600	4.86	63	67.86
Paint door and frame, oil, 2 coats	2.000	Face	2.667	8.54	105	113.54
TOTAL		Ea.	7.356	358.81	307.65	666.46
BI-FOLD, PINE, LOUVERED, 6'-0" X 6'-8"						
Door, pine, louvered, 6'-0" x 6'-8" opening	1.000	Ea.	1.600	276	72.50	348.50
Frame, pine, 4-5/8" jamb	19.000	L.F.	.811	132.05	36.67	168.72
Trim, stock pine, 11/16" x 2-1/2"	38.000	L.F.	1.267	52.82	57.38	110.20
Prime door & frame, oil, brushwork	2.500	Face	2.000	6.08	78.75	84.83
Paint door and frame, oil, 2 coats	2.500	Face	3.333	10.68	131.25	141.93
TOTAL		Ea.	9.011	477.63	376.55	854.18

The costs in this system are based on a cost per each door.

Description	QUAN.	UNIT	LABOR HOURS	COST EACH		
				MAT.	INST.	TOTAL

Closet Door Price Sheet	QUAN.	UNIT	LABOR HOURS	COST EACH		
				MAT.	INST.	TOTAL
Doors, bi-passing, pine, louvered, 4'-0" x 6'-8" opening	1.000	Ea.	1.333	455	60.50	515.50
6'-0" x 6'-8" opening	1.000	Ea.	1.600	560	72.50	632.50
Paneled, 4'-0" x 6'-8" opening	1.000	Ea.	1.333	540	60.50	600.50
6'-0" x 6'-8" opening	1.000	Ea.	1.600	645	72.50	717.50
Flush, birch, hollow core, 4'-0" x 6'-8" opening	1.000	Ea.	1.333	231	60.50	291.50
6'-0" x 6'-8" opening	1.000	Ea.	1.600	277	72.50	349.50
Flush, lauan, hollow core, 4'-0" x 6'-8" opening	1.000	Ea.	1.333	186	60.50	246.50
6'-0" x 6'-8" opening	1.000	Ea.	1.600	218	72.50	290.50
Bi-fold, pine, louvered, 3'-0" x 6'-8" opening	1.000	Ea.	1.231	180	55.50	235.50
6'-0" x 6'-8" opening	1.000	Ea.	1.600	276	72.50	348.50
Paneled, 3'-0" x 6'-8" opening	1.000	Ea.	1.231	180	55.50	235.50
6'-0" x 6'-8" opening	1.000	Ea.	1.600	276	72.50	348.50
Flush, birch, hollow core, 3'-0" x 6'-8" opening	1.000	Ea.	1.231	59	55.50	114.50
6'-0" x 6'-8" opening	1.000	Ea.	1.600	117	72.50	189.50
Flush, lauan, hollow core, 3'-0" x 6'8" opening	1.000	Ea.	1.231	234	55.50	289.50
6'-0" x 6'-8" opening	1.000	Ea.	1.600	440	72.50	512.50
Frame pine, 3'-0" door, 3-5/8" deep	17.000	L.F.	.725	97	33	130
4-5/8" deep	17.000	L.F.	.725	118	33	151
5-5/8" deep	17.000	L.F.	.725	74.50	33	107.50
4'-0" door, 3-5/8" deep	18.000	L.F.	.768	103	34.50	137.50
4-5/8" deep	18.000	L.F.	.768	125	34.50	159.50
5-5/8" deep	18.000	L.F.	.768	79	34.50	113.50
6'-0" door, 3-5/8" deep	19.000	L.F.	.811	108	36.50	144.50
4-5/8" deep	19.000	L.F.	.811	132	36.50	168.50
5-5/8" deep	19.000	L.F.	.811	83	36.50	119.50
Trim both sides, painted 3'-0" x 6'-8" door	34.000	L.F.	1.971	49.50	84	133.50
4'-0" x 6'-8" door	36.000	L.F.	2.086	52	89	141
6'-0" x 6'-8" door	38.000	L.F.	2.203	55	94	149
Paint 2 sides, primer & 2 cts., flush door & frame, 3' x 6'-8" opng	2.000	Face	2.914	10.05	126	136.05
4'-0" x 6'-8" opening	2.000	Face	3.886	13.40	168	181.40
6'-0" x 6'-8" opening	2.000	Face	4.857	16.75	210	226.75
Paneled door & frame, 3'-0" x 6'-8" opening	2.000	Face	6.000	14.30	236	250.30
4'-0" x 6'-8" opening	2.000	Face	8.000	19.05	315	334.05
6'-0" x 6'-8" opening	2.000	Face	10.000	24	395	419
Louvered door & frame, 3'-0" x 6'-8" opening	2.000	Face	6.000	14.30	236	250.30
4'-0" x 6'-8" opening	2.000	Face	8.000	19.05	315	334.05
6'-0" x 6'-8" opening	2.000	Face	10.000	24	395	419

System Description	QUAN.	UNIT	LABOR HOURS	COST PER S.F.		
				MAT.	INST.	TOTAL
Carpet, direct glue-down, nylon, level loop, 26 oz.	1.000	S.F.	.018	2.93	.75	3.68
32 oz.	1.000	S.F.	.018	3.67	.75	4.42
40 oz.	1.000	S.F.	.018	5.45	.75	6.20
Nylon, plush, 20 oz.	1.000	S.F.	.018	1.83	.75	2.58
24 oz.	1.000	S.F.	.018	1.83	.75	2.58
30 oz.	1.000	S.F.	.018	2.69	.75	3.44
42 oz.	1.000	S.F.	.022	4.09	.90	4.99
48 oz.	1.000	S.F.	.022	4.71	.90	5.61
54 oz.	1.000	S.F.	.022	5.15	.90	6.05
Olefin, 15 oz.	1.000	S.F.	.018	.97	.75	1.72
22 oz.	1.000	S.F.	.018	1.14	.75	1.89
Tile, foam backed, needle punch	1.000	S.F.	.014	3.71	.58	4.29
Tufted loop or shag	1.000	S.F.	.014	2.48	.58	3.06
Wool, 36 oz., level loop	1.000	S.F.	.018	12.45	.75	13.20
32 oz., patterned	1.000	S.F.	.020	12.35	.83	13.18
48 oz., patterned	1.000	S.F.	.020	12.60	.83	13.43
Padding, sponge rubber cushion, minimum	1.000	S.F.	.006	.48	.25	.73
Maximum	1.000	S.F.	.006	1.11	.25	1.36
Felt, 32 oz. to 56 oz., minimum	1.000	S.F.	.006	.48	.25	.73
Maximum	1.000	S.F.	.006	.86	.25	1.11
Bonded urethane, 3/8″ thick, minimum	1.000	S.F.	.006	.51	.25	.76
Maximum	1.000	S.F.	.006	.87	.25	1.12
Prime urethane, 1/4″ thick, minimum	1.000	S.F.	.006	.29	.25	.54
Maximum	1.000	S.F.	.006	.54	.25	.79
Stairs, for stairs, add to above carpet prices	1.000	Riser	.267		11.10	11.10
Underlayment plywood, 3/8″ thick	1.000	S.F.	.011	.89	.48	1.37
1/2″ thick	1.000	S.F.	.011	.99	.50	1.49
5/8″ thick	1.000	S.F.	.011	1.20	.52	1.72
3/4″ thick	1.000	S.F.	.012	1.22	.56	1.78
Particle board, 3/8″ thick	1.000	S.F.	.011	.36	.48	.84
1/2″ thick	1.000	S.F.	.011	.41	.50	.91
5/8″ thick	1.000	S.F.	.011	.45	.52	.97
3/4″ thick	1.000	S.F.	.012	.76	.56	1.32
Hardboard, 4′ x 4′, 0.215″ thick	1.000	S.F.	.011	.55	.48	1.03

System Description	QUAN.	UNIT	LABOR HOURS	COST PER S.F.		
				MAT.	INST.	TOTAL
Resilient flooring, asphalt tile on concrete, 1/8" thick						
Color group B	1.000	S.F.	.020	1.24	.83	2.07
Color group C & D	1.000	S.F.	.020	1.36	.83	2.19
Asphalt tile on wood subfloor, 1/8" thick						
Color group B	1.000	S.F.	.020	1.46	.83	2.29
Color group C & D	1.000	S.F.	.020	1.58	.83	2.41
Vinyl composition tile, 12" x 12", 1/16" thick	1.000	S.F.	.016	.87	.67	1.54
Embossed	1.000	S.F.	.016	2.07	.67	2.74
Marbleized	1.000	S.F.	.016	2.07	.67	2.74
Plain	1.000	S.F.	.016	2.66	.67	3.33
.080" thick, embossed	1.000	S.F.	.016	1.30	.67	1.97
Marbleized	1.000	S.F.	.016	2.37	.67	3.04
Plain	1.000	S.F.	.016	2.20	.67	2.87
1/8" thick, marbleized	1.000	S.F.	.016	1.71	.67	2.38
Plain	1.000	S.F.	.016	2.18	.67	2.85
Vinyl tile, 12" x 12", .050" thick, minimum	1.000	S.F.	.016	3.03	.67	3.70
Maximum	1.000	S.F.	.016	6.05	.67	6.72
1/8" thick, minimum	1.000	S.F.	.016	4.24	.67	4.91
Maximum	1.000	S.F.	.016	5.85	.67	6.52
1/8" thick, solid colors	1.000	S.F.	.016	5.65	.67	6.32
Florentine pattern	1.000	S.F.	.016	5.70	.67	6.37
Marbleized or travertine pattern	1.000	S.F.	.016	12.65	.67	13.32
Vinyl sheet goods, backed, .070" thick, minimum	1.000	S.F.	.032	3.58	1.33	4.91
Maximum	1.000	S.F.	.040	3.41	1.67	5.08
.093" thick, minimum	1.000	S.F.	.035	3.58	1.45	5.03
Maximum	1.000	S.F.	.040	4.95	1.67	6.62
.125" thick, minimum	1.000	S.F.	.035	4.13	1.45	5.58
Maximum	1.000	S.F.	.040	6.05	1.67	7.72
Wood, oak, finished in place, 25/32" x 2-1/2" clear	1.000	S.F.	.074	4.26	3.03	7.29
Select	1.000	S.F.	.074	4	3.03	7.03
No. 1 common	1.000	S.F.	.074	5.05	3.03	8.08
Prefinished, oak, 2-1/2" wide	1.000	S.F.	.047	7.05	2.13	9.18
3-1/4" wide	1.000	S.F.	.043	9	1.95	10.95
Ranch plank, oak, random width	1.000	S.F.	.055	8.70	2.49	11.19
Parquet, 5/16" thick, finished in place, oak, minimum	1.000	S.F.	.077	5.45	3.16	8.61
Maximum	1.000	S.F.	.107	6.30	4.52	10.82
Teak, minimum	1.000	S.F.	.077	6.10	3.16	9.26
Maximum	1.000	S.F.	.107	10.05	4.52	14.57
Sleepers, treated, 16" O.C., 1" x 2"	1.000	S.F.	.007	.22	.31	.53
1" x 3"	1.000	S.F.	.008	.34	.36	.70
2" x 4"	1.000	S.F.	.011	.65	.48	1.13
2" x 6"	1.000	S.F.	.012	.88	.56	1.44
Subfloor, plywood, 1/2" thick	1.000	S.F.	.011	.57	.48	1.05
5/8" thick	1.000	S.F.	.012	.75	.54	1.29
3/4" thick	1.000	S.F.	.013	.96	.58	1.54
Ceramic tile, color group 2, 1" x 1"	1.000	S.F.	.087	5.05	3.26	8.31
2" x 2" or 2" x 1"	1.000	S.F.	.084	5.55	3.14	8.69
Color group 1, 8" x 8"		S.F.	.064	3.70	2.38	6.08
12" x 12"		S.F.	.049	4.64	1.83	6.47
16" x 16"		S.F.	.029	6.65	1.08	7.73

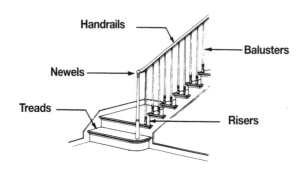

System Description	QUAN.	UNIT	LABOR HOURS	COST EACH		
				MAT.	INST.	TOTAL
7 RISERS, OAK TREADS, BOX STAIRS						
Treads, oak, 1-1/4" x 10" wide, 3' long	6.000	Ea.	2.667	390	120	510
Risers, 3/4" thick, beech	7.000	Ea.	2.625	136.50	118.65	255.15
30" primed pine balusters	12.000	Ea.	1.000	48.36	45.24	93.60
Newels, 3-1/4" wide	2.000	Ea.	2.286	85	103	188
Handrails, oak laminated	7.000	L.F.	.933	248.50	42.35	290.85
Stringers, 2" x 10", 3 each	21.000	L.F.	.306	8.19	13.86	22.05
TOTAL		Ea.	9.817	916.55	443.10	1,359.65
14 RISERS, OAK TREADS, BOX STAIRS						
Treads, oak, 1-1/4" x 10" wide, 3' long	13.000	Ea.	5.778	845	260	1,105
Risers, 3/4" thick, beech	14.000	Ea.	5.250	273	237.30	510.30
30" primed pine balusters	26.000	Ea.	2.167	104.78	98.02	202.80
Newels, 3-1/4" wide	2.000	Ea.	2.286	85	103	188
Handrails, oak, laminated	14.000	L.F.	1.867	497	84.70	581.70
Stringers, 2" x 10", 3 each	42.000	L.F.	5.169	47.46	233.10	280.56
TOTAL		Ea.	22.517	1,852.24	1,016.12	2,868.36
14 RISERS, PINE TREADS, BOX STAIRS						
Treads, pine, 9-1/2" x 3/4" thick	13.000	Ea.	5.778	188.50	260	448.50
Risers, 3/4" thick, pine	14.000	Ea.	5.091	143.64	231	374.64
30" primed pine balusters	26.000	Ea.	2.167	104.78	98.02	202.80
Newels, 3-1/4" wide	2.000	Ea.	2.286	85	103	188
Handrails, oak, laminated	14.000	L.F.	1.867	497	84.70	581.70
Stringers, 2" x 10", 3 each	42.000	L.F.	5.169	47.46	233.10	280.56
TOTAL		Ea.	22.358	1,066.38	1,009.82	2,076.20

Description	QUAN.	UNIT	LABOR HOURS	COST EACH		
				MAT.	INST.	TOTAL

Stairway Price Sheet	QUAN.	UNIT	LABOR HOURS	COST EACH		
				MAT.	INST.	TOTAL
Treads, oak, 1-1/16″ x 9-1/2″, 3′ long, 7 riser stair	6.000	Ea.	2.667	390	120	510
14 riser stair	13.000	Ea.	5.778	845	260	1,105
1-1/16″ x 11-1/2″, 3′ long, 7 riser stair	6.000	Ea.	2.667	390	120	510
14 riser stair	13.000	Ea.	5.778	845	260	1,105
Pine, 3/4″ x 9-1/2″, 3′ long, 7 riser stair	6.000	Ea.	2.667	87	120	207
14 riser stair	13.000	Ea.	5.778	189	260	449
3/4″ x 11-1/4″, 3′ long, 7 riser stair	6.000	Ea.	2.667	132	120	252
14 riser stair	13.000	Ea.	5.778	286	260	546
Risers, oak, 3/4″ x 7-1/2″ high, 7 riser stair	7.000	Ea.	2.625	144	119	263
14 riser stair	14.000	Ea.	5.250	288	237	525
Beech, 3/4″ x 7-1/2″ high, 7 riser stair	7.000	Ea.	2.625	137	119	256
14 riser stair	14.000	Ea.	5.250	273	237	510
Baluster, turned, 30″ high, primed pine, 7 riser stair	12.000	Ea.	3.429	48.50	45	93.50
14 riser stair	26.000	Ea.	7.428	105	98	203
30″ birch, 7 riser stair	12.000	Ea.	3.429	44	41	85
14 riser stair	26.000	Ea.	7.428	95.50	89	184.50
42″ pine, 7 riser stair	12.000	Ea.	3.556	66.50	45	111.50
14 riser stair	26.000	Ea.	7.704	144	98	242
42″ birch, 7 riser stair	12.000	Ea.	3.556	66.50	45	111.50
14 riser stair	26.000	Ea.	7.704	144	98	242
Newels, 3-1/4″ wide, starting, 7 riser stair	2.000	Ea.	2.286	85	103	188
14 riser stair	2.000	Ea.	2.286	85	103	188
Landing, 7 riser stair	2.000	Ea.	3.200	234	145	379
14 riser stair	2.000	Ea.	3.200	234	145	379
Handrails, oak, laminated, 7 riser stair	7.000	L.F.	.933	249	42.50	291.50
14 riser stair	14.000	L.F.	1.867	495	84.50	579.50
Stringers, fir, 2″ x 10″ 7 riser stair	21.000	L.F.	2.585	23.50	117	140.50
14 riser stair	42.000	L.F.	5.169	47.50	233	280.50
2″ x 12″, 7 riser stair	21.000	L.F.	2.585	29	117	146
14 riser stair	42.000	L.F.	5.169	57.50	233	290.50

Special Stairways	QUAN.	UNIT	LABOR HOURS	COST EACH		
				MAT.	INST.	TOTAL
Basement stairs, open risers	1.000	Flight	4.000	700	181	881
Spiral stairs, oak, 4′-6″ diameter, prefabricated, 9′ high	1.000	Flight	10.667	5,125	480	5,605
Aluminum, 5′-0″ diameter stock unit	1.000	Flight	9.956	7,700	610	8,310
Custom unit	1.000	Flight	9.956	14,400	610	15,010
Cast iron, 4′-0″ diameter, minimum	1.000	Flight	9.956	6,850	610	7,460
Maximum	1.000	Flight	17.920	9,300	1,100	10,400
Steel, industrial, pre-erected, 3′-6″ wide, bar rail	1.000	Flight	7.724	7,000	700	7,700
Picket rail	1.000	Flight	7.724	7,850	700	8,550

Division 7
Specialties

System Description	QUAN.	UNIT	LABOR HOURS	COST PER L.F.		
				MAT.	INST.	TOTAL
KITCHEN, ECONOMY GRADE						
Top cabinets, economy grade	1.000	L.F.	.171	38.08	7.68	45.76
Bottom cabinets, economy grade	1.000	L.F.	.256	57.12	11.52	68.64
Square edge, plastic face countertop	1.000	L.F.	.267	27	12.05	39.05
Blocking, wood, 2″ x 4″	1.000	L.F.	.032	.39	1.45	1.84
Soffit, framing, wood, 2″ x 4″	4.000	L.F.	.071	1.56	3.20	4.76
Soffit drywall	2.000	S.F.	.047	.70	2.14	2.84
Drywall painting	2.000	S.F.	.013	.10	.60	.70
TOTAL		L.F.	.857	124.95	38.64	163.59
AVERAGE GRADE						
Top cabinets, average grade	1.000	L.F.	.213	47.60	9.60	57.20
Bottom cabinets, average grade	1.000	L.F.	.320	71.40	14.40	85.80
Solid surface countertop, solid color	1.000	L.F.	.800	66	36	102
Blocking, wood, 2″ x 4″	1.000	L.F.	.032	.39	1.45	1.84
Soffit framing, wood, 2″ x 4″	4.000	L.F.	.071	1.56	3.20	4.76
Soffit drywall	2.000	S.F.	.047	.70	2.14	2.84
Drywall painting	2.000	S.F.	.013	.10	.60	.70
TOTAL		L.F.	1.496	187.75	67.39	255.14
CUSTOM GRADE						
Top cabinets, custom grade	1.000	L.F.	.256	114.40	11.60	126
Bottom cabinets, custom grade	1.000	L.F.	.384	171.60	17.40	189
Solid surface countertop, premium patterned color	1.000	L.F.	1.067	115	48	163
Blocking, wood, 2″ x 4″	1.000	L.F.	.032	.39	1.45	1.84
Soffit framing, wood, 2″ x 4″	4.000	L.F.	.071	1.56	3.20	4.76
Soffit drywall	2.000	S.F.	.047	.70	2.14	2.84
Drywall painting	2.000	S.F.	.013	.10	.60	.70
TOTAL		L.F.	1.870	403.75	84.39	488.14

Description	QUAN.	UNIT	LABOR HOURS	COST PER L.F.		
				MAT.	INST.	TOTAL

Kitchen Price Sheet	QUAN.	UNIT	LABOR HOURS	COST PER L.F.		
				MAT.	INST.	TOTAL
Top cabinets, economy grade	1.000	L.F.	.171	38	7.70	45.70
Average grade	1.000	L.F.	.213	47.50	9.60	57.10
Custom grade	1.000	L.F.	.256	114	11.60	125.60
Bottom cabinets, economy grade	1.000	L.F.	.256	57	11.50	68.50
Average grade	1.000	L.F.	.320	71.50	14.40	85.90
Custom grade	1.000	L.F.	.384	172	17.40	189.40
Counter top, laminated plastic, 7/8″ thick, no splash	1.000	L.F.	.267	21.50	12.05	33.55
With backsplash	1.000	L.F.	.267	28.50	12.05	40.55
1-1/4″ thick, no splash	1.000	L.F.	.286	32	12.90	44.90
With backsplash	1.000	L.F.	.286	31	12.90	43.90
Post formed, laminated plastic	1.000	L.F.	.267	11.10	12.05	23.15
Ceramic tile, with backsplash		L.F.	.427	16.05	7.25	23.30
Marble, with backsplash, minimum	1.000	L.F.	.471	39.50	21.50	61
Maximum	1.000	L.F.	.615	99	28	127
Maple, solid laminated, no backsplash	1.000	L.F.	.286	64.50	12.90	77.40
With backsplash	1.000	L.F.	.286	77	12.90	89.90
Solid Surface, with backsplash, minimum		L.F.	.842	72.50	38	110.50
Maximum		L.F.	1.067	115	48	163
Blocking, wood, 2″ x 4″	1.000	L.F.	.032	.39	1.45	1.84
2″ x 6″	1.000	L.F.	.036	.60	1.63	2.23
2″ x 8″	1.000	L.F.	.040	.83	1.81	2.64
Soffit framing, wood, 2″ x 3″	4.000	L.F.	.064	1.44	2.88	4.32
2″ x 4″	4.000	L.F.	.071	1.56	3.20	4.76
Soffit, drywall, painted	2.000	S.F.	.060	.80	2.74	3.54
Paneling, standard	2.000	S.F.	.064	1.92	2.90	4.82
Deluxe	2.000	S.F.	.091	4.24	4.14	8.38
Sinks, porcelain on cast iron, single bowl, 21″ x 24″	1.000	Ea.	10.334	490	470	960
21″ x 30″	1.000	Ea.	10.334	520	470	990
Double bowl, 20″ x 32″	1.000	Ea.	10.810	575	490	1,065
Stainless steel, single bowl, 16″ x 20″	1.000	Ea.	10.334	685	470	1,155
22″ x 25″	1.000	Ea.	10.334	740	470	1,210
Double bowl, 20″ x 32″	1.000	Ea.	10.810	395	490	885

Kitchen Price Sheet	QUAN.	UNIT	LABOR HOURS	COST PER L.F.		
				MAT.	INST.	TOTAL
Range, free standing, minimum	1.000	Ea.	3.600	395	153	548
Maximum	1.000	Ea.	6.000	2,075	233	2,308
Built-in, minimum	1.000	Ea.	3.333	630	166	796
Maximum	1.000	Ea.	10.000	1,725	460	2,185
Counter top range, 4-burner, minimum	1.000	Ea.	3.333	340	166	506
Maximum	1.000	Ea.	4.667	780	233	1,013
Compactor, built-in, minimum	1.000	Ea.	2.215	545	103	648
Maximum	1.000	Ea.	3.282	640	152	792
Dishwasher, built-in, minimum	1.000	Ea.	6.735	460	340	800
Maximum	1.000	Ea.	9.235	505	465	970
Garbage disposer, minimum	1.000	Ea.	2.810	138	142	280
Maximum	1.000	Ea.	2.810	285	142	427
Microwave oven, minimum	1.000	Ea.	2.615	118	130	248
Maximum	1.000	Ea.	4.615	495	230	725
Range hood, ducted, minimum	1.000	Ea.	4.658	91	218	309
Maximum	1.000	Ea.	5.991	1,025	280	1,305
Ductless, minimum	1.000	Ea.	2.615	96	123	219
Maximum	1.000	Ea.	3.948	1,025	185	1,210
Refrigerator, 16 cu.ft., minimum	1.000	Ea.	2.000	670	67	737
Maximum	1.000	Ea.	3.200	1,075	107	1,182
16 cu.ft. with icemaker, minimum	1.000	Ea.	4.210	870	172	1,042
Maximum	1.000	Ea.	5.410	1,275	212	1,487
19 cu.ft., minimum	1.000	Ea.	2.667	715	89	804
Maximum	1.000	Ea.	4.667	1,250	156	1,406
19 cu.ft. with icemaker, minimum	1.000	Ea.	5.143	965	203	1,168
Maximum	1.000	Ea.	7.143	1,500	270	1,770
Sinks, porcelain on cast iron single bowl, 21″ x 24″	1.000	Ea.	10.334	490	470	960
21″ x 30″	1.000	Ea.	10.334	520	470	990
Double bowl, 20″ x 32″	1.000	Ea.	10.810	575	490	1,065
Stainless steel, single bowl 16″ x 20″	1.000	Ea.	10.334	685	470	1,155
22″ x 25″	1.000	Ea.	10.334	740	470	1,210
Double bowl, 20″ x 32″	1.000	Ea.	10.810	395	490	885
Water heater, electric, 30 gallon	1.000	Ea.	3.636	340	184	524
40 gallon	1.000	Ea.	4.000	365	203	568
Gas, 30 gallon	1.000	Ea.	4.000	665	203	868
75 gallon	1.000	Ea.	5.333	1,350	270	1,620
Wall, packaged terminal heater/air conditioner cabinet, wall sleeve,						
louver, electric heat, thermostat, manual changeover, 208V		Ea.				
6000 BTUH cooling, 8800 BTU heating	1.000	Ea.	2.667	655	123	778
9000 BTUH cooling, 13,900 BTU heating	1.000	Ea.	3.200	755	147	902
12,000 BTUH cooling, 13,900 BTU heating	1.000	Ea.	4.000	810	184	994
15,000 BTUH cooling, 13,900 BTU heating	1.000	Ea.	5.333	905	246	1,151

System Description	QUAN.	UNIT	LABOR HOURS	COST EACH		
				MAT.	INST.	TOTAL
Curtain rods, stainless, 1" diameter, 3' long	1.000	Ea.	.615	36.50	28	64.50
5' long	1.000	Ea.	.615	36.50	28	64.50
Grab bar, 1" diameter, 12" long	1.000	Ea.	.283	24.50	12.80	37.30
36" long	1.000	Ea.	.340	27.50	15.40	42.90
1-1/4" diameter, 12" long	1.000	Ea.	.333	29	15.05	44.05
1-1/2" diameter, 12" long	1.000	Ea.	.383	33.50	17.30	50.80
36" long	1.000	Ea.	.460	37.50	21	58.50
Mirror, 18" x 24"	1.000	Ea.	.400	51.50	18.10	69.60
72" x 24"	1.000	Ea.	1.333	365	60.50	425.50
Medicine chest with mirror, 18" x 24"	1.000	Ea.	.400	249	18.10	267.10
36" x 24"	1.000	Ea.	.600	375	27	402
Toilet tissue dispenser, surface mounted, minimum	1.000	Ea.	.267	18.55	12.05	30.60
Maximum	1.000	Ea.	.400	28	18.10	46.10
Flush mounted, minimum	1.000	Ea.	.293	20.50	13.25	33.75
Maximum	1.000	Ea.	.427	29.50	19.30	48.80
Towel bar, 18" long, minimum	1.000	Ea.	.278	32	12.55	44.55
Maximum	1.000	Ea.	.348	40	15.70	55.70
24" long, minimum	1.000	Ea.	.313	36	14.15	50.15
Maximum	1.000	Ea.	.383	44	17.25	61.25
36" long, minimum	1.000	Ea.	.381	111	17.20	128.20
Maximum	1.000	Ea.	.419	122	18.90	140.90

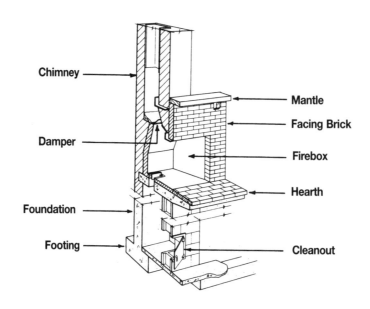

System Description	QUAN.	UNIT	LABOR HOURS	COST EACH		
				MAT.	INST.	TOTAL
MASONRY FIREPLACE						
Footing, 8″ thick, concrete, 4′ x 7′	.700	C.Y.	2.110	109.20	83.33	192.53
Foundation, concrete block, 32″ x 60″ x 4′ deep	1.000	Ea.	5.275	160.20	219	379.20
Fireplace, brick firebox, 30″ x 29″ opening	1.000	Ea.	40.000	560	1,625	2,185
Damper, cast iron, 30″ opening	1.000	Ea.	1.333	92	60.50	152.50
Facing brick, standard size brick, 6′ x 5′	30.000	S.F.	5.217	180	216	396
Hearth, standard size brick, 3′ x 6′	1.000	Ea.	8.000	206	325	531
Chimney, standard size brick, 8″ x 12″ flue, one story house	12.000	V.L.F.	12.000	402	486	888
Mantle, 4″ x 8″, wood	6.000	L.F.	1.333	36	60.30	96.30
Cleanout, cast iron, 8″ x 8″	1.000	Ea.	.667	38.50	30.50	69
TOTAL		Ea.	75.935	1,783.90	3,105.63	4,889.53

The costs in this system are on a cost each basis.

Description	QUAN.	UNIT	LABOR HOURS	COST EACH		
				MAT.	INST.	TOTAL

Masonry Fireplace Price Sheet	QUAN.	UNIT	LABOR HOURS	COST EACH		
				MAT.	INST.	TOTAL
Footing 8" thick, 3' x 6'	.440	C.Y.	1.326	68.50	52.50	121
4' x 7'	.700	C.Y.	2.110	109	83	192
5' x 8'	1.000	C.Y.	3.014	156	119	275
1' thick, 3' x 6'	.670	C.Y.	2.020	105	79.50	184.50
4' x 7'	1.030	C.Y.	3.105	161	123	284
5' x 8'	1.480	C.Y.	4.461	231	177	408
Foundation-concrete block, 24" x 48", 4' deep	1.000	Ea.	4.267	128	175	303
8' deep	1.000	Ea.	8.533	256	350	606
24" x 60", 4' deep	1.000	Ea.	4.978	150	204	354
8' deep	1.000	Ea.	9.956	299	410	709
32" x 48", 4' deep	1.000	Ea.	4.711	142	193	335
8' deep	1.000	Ea.	9.422	283	385	668
32" x 60", 4' deep	1.000	Ea.	5.333	160	219	379
8' deep	1.000	Ea.	10.845	325	445	770
32" x 72", 4' deep	1.000	Ea.	6.133	184	252	436
8' deep	1.000	Ea.	12.267	370	505	875
Fireplace, brick firebox 30" x 29" opening	1.000	Ea.	40.000	560	1,625	2,185
48" x 30" opening	1.000	Ea.	60.000	840	2,450	3,290
Steel fire box with registers, 25" opening	1.000	Ea.	26.667	995	1,100	2,095
48" opening	1.000	Ea.	44.000	1,675	1,800	3,475
Damper, cast iron, 30" opening	1.000	Ea.	1.333	92	60.50	152.50
36" opening	1.000	Ea.	1.556	107	70.50	177.50
Steel, 30" opening	1.000	Ea.	1.333	82.50	60.50	143
36" opening	1.000	Ea.	1.556	96.50	70.50	167
Facing for fireplace, standard size brick, 6' x 5'	30.000	S.F.	5.217	180	216	396
7' x 5'	35.000	S.F.	6.087	210	252	462
8' x 6'	48.000	S.F.	8.348	288	345	633
Fieldstone, 6' x 5'	30.000	S.F.	5.217	625	216	841
7' x 5'	35.000	S.F.	6.087	725	252	977
8' x 6'	48.000	S.F.	8.348	995	345	1,340
Sheetrock on metal, studs, 6' x 5'	30.000	S.F.	.980	22	44	66
7' x 5'	35.000	S.F.	1.143	25.50	51.50	77
8' x 6'	48.000	S.F.	1.568	35	70.50	105.50
Hearth, standard size brick, 3' x 6'	1.000	Ea.	8.000	206	325	531
3' x 7'	1.000	Ea.	9.280	239	375	614
3' x 8'	1.000	Ea.	10.640	274	430	704
Stone, 3' x 6'	1.000	Ea.	8.000	222	325	547
3' x 7'	1.000	Ea.	9.280	258	375	633
3' x 8'	1.000	Ea.	10.640	296	430	726
Chimney, standard size brick , 8" x 12" flue, one story house	12.000	V.L.F.	12.000	400	485	885
Two story house	20.000	V.L.F.	20.000	670	810	1,480
Mantle wood, beams, 4" x 8"	6.000	L.F.	1.333	36	60.50	96.50
4" x 10"	6.000	L.F.	1.371	43	62	105
Ornate, prefabricated, 6' x 3'-6" opening, minimum	1.000	Ea.	1.600	162	72.50	234.50
Maximum	1.000	Ea.	1.600	202	72.50	274.50
Cleanout, door and frame, cast iron, 8" x 8"	1.000	Ea.	.667	38.50	30.50	69
12" x 12"	1.000	Ea.	.800	47	36.50	83.50

Chimney, Flue, Fittings & Framing

Framing

Mantle

Facing Brick

Prefabricated Fireplace

Hearth

System Description	QUAN.	UNIT	LABOR HOURS	COST EACH		
				MAT.	INST.	TOTAL
PREFABRICATED FIREPLACE						
Prefabricated fireplace, metal, minimum	1.000	Ea.	6.154	1,250	278	1,528
Framing, 2″ x 4″ studs, 6′ x 5′	35.000	L.F.	.509	13.65	23.10	36.75
Fire resistant gypsum drywall, unfinished	40.000	S.F.	.320	11.60	14.40	26
Drywall finishing adder	40.000	S.F.	.320	2	14.40	16.40
Facing, brick, standard size brick, 6′ x 5′	30.000	S.F.	5.217	180	216	396
Hearth, standard size brick, 3′ x 6′	1.000	Ea.	8.000	206	325	531
Chimney, one story house, framing, 2″ x 4″ studs	80.000	L.F.	1.164	31.20	52.80	84
Sheathing, plywood, 5/8″ thick	32.000	S.F.	.758	86.40	34.24	120.64
Flue, 10″ metal, insulated pipe	12.000	V.L.F.	4.000	396	181.20	577.20
Fittings, ceiling support	1.000	Ea.	.667	156	30	186
Fittings, joist shield	1.000	Ea.	.667	89.50	30	119.50
Fittings, roof flashing	1.000	Ea.	.667	181	30	211
Mantle beam, wood, 4″ x 8″	6.000	L.F.	1.333	36	60.30	96.30
TOTAL		Ea.	29.776	2,639.35	1,289.44	3,928.79

The costs in this system are on a cost each basis.

Description	QUAN.	UNIT	LABOR HOURS	COST EACH		
				MAT.	INST.	TOTAL

Prefabricated Fireplace Price Sheet	QUAN.	UNIT	LABOR HOURS	COST EACH		
				MAT.	INST.	TOTAL
Prefabricated fireplace, minimum	1.000	Ea.	6.154	1,250	278	1,528
Average	1.000	Ea.	8.000	1,750	360	2,110
Maximum	1.000	Ea.	8.889	3,325	400	3,725
Framing, 2" x 4" studs, fireplace, 6' x 5'	35.000	L.F.	.509	13.65	23	36.65
7' x 5'	40.000	L.F.	.582	15.60	26.50	42.10
8' x 6'	45.000	L.F.	.655	17.55	29.50	47.05
Sheetrock, 1/2" thick, fireplace, 6' x 5'	40.000	S.F.	.640	13.60	29	42.60
7' x 5'	45.000	S.F.	.720	15.30	32.50	47.80
8' x 6'	50.000	S.F.	.800	17	36	53
Facing for fireplace, brick, 6' x 5'	30.000	S.F.	5.217	180	216	396
7' x 5'	35.000	S.F.	6.087	210	252	462
8' x 6'	48.000	S.F.	8.348	288	345	633
Fieldstone, 6' x 5'	30.000	S.F.	5.217	665	216	881
7' x 5'	35.000	S.F.	6.087	775	252	1,027
8' x 6'	48.000	S.F.	8.348	1,075	345	1,420
Hearth, standard size brick, 3' x 6'	1.000	Ea.	8.000	206	325	531
3' x 7'	1.000	Ea.	9.280	239	375	614
3' x 8'	1.000	Ea.	10.640	274	430	704
Stone, 3' x 6'	1.000	Ea.	8.000	222	325	547
3' x 7'	1.000	Ea.	9.280	258	375	633
3' x 8'	1.000	Ea.	10.640	296	430	726
Chimney, framing, 2" x 4", one story house	80.000	L.F.	1.164	31	53	84
Two story house	120.000	L.F.	1.746	47	79	126
Sheathing, plywood, 5/8" thick	32.000	S.F.	.758	86.50	34	120.50
Stucco on plywood	32.000	S.F.	1.125	41.50	49	90.50
Flue, 10" metal pipe, insulated, one story house	12.000	V.L.F.	4.000	395	181	576
Two story house	20.000	V.L.F.	6.667	660	300	960
Fittings, ceiling support	1.000	Ea.	.667	156	30	186
Fittings joist sheild, one story house	1.000	Ea.	.667	89.50	30	119.50
Two story house	2.000	Ea.	1.333	179	60	239
Fittings roof flashing	1.000	Ea.	.667	181	30	211
Mantle, wood beam, 4" x 8"	6.000	L.F.	1.333	36	60.50	96.50
4" x 10"	6.000	L.F.	1.371	43	62	105
Ornate prefabricated, 6' x 3'-6" opening, minimum	1.000	Ea.	1.600	162	72.50	234.50
Maximum	1.000	Ea.	1.600	202	72.50	274.50

System Description	QUAN.	UNIT	LABOR HOURS	COST EACH		
				MAT.	INST.	TOTAL
Economy, lean to, shell only, not including 2' stub wall, fndtn, flrs, heat						
4' x 16'	1.000	Ea.	26.212	2,350	1,200	3,550
4' x 24'	1.000	Ea.	30.259	2,700	1,375	4,075
6' x 10'	1.000	Ea.	16.552	2,575	745	3,320
6' x 16'	1.000	Ea.	23.034	3,600	1,050	4,650
6' x 24'	1.000	Ea.	29.793	4,650	1,350	6,000
8' x 10'	1.000	Ea.	22.069	3,450	995	4,445
8' x 16'	1.000	Ea.	38.400	5,975	1,725	7,700
8' x 24'	1.000	Ea.	49.655	7,750	2,250	10,000
Free standing, 8' x 8'	1.000	Ea.	17.356	2,975	785	3,760
8' x 16'	1.000	Ea.	30.211	5,175	1,375	6,550
8' x 24'	1.000	Ea.	39.051	6,700	1,775	8,475
10' x 10'	1.000	Ea.	18.824	3,850	850	4,700
10' x 16'	1.000	Ea.	24.095	4,925	1,100	6,025
10' x 24'	1.000	Ea.	31.624	6,475	1,425	7,900
14' x 10'	1.000	Ea.	20.741	4,625	940	5,565
14' x 16'	1.000	Ea.	24.889	5,550	1,125	6,675
14' x 24'	1.000	Ea.	33.349	7,425	1,500	8,925
Standard,lean to,shell only,not incl.2'stub wall, fndtn,flrs, heat 4'x10'	1.000	Ea.	28.235	2,525	1,300	3,825
4' x 16'	1.000	Ea.	39.341	3,500	1,800	5,300
4' x 24'	1.000	Ea.	45.412	4,050	2,075	6,125
6' x 10'	1.000	Ea.	24.827	3,875	1,125	5,000
6' x 16'	1.000	Ea.	34.538	5,375	1,550	6,925
6' x 24'	1.000	Ea.	44.689	6,975	2,025	9,000
8' x 10'	1.000	Ea.	33.103	5,150	1,500	6,650
8' x 16'	1.000	Ea.	57.600	8,975	2,600	11,575
8' x 24'	1.000	Ea.	74.482	11,600	3,350	14,950
Free standing, 8' x 8'	1.000	Ea.	26.034	4,475	1,175	5,650
8' x 16'	1.000	Ea.	45.316	7,775	2,050	9,825
8' x 24'	1.000	Ea.	58.577	10,000	2,650	12,650
10' x 10'	1.000	Ea.	28.236	5,775	1,275	7,050
10' x 16'	1.000	Ea.	36.142	7,400	1,625	9,025
10' x 24'	1.000	Ea.	47.436	9,700	2,150	11,850
14' x 10'	1.000	Ea.	31.112	6,925	1,400	8,325
14' x 16'	1.000	Ea.	37.334	8,325	1,700	10,025
14' x 24'	1.000	Ea.	50.030	11,100	2,275	13,375
Deluxe,lean to,shell only,not incl.2'stub wall, fndtn, flrs or heat, 4'x10'	1.000	Ea.	20.645	4,275	940	5,215
4' x 16'	1.000	Ea.	33.032	6,850	1,500	8,350
4' x 24'	1.000	Ea.	49.548	10,300	2,250	12,550
6' x 10'	1.000	Ea.	30.968	6,425	1,400	7,825
6' x 16'	1.000	Ea.	49.548	10,300	2,250	12,550
6' x 24'	1.000	Ea.	74.323	15,400	3,375	18,775
8' x 10'	1.000	Ea.	41.290	8,550	1,875	10,425
8' x 16'	1.000	Ea.	66.065	13,700	3,000	16,700
8' x 24'	1.000	Ea.	99.097	20,500	4,500	25,000
Freestanding, 8' x 8'	1.000	Ea.	18.618	5,400	840	6,240
8' x 16'	1.000	Ea.	37.236	10,800	1,675	12,475
8' x 24'	1.000	Ea.	55.855	16,200	2,525	18,725
10' x 10'	1.000	Ea.	29.091	8,450	1,325	9,775
10' x 16'	1.000	Ea.	46.546	13,500	2,100	15,600
10' x 24'	1.000	Ea.	69.818	20,300	3,150	23,450
14' x 10'	1.000	Ea.	40.727	11,800	1,850	13,650
14' x 16'	1.000	Ea.	65.164	18,900	2,950	21,850
14' x 24'	1.000	Ea.	97.746	28,400	4,425	32,825

System Description	QUAN.	UNIT	LABOR HOURS	COST EACH		
				MAT.	INST.	TOTAL
Swimming pools, vinyl lined, metal sides, sand bottom, 12' x 28'	1.000	Ea.	50.177	3,625	2,350	5,975
12' x 32'	1.000	Ea.	55.366	4,000	2,575	6,575
12' x 36'	1.000	Ea.	60.061	4,350	2,800	7,150
16' x 32'	1.000	Ea.	66.798	4,825	3,100	7,925
16' x 36'	1.000	Ea.	71.190	5,150	3,325	8,475
16' x 40'	1.000	Ea.	74.703	5,400	3,475	8,875
20' x 36'	1.000	Ea.	77.860	5,625	3,625	9,250
20' x 40'	1.000	Ea.	82.135	5,950	3,825	9,775
20' x 44'	1.000	Ea.	90.348	6,525	4,200	10,725
24' x 40'	1.000	Ea.	98.562	7,125	4,600	11,725
24' x 44'	1.000	Ea.	108.418	7,850	5,050	12,900
24' x 48'	1.000	Ea.	118.274	8,550	5,525	14,075
Vinyl lined, concrete sides, 12' x 28'	1.000	Ea.	79.447	5,750	3,700	9,450
12' x 32'	1.000	Ea.	88.818	6,425	4,125	10,550
12' x 36'	1.000	Ea.	97.656	7,075	4,550	11,625
16' x 32'	1.000	Ea.	111.393	8,050	5,175	13,225
16' x 36'	1.000	Ea.	121.354	8,775	5,650	14,425
16' x 40'	1.000	Ea.	130.445	9,425	6,075	15,500
28' x 36'	1.000	Ea.	140.585	10,200	6,525	16,725
20' x 40'	1.000	Ea.	149.336	10,800	6,950	17,750
20' x 44'	1.000	Ea.	164.270	11,900	7,650	19,550
24' x 40'	1.000	Ea.	179.203	13,000	8,350	21,350
24' x 44'	1.000	Ea.	197.124	14,300	9,175	23,475
24' x 48'	1.000	Ea.	215.044	15,600	10,000	25,600
Gunite, bottom and sides, 12' x 28'	1.000	Ea.	129.767	8,400	6,050	14,450
12' x 32'	1.000	Ea.	142.164	9,200	6,600	15,800
12' x 36'	1.000	Ea.	153.028	9,900	7,125	17,025
16' x 32'	1.000	Ea.	167.743	10,900	7,800	18,700
16' x 36'	1.000	Ea.	176.421	11,400	8,200	19,600
16' x 40'	1.000	Ea.	182.368	11,800	8,475	20,275
20' x 36'	1.000	Ea.	187.949	12,200	8,725	20,925
20' x 40'	1.000	Ea.	179.200	16,000	8,325	24,325
20' x 44'	1.000	Ea.	197.120	17,600	9,150	26,750
24' x 40'	1.000	Ea.	215.040	19,200	9,975	29,175
24' x 44'	1.000	Ea.	273.244	17,700	12,700	30,400
24' x 48'	1.000	Ea.	298.077	19,300	13,800	33,100

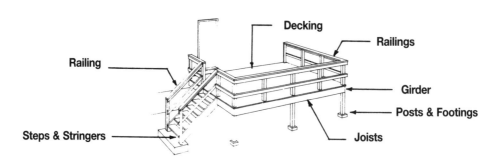

System Description	QUAN.	UNIT	LABOR HOURS	COST PER S.F.		
				MAT.	INST.	TOTAL
8' X 12' DECK, PRESSURE TREATED LUMBER, JOISTS 16" O.C.						
Decking, 2" x 6" lumber	2.080	L.F.	.027	1.25	1.21	2.46
Lumber preservative	2.080	L.F.		.31		.31
Joists, 2" x 8", 16" O.C.	1.000	L.F.	.015	.83	.66	1.49
Lumber preservative	1.000	L.F.		.20		.20
Girder, 2" x 10"	.125	L.F.	.002	.14	.10	.24
Lumber preservative	.125	L.F.		.03		.03
Heavy soil or clay	.250	L.F.	.006		.20	.20
Concrete footings	.250	L.F.	.006	.31	.24	.55
4" x 4" Posts	.250	L.F.	.010	.46	.46	.92
Lumber preservative	.250	L.F.		.05		.05
Framing, pressure treated wood stairs, 3' wide, 8 closed risers	1.000	Set	.080	1.28	3.60	4.88
Railings, 2" x 4"	1.000	L.F.	.026	.39	1.17	1.56
Lumber preservative	1.000	L.F.		.10		.10
TOTAL		S.F.	.172	5.35	7.64	12.99
12' X 16' DECK, PRESSURE TREATED LUMBER, JOISTS 24" O.C.						
Decking, 2" x 6"	2.080	L.F.	.027	1.25	1.21	2.46
Lumber preservative	2.080	L.F.		.31		.31
Joists, 2" x 10", 24" O.C.	.800	L.F.	.014	.90	.64	1.54
Lumber preservative	.800	L.F.		.20		.20
Girder, 2" x 10"	.083	L.F.	.001	.09	.07	.16
Lumber preservative	.083	L.F.		.02		.02
Heavy soil or clay	.122	L.F.	.006		.20	.20
Concrete footings	.122	L.F.	.006	.31	.24	.55
4" x 4" Posts	.122	L.F.	.005	.22	.23	.45
Lumber preservative	.122	L.F.		.02		.02
Framing, pressure treated wood stairs, 3' wide, 8 closed risers	1.000	Set	.040	.64	1.80	2.44
Railings, 2" x 4"	.670	L.F.	.017	.26	.78	1.04
Lumber preservative	.670	L.F.		.07		.07
TOTAL		S.F.	.116	4.29	5.17	9.46
12' X 24' DECK, REDWOOD OR CEDAR, JOISTS 16" O.C.						
Decking, 2" x 6" redwood	2.080	L.F.	.027	11.23	1.21	12.44
Joists, 2" x 10", 16" O.C.	1.000	L.F.	.018	11	.80	11.80
Girder, 2" x 10"	.083	L.F.	.001	.91	.07	.98
Heavy soil or clay	.111	L.F.	.006		.20	.20
Concrete footings	.111	L.F.	.006	.31	.24	.55
Lumber preservative	.111	L.F.		.02		.02
Post, 4" x 4", including concrete footing	.111	L.F.	.009	3.50	.40	3.90
Framing, redwood or cedar stairs, 3' wide, 8 closed risers	1.000	Set	.028	2.49	1.26	3.75
Railings, 2" x 4"	.540	L.F.	.005	1.94	.21	2.15
TOTAL		S.F.	.100	31.40	4.39	35.79

The costs in this system are on a square foot basis.

Wood Deck Price Sheet	QUAN.	UNIT	LABOR HOURS	COST PER S.F.		
				MAT.	INST.	TOTAL
Decking, treated lumber, 1" x 4"	3.430	L.F.	.031	2.84	1.42	4.26
1" x 6"	2.180	L.F.	.033	2.98	1.49	4.47
2" x 4"	3.200	L.F.	.041	1.58	1.86	3.44
2" x 6"	2.080	L.F.	.027	1.56	1.21	2.77
Redwood or cedar,, 1" x 4"	3.430	L.F.	.035	3.31	1.56	4.87
1" x 6"	2.180	L.F.	.036	3.46	1.63	5.09
2" x 4"	3.200	L.F.	.028	11.90	1.28	13.18
2" x 6"	2.080	L.F.	.027	11.25	1.21	12.46
Joists for deck, treated lumber, 2" x 8", 16" O.C.	1.000	L.F.	.015	1.03	.66	1.69
24" O.C.	.800	L.F.	.012	.82	.53	1.35
2" x 10", 16" O.C.	1.000	L.F.	.018	1.38	.80	2.18
24" O.C.	.800	L.F.	.014	1.10	.64	1.74
Redwood or cedar, 2" x 8", 16" O.C.	1.000	L.F.	.015	7.20	.66	7.86
24" O.C.	.800	L.F.	.012	5.75	.53	6.28
2" x 10", 16" O.C.	1.000	L.F.	.018	11	.80	11.80
24" O.C.	.800	L.F.	.014	8.80	.64	9.44
Girder for joists, treated lumber, 2" x 10", 8' x 12' deck	.125	L.F.	.002	.17	.10	.27
12' x 16' deck	.083	L.F.	.001	.11	.07	.18
12' x 24' deck	.083	L.F.	.001	.11	.07	.18
Redwood or cedar, 2" x 10", 8' x 12' deck	.125	L.F.	.002	1.38	.10	1.48
12' x 16' deck	.083	L.F.	.001	.91	.07	.98
12' x 24' deck	.083	L.F.	.001	.91	.07	.98
Posts, 4" x 4", including concrete footing, 8' x 12' deck	.250	S.F.	.022	.82	.90	1.72
12' x 16' deck	.122	L.F.	.017	.55	.67	1.22
12' x 24' deck	.111	L.F.	.017	.53	.65	1.18
Stairs 2" x 10" stringers, treated lumber, 8' x 12' deck	1.000	Set	.020	1.28	3.60	4.88
12' x 16' deck	1.000	Set	.012	.64	1.80	2.44
12' x 24' deck	1.000	Set	.008	.45	1.26	1.71
Redwood or cedar, 8' x 12' deck	1.000	Set	.040	7.10	3.60	10.70
12' x 16' deck	1.000	Set	.020	3.55	1.80	5.35
12' x 24' deck	1.000	Set	.012	2.49	1.26	3.75
Railings 2" x 4", treated lumber, 8' x 12' deck	1.000	L.F.	.026	.49	1.17	1.66
12' x 16' deck	.670	L.F.	.017	.33	.78	1.11
12' x 24' deck	.540	L.F.	.014	.26	.63	.89
Redwood or cedar, 8' x 12' deck	1.000	L.F.	.009	3.62	.39	4.01
12' x 16' deck	.670	L.F.	.006	2.38	.26	2.64
12' x 24' deck	.540	L.F.	.005	1.94	.21	2.15

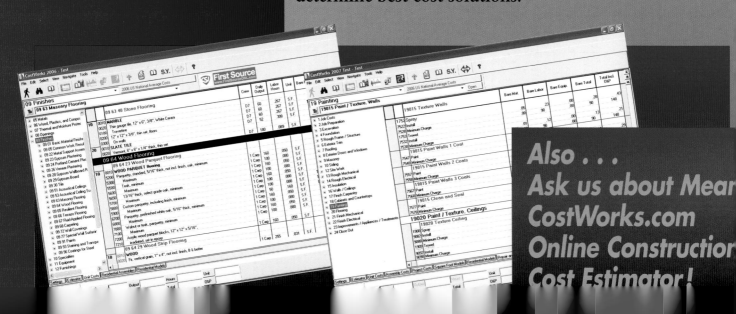

Division 8
Mechanical

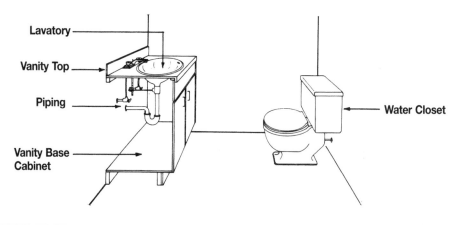

Lavatory

Vanity Top

Piping

Vanity Base Cabinet

Water Closet

System Description	QUAN.	UNIT	LABOR HOURS	COST EACH		
				MAT.	INST.	TOTAL
LAVATORY INSTALLED WITH VANITY, PLUMBING IN 2 WALLS						
Water closet, floor mounted, 2 piece, close coupled, white	1.000	Ea.	3.019	201	138	339
Rough-in, vent, 2" diameter DWV piping	1.000	Ea.	.955	30	43.60	73.60
Waste, 4" diameter DWV piping	1.000	Ea.	.828	39.30	37.65	76.95
Supply, 1/2" diameter type "L" copper supply piping	1.000	Ea.	.593	14.88	30	44.88
Lavatory, 20" x 18", P.E. cast iron white	1.000	Ea.	2.500	239	114	353
Rough-in, vent, 1-1/2" diameter DWV piping	1.000	Ea.	.901	29	41	70
Waste, 2" diameter DWV piping	1.000	Ea.	.955	30	43.60	73.60
Supply, 1/2" diameter type "L" copper supply piping	1.000	Ea.	.988	24.80	50	74.80
Piping, supply, 1/2" diameter type "L" copper supply piping	10.000	L.F.	.988	24.80	50	74.80
Waste, 4" diameter DWV piping	7.000	L.F.	1.931	91.70	87.85	179.55
Vent, 2" diameter DWV piping	12.000	L.F.	2.866	90	130.80	220.80
Vanity base cabinet, 2 door, 30" wide	1.000	Ea.	1.000	259	45	304
Vanity top, plastic & laminated, square edge	2.670	L.F.	.712	92.12	32.17	124.29
TOTAL		Ea.	18.236	1,165.60	843.67	2,009.27
LAVATORY WITH WALL-HUNG LAVATORY, PLUMBING IN 2 WALLS						
Water closet, floor mounted, 2 piece close coupled, white	1.000	Ea.	3.019	201	138	339
Rough-in, vent, 2" diameter DWV piping	1.000	Ea.	.955	30	43.60	73.60
Waste, 4" diameter DWV piping	1.000	Ea.	.828	39.30	37.65	76.95
Supply, 1/2" diameter type "L" copper supply piping	1.000	Ea.	.593	14.88	30	44.88
Lavatory, 20" x 18", P.E. cast iron, wall hung, white	1.000	Ea.	2.000	310	91	401
Rough-in, vent, 1-1/2" diameter DWV piping	1.000	Ea.	.901	29	41	70
Waste, 2" diameter DWV piping	1.000	Ea.	.955	30	43.60	73.60
Supply, 1/2" diameter type "L" copper supply piping	1.000	Ea.	.988	24.80	50	74.80
Piping, supply, 1/2" diameter type "L" copper supply piping	10.000	L.F.	.988	24.80	50	74.80
Waste, 4" diameter DWV piping	7.000	L.F.	1.931	91.70	87.85	179.55
Vent, 2" diameter DWV piping	12.000	L.F.	2.866	90	130.80	220.80
Carrier, steel for studs, no arms	1.000	Ea.	1.143	61.50	58	119.50
TOTAL		Ea.	17.167	946.98	801.50	1,748.48

Description	QUAN.	UNIT	LABOR HOURS	COST EACH		
				MAT.	INST.	TOTAL

Two Fixture Lavatory Price Sheet	QUAN.	UNIT	LABOR HOURS	COST EACH		
				MAT.	INST.	TOTAL
Water closet, close coupled standard 2 piece, white	1.000	Ea.	3.019	201	138	339
Color	1.000	Ea.	3.019	240	138	378
One piece elongated bowl, white	1.000	Ea.	3.019	585	138	723
Color	1.000	Ea.	3.019	720	138	858
Low profile, one piece elongated bowl, white	1.000	Ea.	3.019	845	138	983
Color	1.000	Ea.	3.019	1,100	138	1,238
Rough-in for water closet						
1/2" copper supply, 4" cast iron waste, 2" cast iron vent	1.000	Ea.	2.376	84	111	195
4" PVC waste, 2" PVC vent	1.000	Ea.	2.678	42	125	167
4" copper waste , 2" copper vent	1.000	Ea.	2.520	172	122	294
3" cast iron waste, 1-1/2" cast iron vent	1.000	Ea.	2.244	74.50	105	179.50
3" PVC waste, 1-1/2" PVC vent	1.000	Ea.	2.388	36	116	152
3" copper waste, 1-1/2" copper vent	1.000	Ea.	2.524	162	118	280
1/2" PVC supply, 4" PVC waste, 2" PVC vent	1.000	Ea.	2.974	43	140	183
3" PVC waste, 1-1/2" PVC vent	1.000	Ea.	2.684	36.50	131	167.50
1/2" steel supply, 4" cast iron waste, 2" cast iron vent	1.000	Ea.	2.545	90	120	210
4" cast iron waste, 2" steel vent	1.000	Ea.	2.590	108	122	230
4" PVC waste, 2" PVC vent	1.000	Ea.	2.847	47.50	134	181.50
Lavatory, vanity top mounted, P.E. on cast iron 20" x 18" white	1.000	Ea.	2.500	239	114	353
Color	1.000	Ea.	2.500	270	114	384
Steel, enameled 10" x 17" white	1.000	Ea.	2.759	156	126	282
Color	1.000	Ea.	2.500	162	114	276
Vitreous china 20" x 16", white	1.000	Ea.	2.963	288	135	423
Color	1.000	Ea.	2.963	288	135	423
Wall hung, P.E. on cast iron, 20" x 18", white	1.000	Ea.	2.000	310	91	401
Color	1.000	Ea.	2.000	315	91	406
Vitreous china 19" x 17", white	1.000	Ea.	2.286	193	104	297
Color	1.000	Ea.	2.286	216	104	320
Rough-in supply waste and vent for lavatory						
1/2" copper supply, 2" cast iron waste, 1-1/2" cast iron vent	1.000	Ea.	2.844	84	135	219
2" PVC waste, 1-1/2" PVC vent	1.000	Ea.	2.962	41.50	144	185.50
2" copper waste, 1-1/2" copper vent	1.000	Ea.	2.308	105	117	222
1-1/2" PVC waste, 1-1/4" PVC vent	1.000	Ea.	2.639	40	134	174
1-1/2" copper waste, 1-1/4" copper vent	1.000	Ea.	2.114	86	107	193
1/2" PVC supply, 2" PVC waste, 1-1/2" PVC vent	1.000	Ea.	3.456	43	169	212
1-1/2" PVC waste, 1-1/4" PVC vent	1.000	Ea.	3.133	41.50	159	200.50
1/2" steel supply, 2" cast iron waste, 1-1/2" cast iron vent	1.000	Ea.	3.126	93	149	242
2" cast iron waste, 2" steel vent	1.000	Ea.	3.225	112	154	266
2" PVC waste, 1-1/2" PVC vent	1.000	Ea.	3.244	51	159	210
1-1/2" PVC waste, 1-1/4" PVC vent	1.000	Ea.	2.921	49.50	148	197.50
Piping, supply, 1/2" copper, type "L"	10.000	L.F.	.988	25	50	75
1/2" steel	10.000	L.F.	1.270	34	64.50	98.50
1/2" PVC	10.000	L.F.	1.482	26.50	75	101.50
Waste, 4" cast iron	7.000	L.F.	1.931	91.50	88	179.50
4" copper	7.000	L.F.	2.800	259	128	387
4" PVC	7.000	L.F.	2.333	42.50	106	148.50
Vent, 2" cast iron	12.000	L.F.	2.866	90	131	221
2" copper	12.000	L.F.	2.182	138	110	248
2" PVC	12.000	L.F.	3.254	27.50	148	175.50
2" steel	12.000	Ea.	3.000	143	137	280
Vanity base cabinet, 2 door, 24" x 30"	1.000	Ea.	1.000	259	45	304
24" x 36"	1.000	Ea.	1.200	345	54.50	399.50
Vanity top, laminated plastic, square edge 25" x 32"	2.670	L.F.	.712	92	32	124
25" x 38"	3.170	L.F.	.845	109	38	147
Post formed, laminated plastic, 25" x 32"	2.670	L.F.	.712	29.50	32	61.50
25" x 38"	3.170	L.F.	.845	35	38	73
Cultured marble, 25" x 32" with bowl	1.000	Ea.	2.500	196	114	310
25" x 38" with bowl	1.000	Ea.	2.500	233	114	347
Carrier for lavatory, steel for studs	1.000	Ea.	1.143	61.50	58	119.50
Wood 2" x 8" blocking	1.330	L.F.	.053	1.10	2.41	3.51

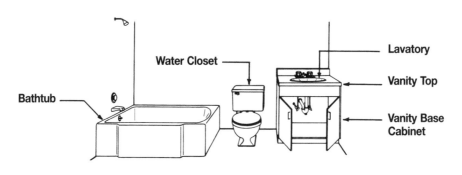

System Description	QUAN.	UNIT	LABOR HOURS	COST EACH		
				MAT.	INST.	TOTAL
BATHROOM INSTALLED WITH VANITY						
Water closet, floor mounted, 2 piece, close coupled, white	1.000	Ea.	3.019	201	138	339
Rough-in, waste, 4" diameter DWV piping	1.000	Ea.	.828	39.30	37.65	76.95
Vent, 2" diameter DWV piping	1.000	Ea.	.955	30	43.60	73.60
Supply, 1/2" diameter type "L" copper supply piping	1.000	Ea.	.593	14.88	30	44.88
Lavatory, 20" x 18", P.E. cast iron with accessories, white	1.000	Ea.	2.500	239	114	353
Rough-in, supply, 1/2" diameter type "L" copper supply piping	1.000	Ea.	.988	24.80	50	74.80
Waste, 1-1/2" diameter DWV piping	1.000	Ea.	1.803	58	82	140
Bathtub, P.E. cast iron, 5' long with accessories, white	1.000	Ea.	3.636	870	166	1,036
Rough-in, waste, 4" diameter DWV piping	1.000	Ea.	.828	39.30	37.65	76.95
Vent, 1-1/2" diameter DWV piping	1.000	Ea.	.593	34.20	30	64.20
Supply, 1/2" diameter type "L" copper supply piping	1.000	Ea.	.988	24.80	50	74.80
Piping, supply, 1/2" diameter type "L" copper supply piping	20.000	L.F.	1.975	49.60	100	149.60
Waste, 4" diameter DWV piping	9.000	L.F.	2.483	117.90	112.95	230.85
Vent, 2" diameter DWV piping	6.000	L.F.	1.500	71.70	68.40	140.10
Vanity base cabinet, 2 door, 30" wide	1.000	Ea.	1.000	259	45	304
Vanity top, plastic laminated square edge	2.670	L.F.	.712	72.09	32.17	104.26
TOTAL		Ea.	24.401	2,145.57	1,137.42	3,282.99
BATHROOM WITH WALL HUNG LAVATORY						
Water closet, floor mounted, 2 piece, close coupled, white	1.000	Ea.	3.019	201	138	339
Rough-in, vent, 2" diameter DWV piping	1.000	Ea.	.955	30	43.60	73.60
Waste, 4" diameter DWV piping	1.000	Ea.	.828	39.30	37.65	76.95
Supply, 1/2" diameter type "L" copper supply piping	1.000	Ea.	.593	14.88	30	44.88
Lavatory, 20" x 18" P.E. cast iron, wall hung, white	1.000	Ea.	2.000	310	91	401
Rough-in, waste, 1-1/2" diameter DWV piping	1.000	Ea.	1.803	58	82	140
Supply, 1/2" diameter type "L" copper supply piping	1.000	Ea.	.988	24.80	50	74.80
Bathtub, P.E. cast iron, 5' long with accessories, white	1.000	Ea.	3.636	870	166	1,036
Rough-in, waste, 4" diameter DWV piping	1.000	Ea.	.828	39.30	37.65	76.95
Supply, 1/2" diameter type "L" copper supply piping	1.000	Ea.	.988	24.80	50	74.80
Vent, 1-1/2" diameter DWV piping	1.000	Ea.	1.482	85.50	75	160.50
Piping, supply, 1/2" diameter type "L" copper supply piping	20.000	L.F.	1.975	49.60	100	149.60
Waste, 4" diameter DWV piping	9.000	L.F.	2.483	117.90	112.95	230.85
Vent, 2" diameter DWV piping	6.000	L.F.	1.500	71.70	68.40	140.10
Carrier, steel, for studs, no arms	1.000	Ea.	1.143	61.50	58	119.50
TOTAL		Ea.	24.221	1,998.28	1,140.25	3,138.53

The costs in this system are a cost each basis, all necessary piping is included.

Three Fixture Bathroom Price Sheet	QUAN.	UNIT	LABOR HOURS	COST EACH		
				MAT.	INST.	TOTAL
Water closet, close coupled standard 2 piece, white	1.000	Ea.	3.019	201	138	339
Color	1.000	Ea.	3.019	240	138	378
One piece, elongated bowl, white	1.000	Ea.	3.019	585	138	723
Color	1.000	Ea.	3.019	720	138	858
Low profile, one piece elongated bowl, white	1.000	Ea.	3.019	845	138	983
Color	1.000	Ea.	3.019	1,100	138	1,238
Rough-in, for water closet						
1/2" copper supply, 4" cast iron waste, 2" cast iron vent	1.000	Ea.	2.376	84	111	195
4" PVC/DWV waste, 2" PVC vent	1.000	Ea.	2.678	42	125	167
4" copper waste, 2" copper vent	1.000	Ea.	2.520	172	122	294
3" cast iron waste, 1-1/2" cast iron vent	1.000	Ea.	2.244	74.50	105	179.50
3" PVC waste, 1-1/2" PVC vent	1.000	Ea.	2.388	36	116	152
3" copper waste, 1-1/2" copper vent	1.000	Ea.	2.014	112	97.50	209.50
1/2" PVC supply, 4" PVC waste, 2" PVC vent	1.000	Ea.	2.974	43	140	183
3" PVC waste, 1-1/2" PVC supply	1.000	Ea.	2.684	36.50	131	167.50
1/2" steel supply, 4" cast iron waste, 2" cast iron vent	1.000	Ea.	2.545	90	120	210
4" cast iron waste, 2" steel vent	1.000	Ea.	2.590	108	122	230
4" PVC waste, 2" PVC vent	1.000	Ea.	2.847	47.50	134	181.50
Lavatory, wall hung, P.E. cast iron 20" x 18", white	1.000	Ea.	2.000	310	91	401
Color	1.000	Ea.	2.000	315	91	406
Vitreous china 19" x 17", white	1.000	Ea.	2.286	193	104	297
Color	1.000	Ea.	2.286	216	104	320
Lavatory, for vanity top, P.E. cast iron 20" x 18"", white	1.000	Ea.	2.500	239	114	353
Color	1.000	Ea.	2.500	270	114	384
Steel, enameled 20" x 17", white	1.000	Ea.	2.759	156	126	282
Color	1.000	Ea.	2.500	162	114	276
Vitreous china 20" x 16", white	1.000	Ea.	2.963	288	135	423
Color	1.000	Ea.	2.963	288	135	423
Rough-in, for lavatory						
1/2" copper supply, 1-1/2" C.I. waste, 1-1/2" C.I. vent	1.000	Ea.	2.791	83	132	215
1-1/2" PVC waste, 1-1/4" PVC vent	1.000	Ea.	2.639	40	134	174
1/2" steel supply, 1-1/4" cast iron waste, 1-1/4" steel vent	1.000	Ea.	2.890	93.50	138	231.50
1-1/4" PVC@ waste, 1-1/4" PVC vent	1.000	Ea.	2.794	49	142	191
1/2" PVC supply, 1-1/2" PVC waste, 1-1/2" PVC vent	1.000	Ea.	3.260	41.50	165	206.50
Bathtub, P.E. cast iron, 5' long corner with fittings, white	1.000	Ea.	3.636	870	166	1,036
Color	1.000	Ea.	3.636	1,075	166	1,241
Rough-in, for bathtub						
1/2" copper supply, 4" cast iron waste, 1-1/2" copper vent	1.000	Ea.	2.409	98.50	118	216.50
4" PVC waste, 1-1/2" PVC vent	1.000	Ea.	2.877	50.50	141	191.50
1/2" steel supply, 4" cast iron waste, 1-1/2" steel vent	1.000	Ea.	2.898	109	139	248
4" PVC waste, 1-1/2" PVC vent	1.000	Ea.	3.159	60	155	215
1/2" PVC supply, 4" PVC waste, 1-1/2" PVC vent	1.000	Ea.	3.371	52	166	218
Piping, supply 1/2" copper	20.000	L.F.	1.975	49.50	100	149.50
1/2" steel	20.000	L.F.	2.540	68	129	197
1/2" PVC	20.000	L.F.	2.963	52.50	150	202.50
Piping, waste, 4" cast iron no hub	9.000	L.F.	2.483	118	113	231
4" PVC/DWV	9.000	L.F.	3.000	54.50	137	191.50
4" copper/DWV	9.000	L.F.	3.600	335	164	499
Piping, vent 2" cast iron no hub	6.000	L.F.	1.433	45	65.50	110.50
2" copper/DWV	6.000	L.F.	1.091	69	55	124
2" PVC/DWV	6.000	L.F.	1.627	13.70	74	87.70
2" steel, galvanized	6.000	L.F.	1.500	71.50	68.50	140
Vanity base cabinet, 2 door, 24" x 30"	1.000	Ea.	1.000	259	45	304
24" x 36"	1.000	Ea.	1.200	345	54.50	399.50
Vanity top, laminated plastic square edge 25" x 32"	2.670	L.F.	.712	72	32	104
25" x 38"	3.160	L.F.	.843	85.50	38	123.50
Cultured marble, 25" x 32", with bowl	1.000	Ea.	2.500	196	114	310
25" x 38", with bowl	1.000	Ea.	2.500	233	114	347
Carrier, for lavatory, steel for studs, no arms	1.000	Ea.	1.143	61.50	58	119.50
Wood, 2" x 8" blocking	1.300	L.F.	.052	1.08	2.35	3.43

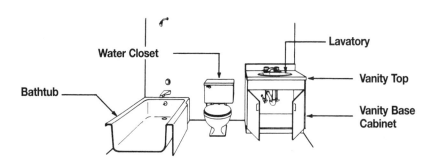

System Description	QUAN.	UNIT	LABOR HOURS	COST EACH		
				MAT.	INST.	TOTAL
BATHROOM WITH LAVATORY INSTALLED IN VANITY						
Water closet, floor mounted, 2 piece, close coupled, white	1.000	Ea.	3.019	201	138	339
Rough-in, waste, 4" diameter DWV piping	1.000	Ea.	.828	39.30	37.65	76.95
Vent, 2" diameter DWV piping	1.000	Ea.	.955	30	43.60	73.60
Supply, 1/2" diameter type "L" copper supply piping	1.000	Ea.	.593	14.88	30	44.88
Lavatory, 20" x 18", P.E. cast iron with accessories, white	1.000	Ea.	2.500	239	114	353
Rough-in, waste, 1-1/2" diameter DWV piping	1.000	Ea.	1.803	58	82	140
Supply, 1/2" diameter type "L" copper supply piping	1.000	Ea.	.988	24.80	50	74.80
Bathtub, P.E. cast iron 5' long with accessories, white	1.000	Ea.	3.636	870	166	1,036
Rough-in, waste, 4" diameter DWV piping	1.000	Ea.	.828	39.30	37.65	76.95
Vent, 1-1/2" diameter DWV piping	1.000	Ea.	.593	34.20	30	64.20
Supply, 1/2" diameter type "L" copper supply piping	1.000	Ea.	.988	24.80	50	74.80
Piping, supply, 1/2" diameter type "L" copper supply piping	10.000	L.F.	.988	24.80	50	74.80
Waste, 4" diameter DWV piping	6.000	L.F.	1.655	78.60	75.30	153.90
Vent, 2" diameter DWV piping	6.000	L.F.	1.500	71.70	68.40	140.10
Vanity base cabinet, 2 door, 30" wide	1.000	Ea.	1.000	259	45	304
Vanity top, plastic laminated square edge	2.670	L.F.	.712	72.09	32.17	104.26
TOTAL		Ea.	22.586	2,081.47	1,049.77	3,131.24
BATHROOM WITH WALL HUNG LAVATORY						
Water closet, floor mounted, 2 piece, close coupled, white	1.000	Ea.	3.019	201	138	339
Rough-in, vent, 2" diameter DWV piping	1.000	Ea.	.955	30	43.60	73.60
Waste, 4" diameter DWV piping	1.000	Ea.	.828	39.30	37.65	76.95
Supply, 1/2" diameter type "L" copper supply piping	1.000	Ea.	.593	14.88	30	44.88
Lavatory, 20" x 18" P.E. cast iron, wall hung, white	1.000	Ea.	2.000	310	91	401
Rough-in, waste, 1-1/2" diameter DWV piping	1.000	Ea.	1.803	58	82	140
Supply, 1/2" diameter type "L" copper supply piping	1.000	Ea.	.988	24.80	50	74.80
Bathtub, P.E. cast iron, 5' long with accessories, white	1.000	Ea.	3.636	870	166	1,036
Rough-in, waste, 4" diameter DWV piping	1.000	Ea.	.828	39.30	37.65	76.95
Supply, 1/2" diameter type "L" copper supply piping	1.000	Ea.	.988	24.80	50	74.80
Vent, 1-1/2" diameter DWV piping	1.000	Ea.	.593	34.20	30	64.20
Piping, supply, 1/2" diameter type "L" copper supply piping	10.000	L.F.	.988	24.80	50	74.80
Waste, 4" diameter DWV piping	6.000	L.F.	1.655	78.60	75.30	153.90
Vent, 2" diameter DWV piping	6.000	L.F.	1.500	71.70	68.40	140.10
Carrier, steel, for studs, no arms	1.000	Ea.	1.143	61.50	58	119.50
TOTAL		Ea.	21.517	1,882.88	1,007.60	2,890.48

The costs in this system are on a cost each basis. All necessary piping is included.

Three Fixture Bathroom Price Sheet	QUAN.	UNIT	LABOR HOURS	COST EACH		
				MAT.	INST.	TOTAL
Water closet, close coupled standard 2 piece, white	1.000	Ea.	3.019	201	138	339
Color	1.000	Ea.	3.019	240	138	378
One piece elongated bowl, white	1.000	Ea.	3.019	585	138	723
Color	1.000	Ea.	3.019	720	138	858
Low profile, one piece elongated bowl, white	1.000	Ea.	3.019	845	138	983
Color	1.000	Ea.	3.019	1,100	138	1,238
Rough-in for water closet						
1/2" copper supply, 4" cast iron waste, 2" cast iron vent	1.000	Ea.	2.376	84	111	195
4" PVC/DWV waste, 2" PVC vent	1.000	Ea.	2.678	42	125	167
4" carrier waste, 2" copper vent	1.000	Ea.	2.520	172	122	294
3" cast iron waste, 1-1/2" cast iron vent	1.000	Ea.	2.244	74.50	105	179.50
3" PVC waste, 1-1/2" PVC vent	1.000	Ea.	2.388	36	116	152
3" copper waste, 1-1/2" copper vent	1.000	Ea.	2.014	112	97.50	209.50
1/2" PVC supply, 4" PVC waste, 2" PVC vent	1.000	Ea.	2.974	43	140	183
3" PVC waste, 1-1/2" PVC supply	1.000	Ea.	2.684	36.50	131	167.50
1/2" steel supply, 4" cast iron waste, 2" cast iron vent	1.000	Ea.	2.545	90	120	210
4" cast iron waste, 2" steel vent	1.000	Ea.	2.590	108	122	230
4" PVC waste, 2" PVC vent	1.000	Ea.	2.847	47.50	134	181.50
Lavatory, wall hung, PE cast iron 20" x 18", white	1.000	Ea.	2.000	310	91	401
Color	1.000	Ea.	2.000	315	91	406
Vitreous china 19" x 17", white	1.000	Ea.	2.286	193	104	297
Color	1.000	Ea.	2.286	216	104	320
Lavatory, for vanity top, PE cast iron 20" x 18", white	1.000	Ea.	2.500	239	114	353
Color	1.000	Ea.	2.500	270	114	384
Steel enameled 20" x 17", white	1.000	Ea.	2.759	156	126	282
Color	1.000	Ea.	2.500	162	114	276
Vitreous china 20" x 16", white	1.000	Ea.	2.963	288	135	423
Color	1.000	Ea.	2.963	288	135	423
Rough-in for lavatory						
1/2" copper supply, 1-1/2" cast iron waste, 1-1/2" cast iron vent	1.000	Ea.	2.791	83	132	215
1-1/2" PVC waste, 1-1/4" PVC vent	1.000	Ea.	2.639	40	134	174
1/2" steel supply, 1-1/4" cast iron waste, 1-1/4" steel vent	1.000	Ea.	2.890	93.50	138	231.50
1-1/4" PVC waste, 1-1/4" PVC vent	1.000	Ea.	2.794	49	142	191
1/2" PVC supply, 1-1/2" PVC waste, 1-1/2" PVC vent	1.000	Ea.	3.260	41.50	165	206.50
Bathtub, PE cast iron, 5' long corner with fittings, white	1.000	Ea.	3.636	870	166	1,036
Color	1.000	Ea.	3.636	1,075	166	1,241
Rough-in for bathtub						
1/2" copper supply, 4" cast iron waste, 1-1/2" copper vent	1.000	Ea.	2.409	98.50	118	216.50
4" PVC waste, 1/2" PVC vent	1.000	Ea.	2.877	50.50	141	191.50
1/2" steel supply, 4" cast iron waste, 1-1/2" steel vent	1.000	Ea.	2.898	109	139	248
4" PVC waste, 1-1/2" PVC vent	1.000	Ea.	3.159	60	155	215
1/2" PVC supply, 4" PVC waste, 1-1/2" PVC vent	1.000	Ea.	3.371	52	166	218
Piping supply, 1/2" copper	10.000	L.F.	.988	25	50	75
1/2" steel	10.000	L.F.	1.270	34	64.50	98.50
1/2" PVC	10.000	L.F.	1.482	26.50	75	101.50
Piping waste, 4" cast iron no hub	6.000	L.F.	1.655	78.50	75.50	154
4" PVC/DWV	6.000	L.F.	2.000	36.50	91	127.50
4" copper/DWV	6.000	L.F.	2.400	222	110	332
Piping vent 2" cast iron no hub	6.000	L.F.	1.433	45	65.50	110.50
2" copper/DWV	6.000	L.F.	1.091	69	55	124
2" PVC/DWV	6.000	L.F.	1.627	13.70	74	87.70
2" steel, galvanized	6.000	L.F.	1.500	71.50	68.50	140
Vanity base cabinet, 2 door, 24" x 30"	1.000	Ea.	1.000	259	45	304
24" x 36"	1.000	Ea.	1.200	345	54.50	399.50
Vanity top, laminated plastic square edge 25" x 32"	2.670	L.F.	.712	72	32	104
25" x 38"	3.160	L.F.	.843	85.50	38	123.50
Cultured marble, 25" x 32", with bowl	1.000	Ea.	2.500	196	114	310
25" x 38", with bowl	1.000	Ea.	2.500	233	114	347
Carrier, for lavatory, steel for studs, no arms	1.000	Ea.	1.143	61.50	58	119.50
Wood, 2" x 8" blocking	1.300	L.F.	.052	1.08	2.35	3.43

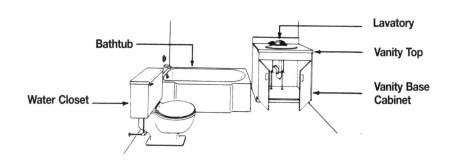

System Description	QUAN.	UNIT	LABOR HOURS	COST EACH		
				MAT.	INST.	TOTAL
BATHROOM WITH LAVATORY INSTALLED IN VANITY						
Water closet, floor mounted, 2 piece, close coupled, white	1.000	Ea.	3.019	201	138	339
Rough-in, vent, 2″ diameter DWV piping	1.000	Ea.	.955	30	43.60	73.60
Waste, 4″ diameter DWV piping	1.000	Ea.	.828	39.30	37.65	76.95
Supply, 1/2″ diameter type "L" copper supply piping	1.000	Ea.	.593	14.88	30	44.88
Lavatory, 20″ x 18″, PE cast iron with accessories, white	1.000	Ea.	2.500	239	114	353
Rough-in, vent, 1-1/2″ diameter DWV piping	1.000	Ea.	1.803	58	82	140
Supply, 1/2″ diameter type "L" copper supply piping	1.000	Ea.	.988	24.80	50	74.80
Bathtub, P.E. cast iron, 5′ long with accessories, white	1.000	Ea.	3.636	870	166	1,036
Rough-in, waste, 4″ diameter DWV piping	1.000	Ea.	.828	39.30	37.65	76.95
Supply, 1/2″ diameter type "L" copper supply piping	1.000	Ea.	.988	24.80	50	74.80
Vent, 1-1/2″ diameter DWV piping	1.000	Ea.	.593	34.20	30	64.20
Piping, supply, 1/2″ diameter type "L" copper supply piping	32.000	L.F.	3.161	79.36	160	239.36
Waste, 4″ diameter DWV piping	12.000	L.F.	3.310	157.20	150.60	307.80
Vent, 2″ diameter DWV piping	6.000	L.F.	1.500	71.70	68.40	140.10
Vanity base cabinet, 2 door, 30″ wide	1.000	Ea.	1.000	259	45	304
Vanity top, plastic laminated square edge	2.670	L.F.	.712	72.09	32.17	104.26
TOTAL		Ea.	26.414	2,214.63	1,235.07	3,449.70
BATHROOM WITH WALL HUNG LAVATORY						
Water closet, floor mounted, 2 piece, close coupled, white	1.000	Ea.	3.019	201	138	339
Rough-in, vent, 2″ diameter DWV piping	1.000	Ea.	.955	30	43.60	73.60
Waste, 4″ diameter DWV piping	1.000	Ea.	.828	39.30	37.65	76.95
Supply, 1/2″ diameter type "L" copper supply piping	1.000	Ea.	.593	14.88	30	44.88
Lavatory, 20″ x 18″ P.E. cast iron, wall hung, white	1.000	Ea.	2.000	310	91	401
Rough-in, waste, 1-1/2″ diameter DWV piping	1.000	Ea.	1.803	58	82	140
Supply, 1/2″ diameter type "L" copper supply piping	1.000	Ea.	.988	24.80	50	74.80
Bathtub, P.E. cast iron, 5′ long with accessories, white	1.000	Ea.	3.636	870	166	1,036
Rough-in, waste, 4″ diameter DWV piping	1.000	Ea.	.828	39.30	37.65	76.95
Supply, 1/2″ diameter type "L" copper supply piping	1.000	Ea.	.988	24.80	50	74.80
Vent, 1-1/2″ diameter DWV piping	1.000	Ea.	.593	34.20	30	64.20
Piping, supply, 1/2″ diameter type "L" copper supply piping	32.000	L.F.	3.161	79.36	160	239.36
Waste, 4″ diameter DWV piping	12.000	L.F.	3.310	157.20	150.60	307.80
Vent, 2″ diameter DWV piping	6.000	L.F.	1.500	71.70	68.40	140.10
Carrier steel, for studs, no arms	1.000	Ea.	1.143	61.50	58	119.50
TOTAL		Ea.	25.345	2,016.04	1,192.90	3,208.94

The costs in this system are on a cost each basis. All necessary piping is included.

Three Fixture Bathroom Price Sheet	QUAN.	UNIT	LABOR HOURS	COST EACH		
				MAT.	INST.	TOTAL
Water closet, close coupled, standard 2 piece, white	1.000	Ea.	3.019	201	138	339
Color	1.000	Ea.	3.019	240	138	378
One piece, elongated bowl, white	1.000	Ea.	3.019	585	138	723
Color	1.000	Ea.	3.019	720	138	858
Low profile, one piece, elongated bowl, white	1.000	Ea.	3.019	845	138	983
Color	1.000	Ea.	3.019	1,100	138	1,238
Rough-in, for water closet						
1/2″ copper supply, 4″ cast iron waste, 2″ cast iron vent	1.000	Ea.	2.376	84	111	195
4″ PVC/DWV waste, 2″ PVC vent	1.000	Ea.	2.678	42	125	167
4″ copper waste, 2″ copper vent	1.000	Ea.	2.520	172	122	294
3″ cast iron waste, 1-1/2″ cast iron vent	1.000	Ea.	2.244	74.50	105	179.50
3″ PVC waste, 1-1/2″ PVC vent	1.000	Ea.	2.388	36	116	152
3″ copper waste, 1-1/2″ copper vent	1.000	Ea.	2.014	112	97.50	209.50
1/2″ PVC supply, 4″ PVC waste, 2″ PVC vent	1.000	Ea.	2.974	43	140	183
3″ PVC waste, 1-1/2″ PVC supply	1.000	Ea.	2.684	36.50	131	167.50
1/2″ steel supply, 4″ cast iron waste, 2″ cast iron vent	1.000	Ea.	2.545	90	120	210
4″ cast iron waste, 2″ steel vent	1.000	Ea.	2.590	108	122	230
4″ PVC waste, 2″ PVC vent	1.000	Ea.	2.847	47.50	134	181.50
Lavatory wall hung, P.E. cast iron, 20″ x 18″, white	1.000	Ea.	2.000	310	91	401
Color	1.000	Ea.	2.000	315	91	406
Vitreous china, 19″ x 17″, white	1.000	Ea.	2.286	193	104	297
Color	1.000	Ea.	2.286	216	104	320
Lavatory, for vanity top, P.E., cast iron, 20″ x 18″, white	1.000	Ea.	2.500	239	114	353
Color	1.000	Ea.	2.500	270	114	384
Steel, enameled, 20″ x 17″, white	1.000	Ea.	2.759	156	126	282
Color	1.000	Ea.	2.500	162	114	276
Vitreous china, 20″ x 16″, white	1.000	Ea.	2.963	288	135	423
Color	1.000	Ea.	2.963	288	135	423
Rough-in, for lavatory						
1/2″ copper supply, 1-1/2″ C.I. waste, 1-1/2″ C.I. vent	1.000	Ea.	2.791	83	132	215
1-1/2″ PVC waste, 1-1/4″ PVC vent	1.000	Ea.	2.639	40	134	174
1/2″ steel supply, 1-1/4″ cast iron waste, 1-1/4″ steel vent	1.000	Ea.	2.890	93.50	138	231.50
1-1/4″ PVC waste, 1-1/4″ PVC vent	1.000	Ea.	2.794	49	142	191
1/2″ PVC supply, 1-1/2″ PVC waste, 1-1/2″ PVC vent	1.000	Ea.	3.260	41.50	165	206.50
Bathtub, P.E. cast iron, 5′ long corner with fittings, white	1.000	Ea.	3.636	870	166	1,036
Color	1.000	Ea.	3.636	1,075	166	1,241
Rough-in, for bathtub						
1/2″ copper supply, 4″ cast iron waste, 1-1/2″ copper vent	1.000	Ea.	2.409	98.50	118	216.50
4″ PVC waste, 1/2″ PVC vent	1.000	Ea.	2.877	50.50	141	191.50
1/2″ steel supply, 4″ cast iron waste, 1-1/2″ steel vent	1.000	Ea.	2.898	109	139	248
4″ PVC waste, 1-1/2″ PVC vent	1.000	Ea.	3.159	60	155	215
1/2″ PVC supply, 4″ PVC waste, 1-1/2″ PVC vent	1.000	Ea.	3.371	52	166	218
Piping, supply, 1/2″ copper	32.000	L.F.	3.161	79.50	160	239.50
1/2″ steel	32.000	L.F.	4.063	109	206	315
1/2″ PVC	32.000	L.F.	4.741	84	240	324
Piping, waste, 4″ cast iron no hub	12.000	L.F.	3.310	157	151	308
4″ PVC/DWV	12.000	L.F.	4.000	72.50	182	254.50
4″ copper/DWV	12.000	L.F.	4.800	445	219	664
Piping, vent, 2″ cast iron no hub	6.000	L.F.	1.433	45	65.50	110.50
2″ copper/DWV	6.000	L.F.	1.091	69	55	124
2″ PVC/DWV	6.000	L.F.	1.627	13.70	74	87.70
2″ steel, galvanized	6.000	L.F.	1.500	71.50	68.50	140
Vanity base cabinet, 2 door, 24″ x 30″	1.000	Ea.	1.000	259	45	304
24″ x 36″	1.000	Ea.	1.200	345	54.50	399.50
Vanity top, laminated plastic square edge, 25″ x 32″	2.670	L.F.	.712	72	32	104
25″ x 38″	3.160	L.F.	.843	85.50	38	123.50
Cultured marble, 25″ x 32″, with bowl	1.000	Ea.	2.500	196	114	310
25″ x 38″, with bowl	1.000	Ea.	2.500	233	114	347
Carrier, for lavatory, steel for studs, no arms	1.000	Ea.	1.143	61.50	58	119.50
Wood, 2″ x 8″ blocking	1.300	L.F.	.052	1.08	2.35	3.43

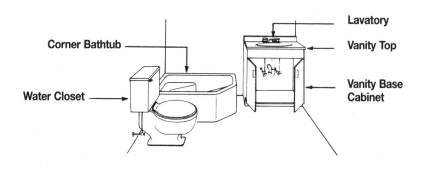

System Description	QUAN.	UNIT	LABOR HOURS	COST EACH		
				MAT.	INST.	TOTAL
BATHROOM WITH LAVATORY INSTALLED IN VANITY						
Water closet, floor mounted, 2 piece, close coupled, white	1.000	Ea.	3.019	201	138	339
Rough-in, vent, 2″ diameter DWV piping	1.000	Ea.	.955	30	43.60	73.60
Waste, 4″ diameter DWV piping	1.000	Ea.	.828	39.30	37.65	76.95
Supply, 1/2″ diameter type "L" copper supply piping	1.000	Ea.	.593	14.88	30	44.88
Lavatory, 20″ x 18″, P.E. cast iron with fittings, white	1.000	Ea.	2.500	239	114	353
Rough-in, waste, 1-1/2″ diameter DWV piping	1.000	Ea.	1.803	58	82	140
Supply, 1/2″ diameter type "L" copper supply piping	1.000	Ea.	.988	24.80	50	74.80
Bathtub, P.E. cast iron, corner with fittings, white	1.000	Ea.	3.636	1,925	166	2,091
Rough-in, waste, 4″ diameter DWV piping	1.000	Ea.	.828	39.30	37.65	76.95
Supply, 1/2″ diameter type "L" copper supply piping	1.000	Ea.	.988	24.80	50	74.80
Vent, 1-1/2″ diameter DWV piping	1.000	Ea.	.593	34.20	30	64.20
Piping, supply, 1/2″ diameter type "L" copper supply piping	32.000	L.F.	3.161	79.36	160	239.36
Waste, 4″ diameter DWV piping	12.000	L.F.	3.310	157.20	150.60	307.80
Vent, 2″ diameter DWV piping	6.000	L.F.	1.500	71.70	68.40	140.10
Vanity base cabinet, 2 door, 30″ wide	1.000	Ea.	1.000	259	45	304
Vanity top, plastic laminated, square edge	2.670	L.F.	.712	92.12	32.17	124.29
TOTAL		Ea.	26.414	3,289.66	1,235.07	4,524.73
BATHROOM WITH WALL HUNG LAVATORY						
Water closet, floor mounted, 2 piece, close coupled, white	1.000	Ea.	3.019	201	138	339
Rough-in, vent, 2″ diameter DWV piping	1.000	Ea.	.955	30	43.60	73.60
Waste, 4″ diameter DWV piping	1.000	Ea.	.828	39.30	37.65	76.95
Supply, 1/2″ diameter type "L" copper supply piping	1.000	Ea.	.593	14.88	30	44.88
Lavatory, 20″ x 18″, P.E. cast iron, with fittings, white	1.000	Ea.	2.000	310	91	401
Rough-in, waste, 1-1/2″ diameter DWV piping	1.000	Ea.	1.803	58	82	140
Supply, 1/2″ diameter type "L" copper supply piping	1.000	Ea.	.988	24.80	50	74.80
Bathtub, P.E. cast iron, corner, with fittings, white	1.000	Ea.	3.636	1,925	166	2,091
Rough-in, waste, 4″ diameter DWV piping	1.000	Ea.	.828	39.30	37.65	76.95
Supply, 1/2″ diameter type "L" copper supply piping	1.000	Ea.	.988	24.80	50	74.80
Vent, 1-1/2″ diameter DWV piping	1.000	Ea.	.593	34.20	30	64.20
Piping, supply, 1/2″ diameter type "L" copper supply piping	32.000	L.F.	3.161	79.36	160	239.36
Waste, 4″ diameter DWV piping	12.000	L.F.	3.310	157.20	150.60	307.80
Vent, 2″ diameter DWV piping	6.000	L.F.	1.500	71.70	68.40	140.10
Carrier, steel, for studs, no arms	1.000	Ea.	1.143	61.50	58	119.50
TOTAL		Ea.	25.345	3,071.04	1,192.90	4,263.94

The costs in this system are on a cost each basis. All necessary piping is included.

Three Fixture Bathroom Price Sheet	QUAN.	UNIT	LABOR HOURS	COST EACH		
				MAT.	INST.	TOTAL
Water closet, close coupled, standard 2 piece, white	1.000	Ea.	3.019	201	138	339
Color	1.000	Ea.	3.019	240	138	378
One piece elongated bowl, white	1.000	Ea.	3.019	585	138	723
Color	1.000	Ea.	3.019	720	138	858
Low profile, one piece elongated bowl, white	1.000	Ea.	3.019	845	138	983
Color	1.000	Ea.	3.019	1,100	138	1,238
Rough-in, for water closet						
1/2" copper supply, 4" cast iron waste, 2" cast iron vent	1.000	Ea.	2.376	84	111	195
4" PVC/DWV waste, 2" PVC vent	1.000	Ea.	2.678	42	125	167
4" copper waste, 2" copper vent	1.000	Ea.	2.520	172	122	294
3" cast iron waste, 1-1/2" cast iron vent	1.000	Ea.	2.244	74.50	105	179.50
3" PVC waste, 1-1/2" PVC vent	1.000	Ea.	2.388	36	116	152
3" copper waste, 1-1/2" copper vent	1.000	Ea.	2.014	112	97.50	209.50
1/2" PVC supply, 4" PVC waste, 2" PVC vent	1.000	Ea.	2.974	43	140	183
3" PVC waste, 1-1/2" PVC supply	1.000	Ea.	2.684	36.50	131	167.50
1/2" steel supply, 4" cast iron waste, 2" cast iron vent	1.000	Ea.	2.545	90	120	210
4" cast iron waste, 2" steel vent	1.000	Ea.	2.590	108	122	230
4" PVC waste, 2" PVC vent	1.000	Ea.	2.847	47.50	134	181.50
Lavatory, wall hung P.E. cast iron 20" x 18", white	1.000	Ea.	2.000	310	91	401
Color	1.000	Ea.	2.000	315	91	406
Vitreous china 19" x 17", white	1.000	Ea.	2.286	193	104	297
Color	1.000	Ea.	2.286	216	104	320
Lavatory, for vanity top, P.E., cast iron, 20" x 18", white	1.000	Ea.	2.500	239	114	353
Color	1.000	Ea.	2.500	270	114	384
Steel enameled 20" x 17", white	1.000	Ea.	2.759	156	126	282
Color	1.000	Ea.	2.500	162	114	276
Vitreous china 20" x 16", white	1.000	Ea.	2.963	288	135	423
Color	1.000	Ea.	2.963	288	135	423
Rough-in, for lavatory						
1/2" copper supply, 1-1/2" cast iron waste, 1-1/2" cast iron vent	1.000	Ea.	2.791	83	132	215
1-1/2" PVC waste, 1-1/4" PVC vent	1.000	Ea.	2.639	40	134	174
1/2" steel supply, 1-1/4" cast iron waste, 1-1/4" steel vent	1.000	Ea.	2.890	93.50	138	231.50
1-1/4" PVC waste, 1-1/4" PVC vent	1.000	Ea.	2.794	49	142	191
1/2" PVC supply, 1-1/2" PVC waste, 1-1/2" PVC vent	1.000	Ea.	3.260	41.50	165	206.50
Bathtub, P.E. cast iron, corner with fittings, white	1.000	Ea.	3.636	1,925	166	2,091
Color	1.000	Ea.	4.000	2,150	182	2,332
Rough-in, for bathtub						
1/2" copper supply, 4" cast iron waste, 1-1/2" copper vent	1.000	Ea.	2.409	98.50	118	216.50
4" PVC waste, 1-1/2" PVC vent	1.000	Ea.	2.877	50.50	141	191.50
1/2" steel supply, 4" cast iron waste, 1-1/2" steel vent	1.000	Ea.	2.898	109	139	248
4" PVC waste, 1-1/2" PVC vent	1.000	Ea.	3.159	60	155	215
1/2" PVC supply, 4" PVC waste, 1-1/2" PVC vent	1.000	Ea.	3.371	52	166	218
Piping, supply, 1/2" copper	32.000	L.F.	3.161	79.50	160	239.50
1/2" steel	32.000	L.F.	4.063	109	206	315
1/2" PVC	32.000	L.F.	4.741	84	240	324
Piping, waste, 4" cast iron, no hub	12.000	L.F.	3.310	157	151	308
4" PVC/DWV	12.000	L.F.	4.000	72.50	182	254.50
4" copper/DWV	12.000	L.F.	4.800	445	219	664
Piping, vent 2" cast iron, no hub	6.000	L.F.	1.433	45	65.50	110.50
2" copper/DWV	6.000	L.F.	1.091	69	55	124
2" PVC/DWV	6.000	L.F.	1.627	13.70	74	87.70
2" steel, galvanized	6.000	L.F.	1.500	71.50	68.50	140
Vanity base cabinet, 2 door, 24" x 30"	1.000	Ea.	1.000	259	45	304
24" x 36"	1.000	Ea.	1.200	345	54.50	399.50
Vanity top, laminated plastic square edge 25" x 32"	2.670	L.F.	.712	92	32	124
25" x 38"	3.160	L.F.	.843	109	38	147
Cultured marble, 25" x 32", with bowl	1.000	Ea.	2.500	196	114	310
25" x 38", with bowl	1.000	Ea.	2.500	233	114	347
Carrier, for lavatory, steel for studs, no arms	1.000	Ea.	1.143	61.50	58	119.50
Wood, 2" x 8" blocking	1.300	L.F.	.053	1.10	2.41	3.51

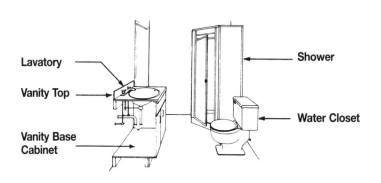

System Description	QUAN.	UNIT	LABOR HOURS	COST EACH		
				MAT.	INST.	TOTAL
BATHROOM WITH SHOWER, LAVATORY INSTALLED IN VANITY						
Water closet, floor mounted, 2 piece, close coupled, white	1.000	Ea.	3.019	201	138	339
Rough-in, vent, 2" diameter DWV piping	1.000	Ea.	.955	30	43.60	73.60
Waste, 4" diameter DWV piping	1.000	Ea.	.828	39.30	37.65	76.95
Supply, 1/2" diameter type "L" copper supply piping	1.000	Ea.	.593	14.88	30	44.88
Lavatory, 20" x 18" P.E. cast iron with fittings, white	1.000	Ea.	2.500	239	114	353
Rough-in, waste, 1-1/2" diameter DWV piping	1.000	Ea.	1.803	58	82	140
Supply, 1/2" diameter type "L" copper supply piping	1.000	Ea.	.988	24.80	50	74.80
Shower, steel enameled, stone base, corner, white	1.000	Ea.	3.200	400	146	546
Shower mixing valve	1.000	Ea.	1.333	124	67.50	191.50
Shower door	1.000	Ea.	1.000	238	50.50	288.50
Rough-in, vent, 1-1/2" diameter DWV piping	1.000	Ea.	.225	7.25	10.25	17.50
Waste, 2" diameter DWV piping	1.000	Ea.	1.433	45	65.40	110.40
Supply, 1/2" diameter type "L" copper supply piping	1.000	Ea.	1.580	39.68	80	119.68
Piping, supply, 1/2" diameter type "L" copper supply piping	36.000	L.F.	4.148	104.16	210	314.16
Waste, 4" diameter DWV piping	7.000	L.F.	2.759	131	125.50	256.50
Vent, 2" diameter DWV piping	6.000	L.F.	2.250	107.55	102.60	210.15
Vanity base 2 door, 30" wide	1.000	Ea.	1.000	259	45	304
Vanity top, plastic laminated, square edge	2.170	L.F.	.712	76.10	32.17	108.27
TOTAL		Ea.	30.326	2,138.72	1,430.17	3,568.89
BATHROOM WITH SHOWER, WALL HUNG LAVATORY						
Water closet, floor mounted, close coupled	1.000	Ea.	3.019	201	138	339
Rough-in, vent, 2" diameter DWV piping	1.000	Ea.	.955	30	43.60	73.60
Waste, 4" diameter DWV piping	1.000	Ea.	.828	39.30	37.65	76.95
Supply, 1/2" diameter type "L" copper supply piping	1.000	Ea.	.593	14.88	30	44.88
Lavatory, 20" x 18" P.E. cast iron with fittings, white	1.000	Ea.	2.000	310	91	401
Rough-in, waste, 1-1/2" diameter DWV piping	1.000	Ea.	1.803	58	82	140
Supply, 1/2" diameter type "L" copper supply piping	1.000	Ea.	.988	24.80	50	74.80
Shower, steel enameled, stone base, white	1.000	Ea.	3.200	400	146	546
Mixing valve	1.000	Ea.	1.333	124	67.50	191.50
Shower door	1.000	Ea.	1.000	238	50.50	288.50
Rough-in, vent, 1-1/2" diameter DWV piping	1.000	Ea.	.225	7.25	10.25	17.50
Waste, 2" diameter DWV piping	1.000	Ea.	1.433	45	65.40	110.40
Supply, 1/2" diameter type "L" copper supply piping	1.000	Ea.	1.580	39.68	80	119.68
Piping, supply, 1/2" diameter type "L" copper supply piping	36.000	L.F.	4.148	104.16	210	314.16
Waste, 4" diameter DWV piping	7.000	L.F.	2.759	131	125.50	256.50
Vent, 2" diameter DWV piping	6.000	L.F.	2.250	107.55	102.60	210.15
Carrier, steel, for studs, no arms	1.000	Ea.	1.143	61.50	58	119.50
TOTAL		Ea.	29.257	1,936.12	1,388	3,324.12

The costs in this system are on a cost each basis. All necessary piping is included.

Three Fixture Bathroom Price Sheet	QUAN.	UNIT	LABOR HOURS	COST EACH		
				MAT.	INST.	TOTAL
Water closet, close coupled, standard 2 piece, white	1.000	Ea.	3.019	201	138	339
Color	1.000	Ea.	3.019	240	138	378
One piece elongated bowl, white	1.000	Ea.	3.019	585	138	723
Color	1.000	Ea.	3.019	720	138	858
Low profile, one piece elongated bowl, white	1.000	Ea.	3.019	845	138	983
Color	1.000	Ea.	3.019	1,100	138	1,238
Rough-in, for water closet						
1/2" copper supply, 4" cast iron waste, 2" cast iron vent	1.000	Ea.	2.376	84	111	195
4" PVC/DWV waste, 2" PVC vent	1.000	Ea.	2.678	42	125	167
4" copper waste, 2" copper vent	1.000	Ea.	2.520	172	122	294
3" cast iron waste, 1-1/2" cast iron vent	1.000	Ea.	2.244	74.50	105	179.50
3" PVC waste, 1-1/2" PVC vent	1.000	Ea.	2.388	36	116	152
3" copper waste, 1-1/2" copper vent	1.000	Ea.	2.014	112	97.50	209.50
1/2" PVC supply, 4" PVC waste, 2" PVC vent	1.000	Ea.	2.974	43	140	183
3" PVC waste, 1-1/2" PVC supply	1.000	Ea.	2.684	36.50	131	167.50
1/2" steel supply, 4" cast iron waste, 2" cast iron vent	1.000	Ea.	2.545	90	120	210
4" cast iron waste, 2" steel vent	1.000	Ea.	2.590	108	122	230
4" PVC waste, 2" PVC vent	1.000	Ea.	2.847	47.50	134	181.50
Lavatory, wall hung, P.E. cast iron 20" x 18", white	1.000	Ea.	2.000	310	91	401
Color	1.000	Ea.	2.000	315	91	406
Vitreous china 19" x 17", white	1.000	Ea.	2.286	193	104	297
Color	1.000	Ea.	2.286	216	104	320
Lavatory, for vanity top, P.E. cast iron 20" x 18", white	1.000	Ea.	2.500	239	114	353
Color	1.000	Ea.	2.500	270	114	384
Steel enameled 20" x 17", white	1.000	Ea.	2.759	156	126	282
Color	1.000	Ea.	2.500	162	114	276
Vitreous china 20" x 16", white	1.000	Ea.	2.963	288	135	423
Color	1.000	Ea.	2.963	288	135	423
Rough-in, for lavatory						
1/2" copper supply, 1-1/2" cast iron waste, 1-1/2" cast iron vent	1.000	Ea.	2.791	83	132	215
1-1/2" PVC waste, 1-1/2" PVC vent	1.000	Ea.	2.639	40	134	174
1/2" steel supply, 1-1/4" cast iron waste, 1-1/4" steel vent	1.000	Ea.	2.890	93.50	138	231.50
1-1/4" PVC waste, 1-1/4" PVC vent	1.000	Ea.	2.921	49.50	148	197.50
1/2" PVC supply, 1-1/2" PVC waste, 1-1/2" PVC vent	1.000	Ea.	3.260	41.50	165	206.50
Shower, steel enameled stone base, 32" x 32", white	1.000	Ea.	8.000	400	146	546
Color	1.000	Ea.	7.822	900	134	1,034
36" x 36" white	1.000	Ea.	8.889	960	152	1,112
Color	1.000	Ea.	8.889	1,025	152	1,177
Rough-in, for shower						
1/2" copper supply, 4" cast iron waste, 1-1/2" copper vent	1.000	Ea.	3.238	92	156	248
4" PVC waste, 1-1/2" PVC vent	1.000	Ea.	3.429	55.50	165	220.50
1/2" steel supply, 4" cast iron waste, 1-1/2" steel vent	1.000	Ea.	3.665	109	178	287
4" PVC waste, 1-1/2" PVC vent	1.000	Ea.	3.881	70	189	259
1/2" PVC supply, 4" PVC waste, 1-1/2" PVC vent	1.000	Ea.	4.219	57.50	205	262.50
Piping, supply, 1/2" copper	36.000	L.F.	4.148	104	210	314
1/2" steel	36.000	L.F.	5.333	143	271	414
1/2" PVC	36.000	L.F.	6.222	110	315	425
Piping, waste, 4" cast iron no hub	7.000	L.F.	2.759	131	126	257
4" PVC/DWV	7.000	L.F.	3.333	60.50	152	212.50
4" copper/DWV	7.000	L.F.	4.000	370	183	553
Piping, vent, 2" cast iron no hub	6.000	L.F.	2.149	67.50	98	165.50
2" copper/DWV	6.000	L.F.	1.636	104	83	187
2" PVC/DWV	6.000	L.F.	2.441	20.50	111	131.50
2" steel, galvanized	6.000	L.F.	2.250	108	103	211
Vanity base cabinet, 2 door, 24" x 30"	1.000	Ea.	1.000	259	45	304
24" x 36"	1.000	Ea.	1.200	345	54.50	399.50
Vanity top, laminated plastic square edge, 25" x 32"	2.170	L.F.	.712	76	32	108
25" x 38"	2.670	L.F.	.845	90.50	38	128.50
Carrier, for lavatory, steel for studs, no arms	1.000	Ea.	1.143	61.50	58	119.50
Wood, 2" x 8" blocking	1.300	L.F.	.052	1.08	2.35	3.43

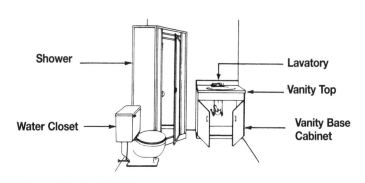

System Description	QUAN.	UNIT	LABOR HOURS	COST EACH		
				MAT.	INST.	TOTAL
BATHROOM WITH LAVATORY INSTALLED IN VANITY						
Water closet, floor mounted, 2 piece, close coupled, white	1.000	Ea.	3.019	201	138	339
Rough-in, vent, 2" diameter DWV piping	1.000	Ea.	.955	30	43.60	73.60
Waste, 4" diameter DWV piping	1.000	Ea.	.828	39.30	37.65	76.95
Supply, 1/2" diameter type "L" copper supply piping	1.000	Ea.	.593	14.88	30	44.88
Lavatory, 20" x 18", P.E. cast iron with fittings, white	1.000	Ea.	2.500	239	114	353
Rough-in, waste, 1-1/2" diameter DWV piping	1.000	Ea.	1.803	58	82	140
Supply, 1/2" diameter type "L" copper supply piping	1.000	Ea.	.988	24.80	50	74.80
Shower, steel enameled, stone base, corner, white	1.000	Ea.	3.200	400	146	546
Mixing valve	1.000	Ea.	1.333	124	67.50	191.50
Shower door	1.000	Ea.	1.000	238	50.50	288.50
Rough-in, vent, 1-1/2" diameter DWV piping	1.000	Ea.	.225	7.25	10.25	17.50
Waste, 2" diameter DWV piping	1.000	Ea.	1.433	45	65.40	110.40
Supply, 1/2" diameter type "L" copper supply piping	1.000	Ea.	1.580	39.68	80	119.68
Piping, supply, 1/2" diameter type "L" copper supply piping	36.000	L.F.	3.556	89.28	180	269.28
Waste, 4" diameter DWV piping	7.000	L.F.	1.931	91.70	87.85	179.55
Vent, 2" diameter DWV piping	6.000	L.F.	1.500	71.70	68.40	140.10
Vanity base, 2 door, 30" wide	1.000	Ea.	1.000	259	45	304
Vanity top, plastic laminated, square edge	2.670	L.F.	.712	72.09	32.17	104.26
TOTAL		Ea.	28.156	2,044.68	1,328.32	3,373
BATHROOM, WITH WALL HUNG LAVATORY						
Water closet, floor mounted, 2 piece, close coupled, white	1.000	Ea.	3.019	201	138	339
Rough-in, vent, 2" diameter DWV piping	1.000	Ea.	.955	30	43.60	73.60
Waste, 4" diameter DWV piping	1.000	Ea.	.828	39.30	37.65	76.95
Supply, 1/2" diameter type "L" copper supply piping	1.000	Ea.	.593	14.88	30	44.88
Lavatory, wall hung, 20" x 18" P.E. cast iron with fittings, white	1.000	Ea.	2.000	310	91	401
Rough-in, waste, 1-1/2" diameter DWV piping	1.000	Ea.	1.803	58	82	140
Supply, 1/2" diameter type "L" copper supply piping	1.000	Ea.	.988	24.80	50	74.80
Shower, steel enameled, stone base, corner, white	1.000	Ea.	3.200	400	146	546
Mixing valve	1.000	Ea.	1.333	124	67.50	191.50
Shower door	1.000	Ea.	1.000	238	50.50	288.50
Rough-in, waste, 1-1/2" diameter DWV piping	1.000	Ea.	.225	7.25	10.25	17.50
Waste, 2" diameter DWV piping	1.000	Ea.	1.433	45	65.40	110.40
Supply, 1/2" diameter type "L" copper supply piping	1.000	Ea.	1.580	39.68	80	119.68
Piping, supply, 1/2" diameter type "L" copper supply piping	36.000	L.F.	3.556	89.28	180	269.28
Waste, 4" diameter DWV piping	7.000	L.F.	1.931	91.70	87.85	179.55
Vent, 2" diameter DWV piping	6.000	L.F.	1.500	71.70	68.40	140.10
Carrier, steel, for studs, no arms	1.000	Ea.	1.143	61.50	58	119.50
TOTAL		Ea.	27.087	1,846.09	1,286.15	3,132.24

The costs in this system are on a cost each basis. All necessary piping is included.

Three Fixture Bathroom Price Sheet	QUAN.	UNIT	LABOR HOURS	COST EACH		
				MAT.	INST.	TOTAL
Water closet, close coupled, standard 2 piece, white	1.000	Ea.	3.019	201	138	339
Color	1.000	Ea.	3.019	240	138	378
One piece elongated bowl, white	1.000	Ea.	3.019	585	138	723
Color	1.000	Ea.	3.019	720	138	858
Low profile one piece elongated bowl, white	1.000	Ea.	3.019	845	138	983
Color	1.000	Ea.	3.623	1,100	138	1,238
Rough-in, for water closet						
1/2" copper supply, 4" cast iron waste, 2" cast iron vent	1.000	Ea.	2.376	84	111	195
4" P.V.C./DWV waste, 2" PVC vent	1.000	Ea.	2.678	42	125	167
4" copper waste, 2" copper vent	1.000	Ea.	2.520	172	122	294
3" cast iron waste, 1-1/2" cast iron vent	1.000	Ea.	2.244	74.50	105	179.50
3" PVC waste, 1-1/2" PVC vent	1.000	Ea.	2.388	36	116	152
3" copper waste, 1-1/2" copper vent	1.000	Ea.	2.014	112	97.50	209.50
1/2" P.V.C. supply, 4" P.V.C. waste, 2" P.V.C. vent	1.000	Ea.	2.974	43	140	183
3" P.V.C. waste, 1-1/2" P.V.C. vent	1.000	Ea.	2.684	36.50	131	167.50
1/2" steel supply, 4" cast iron waste, 2" cast iron vent	1.000	Ea.	2.545	90	120	210
4" cast iron waste, 2" steel vent	1.000	Ea.	2.590	108	122	230
4" P.V.C. waste, 2" P.V.C. vent	1.000	Ea.	2.847	47.50	134	181.50
Lavatory, wall hung P.E. cast iron 20" x 18", white	1.000	Ea.	2.000	310	91	401
Color	1.000	Ea.	2.000	315	91	406
Vitreous china 19" x 17", white	1.000	Ea.	2.286	193	104	297
Color	1.000	Ea.	2.286	216	104	320
Lavatory, for vanity top P.E. cast iron 20" x 18", white	1.000	Ea.	2.500	239	114	353
Color	1.000	Ea.	2.500	270	114	384
Steel enameled 20" x 17", white	1.000	Ea.	2.759	156	126	282
Color	1.000	Ea.	2.500	162	114	276
Vitreous china 20" x 16", white	1.000	Ea.	2.963	288	135	423
Color	1.000	Ea.	2.963	288	135	423
Rough-in, for lavatory						
1/2" copper supply, 1-1/2" cast iron waste, 1-1/2" cast iron vent	1.000	Ea.	2.791	83	132	215
1-1/2" P.V.C. waste, 1-1/2" P.V.C. vent	1.000	Ea.	2.639	40	134	174
1/2" steel supply, 1-1/2" cast iron waste, 1-1/4" steel vent	1.000	Ea.	2.890	93.50	138	231.50
1-1/2" P.V.C. waste, 1-1/4" P.V.C. vent	1.000	Ea.	2.921	49.50	148	197.50
1/2" P.V.C. supply, 1-1/2" P.V.C. waste, 1-1/2" P.V.C. vent	1.000	Ea.	3.260	41.50	165	206.50
Shower, steel enameled stone base, 32" x 32", white	1.000	Ea.	8.000	400	146	546
Color	1.000	Ea.	7.822	900	134	1,034
36" x 36", white	1.000	Ea.	8.889	960	152	1,112
Color	1.000	Ea.	8.889	1,025	152	1,177
Rough-in, for shower						
1/2" copper supply, 2" cast iron waste, 1-1/2" copper vent	1.000	Ea.	3.161	93	153	246
2" P.V.C. waste, 1-1/2" P.V.C. vent	1.000	Ea.	3.429	55.50	165	220.50
1/2" steel supply, 2" cast iron waste, 1-1/2" steel vent	1.000	Ea.	3.887	142	188	330
2" P.V.C. waste, 1-1/2" P.V.C. vent	1.000	Ea.	3.881	70	189	259
1/2" P.V.C. supply, 2" P.V.C. waste, 1-1/2" P.V.C. vent	1.000	Ea.	4.219	57.50	205	262.50
Piping, supply, 1/2" copper	36.000	L.F.	3.556	89.50	180	269.50
1/2" steel	36.000	L.F.	4.571	123	232	355
1/2" P.V.C.	36.000	L.F.	5.333	94.50	270	364.50
Waste, 4" cast iron, no hub	7.000	L.F.	1.931	91.50	88	179.50
4" P.V.C./DWV	7.000	L.F.	2.333	42.50	106	148.50
4" copper/DWV	7.000	L.F.	2.800	259	128	387
Vent, 2" cast iron, no hub	6.000	L.F.	1.091	69	55	124
2" copper/DWV	6.000	L.F.	1.091	69	55	124
2" P.V.C./DWV	6.000	L.F.	1.627	13.70	74	87.70
2" steel, galvanized	6.000	L.F.	1.500	71.50	68.50	140
Vanity base cabinet, 2 door, 24" x 30"	1.000	Ea.	1.000	259	45	304
24" x 36"	1.000	Ea.	1.200	345	54.50	399.50
Vanity top, laminated plastic square edge, 25" x 32"	2.670	L.F.	.712	72	32	104
25" x 38"	3.170	L.F.	.845	85.50	38	123.50
Carrier , for lavatory, steel, for studs, no arms	1.000	Ea.	1.143	61.50	58	119.50
Wood, 2" x 8" blocking	1.300	L.F.	.052	1.08	2.35	3.43

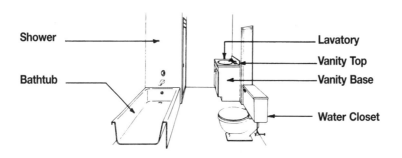

System Description	QUAN.	UNIT	LABOR HOURS	COST EACH		
				MAT.	INST.	TOTAL
BATHROOM WITH LAVATORY INSTALLED IN VANITY						
Water closet, floor mounted, 2 piece, close coupled, white	1.000	Ea.	3.019	201	138	339
Rough-in, vent, 2″ diameter DWV piping	1.000	Ea.	.955	30	43.60	73.60
Waste, 4″ diameter DWV piping	1.000	Ea.	.828	39.30	37.65	76.95
Supply, 1/2″ diameter type "L" copper supply piping	1.000	Ea.	.593	14.88	30	44.88
Lavatory, 20″ x 18″ P.E. cast iron with fittings, white	1.000	Ea.	2.500	239	114	353
Shower, steel, enameled, stone base, corner, white	1.000	Ea.	3.333	845	152	997
Mixing valve	1.000	Ea.	1.333	124	67.50	191.50
Shower door	1.000	Ea.	1.000	238	50.50	288.50
Rough-in, waste, 1-1/2″ diameter DWV piping	2.000	Ea.	4.507	145	205	350
Supply, 1/2″ diameter type "L" copper supply piping	2.000	Ea.	3.161	79.36	160	239.36
Bathtub, P.E. cast iron, 5′ long with fittings, white	1.000	Ea.	3.636	870	166	1,036
Rough-in, waste, 4″ diameter DWV piping	1.000	Ea.	.828	39.30	37.65	76.95
Supply, 1/2″ diameter type "L" copper supply piping	1.000	Ea.	.988	24.80	50	74.80
Vent, 1-1/2″ diameter DWV piping	1.000	Ea.	.593	34.20	30	64.20
Piping, supply, 1/2″ diameter type "L" copper supply piping	42.000	L.F.	4.148	104.16	210	314.16
Waste, 4″ diameter DWV piping	10.000	L.F.	2.759	131	125.50	256.50
Vent, 2″ diameter DWV piping	13.000	L.F.	3.250	155.35	148.20	303.55
Vanity base, 2 doors, 30″ wide	1.000	Ea.	1.000	259	45	304
Vanity top, plastic laminated, square edge	2.670	L.F.	.712	72.09	32.17	104.26
TOTAL		Ea.	39.143	3,645.44	1,842.77	5,488.21
BATHROOM WITH WALL HUNG LAVATORY						
Water closet, floor mounted, 2 piece, close coupled, white	1.000	Ea.	3.019	201	138	339
Rough-in, vent, 2″ diameter DWV piping	1.000	Ea.	.955	30	43.60	73.60
Waste, 4″ diameter DWV piping	1.000	Ea.	.828	39.30	37.65	76.95
Supply, 1/2″ diameter type "L" copper supply piping	1.000	Ea.	.593	14.88	30	44.88
Lavatory, 20″ x 18″ P.E. cast iron with fittings, white	1.000	Ea.	2.000	310	91	401
Shower, steel enameled, stone base, corner , white	1.000	Ea.	3.333	845	152	997
Mixing valve	1.000	Ea.	1.333	124	67.50	191.50
Shower door	1.000	Ea.	1.000	238	50.50	288.50
Rough-in, waste, 1-1/2″ diameter DWV piping	2.000	Ea.	4.507	145	205	350
Supply, 1/2″ diameter type "L" copper supply piping	2.000	Ea.	3.161	79.36	160	239.36
Bathtub, P.E. cast iron, 5′ long with fittings, white	1.000	Ea.	3.636	870	166	1,036
Rough-in, waste, 4″ diameter DWV piping	1.000	Ea.	.828	39.30	37.65	76.95
Supply, 1/2″ diameter type "L" copper supply piping	1.000	Ea.	.988	24.80	50	74.80
Vent, 1-1/2″ diameter copper DWV piping	1.000	Ea.	.593	34.20	30	64.20
Piping, supply, 1/2″ diameter type "L" copper supply piping	42.000	L.F.	4.148	104.16	210	314.16
Waste, 4″ diameter DWV piping	10.000	L.F.	2.759	131	125.50	256.50
Vent, 2″ diameter DWV piping	13.000	L.F.	3.250	155.35	148.20	303.55
Carrier, steel, for studs, no arms	1.000	Ea.	1.143	61.50	58	119.50
TOTAL		Ea.	38.074	3,446.85	1,800.60	5,247.45

The costs in this system are on a cost each basis. All necessary piping is included.

Four Fixture Bathroom Price Sheet	QUAN.	UNIT	LABOR HOURS	COST EACH		
				MAT.	INST.	TOTAL
Water closet, close coupled, standard 2 piece, white	1.000	Ea.	3.019	201	138	339
Color	1.000	Ea.	3.019	240	138	378
One piece elongated bowl, white	1.000	Ea.	3.019	585	138	723
Color	1.000	Ea.	3.019	720	138	858
Low profile, one piece elongated bowl, white	1.000	Ea.	3.019	845	138	983
Color	1.000	Ea.	3.019	1,100	138	1,238
1/2" copper supply, 4" cast iron waste, 2" cast iron vent	1.000	Ea.	2.376	84	111	195
4" PVC/DWV waste, 2" PVC vent	1.000	Ea.	2.678	42	125	167
4" copper waste, 2" copper vent	1.000	Ea.	2.520	172	122	294
3" cast iron waste, 1-1/2" cast iron vent	1.000	Ea.	2.244	74.50	105	179.50
3" P.V.C. waste, 1-1/2" P.V.C. vent	1.000	Ea.	2.388	36	116	152
3" copper waste, 1-1/2" copper vent	1.000	Ea.	2.014	112	97.50	209.50
1/2" P.V.C. supply, 4" P.V.C. waste, 2" P.V.C. vent	1.000	Ea.	2.974	43	140	183
3" P.V.C. waste, 1-1/2" P.V.C. vent	1.000	Ea.	2.684	36.50	131	167.50
1/2" steel supply, 4" cast iron waste, 2" cast iron vent	1.000	Ea.	2.545	90	120	210
4" cast iron waste, 2" steel vent	1.000	Ea.	2.590	108	122	230
4" P.V.C. waste, 2" P.V.C. vent	1.000	Ea.	2.847	47.50	134	181.50
Lavatory, wall hung P.E. cast iron 20" x 18", white	1.000	Ea.	2.000	310	91	401
Color	1.000	Ea.	2.000	315	91	406
Vitreous china 19" x 17", white	1.000	Ea.	2.286	193	104	297
Color	1.000	Ea.	2.286	216	104	320
Lavatory for vanity top, P.E. cast iron 20" x 18", white	1.000	Ea.	2.500	239	114	353
Color	1.000	Ea.	2.500	270	114	384
Steel enameled, 20" x 17", white	1.000	Ea.	2.759	156	126	282
Color	1.000	Ea.	2.500	162	114	276
Vitreous china 20" x 16", white	1.000	Ea.	2.963	288	135	423
Color	1.000	Ea.	2.963	288	135	423
Shower, steel enameled stone base, 36" square, white	1.000	Ea.	8.889	845	152	997
Color	1.000	Ea.	8.889	950	152	1,102
Rough-in, for lavatory or shower						
1/2" copper supply, 1-1/2" cast iron waste, 1-1/2" cast iron vent	1.000	Ea.	3.834	112	183	295
1-1/2" P.V.C. waste, 1-1/4" P.V.C. vent	1.000	Ea.	3.675	58.50	186	244.50
1/2" steel supply, 1-1/4" cast iron waste, 1-1/4" steel vent	1.000	Ea.	4.103	128	198	326
1-1/4" P.V.C. waste, 1-1/4" P.V.C. vent	1.000	Ea.	3.937	73.50	200	273.50
1/2" P.V.C. supply, 1-1/2" P.V.C. waste, 1-1/2" P.V.C. vent	1.000	Ea.	4.592	61	233	294
Bathtub, P.E. cast iron, 5' long with fittings, white	1.000	Ea.	3.636	870	166	1,036
Color	1.000	Ea.	3.636	1,075	166	1,241
Steel, enameled 5' long with fittings, white	1.000	Ea.	2.909	365	133	498
Color	1.000	Ea.	2.909	365	133	498
Rough-in, for bathtub						
1/2" copper supply, 4" cast iron waste, 1-1/2" copper vent	1.000	Ea.	2.409	98.50	118	216.50
4" P.V.C. waste, 1-1/2" P.V.C. vent	1.000	Ea.	2.877	50.50	141	191.50
1/2" steel supply, 4" cast iron waste, 1-1/2" steel vent	1.000	Ea.	2.898	109	139	248
4" P.V.C. waste, 1-1/2" P.V.C. vent	1.000	Ea.	3.159	60	155	215
1/2" P.V.C. supply, 4" P.V.C. waste, 1-1/2" P.V.C. vent	1.000	Ea.	3.371	52	166	218
Piping, supply, 1/2" copper	42.000	L.F.	4.148	104	210	314
1/2" steel	42.000	L.F.	5.333	143	271	414
1/2" P.V.C.	42.000	L.F.	6.222	110	315	425
Waste, 4" cast iron, no hub	10.000	L.F.	2.759	131	126	257
4" P.V.C./DWV	10.000	L.F.	3.333	60.50	152	212.50
4" copper/DWV	10.000	Ea.	4.000	370	183	553
Vent 2" cast iron, no hub	13.000	L.F.	3.105	97.50	142	239.50
2" copper/DWV	13.000	L.F.	2.364	150	120	270
2" P.V.C./DWV	13.000	L.F.	3.525	29.50	161	190.50
2" steel, galvanized	13.000	L.F.	3.250	155	148	303
Vanity base cabinet, 2 doors, 30" wide	1.000	Ea.	1.000	259	45	304
Vanity top, plastic laminated, square edge	2.670	L.F.	.712	72	32	104
Carrier, steel for studs, no arms	1.000	Ea.	1.143	61.50	58	119.50
Wood, 2" x 8" blocking	1.300	L.F.	.052	1.08	2.35	3.43

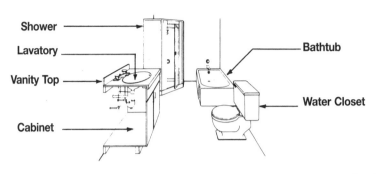

System Description	QUAN.	UNIT	LABOR HOURS	COST EACH		
				MAT.	INST.	TOTAL
BATHROOM WITH LAVATORY INSTALLED IN VANITY						
Water closet, floor mounted, 2 piece, close coupled, white	1.000	Ea.	3.019	201	138	339
Rough-in, vent, 2" diameter DWV piping	1.000	Ea.	.955	30	43.60	73.60
Waste, 4" diameter DWV piping	1.000	Ea.	.828	39.30	37.65	76.95
Supply, 1/2" diameter type "L" copper supply piping	1.000	Ea.	.593	14.88	30	44.88
Lavatory, 20" x 18" P.E. cast iron with fittings, white	1.000	Ea.	2.500	239	114	353
Shower, steel, enameled, stone base, corner, white	1.000	Ea.	3.333	845	152	997
Mixing valve	1.000	Ea.	1.333	124	67.50	191.50
Shower door	1.000	Ea.	1.000	238	50.50	288.50
Rough-in, waste, 1-1/2" diameter DWV piping	2.000	Ea.	4.507	145	205	350
Supply, 1/2" diameter type "L" copper supply piping	2.000	Ea.	3.161	79.36	160	239.36
Bathtub, P.E. cast iron, 5' long with fittings, white	1.000	Ea.	3.636	870	166	1,036
Rough-in, waste, 4" diameter DWV piping	1.000	Ea.	.828	39.30	37.65	76.95
Supply, 1/2" diameter type "L" copper supply piping	1.000	Ea.	.988	24.80	50	74.80
Vent, 1-1/2" diameter DWV piping	1.000	Ea.	.593	34.20	30	64.20
Piping, supply, 1/2" diameter type "L" copper supply piping	42.000	L.F.	4.939	124	250	374
Waste, 4" diameter DWV piping	10.000	L.F.	4.138	196.50	188.25	384.75
Vent, 2" diameter DWV piping	13.000	L.F.	4.500	215.10	205.20	420.30
Vanity base, 2 doors, 30" wide	1.000	Ea.	1.000	259	45	304
Vanity top, plastic laminated, square edge	2.670	L.F.	.712	76.10	32.17	108.27
TOTAL		Ea.	42.563	3,794.54	2,002.52	5,797.06
BATHROOM WITH WALL HUNG LAVATORY						
Water closet, floor mounted, 2 piece, close coupled, white	1.000	Ea.	3.019	201	138	339
Rough-in, vent, 2" diameter DWV piping	1.000	Ea.	.955	30	43.60	73.60
Waste, 4" diameter DWV piping	1.000	Ea.	.828	39.30	37.65	76.95
Supply, 1/2" diameter type "L" copper supply piping	1.000	Ea.	.593	14.88	30	44.88
Lavatory, 20" x 18" P.E. cast iron with fittings, white	1.000	Ea.	2.000	310	91	401
Shower, steel enameled, stone base, corner, white	1.000	Ea.	3.333	845	152	997
Mixing valve	1.000	Ea.	1.333	124	67.50	191.50
Shower door	1.000	Ea.	1.000	238	50.50	288.50
Rough-in, waste, 1-1/2" diameter DWV piping	2.000	Ea.	4.507	145	205	350
Supply, 1/2" diameter type "L" copper supply piping	2.000	Ea.	3.161	79.36	160	239.36
Bathtub, P.E. cast iron, 5' long with fittings, white	1.000	Ea.	3.636	870	166	1,036
Rough-in, waste, 4" diameter DWV piping	1.000	Ea.	.828	39.30	37.65	76.95
Supply, 1/2" diameter type "L" copper supply piping	1.000	Ea.	.988	24.80	50	74.80
Vent, 1-1/2" diameter DWV piping	1.000	Ea.	.593	34.20	30	64.20
Piping, supply, 1/2" diameter type "L" copper supply piping	42.000	L.F.	4.939	124	250	374
Waste, 4" diameter DWV piping	10.000	L.F.	4.138	196.50	188.25	384.75
Vent, 2" diameter DWV piping	13.000	L.F.	4.500	215.10	205.20	420.30
Carrier, steel for studs, no arms	1.000	Ea.	1.143	61.50	58	119.50
TOTAL		Ea.	41.494	3,591.94	1,960.35	5,552.29

The costs in this system are on a cost each basis. All necessary piping is included.

Four Fixture Bathroom Price Sheet	QUAN.	UNIT	LABOR HOURS	COST EACH		
				MAT.	INST.	TOTAL
Water closet, close coupled, standard 2 piece, white	1.000	Ea.	3.019	201	138	339
Color	1.000	Ea.	3.019	240	138	378
One piece, elongated bowl, white	1.000	Ea.	3.019	585	138	723
Color	1.000	Ea.	3.019	720	138	858
Low profile, one piece elongated bowl, white	1.000	Ea.	3.019	845	138	983
Color	1.000	Ea.	3.019	1,100	138	1,238
Rough-in, for water closet						
1/2" copper supply, 4" cast iron waste, 2" cast iron vent	1.000	Ea.	2.376	84	111	195
4" PVC/DWV waste, 2" PVC vent	1.000	Ea.	2.678	42	125	167
4" copper waste, 2" copper vent	1.000	Ea.	2.520	172	122	294
3" cast iron waste, 1-1/2" cast iron vent	1.000	Ea.	2.244	74.50	105	179.50
3" PVC waste, 1-1/2" PVC vent	1.000	Ea.	2.388	36	116	152
3" PVC waste, 1-1/2" PVC vent	1.000	Ea.	2.014	112	97.50	209.50
1/2" PVC supply, 4" PVC waste, 2" PVC vent	1.000	Ea.	2.974	43	140	183
3" PVC waste, 1-1/2" PVC vent	1.000	Ea.	2.684	36.50	131	167.50
1/2" steel supply, 4" cast iron waste, 2" cast iron vent	1.000	Ea.	2.545	90	120	210
4" cast iron waste, 2" steel vent	1.000	Ea.	2.590	108	122	230
4" PVC waste, 2" PVC vent	1.000	Ea.	2.847	47.50	134	181.50
Lavatory wall hung, P.E. cast iron 20" x 18", white	1.000	Ea.	2.000	310	91	401
Color	1.000	Ea.	2.000	315	91	406
Vitreous china 19" x 17", white	1.000	Ea.	2.286	193	104	297
Color	1.000	Ea.	2.286	216	104	320
Lavatory for vanity top, P.E. cast iron, 20" x 18", white	1.000	Ea.	2.500	239	114	353
Color	1.000	Ea.	2.500	270	114	384
Steel, enameled 20" x 17", white	1.000	Ea.	2.759	156	126	282
Color	1.000	Ea.	2.500	162	114	276
Vitreous china 20" x 16", white	1.000	Ea.	2.963	288	135	423
Color	1.000	Ea.	2.963	288	135	423
Shower, steel enameled, stone base 36" square, white	1.000	Ea.	8.889	845	152	997
Color	1.000	Ea.	8.889	950	152	1,102
Rough-in, for lavatory and shower						
1/2" copper supply, 1-1/2" cast iron waste, 1-1/2" cast iron vent	1.000	Ea.	7.668	224	365	589
1-1/2" PVC waste, 1-1/4" PVC vent	1.000	Ea.	7.352	117	370	487
1/2" steel supply, 1-1/4" cast iron waste, 1-1/4" steel vent	1.000	Ea.	8.205	257	395	652
1-1/4" PVC waste, 1-1/4" PVC vent	1.000	Ea.	7.873	147	400	547
1/2" PVC supply, 1-1/2" PVC waste, 1-1/2" PVC vent	1.000	Ea.	9.185	122	465	587
Bathtub, P.E. cast iron, 5' long with fittings, white	1.000	Ea.	3.636	870	166	1,036
Color	1.000	Ea.	3.636	1,075	166	1,241
Steel enameled, 5' long with fittings, white	1.000	Ea.	2.909	365	133	498
Color	1.000	Ea.	2.909	365	133	498
Rough-in, for bathtub						
1/2" copper supply, 4" cast iron waste, 1-1/2" copper vent	1.000	Ea.	2.409	98.50	118	216.50
4" PVC waste, 1-1/2" PVC vent	1.000	Ea.	2.877	50.50	141	191.50
1/2" steel supply, 4" cast iron waste, 1-1/2" steel vent	1.000	Ea.	2.898	109	139	248
4" PVC waste, 1-1/2" PVC vent	1.000	Ea.	3.159	60	155	215
1/2" PVC supply, 4" PVC waste, 1-1/2" PVC vent	1.000	Ea.	3.371	52	166	218
Piping supply, 1/2" copper	42.000	L.F.	4.148	104	210	314
1/2" steel	42.000	L.F.	5.333	143	271	414
1/2" PVC	42.000	L.F.	6.222	110	315	425
Piping, waste, 4" cast iron, no hub	10.000	L.F.	3.586	170	163	333
4" PVC/DWV	10.000	L.F.	4.333	78.50	198	276.50
4" copper/DWV	10.000	L.F.	5.200	480	237	717
Piping, vent, 2" cast iron, no hub	13.000	L.F.	3.105	97.50	142	239.50
2" copper/DWV	13.000	L.F.	2.364	150	120	270
2" PVC/DWV	13.000	L.F.	3.525	29.50	161	190.50
2" steel, galvanized	13.000	L.F.	3.250	155	148	303
Vanity base cabinet, 2 doors, 30" wide	1.000	Ea.	1.000	259	45	304
Vanity top, plastic laminated, square edge	3.160	L.F.	.843	85.50	38	123.50
Carrier, steel, for studs, no arms	1.000	Ea.	1.143	61.50	58	119.50
Wood, 2" x 8" blocking	1.300	L.F.	.052	1.08	2.35	3.43

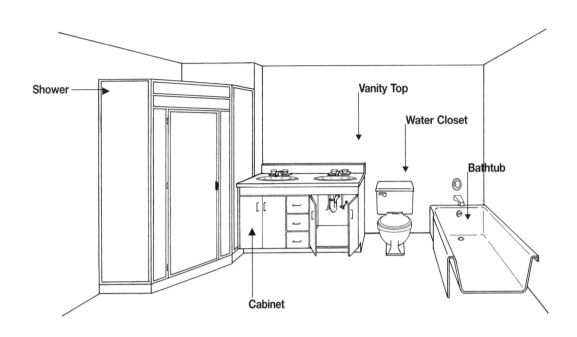

Shower

Vanity Top

Water Closet

Bathtub

Cabinet

System Description	QUAN.	UNIT	LABOR HOURS	COST EACH		
				MAT.	INST.	TOTAL
BATHROOM WITH SHOWER, BATHTUB, LAVATORIES IN VANITY						
Water closet, floor mounted, 1 piece combination, white	1.000	Ea.	3.019	845	138	983
Rough-in, vent, 2" diameter DWV piping	1.000	Ea.	.955	30	43.60	73.60
Waste, 4" diameter DWV piping	1.000	Ea.	.828	39.30	37.65	76.95
Supply, 1/2" diameter type "L" copper supply piping	1.000	Ea.	.593	14.88	30	44.88
Lavatory, 20" x 16", vitreous china oval, with fittings, white	2.000	Ea.	5.926	576	270	846
Shower, steel enameled, stone base, corner, white	1.000	Ea.	3.333	845	152	997
Mixing valve	1.000	Ea.	1.333	124	67.50	191.50
Shower door	1.000	Ea.	1.000	238	50.50	288.50
Rough-in, waste, 1-1/2" diameter DWV piping	3.000	Ea.	5.408	174	246	420
Supply, 1/2" diameter type "L" copper supply piping	3.000	Ea.	2.963	74.40	150	224.40
Bathtub, P.E. cast iron, 5' long with fittings, white	1.000	Ea.	3.636	870	166	1,036
Rough-in, waste, 4" diameter DWV piping	1.000	Ea.	1.103	52.40	50.20	102.60
Supply, 1/2" diameter type "L" copper supply piping	1.000	Ea.	.988	24.80	50	74.80
Vent, 1-1/2" diameter copper DWV piping	1.000	Ea.	.593	34.20	30	64.20
Piping, supply, 1/2" diameter type "L" copper supply piping	42.000	L.F.	4.148	104.16	210	314.16
Waste, 4" diameter DWV piping	10.000	L.F.	2.759	131	125.50	256.50
Vent, 2" diameter DWV piping	13.000	L.F.	3.250	155.35	148.20	303.55
Vanity base, 2 door, 24" x 48"	1.000	Ea.	1.400	410	63.50	473.50
Vanity top, plastic laminated, square edge	4.170	L.F.	1.112	112.59	50.25	162.84
TOTAL		Ea.	44.347	4,855.08	2,078.90	6,933.98

The costs in this system are on a cost each basis. All necessary piping
is included.

Description	QUAN.	UNIT	LABOR HOURS	COST EACH		
				MAT.	INST.	TOTAL

Five Fixture Bathroom Price Sheet	QUAN.	UNIT	LABOR HOURS	COST EACH		
				MAT.	INST.	TOTAL
Water closet, close coupled, standard 2 piece, white	1.000	Ea.	3.019	201	138	339
Color	1.000	Ea.	3.019	240	138	378
One piece elongated bowl, white	1.000	Ea.	3.019	585	138	723
Color	1.000	Ea.	3.019	720	138	858
Low profile, one piece elongated bowl, white	1.000	Ea.	3.019	845	138	983
Color	1.000	Ea.	3.019	1,100	138	1,238
Rough-in, supply, waste and vent for water closet						
1/2" copper supply, 4" cast iron waste, 2" cast iron vent	1.000	Ea.	2.376	84	111	195
4" P.V.C./DWV waste, 2" P.V.C. vent	1.000	Ea.	2.678	42	125	167
4" copper waste, 2" copper vent	1.000	Ea.	2.520	172	122	294
3" cast iron waste, 1-1/2" cast iron vent	1.000	Ea.	2.244	74.50	105	179.50
3" P.V.C. waste, 1-1/2" P.V.C. vent	1.000	Ea.	2.388	36	116	152
3" copper waste, 1-1/2" copper vent	1.000	Ea.	2.014	112	97.50	209.50
1/2" P.V.C. supply, 4" P.V.C. waste, 2" P.V.C. vent	1.000	Ea.	2.974	43	140	183
3" P.V.C. waste, 1-1/2" P.V.C. supply	1.000	Ea.	2.684	36.50	131	167.50
1/2" steel supply, 4" cast iron waste, 2" cast iron vent	1.000	Ea.	2.545	90	120	210
4" cast iron waste, 2" steel vent	1.000	Ea.	2.590	108	122	230
4" P.V.C. waste, 2" P.V.C. vent	1.000	Ea.	2.847	47.50	134	181.50
Lavatory, wall hung, P.E. cast iron 20" x 18", white	2.000	Ea.	4.000	620	182	802
Color	2.000	Ea.	4.000	630	182	812
Vitreous china, 19" x 17", white	2.000	Ea.	4.571	385	208	593
Color	2.000	Ea.	4.571	430	208	638
Lavatory, for vanity top, P.E. cast iron, 20" x 18", white	2.000	Ea.	5.000	480	228	708
Color	2.000	Ea.	5.000	540	228	768
Steel enameled 20" x 17", white	2.000	Ea.	5.517	310	252	562
Color	2.000	Ea.	5.000	325	228	553
Vitreous china 20" x 16", white	2.000	Ea.	5.926	575	270	845
Color	2.000	Ea.	5.926	575	270	845
Shower, steel enameled, stone base 36" square, white	1.000	Ea.	8.889	845	152	997
Color	1.000	Ea.	8.889	950	152	1,102
Rough-in, for lavatory or shower						
1/2" copper supply, 1-1/2" cast iron waste, 1-1/2" cast iron vent	3.000	Ea.	8.371	248	395	643
1-1/2" P.V.C. waste, 1-1/4" P.V.C. vent	3.000	Ea.	7.916	120	400	520
1/2" steel supply, 1-1/4" cast iron waste, 1-1/4" steel vent	3.000	Ea.	8.670	280	415	695
1-1/4" P.V.C. waste, 1-1/4" P.V.C. vent	3.000	Ea.	8.381	148	425	573
1/2" P.V.C. supply, 1-1/2" P.V.C. waste, 1-1/2" P.V.C. vent	3.000	Ea.	9.778	125	495	620
Bathtub, P.E. cast iron 5' long with fittings, white	1.000	Ea.	3.636	870	166	1,036
Color	1.000	Ea.	3.636	1,075	166	1,241
Steel, enameled 5' long with fittings, white	1.000	Ea.	2.909	365	133	498
Color	1.000	Ea.	2.909	365	133	498
Rough-in, for bathtub						
1/2" copper supply, 4" cast iron waste, 1-1/2" copper vent	1.000	Ea.	2.684	111	130	241
4" P.V.C. waste, 1-1/2" P.V.C. vent	1.000	Ea.	3.210	56.50	156	212.50
1/2" steel supply, 4" cast iron waste, 1-1/2" steel vent	1.000	Ea.	3.173	122	151	273
4" P.V.C. waste, 1-1/2" P.V.C. vent	1.000	Ea.	3.492	66	170	236
1/2" P.V.C. supply, 4" P.V.C. waste, 1-1/2" P.V.C. vent	1.000	Ea.	3.704	58	181	239
Piping, supply, 1/2" copper	42.000	L.F.	4.148	104	210	314
1/2" steel	42.000	L.F.	5.333	143	271	414
1/2" P.V.C.	42.000	L.F.	6.222	110	315	425
Piping, waste, 4" cast iron, no hub	10.000	L.F.	2.759	131	126	257
4" P.V.C./DWV	10.000	L.F.	3.333	60.50	152	212.50
4" copper/DWV	10.000	L.F.	4.000	370	183	553
Piping, vent, 2" cast iron, no hub	13.000	L.F.	3.105	97.50	142	239.50
2" copper/DWV	13.000	L.F.	2.364	150	120	270
2" P.V.C./DWV	13.000	L.F.	3.525	29.50	161	190.50
2" steel, galvanized	13.000	L.F.	3.250	155	148	303
Vanity base cabinet, 2 doors, 24" x 48"	1.000	Ea.	1.400	410	63.50	473.50
Vanity top, plastic laminated, square edge	4.170	L.F.	1.112	113	50.50	163.50
Carrier, steel, for studs, no arms	1.000	Ea.	1.143	61.50	58	119.50
Wood, 2" x 8" blocking	1.300	L.F.	.052	1.08	2.35	3.43

Floor Registers
Register Elbows
Lateral Ducts
Return Air Grille
Return Air Duct
Supply Duct
Plenum
Furnace

System Description	QUAN.	UNIT	LABOR HOURS	COST PER SYSTEM		
				MAT.	INST.	TOTAL
HEATING ONLY, GAS FIRED HOT AIR, ONE ZONE, 1200 S.F. BUILDING						
Furnace, gas, up flow	1.000	Ea.	5.000	720	226	946
Intermittent pilot	1.000	Ea.		157		157
Supply duct, rigid fiberglass	176.000	S.F.	12.068	140.80	566.72	707.52
Return duct, sheet metal, galvanized	158.000	Lb.	16.137	104.28	756.82	861.10
Lateral ducts, 6" flexible fiberglass	144.000	L.F.	8.862	341.28	400.32	741.60
Register, elbows	12.000	Ea.	3.200	330	144.60	474.60
Floor registers, enameled steel	12.000	Ea.	3.000	264	151.20	415.20
Floor grille, return air	2.000	Ea.	.727	47	36.60	83.60
Thermostat	1.000	Ea.	1.000	29.50	50.50	80
Plenum	1.000	Ea.	1.000	88	45.50	133.50
TOTAL		System	50.994	2,221.86	2,378.26	4,600.12
HEATING/COOLING, GAS FIRED FORCED AIR, ONE ZONE, 1200 S.F. BUILDING						
Furnace, including plenum, compressor, coil	1.000	Ea.	14.720	4,623	667	5,290
Intermittent pilot	1.000	Ea.		157		157
Supply duct, rigid fiberglass	176.000	S.F.	12.068	140.80	566.72	707.52
Return duct, sheet metal, galvanized	158.000	Lb.	16.137	104.28	756.82	861.10
Lateral duct, 6" flexible fiberglass	144.000	L.F.	8.862	341.28	400.32	741.60
Register elbows	12.000	Ea.	3.200	330	144.60	474.60
Floor registers, enameled steel	12.000	Ea.	3.000	264	151.20	415.20
Floor grille return air	2.000	Ea.	.727	47	36.60	83.60
Thermostat	1.000	Ea.	1.000	29.50	50.50	80
Refrigeration piping, 25 ft. (pre-charged)	1.000	Ea.		237		237
TOTAL		System	59.714	6,273.86	2,773.76	9,047.62

The costs in these systems are based on complete system basis. For larger buildings use the price sheet on the opposite page.

Description	QUAN.	UNIT	LABOR HOURS	COST PER SYSTEM		
				MAT.	INST.	TOTAL

Gas Heating/Cooling Price Sheet	QUAN.	UNIT	LABOR HOURS	COST EACH MAT.	COST EACH INST.	COST EACH TOTAL
Furnace, heating only, 100 MBH, area to 1200 S.F.	1.000	Ea.	5.000	720	226	946
120 MBH, area to 1500 S.F.	1.000	Ea.	5.000	720	226	946
160 MBH, area to 2000 S.F.	1.000	Ea.	5.714	735	259	994
200 MBH, area to 2400 S.F.	1.000	Ea.	6.154	2,525	278	2,803
Heating/cooling, 100 MBH heat, 36 MBH cool, to 1200 S.F.	1.000	Ea.	16.000	5,025	725	5,750
120 MBH heat, 42 MBH cool, to 1500 S.F.	1.000	Ea.	18.462	5,350	865	6,215
144 MBH heat, 47 MBH cool, to 2000 S.F.	1.000	Ea.	20.000	6,175	940	7,115
200 MBH heat, 60 MBH cool, to 2400 S.F.	1.000	Ea.	34.286	1,500	1,600	3,100
Intermittent pilot, 100 MBH furnace	1.000	Ea.		157		157
200 MBH furnace	1.000	Ea.		157		157
Supply duct, rectangular, area to 1200 S.F., rigid fiberglass	176.000	S.F.	12.068	141	565	706
Sheet metal insulated	228.000	Lb.	31.331	274	1,450	1,724
Area to 1500 S.F., rigid fiberglass	176.000	S.F.	12.068	141	565	706
Sheet metal insulated	228.000	Lb.	31.331	274	1,450	1,724
Area to 2400 S.F., rigid fiberglass	205.000	S.F.	14.057	164	660	824
Sheet metal insulated	271.000	Lb.	37.048	320	1,700	2,020
Round flexible, insulated 6″ diameter, to 1200 S.F.	156.000	L.F.	9.600	370	435	805
To 1500 S.F.	184.000	L.F.	11.323	435	510	945
8″ diameter, to 2000 S.F.	269.000	L.F.	23.911	790	1,075	1,865
To 2400 S.F.	248.000	L.F.	22.045	725	995	1,720
Return duct, sheet metal galvanized, to 1500 S.F.	158.000	Lb.	16.137	104	755	859
To 2400 S.F.	191.000	Lb.	19.507	126	915	1,041
Lateral ducts, flexible round 6″ insulated, to 1200 S.F.	144.000	L.F.	8.862	340	400	740
To 1500 S.F.	172.000	L.F.	10.585	410	480	890
To 2000 S.F.	261.000	L.F.	16.062	620	725	1,345
To 2400 S.F.	300.000	L.F.	18.462	710	835	1,545
Spiral steel insulated, to 1200 S.F.	144.000	L.F.	20.067	480	895	1,375
To 1500 S.F.	172.000	L.F.	23.952	575	1,075	1,650
To 2000 S.F.	261.000	L.F.	36.352	875	1,625	2,500
To 2400 S.F.	300.000	L.F.	41.825	1,000	1,850	2,850
Rectangular sheet metal galvanized insulated, to 1200 S.F.	228.000	Lb.	39.056	390	1,775	2,165
To 1500 S.F.	344.000	Lb.	53.966	515	2,475	2,990
To 2000 S.F.	522.000	Lb.	81.926	785	3,750	4,535
To 2400 S.F.	600.000	Lb.	94.189	900	4,325	5,225
Register elbows, to 1500 S.F.	12.000	Ea.	3.200	330	145	475
To 2400 S.F.	14.000	Ea.	3.733	385	169	554
Floor registers, enameled steel w/damper, to 1500 S.F.	12.000	Ea.	3.000	264	151	415
To 2400 S.F.	14.000	Ea.	4.308	365	217	582
Return air grille, area to 1500 S.F. 12″ x 12″	2.000	Ea.	.727	47	36.50	83.50
Area to 2400 S.F. 8″ x 16″	2.000	Ea.	.444	42	22.50	64.50
Area to 2400 S.F. 8″ x 16″	2.000	Ea.	.727	47	36.50	83.50
16″ x 16″	1.000	Ea.	.364	34	18.30	52.30
Thermostat, manual, 1 set back	1.000	Ea.	1.000	29.50	50.50	80
Electric, timed, 1 set back	1.000	Ea.	1.000	104	50.50	154.50
2 set back	1.000	Ea.	1.000	229	50.50	279.50
Plenum, heating only, 100 M.B.H.	1.000	Ea.	1.000	88	45.50	133.50
120 MBH	1.000	Ea.	1.000	88	45.50	133.50
160 MBH	1.000	Ea.	1.000	88	45.50	133.50
200 MBH	1.000	Ea.	1.000	88	45.50	133.50
Refrigeration piping, 3/8″	25.000	L.F.		27.50		27.50
3/4″	25.000	L.F.		57		57
7/8″	25.000	L.F.		66.50		66.50
Refrigerant piping, 25 ft. (precharged)	1.000	Ea.		237		237
Diffusers, ceiling, 6″ diameter, to 1500 S.F.	10.000	Ea.	4.444	210	225	435
To 2400 S.F.	12.000	Ea.	6.000	276	300	576
Floor, aluminum, adjustable, 2-1/4″ x 12″ to 1500 S.F.	12.000	Ea.	3.000	193	151	344
To 2400 S.F.	14.000	Ea.	3.500	225	176	401
Side wall, aluminum, adjustable, 8″ x 4″, to 1500 S.F.	12.000	Ea.	3.000	440	151	591
5″ x 10″ to 2400 S.F.	12.000	Ea.	3.692	570	186	756

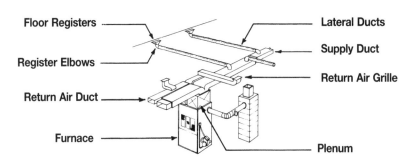

Floor Registers — Lateral Ducts
Register Elbows — Supply Duct
Return Air Duct — Return Air Grille
Furnace — Return Air Grille
Plenum

System Description	QUAN.	UNIT	LABOR HOURS	COST PER SYSTEM		
				MAT.	INST.	TOTAL
HEATING ONLY, OIL FIRED HOT AIR, ONE ZONE, 1200 S.F. BUILDING						
Furnace, oil fired, atomizing gun type burner	1.000	Ea.	4.571	1,850	207	2,057
3/8" diameter copper supply pipe	1.000	Ea.	2.759	50.40	139.80	190.20
Shut off valve	1.000	Ea.	.333	11.30	16.90	28.20
Oil tank, 275 gallon, on legs	1.000	Ea.	3.200	360	147	507
Supply duct, rigid fiberglass	176.000	S.F.	12.068	140.80	566.72	707.52
Return duct, sheet metal, galvanized	158.000	Lb.	16.137	104.28	756.82	861.10
Lateral ducts, 6" flexible fiberglass	144.000	L.F.	8.862	341.28	400.32	741.60
Register elbows	12.000	Ea.	3.200	330	144.60	474.60
Floor register, enameled steel	12.000	Ea.	3.000	264	151.20	415.20
Floor grille, return air	2.000	Ea.	.727	47	36.60	83.60
Thermostat	1.000	Ea.	1.000	29.50	50.50	80
TOTAL		System	55.857	3,528.56	2,617.46	6,146.02
HEATING/COOLING, OIL FIRED, FORCED AIR, ONE ZONE, 1200 S.F. BUILDING						
Furnace, including plenum, compressor, coil	1.000	Ea.	16.000	5,350	725	6,075
3/8" diameter copper supply pipe	1.000	Ea.	2.759	50.40	139.80	190.20
Shut off valve	1.000	Ea.	.333	11.30	16.90	28.20
Oil tank, 275 gallon on legs	1.000	Ea.	3.200	360	147	507
Supply duct, rigid fiberglass	176.000	S.F.	12.068	140.80	566.72	707.52
Return duct, sheet metal, galvanized	158.000	Lb.	16.137	104.28	756.82	861.10
Lateral ducts, 6" flexible fiberglass	144.000	L.F.	8.862	341.28	400.32	741.60
Register elbows	12.000	Ea.	3.200	330	144.60	474.60
Floor registers, enameled steel	12.000	Ea.	3.000	264	151.20	415.20
Floor grille, return air	2.000	Ea.	.727	47	36.60	83.60
Refrigeration piping (precharged)	25.000	L.F.		237		237
TOTAL		System	66.286	7,236.06	3,084.96	10,321.02

Description	QUAN.	UNIT	LABOR HOURS	COST EACH		
				MAT.	INST.	TOTAL

Oil Fired Heating/Cooling	QUAN.	UNIT	LABOR HOURS	COST EACH		
				MAT.	INST.	TOTAL
Furnace, heating, 95.2 MBH, area to 1200 S.F.	1.000	Ea.	4.706	1,875	213	2,088
123.2 MBH, area to 1500 S.F.	1.000	Ea.	5.000	1,950	226	2,176
151.2 MBH, area to 2000 S.F.	1.000	Ea.	5.333	2,250	241	2,491
200 MBH, area to 2400 S.F.	1.000	Ea.	6.154	2,675	278	2,953
Heating/cooling, 95.2 MBH heat, 36 MBH cool, to 1200 S.F.	1.000	Ea.	16.000	5,350	725	6,075
112 MBH heat, 42 MBH cool, to 1500 S.F.	1.000	Ea.	24.000	8,025	1,100	9,125
151 MBH heat, 47 MBH cool, to 2000 S.F.	1.000	Ea.	20.800	6,950	945	7,895
184.8 MBH heat, 60 MBH cool, to 2400 S.F.	1.000	Ea.	24.000	2,675	1,125	3,800
Oil piping to furnace, 3/8" dia., copper	1.000	Ea.	3.412	169	171	340
Oil tank, on legs above ground, 275 gallons	1.000	Ea.	3.200	360	147	507
550 gallons	1.000	Ea.	5.926	2,275	273	2,548
Below ground, 275 gallons	1.000	Ea.	3.200	360	147	507
550 gallons	1.000	Ea.	5.926	2,275	273	2,548
1000 gallons	1.000	Ea.	6.400	2,800	295	3,095
Supply duct, rectangular, area to 1200 S.F., rigid fiberglass	176.000	S.F.	12.068	141	565	706
Sheet metal, insulated	228.000	Lb.	31.331	274	1,450	1,724
Area to 1500 S.F., rigid fiberglass	176.000	S.F.	12.068	141	565	706
Sheet metal, insulated	228.000	Lb.	31.331	274	1,450	1,724
Area to 2400 S.F., rigid fiberglass	205.000	S.F.	14.057	164	660	824
Sheet metal, insulated	271.000	Lb.	37.048	320	1,700	2,020
Round flexible, insulated, 6" diameter to 1200 S.F.	156.000	L.F.	9.600	370	435	805
To 1500 S.F.	184.000	L.F.	11.323	435	510	945
8" diameter to 2000 S.F.	269.000	L.F.	23.911	790	1,075	1,865
To 2400 S.F.	269.000	L.F.	22.045	725	995	1,720
Return duct, sheet metal galvanized, to 1500 S.F.	158.000	Lb.	16.137	104	755	859
To 2400 S.F.	191.000	Lb.	19.507	126	915	1,041
Lateral ducts, flexible round, 6", insulated to 1200 S.F.	144.000	L.F.	8.862	340	400	740
To 1500 S.F.	172.000	L.F.	10.585	410	480	890
To 2000 S.F.	261.000	L.F.	16.062	620	725	1,345
To 2400 S.F.	300.000	L.F.	18.462	710	835	1,545
Spiral steel, insulated to 1200 S.F.	144.000	L.F.	20.067	480	895	1,375
To 1500 S.F.	172.000	L.F.	23.952	575	1,075	1,650
To 2000 S.F.	261.000	L.F.	36.352	875	1,625	2,500
To 2400 S.F.	300.000	L.F.	41.825	1,000	1,850	2,850
Rectangular sheet metal galvanized insulated, to 1200 S.F.	288.000	Lb.	45.183	430	2,075	2,505
To 1500 S.F.	344.000	Lb.	53.966	515	2,475	2,990
To 2000 S.F.	522.000	Lb.	81.926	785	3,750	4,535
To 2400 S.F.	600.000	Lb.	94.189	900	4,325	5,225
Register elbows, to 1500 S.F.	12.000	Ea.	3.200	330	145	475
To 2400 S.F.	14.000	Ea.	3.733	385	169	554
Floor registers, enameled steel w/damper, to 1500 S.F.	12.000	Ea.	3.000	264	151	415
To 2400 S.F.	14.000	Ea.	4.308	365	217	582
Return air grille, area to 1500 S.F., 12" x 12"	2.000	Ea.	.727	47	36.50	83.50
12" x 24"	1.000	Ea.	.444	42	22.50	64.50
Area to 2400 S.F., 8" x 16"	2.000	Ea.	.727	47	36.50	83.50
16" x 16"	1.000	Ea.	.364	34	18.30	52.30
Thermostat, manual, 1 set back	1.000	Ea.	1.000	29.50	50.50	80
Electric, timed, 1 set back	1.000	Ea.	1.000	104	50.50	154.50
2 set back	1.000	Ea.	1.000	229	50.50	279.50
Refrigeration piping, 3/8"	25.000	L.F.		27.50		27.50
3/4"	25.000	L.F.		57		57
Diffusers, ceiling, 6" diameter, to 1500 S.F.	10.000	Ea.	4.444	210	225	435
To 2400 S.F.	12.000	Ea.	6.000	276	300	576
Floor, aluminum, adjustable, 2-1/4" x 12" to 1500 S.F.	12.000	Ea.	3.000	193	151	344
To 2400 S.F.	14.000	Ea.	3.500	225	176	401
Side wall, aluminum, adjustable, 8" x 4", to 1500 S.F.	12.000	Ea.	3.000	440	151	591
5" x 10" to 2400 S.F.	12.000	Ea.	3.692	570	186	756

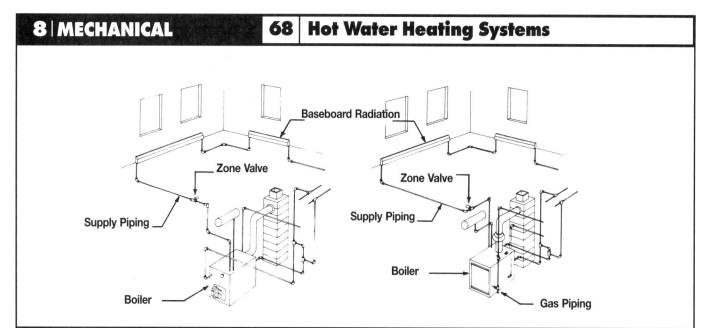

System Description	QUAN.	UNIT	LABOR HOURS	COST EACH		
				MAT.	INST.	TOTAL
OIL FIRED HOT WATER HEATING SYSTEM, AREA TO 1200 S.F.						
Boiler package, oil fired, 97 MBH, area to 1200 S.F. building	1.000	Ea.	15.000	1,625	665	2,290
3/8" diameter copper supply pipe	1.000	Ea.	2.759	50.40	139.80	190.20
Shut off valve	1.000	Ea.	.333	11.30	16.90	28.20
Oil tank, 275 gallon, with black iron filler pipe	1.000	Ea.	3.200	360	147	507
Supply piping, 3/4" copper tubing	176.000	L.F.	18.526	679.36	941.60	1,620.96
Supply fittings, copper 3/4"	36.000	Ea.	15.158	80.64	774	854.64
Supply valves, 3/4"	2.000	Ea.	.800	177	41	218
Baseboard radiation, 3/4"	106.000	L.F.	35.333	501.38	1,627.10	2,128.48
Zone valve	1.000	Ea.	.400	151	20.50	171.50
TOTAL		Ea.	91.509	3,636.08	4,372.90	8,008.98
OIL FIRED HOT WATER HEATING SYSTEM, AREA TO 2400 S.F.						
Boiler package, oil fired, 225 MBH, area to 2400 S.F. building	1.000	Ea.	25.105	5,150	1,125	6,275
3/8" diameter copper supply pipe	1.000	Ea.	2.759	50.40	139.80	190.20
Shut off valve	1.000	Ea.	.333	11.30	16.90	28.20
Oil tank, 550 gallon, with black iron pipe filler pipe	1.000	Ea.	5.926	2,275	273	2,548
Supply piping, 3/4" copper tubing	228.000	L.F.	23.999	880.08	1,219.80	2,099.88
Supply fittings, copper	46.000	Ea.	19.368	103.04	989	1,092.04
Supply valves	2.000	Ea.	.800	177	41	218
Baseboard radiation	212.000	L.F.	70.666	1,002.76	3,254.20	4,256.96
Zone valve	1.000	Ea.	.400	151	20.50	171.50
TOTAL		Ea.	149.356	9,800.58	7,079.20	16,879.78

The costs in this system are on a cost each basis. The costs represent total cost for the system based on a gross square foot of plan area.

Description	QUAN.	UNIT	LABOR HOURS	COST EACH		
				MAT.	INST.	TOTAL

Hot Water Heating Price Sheet	QUAN.	UNIT	LABOR HOURS	COST EACH		
				MAT.	INST.	TOTAL
Boiler, oil fired, 97 MBH, area to 1200 S.F.	1.000	Ea.	15.000	1,625	665	2,290
118 MBH, area to 1500 S.F.	1.000	Ea.	16.506	1,925	730	2,655
161 MBH, area to 2000 S.F.	1.000	Ea.	18.405	4,900	815	5,715
215 MBH, area to 2400 S.F.	1.000	Ea.	19.704	2,850	1,725	4,575
Oil piping, (valve & filter), 3/8" copper	1.000	Ea.	3.289	61.50	157	218.50
1/4" copper	1.000	Ea.	3.242	78	163	241
Oil tank, filler pipe and cap on legs, 275 gallon	1.000	Ea.	3.200	360	147	507
550 gallon	1.000	Ea.	5.926	2,275	273	2,548
Buried underground, 275 gallon	1.000	Ea.	3.200	360	147	507
550 gallon	1.000	Ea.	5.926	2,275	273	2,548
1000 gallon	1.000	Ea.	6.400	2,800	295	3,095
Supply piping copper, area to 1200 S.F., 1/2" tubing	176.000	L.F.	17.384	435	880	1,315
3/4" tubing	176.000	L.F.	18.526	680	940	1,620
Area to 1500 S.F., 1/2" tubing	186.000	L.F.	18.371	460	930	1,390
3/4" tubing	186.000	L.F.	19.578	720	995	1,715
Area to 2000 S.F., 1/2" tubing	204.000	L.F.	20.149	505	1,025	1,530
3/4" tubing	204.000	L.F.	21.473	785	1,100	1,885
Area to 2400 S.F., 1/2" tubing	228.000	L.F.	22.520	565	1,150	1,715
3/4" tubing	228.000	L.F.	23.999	880	1,225	2,105
Supply pipe fittings copper, area to 1200 S.F., 1/2"	36.000	Ea.	14.400	36.50	740	776.50
3/4"	36.000	Ea.	15.158	80.50	775	855.50
Area to 1500 S.F., 1/2"	40.000	Ea.	16.000	40.50	820	860.50
3/4"	40.000	Ea.	16.842	89.50	860	949.50
Area to 2000 S.F., 1/2"	44.000	Ea.	17.600	44.50	900	944.50
3/4"	44.000	Ea.	18.526	98.50	945	1,043.50
Area to 2400, S.F., 1/2"	46.000	Ea.	18.400	46.50	945	991.50
3/4"	46.000	Ea.	19.368	103	990	1,093
Supply valves, 1/2" pipe size	2.000	Ea.	.667	132	34	166
3/4"	2.000	Ea.	.800	177	41	218
Baseboard radiation, area to 1200 S.F., 1/2" tubing	106.000	L.F.	28.267	835	1,300	2,135
3/4" tubing	106.000	L.F.	35.333	500	1,625	2,125
Area to 1500 S.F., 1/2" tubing	134.000	L.F.	35.734	1,050	1,650	2,700
3/4" tubing	134.000	L.F.	44.666	635	2,050	2,685
Area to 2000 S.F., 1/2" tubing	178.000	L.F.	47.467	1,400	2,200	3,600
3/4" tubing	178.000	L.F.	59.333	840	2,725	3,565
Area to 2400 S.F., 1/2" tubing	212.000	L.F.	56.534	1,675	2,600	4,275
3/4" tubing	212.000	L.F.	70.666	1,000	3,250	4,250
Zone valves, 1/2" tubing	1.000	Ea.	.400	151	20.50	171.50
3/4" tubing	1.000	Ea.	.400	151	20.50	171.50

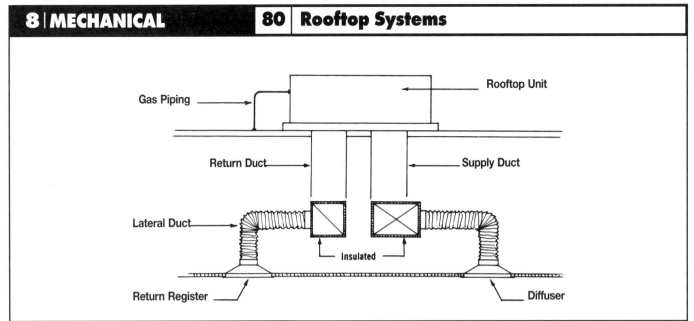

System Description	QUAN.	UNIT	LABOR HOURS	COST EACH		
				MAT.	INST.	TOTAL
ROOFTOP HEATING/COOLING UNIT, AREA TO 2000 S.F.						
Rooftop unit, single zone, electric cool, gas heat, to 2000 s.f.	1.000	Ea.	28.521	4,300	1,325	5,625
Gas piping	34.500	L.F.	5.207	143.87	263.93	407.80
Duct, supply and return, galvanized steel	38.000	Lb.	3.881	25.08	182.02	207.10
Insulation, ductwork	33.000	S.F.	1.508	23.10	66.33	89.43
Lateral duct, flexible duct 12" diameter, insulated	72.000	L.F.	11.520	309.60	522	831.60
Diffusers	4.000	Ea.	4.571	1,124	230	1,354
Return registers	1.000	Ea.	.727	112	36.50	148.50
TOTAL		Ea.	55.935	6,037.65	2,625.78	8,663.43
ROOFTOP HEATING/COOLING UNIT, AREA TO 5000 S.F.						
Rooftop unit, single zone, electric cool, gas heat, to 5000 s.f.	1.000	Ea.	42.032	13,300	1,875	15,175
Gas piping	86.250	L.F.	13.019	359.66	659.81	1,019.47
Duct supply and return, galvanized steel	95.000	Lb.	9.702	62.70	455.05	517.75
Insulation, ductwork	82.000	S.F.	3.748	57.40	164.82	222.22
Lateral duct, flexible duct, 12" diameter, insulated	180.000	L.F.	28.800	774	1,305	2,079
Diffusers	10.000	Ea.	11.429	2,810	575	3,385
Return registers	3.000	Ea.	2.182	336	109.50	445.50
TOTAL		Ea.	110.912	17,699.76	5,144.18	22,843.94

Description	QUAN.	UNIT	LABOR HOURS	COST EACH		
				MAT.	INST.	TOTAL

Rooftop Price Sheet	QUAN.	UNIT	LABOR HOURS	COST EACH		
				MAT.	INST.	TOTAL
Rooftop unit, single zone, electric cool, gas heat to 2000 S.F.	1.000	Ea.	28.521	4,300	1,325	5,625
Area to 3000 S.F.	1.000	Ea.	35.982	8,575	1,600	10,175
Area to 5000 S.F.	1.000	Ea.	42.032	13,300	1,875	15,175
Area to 10000 S.F.	1.000	Ea.	68.376	27,500	3,150	30,650
Gas piping, area 2000 through 4000 S.F.	34.500	L.F.	5.207	144	264	408
Area 5000 to 10000 S.F.	86.250	L.F.	13.019	360	660	1,020
Duct, supply and return, galvanized steel, to 2000 S.F.	38.000	Lb.	3.881	25	182	207
Area to 3000 S.F.	57.000	Lb.	5.821	37.50	273	310.50
Area to 5000 S.F.	95.000	Lb.	9.702	62.50	455	517.50
Area to 10000 S.F.	190.000	Lb.	19.405	125	910	1,035
Rigid fiberglass, area to 2000 S.F.	33.000	S.F.	2.263	26.50	106	132.50
Area to 3000 S.F.	49.000	S.F.	3.360	39	158	197
Area to 5000 S.F.	82.000	S.F.	5.623	65.50	264	329.50
Area to 10000 S.F.	164.000	S.F.	11.245	131	530	661
Insulation, supply and return, blanket type, area to 2000 S.F.	33.000	S.F.	1.508	23	66.50	89.50
Area to 3000 S.F.	49.000	S.F.	2.240	34.50	98.50	133
Area to 5000 S.F.	82.000	S.F.	3.748	57.50	165	222.50
Area to 10000 S.F.	164.000	S.F.	7.496	115	330	445
Lateral ducts, flexible round, 12" insulated, to 2000 S.F.	72.000	L.F.	11.520	310	520	830
Area to 3000 S.F.	108.000	L.F.	17.280	465	785	1,250
Area to 5000 S.F.	180.000	L.F.	28.800	775	1,300	2,075
Area to 10000 S.F.	360.000	L.F.	57.600	1,550	2,600	4,150
Rectangular, galvanized steel, to 2000 S.F.	239.000	Lb.	24.409	158	1,150	1,308
Area to 3000 S.F.	360.000	Lb.	36.767	238	1,725	1,963
Area to 5000 S.F.	599.000	Lb.	61.176	395	2,875	3,270
Area to 10000 S.F.	998.000	Lb.	101.926	660	4,775	5,435
Diffusers, ceiling, 1 to 4 way blow, 24" x 24", to 2000 S.F.	4.000	Ea.	4.571	1,125	230	1,355
Area to 3000 S.F.	6.000	Ea.	6.857	1,675	345	2,020
Area to 5000 S.F.	10.000	Ea.	11.429	2,800	575	3,375
Area to 10000 S.F.	20.000	Ea.	22.857	5,625	1,150	6,775
Return grilles, 24" x 24", to 2000 S.F.	1.000	Ea.	.727	112	36.50	148.50
Area to 3000 S.F.	2.000	Ea.	1.455	224	73	297
Area to 5000 S.F.	3.000	Ea.	2.182	335	110	445
Area to 10000 S.F.	5.000	Ea.	3.636	560	183	743

Division 9
Electrical

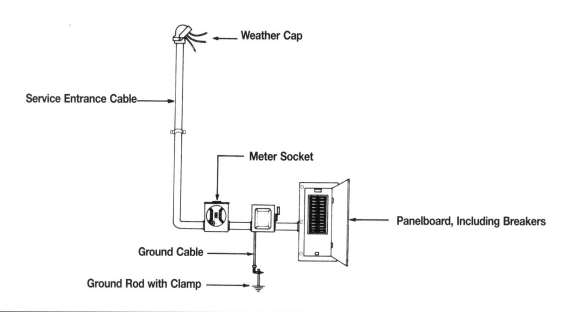

System Description	QUAN.	UNIT	LABOR HOURS	COST EACH		
				MAT.	INST.	TOTAL
100 AMP SERVICE						
Weather cap	1.000	Ea.	.667	13.40	33	46.40
Service entrance cable	10.000	L.F.	.762	50.50	37.90	88.40
Meter socket	1.000	Ea.	2.500	44	124	168
Ground rod with clamp	1.000	Ea.	1.455	16.25	72.50	88.75
Ground cable	5.000	L.F.	.250	9.65	12.45	22.10
Panel board, 12 circuit	1.000	Ea.	6.667	257	330	587
TOTAL		Ea.	12.301	390.80	609.85	1,000.65
200 AMP SERVICE						
Weather cap	1.000	Ea.	1.000	37	49.50	86.50
Service entrance cable	10.000	L.F.	1.143	64.50	57	121.50
Meter socket	1.000	Ea.	4.211	74	209	283
Ground rod with clamp	1.000	Ea.	1.818	36	90.50	126.50
Ground cable	10.000	L.F.	.500	19.30	24.90	44.20
3/4" EMT	5.000	L.F.	.308	5	15.30	20.30
Panel board, 24 circuit	1.000	Ea.	12.308	585	515	1,100
TOTAL		Ea.	21.288	820.80	961.20	1,782
400 AMP SERVICE						
Weather cap	1.000	Ea.	2.963	395	147	542
Service entrance cable	180.000	L.F.	5.760	727.20	286.20	1,013.40
Meter socket	1.000	Ea.	4.211	74	209	283
Ground rod with clamp	1.000	Ea.	2.000	101	99.50	200.50
Ground cable	20.000	L.F.	.485	51.40	24	75.40
3/4" greenfield	20.000	L.F.	1.000	13.20	49.80	63
Current transformer cabinet	1.000	Ea.	6.154	231	305	536
Panel board, 42 circuit	1.000	Ea.	33.333	3,050	1,650	4,700
TOTAL		Ea.	55.906	4,642.80	2,770.50	7,413.30

Thermostat

Electric Baseboard

System Description	QUAN.	UNIT	LABOR HOURS	COST EACH		
				MAT.	INST.	TOTAL
4' BASEBOARD HEATER						
Electric baseboard heater, 4' long	1.000	Ea.	1.194	56	59.50	115.50
Thermostat, integral	1.000	Ea.	.500	22.50	25	47.50
Romex, 12-3 with ground	40.000	L.F.	1.600	30.80	79.60	110.40
Panel board breaker, 20 Amp	1.000	Ea.	.300	10.95	14.85	25.80
TOTAL		Ea.	3.594	120.25	178.95	299.20
6' BASEBOARD HEATER						
Electric baseboard heater, 6' long	1.000	Ea.	1.600	73.50	79.50	153
Thermostat, integral	1.000	Ea.	.500	22.50	25	47.50
Romex, 12-3 with ground	40.000	L.F.	1.600	30.80	79.60	110.40
Panel board breaker, 20 Amp	1.000	Ea.	.400	14.60	19.80	34.40
TOTAL		Ea.	4.100	141.40	203.90	345.30
8' BASEBOARD HEATER						
Electric baseboard heater, 8' long	1.000	Ea.	2.000	92.50	99.50	192
Thermostat, integral	1.000	Ea.	.500	22.50	25	47.50
Romex, 12-3 with ground	40.000	L.F.	1.600	30.80	79.60	110.40
Panel board breaker, 20 Amp	1.000	Ea.	.500	18.25	24.75	43
TOTAL		Ea.	4.600	164.05	228.85	392.90
10' BASEBOARD HEATER						
Electric baseboard heater, 10' long	1.000	Ea.	2.424	193	120	313
Thermostat, integral	1.000	Ea.	.500	22.50	25	47.50
Romex, 12-3 with ground	40.000	L.F.	1.600	30.80	79.60	110.40
Panel board breaker, 20 Amp	1.000	Ea.	.750	27.38	37.13	64.51
TOTAL		Ea.	5.274	273.68	261.73	535.41

The costs in this system are on a cost each basis and include all necessary conduit fittings.

Description	QUAN.	UNIT	LABOR HOURS	COST EACH		
				MAT.	INST.	TOTAL

System Description	QUAN.	UNIT	LABOR HOURS	COST EACH		
				MAT.	INST.	TOTAL
Air conditioning receptacles						
Using non-metallic sheathed cable	1.000	Ea.	.800	24	40	64
Using BX cable	1.000	Ea.	.964	38	48	86
Using EMT conduit	1.000	Ea.	1.194	47	59.50	106.50
Disposal wiring						
Using non-metallic sheathed cable	1.000	Ea.	.889	19.60	44	63.60
Using BX cable	1.000	Ea.	1.067	32.50	53	85.50
Using EMT conduit	1.000	Ea.	1.333	43.50	66.50	110
Dryer circuit						
Using non-metallic sheathed cable	1.000	Ea.	1.455	51.50	72.50	124
Using BX cable	1.000	Ea.	1.739	60	86.50	146.50
Using EMT conduit	1.000	Ea.	2.162	61	107	168
Duplex receptacles						
Using non-metallic sheathed cable	1.000	Ea.	.615	24	30.50	54.50
Using BX cable	1.000	Ea.	.741	38	37	75
Using EMT conduit	1.000	Ea.	.920	47	45.50	92.50
Exhaust fan wiring						
Using non-metallic sheathed cable	1.000	Ea.	.800	21.50	40	61.50
Using BX cable	1.000	Ea.	.964	35.50	48	83.50
Using EMT conduit	1.000	Ea.	1.194	44.50	59.50	104
Furnace circuit & switch						
Using non-metallic sheathed cable	1.000	Ea.	1.333	26.50	66.50	93
Using BX cable	1.000	Ea.	1.600	43.50	79.50	123
Using EMT conduit	1.000	Ea.	2.000	48	99.50	147.50
Ground fault						
Using non-metallic sheathed cable	1.000	Ea.	1.000	55.50	49.50	105
Using BX cable	1.000	Ea.	1.212	69.50	60	129.50
Using EMT conduit	1.000	Ea.	1.481	86.50	73.50	160
Heater circuits						
Using non-metallic sheathed cable	1.000	Ea.	1.000	28.50	49.50	78
Using BX cable	1.000	Ea.	1.212	36	60	96
Using EMT conduit	1.000	Ea.	1.481	44	73.50	117.50
Lighting wiring						
Using non-metallic sheathed cable	1.000	Ea.	.500	29.50	25	54.50
Using BX cable	1.000	Ea.	.602	37	30	67
Using EMT conduit	1.000	Ea.	.748	42.50	37	79.50
Range circuits						
Using non-metallic sheathed cable	1.000	Ea.	2.000	97.50	99.50	197
Using BX cable	1.000	Ea.	2.424	160	120	280
Using EMT conduit	1.000	Ea.	2.963	101	147	248
Switches, single pole						
Using non-metallic sheathed cable	1.000	Ea.	.500	21.50	25	46.50
Using BX cable	1.000	Ea.	.602	35.50	30	65.50
Using EMT conduit	1.000	Ea.	.748	44.50	37	81.50
Switches, 3-way						
Using non-metallic sheathed cable	1.000	Ea.	.667	27.50	33	60.50
Using BX cable	1.000	Ea.	.800	39.50	40	79.50
Using EMT conduit	1.000	Ea.	1.333	58	66.50	124.50
Water heater						
Using non-metallic sheathed cable	1.000	Ea.	1.600	34	79.50	113.50
Using BX cable	1.000	Ea.	1.905	57	94.50	151.50
Using EMT conduit	1.000	Ea.	2.353	50.50	117	167.50
Weatherproof receptacle						
Using non-metallic sheathed cable	1.000	Ea.	1.333	150	66.50	216.50
Using BX cable	1.000	Ea.	1.600	157	79.50	236.50
Using EMT conduit	1.000	Ea.	2.000	166	99.50	265.50

System Description	QUAN.	UNIT	LABOR HOURS	COST EACH		
				MAT.	INST.	TOTAL
Fluorescent strip, 4' long, 1 light, average	1.000	Ea.	.941	33.50	47	80.50
Deluxe	1.000	Ea.	1.129	40	56.50	96.50
2 lights, average	1.000	Ea.	1.000	36	49.50	85.50
Deluxe	1.000	Ea.	1.200	43	59.50	102.50
8' long, 1 light, average	1.000	Ea.	1.194	50.50	59.50	110
Deluxe	1.000	Ea.	1.433	60.50	71.50	132
2 lights, average	1.000	Ea.	1.290	60.50	64	124.50
Deluxe	1.000	Ea.	1.548	72.50	77	149.50
Surface mounted, 4' x 1', economy	1.000	Ea.	.914	65	45.50	110.50
Average	1.000	Ea.	1.143	81	57	138
Deluxe	1.000	Ea.	1.371	97	68.50	165.50
4' x 2', economy	1.000	Ea.	1.208	82.50	60	142.50
Average	1.000	Ea.	1.509	103	75	178
Deluxe	1.000	Ea.	1.811	124	90	214
Recessed, 4'x 1', 2 lamps, economy	1.000	Ea.	1.123	46	56	102
Average	1.000	Ea.	1.404	57.50	70	127.50
Deluxe	1.000	Ea.	1.684	69	84	153
4' x 2', 4' lamps, economy	1.000	Ea.	1.362	55.50	67.50	123
Average	1.000	Ea.	1.702	69.50	84.50	154
Deluxe	1.000	Ea.	2.043	83.50	101	184.50
Incandescent, exterior, 150W, single spot	1.000	Ea.	.500	23	25	48
Double spot	1.000	Ea.	1.167	86.50	58	144.50
Recessed, 100W, economy	1.000	Ea.	.800	58	39.50	97.50
Average	1.000	Ea.	1.000	72.50	49.50	122
Deluxe	1.000	Ea.	1.200	87	59.50	146.50
150W, economy	1.000	Ea.	.800	85.50	39.50	125
Average	1.000	Ea.	1.000	107	49.50	156.50
Deluxe	1.000	Ea.	1.200	128	59.50	187.50
Surface mounted, 60W, economy	1.000	Ea.	.800	46.50	40	86.50
Average	1.000	Ea.	1.000	52	49.50	101.50
Deluxe	1.000	Ea.	1.194	70	59.50	129.50
Metal halide, recessed 2' x 2' 250W	1.000	Ea.	2.500	335	124	459
2' x 2', 400W	1.000	Ea.	2.759	390	137	527
Surface mounted, 2' x 2', 250W	1.000	Ea.	2.963	350	147	497
2' x 2', 400W	1.000	Ea.	3.333	415	166	581
High bay, single, unit, 400W	1.000	Ea.	3.478	420	173	593
Twin unit, 400W	1.000	Ea.	5.000	845	249	1,094
Low bay, 250W	1.000	Ea.	2.500	390	124	514

Location Factors

Costs shown in *RSMeans Residential Cost Data* are based on National Averages for materials and installation. To adjust these costs to a specific location, simply multiply the base cost by the factor for that city. The data is arranged alphabetically by state and postal zip code numbers. For a city not listed, use the factor for a nearby city with similar economic characteristics.

STATE	CITY	Residential
ALABAMA		
350-352	Birmingham	.88
354	Tuscaloosa	.79
355	Jasper	.73
356	Decatur	.79
357-358	Huntsville	.85
359	Gadsden	.76
360-361	Montgomery	.78
362	Anniston	.74
363	Dothan	.77
364	Evergreen	.75
365-366	Mobile	.83
367	Selma	.75
368	Phenix City	.76
369	Butler	.76
ALASKA		
995-996	Anchorage	1.27
997	Fairbanks	1.29
998	Juneau	1.26
999	Ketchikan	1.30
ARIZONA		
850,853	Phoenix	.86
852	Mesa/Tempe	.83
855	Globe	.79
856-857	Tucson	.85
859	Show Low	.81
860	Flagstaff	.86
863	Prescott	.80
864	Kingman	.83
865	Chambers	.80
ARKANSAS		
716	Pine Bluff	.81
717	Camden	.69
718	Texarkana	.74
719	Hot Springs	.69
720-722	Little Rock	.85
723	West Memphis	.79
724	Jonesboro	.78
725	Batesville	.75
726	Harrison	.76
727	Fayetteville	.71
728	Russellville	.76
729	Fort Smith	.78
CALIFORNIA		
900-902	Los Angeles	1.08
903-905	Inglewood	1.04
906-908	Long Beach	1.03
910-912	Pasadena	1.04
913-916	Van Nuys	1.07
917-918	Alhambra	1.08
919-921	San Diego	1.06
922	Palm Springs	1.04
923-924	San Bernardino	1.04
925	Riverside	1.08
926-927	Santa Ana	1.05
928	Anaheim	1.08
930	Oxnard	1.09
931	Santa Barbara	1.08
932-933	Bakersfield	1.06
934	San Luis Obispo	1.07
935	Mojave	1.05
936-938	Fresno	1.09
939	Salinas	1.10
940-941	San Francisco	1.25
942,956-958	Sacramento	1.11
943	Palo Alto	1.18
944	San Mateo	1.23
945	Vallejo	1.16
946	Oakland	1.22
947	Berkeley	1.24
948	Richmond	1.25
949	San Rafael	1.23
950	Santa Cruz	1.14
951	San Jose	1.21
952	Stockton	1.08
953	Modesto	1.08

STATE	CITY	Residential
CALIFORNIA (CONT'D)		
954	Santa Rosa	1.17
955	Eureka	1.11
959	Marysville	1.09
960	Redding	1.09
961	Susanville	1.09
COLORADO		
800-802	Denver	.93
803	Boulder	.93
804	Golden	.91
805	Fort Collins	.89
806	Greeley	.79
807	Fort Morgan	.92
808-809	Colorado Springs	.90
810	Pueblo	.91
811	Alamosa	.88
812	Salida	.90
813	Durango	.91
814	Montrose	.87
815	Grand Junction	.91
816	Glenwood Springs	.90
CONNECTICUT		
060	New Britain	1.11
061	Hartford	1.11
062	Willimantic	1.11
063	New London	1.10
064	Meriden	1.11
065	New Haven	1.11
066	Bridgeport	1.12
067	Waterbury	1.11
068	Norwalk	1.11
069	Stamford	1.12
D.C.		
200-205	Washington	.96
DELAWARE		
197	Newark	1.04
198	Wilmington	1.05
199	Dover	1.03
FLORIDA		
320,322	Jacksonville	.82
321	Daytona Beach	.90
323	Tallahassee	.78
324	Panama City	.75
325	Pensacola	.82
326,344	Gainesville	.81
327-328,347	Orlando	.90
329	Melbourne	.91
330-332,340	Miami	.87
333	Fort Lauderdale	.85
334,349	West Palm Beach	.85
335-336,346	Tampa	.92
337	St. Petersburg	.79
338	Lakeland	.89
339,341	Fort Myers	.87
342	Sarasota	.90
GEORGIA		
300-303,399	Atlanta	.89
304	Statesboro	.71
305	Gainesville	.79
306	Athens	.79
307	Dalton	.75
308-309	Augusta	.80
310-312	Macon	.81
313-314	Savannah	.82
315	Waycross	.75
316	Valdosta	.73
317,398	Albany	.78
318-319	Columbus	.83
HAWAII		
967	Hilo	1.22
968	Honolulu	1.25

Location Factors

STATE	CITY	Residential
STATES & POSS.		
969	Guam	.99
IDAHO		
832	Pocatello	.86
833	Twin Falls	.73
834	Idaho Falls	.75
835	Lewiston	.97
836-837	Boise	.87
838	Coeur d'Alene	.95
ILLINOIS		
600-603	North Suburban	1.10
604	Joliet	1.11
605	South Suburban	1.10
606-608	Chicago	1.19
609	Kankakee	.99
610-611	Rockford	1.06
612	Rock Island	.97
613	La Salle	1.06
614	Galesburg	1.00
615-616	Peoria	.99
617	Bloomington	.98
618-619	Champaign	1.00
620-622	East St. Louis	.99
623	Quincy	.99
624	Effingham	.99
625	Decatur	.97
626-627	Springfield	.96
628	Centralia	1.00
629	Carbondale	.96
INDIANA		
460	Anderson	.91
461-462	Indianapolis	.94
463-464	Gary	1.03
465-466	South Bend	.91
467-468	Fort Wayne	.90
469	Kokomo	.92
470	Lawrenceburg	.87
471	New Albany	.87
472	Columbus	.92
473	Muncie	.91
474	Bloomington	.94
475	Washington	.91
476-477	Evansville	.90
478	Terre Haute	.90
479	Lafayette	.92
IOWA		
500-503,509	Des Moines	.89
504	Mason City	.77
505	Fort Dodge	.76
506-507	Waterloo	.78
508	Creston	.80
510-511	Sioux City	.85
512	Sibley	.72
513	Spencer	.74
514	Carroll	.74
515	Council Bluffs	.82
516	Shenandoah	.74
520	Dubuque	.85
521	Decorah	.75
522-524	Cedar Rapids	.93
525	Ottumwa	.83
526	Burlington	.86
527-528	Davenport	.97
KANSAS		
660-662	Kansas City	.98
664-666	Topeka	.79
667	Fort Scott	.88
668	Emporia	.74
669	Belleville	.79
670-672	Wichita	.79
673	Independence	.84
674	Salina	.77
675	Hutchinson	.79
676	Hays	.82
677	Colby	.83
678	Dodge City	.81
679	Liberal	.80
KENTUCKY		
400-402	Louisville	.90
403-405	Lexington	.88

STATE	CITY	Residential
KENTUCKY (CONT'D)		
406	Frankfort	.86
407-409	Corbin	.77
410	Covington	.99
411-412	Ashland	.92
413-414	Campton	.78
415-416	Pikeville	.84
417-418	Hazard	.73
420	Paducah	.89
421-422	Bowling Green	.89
423	Owensboro	.88
424	Henderson	.90
425-426	Somerset	.77
427	Elizabethtown	.86
LOUISIANA		
700-701	New Orleans	.87
703	Thibodaux	.84
704	Hammond	.79
705	Lafayette	.82
706	Lake Charles	.83
707-708	Baton Rouge	.85
710-711	Shreveport	.78
712	Monroe	.74
713-714	Alexandria	.74
MAINE		
039	Kittery	.87
040-041	Portland	.89
042	Lewiston	.88
043	Augusta	.89
044	Bangor	.87
045	Bath	.87
046	Machias	.88
047	Houlton	.89
048	Rockland	.88
049	Waterville	.87
MARYLAND		
206	Waldorf	.85
207-208	College Park	.88
209	Silver Spring	.86
210-212	Baltimore	.90
214	Annapolis	.84
215	Cumberland	.85
216	Easton	.68
217	Hagerstown	.85
218	Salisbury	.74
219	Elkton	.80
MASSACHUSETTS		
010-011	Springfield	1.04
012	Pittsfield	1.02
013	Greenfield	1.01
014	Fitchburg	1.12
015-016	Worcester	1.13
017	Framingham	1.13
018	Lowell	1.13
019	Lawrence	1.13
020-022, 024	Boston	1.21
023	Brockton	1.12
025	Buzzards Bay	1.10
026	Hyannis	1.10
027	New Bedford	1.12
MICHIGAN		
480,483	Royal Oak	1.02
481	Ann Arbor	1.03
482	Detroit	1.06
484-485	Flint	.97
486	Saginaw	.93
487	Bay City	.94
488-489	Lansing	.95
490	Battle Creek	.92
491	Kalamazoo	.91
492	Jackson	.93
493,495	Grand Rapids	.80
494	Muskegan	.88
496	Traverse City	.79
497	Gaylord	.82
498-499	Iron mountain	.89
MINNESOTA		
550-551	Saint Paul	1.12
553-555	Minneapolis	1.16
556-558	Duluth	1.08

Location Factors

STATE	CITY	Residential
MINNESOTA (CONT'd)		
559	Rochester	1.05
560	Mankato	1.02
561	Windom	.83
562	Willmar	.84
563	St. Cloud	1.07
564	Brainerd	.98
565	Detroit Lakes	.96
566	Bemidji	.96
567	Thief River Falls	.95
MISSISSIPPI		
386	Clarksdale	.75
387	Greenville	.82
388	Tupelo	.76
389	Greenwood	.78
390-392	Jackson	.83
393	Meridian	.80
394	Laurel	.77
395	Biloxi	.83
396	Mccomb	.78
397	Columbus	.76
MISSOURI		
630-631	St. Louis	1.03
633	Bowling Green	.95
634	Hannibal	.86
635	Kirksville	.80
636	Flat River	.94
637	Cape Girardeau	.88
638	Sikeston	.83
639	Poplar Bluff	.83
640-641	Kansas City	1.03
644-645	St. Joseph	.95
646	Chillicothe	.88
647	Harrisonville	.98
648	Joplin	.84
650-651	Jefferson City	.88
652	Columbia	.88
653	Sedalia	.86
654-655	Rolla	.88
656-658	Springfield	.87
MONTANA		
590-591	Billings	.87
592	Wolf Point	.83
593	Miles City	.85
594	Great Falls	.89
595	Havre	.80
596	Helena	.86
597	Butte	.85
598	Missoula	.82
599	Kalispell	.81
NEBRASKA		
680-681	Omaha	.91
683-685	Lincoln	.87
686	Columbus	.85
687	Norfolk	.89
688	Grand Island	.89
689	Hastings	.91
690	Mccook	.83
691	North Platte	.89
692	Valentine	.83
693	Alliance	.83
NEVADA		
889-891	Las Vegas	1.02
893	Ely	.87
894-895	Reno	.94
897	Carson City	.95
898	Elko	.92
NEW HAMPSHIRE		
030	Nashua	.95
031	Manchester	.95
032-033	Concord	.93
034	Keene	.76
035	Littleton	.82
036	Charleston	.74
037	Claremont	.75
038	Portsmouth	.94

STATE	CITY	Residential
NEW JERSEY		
070-071	Newark	1.12
072	Elizabeth	1.15
073	Jersey City	1.11
074-075	Paterson	1.12
076	Hackensack	1.11
077	Long Branch	1.12
078	Dover	1.12
079	Summit	1.12
080,083	Vineland	1.09
081	Camden	1.10
082,084	Atlantic City	1.13
085-086	Trenton	1.11
087	Point Pleasant	1.10
088-089	New Brunswick	1.12
NEW MEXICO		
870-872	Albuquerque	.85
873	Gallup	.85
874	Farmington	.85
875	Santa Fe	.86
877	Las Vegas	.85
878	Socorro	.85
879	Truth/Consequences	.84
880	Las Cruces	.83
881	Clovis	.85
882	Roswell	.85
883	Carrizozo	.85
884	Tucumcari	.86
NEW YORK		
100-102	New York	1.34
103	Staten Island	1.27
104	Bronx	1.29
105	Mount Vernon	1.14
106	White Plains	1.17
107	Yonkers	1.18
108	New Rochelle	1.18
109	Suffern	1.11
110	Queens	1.28
111	Long Island City	1.31
112	Brooklyn	1.32
113	Flushing	1.30
114	Jamaica	1.29
115,117,118	Hicksville	1.18
116	Far Rockaway	1.29
119	Riverhead	1.19
120-122	Albany	.94
123	Schenectady	.95
124	Kingston	1.03
125-126	Poughkeepsie	1.05
127	Monticello	1.05
128	Glens Falls	.88
129	Plattsburgh	.92
130-132	Syracuse	.96
133-135	Utica	.92
136	Watertown	.89
137-139	Binghamton	.94
140-142	Buffalo	1.03
143	Niagara Falls	1.00
144-146	Rochester	.97
147	Jamestown	.88
148-149	Elmira	.85
NORTH CAROLINA		
270,272-274	Greensboro	.84
271	Winston-Salem	.84
275-276	Raleigh	.85
277	Durham	.84
278	Rocky Mount	.74
279	Elizabeth City	.75
280	Gastonia	.85
281-282	Charlotte	.86
283	Fayetteville	.83
284	Wilmington	.82
285	Kinston	.74
286	Hickory	.79
287-288	Asheville	.82
289	Murphy	.73
NORTH DAKOTA		
580-581	Fargo	.79
582	Grand Forks	.75
583	Devils Lake	.78
584	Jamestown	.73
585	Bismarck	.78

Location Factors

STATE	CITY	Residential
NORTH DAKOTA (CONT'D)		
586	Dickinson	.77
587	Minot	.82
588	Williston	.77
OHIO		
430-432	Columbus	.94
433	Marion	.90
434-436	Toledo	1.01
437-438	Zanesville	.90
439	Steubenville	.95
440	Lorain	.99
441	Cleveland	1.01
442-443	Akron	.98
444-445	Youngstown	.96
446-447	Canton	.94
448-449	Mansfield	.94
450	Hamilton	.93
451-452	Cincinnati	.93
453-454	Dayton	.93
455	Springfield	.94
456	Chillicothe	.97
457	Athens	.89
458	Lima	.91
OKLAHOMA		
730-731	Oklahoma City	.79
734	Ardmore	.78
735	Lawton	.81
736	Clinton	.77
737	Enid	.77
738	Woodward	.76
739	Guymon	.67
740-741	Tulsa	.78
743	Miami	.82
744	Muskogee	.72
745	Mcalester	.74
746	Ponca City	.77
747	Durant	.77
748	Shawnee	.75
749	Poteau	.78
OREGON		
970-972	Portland	1.02
973	Salem	1.00
974	Eugene	1.01
975	Medford	1.00
976	Klamath Falls	1.01
977	Bend	1.02
978	Pendleton	1.00
979	Vale	.99
PENNSYLVANIA		
150-152	Pittsburgh	.97
153	Washington	.93
154	Uniontown	.89
155	Bedford	.88
156	Greensburg	.93
157	Indiana	.90
158	Dubois	.89
159	Johnstown	.89
160	Butler	.92
161	New Castle	.91
162	Kittanning	.93
163	Oil City	.90
164-165	Erie	.94
166	Altoona	.87
167	Bradford	.90
168	State College	.90
169	Wellsboro	.89
170-171	Harrisburg	.94
172	Chambersburg	.89
173-174	York	.91
175-176	Lancaster	.91
177	Williamsport	.84
178	Sunbury	.91
179	Pottsville	.90
180	Lehigh Valley	1.01
181	Allentown	1.04
182	Hazleton	.90
183	Stroudsburg	.91
184-185	Scranton	.96
186-187	Wilkes-Barre	.92
188	Montrose	.90
189	Doylestown	1.05

STATE	CITY	Residential
PENNSYLVANIA (CONT'D)		
190-191	Philadelphia	1.18
193	Westchester	1.11
194	Norristown	1.10
195-196	Reading	.97
PUERTO RICO		
009	San Juan	.75
RHODE ISLAND		
028	Newport	1.07
029	Providence	1.07
SOUTH CAROLINA		
290-292	Columbia	.85
293	Spartanburg	.85
294	Charleston	.88
295	Florence	.80
296	Greenville	.84
297	Rock Hill	.83
298	Aiken	.99
299	Beaufort	.83
SOUTH DAKOTA		
570-571	Sioux Falls	.78
572	Watertown	.74
573	Mitchell	.76
574	Aberdeen	.78
575	Pierre	.75
576	Mobridge	.74
577	Rapid City	.76
TENNESSEE		
370-372	Nashville	.83
373-374	Chattanooga	.76
375,380-381	Memphis	.82
376	Johnson City	.71
377-379	Knoxville	.73
382	Mckenzie	.72
383	Jackson	.70
384	Columbia	.72
385	Cookeville	.71
TEXAS		
750	Mckinney	.74
751	Waxahackie	.75
752-753	Dallas	.82
754	Greenville	.68
755	Texarkana	.72
756	Longview	.67
757	Tyler	.73
758	Palestine	.66
759	Lufkin	.70
760-761	Fort Worth	.81
762	Denton	.76
763	Wichita Falls	.79
764	Eastland	.72
765	Temple	.74
766-767	Waco	.77
768	Brownwood	.68
769	San Angelo	.71
770-772	Houston	.84
773	Huntsville	.68
774	Wharton	.70
775	Galveston	.83
776-777	Beaumont	.81
778	Bryan	.73
779	Victoria	.73
780	Laredo	.73
781-782	San Antonio	.80
783-784	Corpus Christi	.77
785	Mc Allen	.75
786-787	Austin	.79
788	Del Rio	.66
789	Giddings	.69
790-791	Amarillo	.77
792	Childress	.75
793-794	Lubbock	.75
795-796	Abilene	.74
797	Midland	.75
798-799,885	El Paso	.74
UTAH		
840-841	Salt Lake City	.81
842,844	Ogden	.79
843	Logan	.79

267

Location Factors

STATE	CITY	Residential
UTAH (CONT'D)		
845	Price	.71
846-847	Provo	.81
VERMONT		
050	White River Jct.	.76
051	Bellows Falls	.79
052	Bennington	.81
053	Brattleboro	.81
054	Burlington	.82
056	Montpelier	.83
057	Rutland	.82
058	St. Johnsbury	.79
059	Guildhall	.78
VIRGINIA		
220-221	Fairfax	1.02
222	Arlington	1.04
223	Alexandria	1.07
224-225	Fredericksburg	.94
226	Winchester	.92
227	Culpeper	1.00
228	Harrisonburg	.90
229	Charlottesville	.91
230-232	Richmond	.99
233-235	Norfolk	1.00
236	Newport News	1.00
237	Portsmouth	.92
238	Petersburg	.98
239	Farmville	.90
240-241	Roanoke	.98
242	Bristol	.85
243	Pulaski	.84
244	Staunton	.92
245	Lynchburg	.97
246	Grundy	.84
WASHINGTON		
980-981,987	Seattle	1.02
982	Everett	1.05
983-984	Tacoma	1.01
985	Olympia	1.00
986	Vancouver	.99
988	Wenatchee	.94
989	Yakima	.97
990-992	Spokane	1.00
993	Richland	.98
994	Clarkston	.98
WEST VIRGINIA		
247-248	Bluefield	.88
249	Lewisburg	.89
250-253	Charleston	.95
254	Martinsburg	.86
255-257	Huntington	.96
258-259	Beckley	.90
260	Wheeling	.93
261	Parkersburg	.91
262	Buckhannon	.92
263-264	Clarksburg	.91
265	Morgantown	.92
266	Gassaway	.92
267	Romney	.88
268	Petersburg	.90
WISCONSIN		
530,532	Milwaukee	1.08
531	Kenosha	1.05
534	Racine	1.04
535	Beloit	1.00
537	Madison	1.00
538	Lancaster	.98
539	Portage	.98
540	New Richmond	1.00
541-543	Green Bay	1.01
544	Wausau	.95
545	Rhinelander	.96
546	La Crosse	.95
547	Eau Claire	.99
548	Superior	.99
549	Oshkosh	.96
WYOMING		
820	Cheyenne	.83
821	Yellowstone Nat. Pk.	.75
822	Wheatland	.75

STATE	CITY	Residential
WYOMING (CONT'D)		
823	Rawlins	.75
824	Worland	.74
825	Riverton	.74
826	Casper	.77
827	Newcastle	.74
828	Sheridan	.80
829-831	Rock Springs	.79
CANADIAN FACTORS (reflect Canadian currency)		
ALBERTA		
	Calgary	1.13
	Edmonton	1.13
	Fort McMurray	1.16
	Lethbridge	1.13
	Lloydminster	1.08
	Medicine Hat	1.08
	Red Deer	1.08
BRITISH COLUMBIA		
	Kamloops	1.06
	Prince George	1.06
	Vancouver	1.07
	Victoria	1.01
MANITOBA		
	Brandon	1.03
	Portage la Prairie	1.03
	Winnipeg	1.03
NEW BRUNSWICK		
	Bathurst	.96
	Dalhousie	.95
	Fredericton	1.03
	Moncton	.96
	Newcastle	.96
	St. John	1.03
NEWFOUNDLAND		
	Corner Brook	.97
	St Johns	.99
NORTHWEST TERRITORIES		
	Yellowknife	1.08
NOVA SCOTIA		
	Bridgewater	.98
	Dartmouth	.99
	Halifax	1.01
	New Glasgow	.98
	Sydney	.97
	Truro	.98
	Yarmouth	.98
ONTARIO		
	Barrie	1.14
	Brantford	1.16
	Cornwall	1.16
	Hamilton	1.18
	Kingston	1.16
	Kitchener	1.11
	London	1.15
	North Bay	1.12
	Oshawa	1.15
	Ottawa	1.17
	Owen Sound	1.13
	Peterborough	1.13
	Sarnia	1.16
	Sault Ste Marie	1.09
	St. Catharines	1.11
	Sudbury	1.09
	Thunder Bay	1.14
	Timmins	1.12
	Toronto	1.19
	Windsor	1.13
PRINCE EDWARD ISLAND		
	Charlottetown	.93
	Summerside	.93
QUEBEC		
	Cap-de-la-Madeleine	1.15
	Charlesbourg	1.15
	Chicoutimi	1.18
	Gatineau	1.14
	Granby	1.14

Location Factors

STATE	CITY	Residential
QUEBEC (CONT'D)		
	Hull	1.14
	Joliette	1.15
	Laval	1.14
	Montreal	1.18
	Quebec	1.20
	Rimouski	1.18
	Rouyn-Noranda	1.14
	Saint Hyacinthe	1.14
	Sherbrooke	1.14
	Sorel	1.15
	St Jerome	1.14
	Trois Rivieres	1.15
SASKATCHEWAN		
	Moose Jaw	.95
	Prince Albert	.94
	Regina	.97
	Saskatoon	.96
YUKON		
	Whitehorse	.94

A	Area Square Feet; Ampere
ABS	Acrylonitrile Butadiene Stryrene; Asbestos Bonded Steel
A.C.	Alternating Current; Air-Conditioning; Asbestos Cement; Plywood Grade A & C
A.C.I.	American Concrete Institute
AD	Plywood, Grade A & D
Addit.	Additional
Adj.	Adjustable
af	Audio-frequency
A.G.A.	American Gas Association
Agg.	Aggregate
A.H.	Ampere Hours
A hr.	Ampere-hour
A.H.U.	Air Handling Unit
A.I.A.	American Institute of Architects
AIC	Ampere Interrupting Capacity
Allow.	Allowance
alt.	Altitude
Alum.	Aluminum
a.m.	Ante Meridiem
Amp.	Ampere
Anod.	Anodized
Approx.	Approximate
Apt.	Apartment
Asb.	Asbestos
A.S.B.C.	American Standard Building Code
Asbe.	Asbestos Worker
A.S.H.R.A.E.	American Society of Heating, Refrig. & AC Engineers
A.S.M.E.	American Society of Mechanical Engineers
A.S.T.M.	American Society for Testing and Materials
Attchmt.	Attachment
Avg.	Average
A.W.G.	American Wire Gauge
AWWA	American Water Works Assoc.
Bbl.	Barrel
B&B	Grade B and Better; Balled & Burlapped
B.&S.	Bell and Spigot
B.&W.	Black and White
b.c.c.	Body-centered Cubic
B.C.Y.	Bank Cubic Yards
BE	Bevel End
B.F.	Board Feet
Bg. cem.	Bag of Cement
BHP	Boiler Horsepower; Brake Horsepower
B.I.	Black Iron
Bit.; Bitum.	Bituminous
Bk.	Backed
Bkrs.	Breakers
Bldg.	Building
Blk.	Block
Bm.	Beam
Boil.	Boilermaker
B.P.M.	Blows per Minute
BR	Bedroom
Brg.	Bearing
Brhe.	Bricklayer Helper
Bric.	Bricklayer
Brk.	Brick
Brng.	Bearing
Brs.	Brass
Brz.	Bronze
Bsn.	Basin
Btr.	Better
BTU	British Thermal Unit
BTUH	BTU per Hour
B.U.R.	Built-up Roofing
BX	Interlocked Armored Cable
c	Conductivity, Copper Sweat
C	Hundred; Centigrade
C/C	Center to Center, Cedar on Cedar
Cab.	Cabinet
Cair.	Air Tool Laborer
Calc	Calculated
Cap.	Capacity
Carp.	Carpenter
C.B.	Circuit Breaker
C.C.A.	Chromate Copper Arsenate
C.C.F.	Hundred Cubic Feet
cd	Candela
cd/sf	Candela per Square Foot
CD	Grade of Plywood Face & Back
CDX	Plywood, Grade C & D, exterior glue
Cefi.	Cement Finisher
Cem.	Cement
CF	Hundred Feet
C.F.	Cubic Feet
CFM	Cubic Feet per Minute
c.g.	Center of Gravity
CHW	Chilled Water; Commercial Hot Water
C.I.	Cast Iron
C.I.P.	Cast in Place
Circ.	Circuit
C.L.	Carload Lot
Clab.	Common Laborer
Clam	Common maintenance laborer
C.L.F.	Hundred Linear Feet
CLF	Current Limiting Fuse
CLP	Cross Linked Polyethylene
cm	Centimeter
CMP	Corr. Metal Pipe
C.M.U.	Concrete Masonry Unit
CN	Change Notice
Col.	Column
CO_2	Carbon Dioxide
Comb.	Combination
Compr.	Compressor
Conc.	Concrete
Cont.	Continuous; Continued
Corr.	Corrugated
Cos	Cosine
Cot	Cotangent
Cov.	Cover
C/P	Cedar on Paneling
CPA	Control Point Adjustment
Cplg.	Coupling
C.P.M.	Critical Path Method
CPVC	Chlorinated Polyvinyl Chloride
C.Pr.	Hundred Pair
CRC	Cold Rolled Channel
Creos.	Creosote
Crpt.	Carpet & Linoleum Layer
CRT	Cathode-ray Tube
CS	Carbon Steel, Constant Shear Bar Joist
Csc	Cosecant
C.S.F.	Hundred Square Feet
CSI	Construction Specifications Institute
C.T.	Current Transformer
CTS	Copper Tube Size
Cu	Copper, Cubic
Cu. Ft.	Cubic Foot
cw	Continuous Wave
C.W.	Cool White; Cold Water
Cwt.	100 Pounds
C.W.X.	Cool White Deluxe
C.Y.	Cubic Yard (27 cubic feet)
C.Y./Hr.	Cubic Yard per Hour
Cyl.	Cylinder
d	Penny (nail size)
D	Deep; Depth; Discharge
Dis.;Disch.	Discharge
Db.	Decibel
Dbl.	Double
DC	Direct Current
DDC	Direct Digital Control
Demob.	Demobilization
d.f.u.	Drainage Fixture Units
D.H.	Double Hung
DHW	Domestic Hot Water
Diag.	Diagonal
Diam.	Diameter
Distrib.	Distribution
Div.	Division
Dk.	Deck
D.L.	Dead Load; Diesel
DLH	Deep Long Span Bar Joist
Do.	Ditto
Dp.	Depth
D.P.S.T.	Double Pole, Single Throw
Dr.	Driver
Drink.	Drinking
D.S.	Double Strength
D.S.A.	Double Strength A Grade
D.S.B.	Double Strength B Grade
Dty.	Duty
DWV	Drain Waste Vent
DX	Deluxe White, Direct Expansion
dyn	Dyne
e	Eccentricity
E	Equipment Only; East
Ea.	Each
E.B.	Encased Burial
Econ.	Economy
E.C.Y	Embankment Cubic Yards
EDP	Electronic Data Processing
EIFS	Exterior Insulation Finish System
E.D.R.	Equiv. Direct Radiation
Eq.	Equation
Elec.	Electrician; Electrical
Elev.	Elevator; Elevating
EMT	Electrical Metallic Conduit; Thin Wall Conduit
Eng.	Engine, Engineered
EPDM	Ethylene Propylene Diene Monomer
EPS	Expanded Polystyrene
Eqhv.	Equip. Oper., Heavy
Eqlt.	Equip. Oper., Light
Eqmd.	Equip. Oper., Medium
Eqmm.	Equip. Oper., Master Mechanic
Eqol.	Equip. Oper., Oilers
Equip.	Equipment
ERW	Electric Resistance Welded
E.S.	Energy Saver
Est.	Estimated
esu	Electrostatic Units
E.W.	Each Way
EWT	Entering Water Temperature
Excav.	Excavation
Exp.	Expansion, Exposure
Ext.	Exterior
Extru.	Extrusion
f.	Fiber stress
F	Fahrenheit; Female; Fill
Fab.	Fabricated
FBGS	Fiberglass
F.C.	Footcandles
f.c.c.	Face-centered Cubic
f'c.	Compressive Stress in Concrete; Extreme Compressive Stress
F.E.	Front End
FEP	Fluorinated Ethylene Propylene (Teflon)
F.G.	Flat Grain
F.H.A.	Federal Housing Administration
Fig.	Figure
Fin.	Finished
Fixt.	Fixture
Fl. Oz.	Fluid Ounces
Flr.	Floor
F.M.	Frequency Modulation; Factory Mutual
Fmg.	Framing
Fndtn.	Foundation
Fori.	Foreman, Inside

Foro.	Foreman, Outside	J.I.C.	Joint Industrial Council	M.C.F.M.	Thousand Cubic Feet per Minute
Fount.	Fountain	K	Thousand; Thousand Pounds;	M.C.M.	Thousand Circular Mils
FPM	Feet per Minute		Heavy Wall Copper Tubing, Kelvin	M.C.P.	Motor Circuit Protector
FPT	Female Pipe Thread	K.A.H.	Thousand Amp. Hours	MD	Medium Duty
Fr.	Frame	KCMIL	Thousand Circular Mils	M.D.O.	Medium Density Overlaid
F.R.	Fire Rating	KD	Knock Down	Med.	Medium
FRK	Foil Reinforced Kraft	K.D.A.T.	Kiln Dried After Treatment	MF	Thousand Feet
FRP	Fiberglass Reinforced Plastic	kg	Kilogram	M.F.B.M.	Thousand Feet Board Measure
FS	Forged Steel	kG	Kilogauss	Mfg.	Manufacturing
FSC	Cast Body; Cast Switch Box	kgf	Kilogram Force	Mfrs.	Manufacturers
Ft.	Foot; Feet	kHz	Kilohertz	mg	Milligram
Ftng.	Fitting	Kip.	1000 Pounds	MGD	Million Gallons per Day
Ftg.	Footing	KJ	Kiljoule	MGPH	Thousand Gallons per Hour
Ft. Lb.	Foot Pound	K.L.	Effective Length Factor	MH, M.H.	Manhole; Metal Halide; Man-Hour
Furn.	Furniture	K.L.F.	Kips per Linear Foot	MHz	Megahertz
FVNR	Full Voltage Non-Reversing	Km	Kilometer	Mi.	Mile
FXM	Female by Male	K.S.F.	Kips per Square Foot	MI	Malleable Iron; Mineral Insulated
Fy.	Minimum Yield Stress of Steel	K.S.I.	Kips per Square Inch	mm	Millimeter
g	Gram	kV	Kilovolt	Mill.	Millwright
G	Gauss	kVA	Kilovolt Ampere	Min., min.	Minimum, minute
Ga.	Gauge	K.V.A.R.	Kilovar (Reactance)	Misc.	Miscellaneous
Gal.	Gallon	KW	Kilowatt	ml	Milliliter, Mainline
Gal./Min.	Gallon per Minute	KWh	Kilowatt-hour	M.L.F.	Thousand Linear Feet
Galv.	Galvanized	L	Labor Only; Length; Long;	Mo.	Month
Gen.	General		Medium Wall Copper Tubing	Mobil.	Mobilization
G.F.I.	Ground Fault Interrupter	Lab.	Labor	Mog.	Mogul Base
Glaz.	Glazier	lat	Latitude	MPH	Miles per Hour
GPD	Gallons per Day	Lath.	Lather	MPT	Male Pipe Thread
GPH	Gallons per Hour	Lav.	Lavatory	MRT	Mile Round Trip
GPM	Gallons per Minute	lb.; #	Pound	ms	Millisecond
GR	Grade	L.B.	Load Bearing; L Conduit Body	M.S.F.	Thousand Square Feet
Gran.	Granular	L. & E.	Labor & Equipment	Mstz.	Mosaic & Terrazzo Worker
Grnd.	Ground	lb./hr.	Pounds per Hour	M.S.Y.	Thousand Square Yards
H	High; High Strength Bar Joist;	lb./L.F.	Pounds per Linear Foot	Mtd.	Mounted
	Henry	lbf/sq.in.	Pound-force per Square Inch	Mthe.	Mosaic & Terrazzo Helper
H.C.	High Capacity	L.C.L.	Less than Carload Lot	Mtng.	Mounting
H.D.	Heavy Duty; High Density	L.C.Y.	Loose Cubic Yard	Mult.	Multi; Multiply
H.D.O.	High Density Overlaid	Ld.	Load	M.V.A.	Million Volt Amperes
Hdr.	Header	LE	Lead Equivalent	M.V.A.R.	Million Volt Amperes Reactance
Hdwe.	Hardware	LED	Light Emitting Diode	MV	Megavolt
Help.	Helper Average	L.F.	Linear Foot	MW	Megawatt
HEPA	High Efficiency Particulate Air	L.F. Nose	Linear Foot of Stair Nosing	MXM	Male by Male
	Filter	L.F. Rsr	Linear Foot of Stair Riser	MYD	Thousand Yards
Hg	Mercury	Lg.	Long; Length; Large	N	Natural; North
HIC	High Interrupting Capacity	L & H	Light and Heat	nA	Nanoampere
HM	Hollow Metal	LH	Long Span Bar Joist	NA	Not Available; Not Applicable
H.O.	High Output	L.H.	Labor Hours	N.B.C.	National Building Code
Horiz.	Horizontal	L.L.	Live Load	NC	Normally Closed
H.P.	Horsepower; High Pressure	L.L.D.	Lamp Lumen Depreciation	N.E.M.A.	National Electrical Manufacturers
H.P.F.	High Power Factor	lm	Lumen		Assoc.
Hr.	Hour	lm/sf	Lumen per Square Foot	NEHB	Bolted Circuit Breaker to 600V.
Hrs./Day	Hours per Day	lm/W	Lumen per Watt	N.L.B.	Non-Load-Bearing
HSC	High Short Circuit	L.O.A.	Length Over All	NM	Non-Metallic Cable
Ht.	Height	log	Logarithm	nm	Nanometer
Htg.	Heating	L-O-L	Lateralolet	No.	Number
Htrs.	Heaters	L.P.	Liquefied Petroleum; Low Pressure	NO	Normally Open
HVAC	Heating, Ventilation & Air-	L.P.F.	Low Power Factor	N.O.C.	Not Otherwise Classified
	Conditioning	LR	Long Radius	Nose.	Nosing
Hvy.	Heavy	L.S.	Lump Sum	N.P.T.	National Pipe Thread
HW	Hot Water	Lt.	Light	NQOD	Combination Plug-on/Bolt on
Hyd.;Hydr.	Hydraulic	Lt. Ga.	Light Gauge		Circuit Breaker to 240V.
Hz.	Hertz (cycles)	L.T.L.	Less than Truckload Lot	N.R.C.	Noise Reduction Coefficient
I.	Moment of Inertia	Lt. Wt.	Lightweight	N.R.S.	Non Rising Stem
I.C.	Interrupting Capacity	L.V.	Low Voltage	ns	Nanosecond
ID	Inside Diameter	M	Thousand; Material; Male;	nW	Nanowatt
I.D.	Inside Dimension; Identification		Light Wall Copper Tubing	OB	Opposing Blade
I.F.	Inside Frosted	M^2CA	Meters Squared Contact Area	OC	On Center
I.M.C.	Intermediate Metal Conduit	m/hr; M.H.	Man-hour	OD	Outside Diameter
In.	Inch	mA	Milliampere	O.D.	Outside Dimension
Incan.	Incandescent	Mach.	Machine	ODS	Overhead Distribution System
Incl.	Included; Including	Mag. Str.	Magnetic Starter	O.G.	Ogee
Int.	Interior	Maint.	Maintenance	O.H.	Overhead
Inst.	Installation	Marb.	Marble Setter	O&P	Overhead and Profit
Insul.	Insulation/Insulated	Mat; Mat'l.	Material	Oper.	Operator
I.P.	Iron Pipe	Max.	Maximum	Opng.	Opening
I.P.S.	Iron Pipe Size	MBF	Thousand Board Feet	Orna.	Ornamental
I.P.T.	Iron Pipe Threaded	MBH	Thousand BTU's per hr.	OSB	Oriented Strand Board
I.W.	Indirect Waste	MC	Metal Clad Cable	O.S.&Y.	Outside Screw and Yoke
J	Joule	M.C.F.	Thousand Cubic Feet	Ovhd.	Overhead

271

OWG	Oil, Water or Gas	SC	Screw Cover	Tilh.	Tile Layer, Helper
Oz.	Ounce	SCFM	Standard Cubic Feet per Minute	THHN	Nylon Jacketed Wire
P.	Pole; Applied Load; Projection	Scaf.	Scaffold	THW.	Insulated Strand Wire
p.	Page	Sch.; Sched.	Schedule	THWN;	Nylon Jacketed Wire
Pape.	Paperhanger	S.C.R.	Modular Brick	T.L.	Truckload
P.A.P.R.	Powered Air Purifying Respirator	S.D.	Sound Deadening	T.M.	Track Mounted
PAR	Parabolic Reflector	S.D.R.	Standard Dimension Ratio	Tot.	Total
Pc., Pcs.	Piece, Pieces	S.E.	Surfaced Edge	T-O-L	Threadolet
P.C.	Portland Cement; Power Connector	Sel.	Select	T.S.	Trigger Start
P.C.F.	Pounds per Cubic Foot	S.E.R.; S.E.U.	Service Entrance Cable	Tr.	Trade
P.C.M.	Phase Contrast Microscopy	S.F.	Square Foot	Transf.	Transformer
P.E.	Professional Engineer;	S.F.C.A.	Square Foot Contact Area	Trhv.	Truck Driver, Heavy
	Porcelain Enamel;	S.F. Flr.	Square Foot of Floor	Trlr	Trailer
	Polyethylene; Plain End	S.F.G.	Square Foot of Ground	Trlt.	Truck Driver, Light
Perf.	Perforated	S.F. Hor.	Square Foot Horizontal	TTY	Teletypewriter
Ph.	Phase	S.F.R.	Square Feet of Radiation	TV	Television
P.I.	Pressure Injected	S.F. Shlf.	Square Foot of Shelf	T.W.	Thermoplastic Water Resistant
Pile.	Pile Driver	S4S	Surface 4 Sides		Wire
Pkg.	Package	Shee.	Sheet Metal Worker	UCI	Uniform Construction Index
Pl.	Plate	Sin.	Sine	UF	Underground Feeder
Plah.	Plasterer Helper	Skwk.	Skilled Worker	UGND	Underground Feeder
Plas.	Plasterer	SL	Saran Lined	U.H.F.	Ultra High Frequency
Pluh.	Plumbers Helper	S.L.	Slimline	U.L.	Underwriters Laboratory
Plum.	Plumber	Sldr.	Solder	Uld.	unloading
Ply.	Plywood	SLH	Super Long Span Bar Joist	Unfin.	Unfinished
p.m.	Post Meridiem	S.N.	Solid Neutral	URD	Underground Residential
Pntd.	Painted	S-O-L	Socketolet		Distribution
Pord.	Painter, Ordinary	sp	Standpipe	US	United States
pp	Pages	S.P.	Static Pressure; Single Pole; Self-	USP	United States Primed
PP; PPL	Polypropylene		Propelled	UTP	Unshielded Twisted Pair
P.P.M.	Parts per Million	Spri.	Sprinkler Installer	V	Volt
Pr.	Pair	spwg	Static Pressure Water Gauge	V.A.	Volt Amperes
P.E.S.B.	Pre-engineered Steel Building	S.P.D.T.	Single Pole, Double Throw	V.C.T.	Vinyl Composition Tile
Prefab.	Prefabricated	SPF	Spruce Pine Fir	VAV	Variable Air Volume
Prefin.	Prefinished	S.P.S.T.	Single Pole, Single Throw	VC	Veneer Core
Prop.	Propelled	SPT	Standard Pipe Thread	Vent.	Ventilation
PSF; psf	Pounds per Square Foot	Sq.	Square; 100 Square Feet	Vert.	Vertical
PSI; psi	Pounds per Square Inch	Sq. Hd.	Square Head	V.F.	Vinyl Faced
PSIG	Pounds per Square Inch Gauge	Sq. In.	Square Inch	V.G.	Vertical Grain
PSP	Plastic Sewer Pipe	S.S.	Single Strength; Stainless Steel	V.H.F.	Very High Frequency
Pspr.	Painter, Spray	S.S.B.	Single Strength B Grade	VHO	Very High Output
Psst.	Painter, Structural Steel	sst	Stainless Steel	Vib.	Vibrating
P.T.	Potential Transformer	Sswk.	Structural Steel Worker	V.L.F.	Vertical Linear Foot
P. & T.	Pressure & Temperature	Sswl.	Structural Steel Welder	Vol.	Volume
Ptd.	Painted	St.; Stl.	Steel	VRP	Vinyl Reinforced Polyester
Ptns.	Partitions	S.T.C.	Sound Transmission Coefficient	W	Wire; Watt; Wide; West
Pu	Ultimate Load	Std.	Standard	w/	With
PVC	Polyvinyl Chloride	STK	Select Tight Knot	W.C.	Water Column; Water Closet
Pvmt.	Pavement	STP	Standard Temperature & Pressure	W.F.	Wide Flange
Pwr.	Power	Stpi.	Steamfitter, Pipefitter	W.G.	Water Gauge
Q	Quantity Heat Flow	Str.	Strength; Starter; Straight	Wldg.	Welding
Quan.; Qty.	Quantity	Strd.	Stranded	W. Mile	Wire Mile
Q.C.	Quick Coupling	Struct.	Structural	W-O-L	Weldolet
r	Radius of Gyration	Sty.	Story	W.R.	Water Resistant
R	Resistance	Subj.	Subject	Wrck.	Wrecker
R.C.P.	Reinforced Concrete Pipe	Subs.	Subcontractors	W.S.P.	Water, Steam, Petroleum
Rect.	Rectangle	Surf.	Surface	WT., Wt.	Weight
Reg.	Regular	Sw.	Switch	WWF	Welded Wire Fabric
Reinf.	Reinforced	Swbd.	Switchboard	XFER	Transfer
Req'd.	Required	S.Y.	Square Yard	XFMR	Transformer
Res.	Resistant	Syn.	Synthetic	XHD	Extra Heavy Duty
Resi.	Residential	S.Y.P.	Southern Yellow Pine	XHHW; XLPE	Cross-Linked Polyethylene Wire
Rgh.	Rough	Sys.	System		Insulation
RGS	Rigid Galvanized Steel	t.	Thickness	XLP	Cross-linked Polyethylene
R.H.W.	Rubber, Heat & Water Resistant;	T	Temperature; Ton	Y	Wye
	Residential Hot Water	Tan	Tangent	yd	Yard
rms	Root Mean Square	T.C.	Terra Cotta	yr	Year
Rnd.	Round	T & C	Threaded and Coupled	Δ	Delta
Rodm.	Rodman	T.D.	Temperature Difference	%	Percent
Rofc.	Roofer, Composition	Tdd	Telecommunications Device for	~	Approximately
Rofp.	Roofer, Precast		the Deaf	Ø	Phase
Rohe.	Roofer Helpers (Composition)	T.E.M.	Transmission Electron Microscopy	@	At
Rots.	Roofer, Tile & Slate	TFE	Tetrafluoroethylene (Teflon)	#	Pound; Number
R.O.W.	Right of Way	T. & G.	Tongue & Groove;	<	Less Than
RPM	Revolutions per Minute		Tar & Gravel	>	Greater Than
R.S.	Rapid Start	Th.; Thk.	Thick		
Rsr	Riser	Thn.	Thin		
RT	Round Trip	Thrded	Threaded		
S.	Suction; Single Entrance; South	Tilf.	Tile Layer, Floor		

Index

Index

Notes

For more information visit
the RSMeans Website at
www.rsmeans.com

Contractor's Pricing Guides

Contractor's Pricing Guide: Residential Detailed Costs 2008

Every aspect of residential construction, from overhead costs to residential lighting and wiring, is in here. All the detail you need to accurately estimate the costs of your work with or without markups—labor-hours, typical crews, and equipment are included as well. When you need a detailed estimate, this publication has all the costs to help you come up with a complete, on the money, price you can rely on to win profitable work.

Unit Prices Now Updated to MasterFormat 2004!

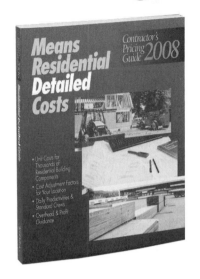

$39.95 per copy
Available Nov. 2007
Catalog no. 60338

Contractor's Pricing Guide: Residential Repair & Remodeling Costs 2008

This book provides total unit price costs for every aspect of the most common repair and remodeling projects. Organized in the order of construction by component and activity, it includes demolition and installation, cleaning, painting, and more. With simplified estimating methods, clear, concise descriptions, and technical specifications for each component, the book is a valuable tool for contractors who want to speed up their estimating time, while making sure their costs are on target.

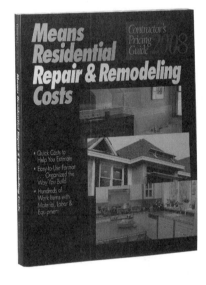

$39.95 per copy
Available Nov. 2007
Catalog no. 60348

Contractor's Pricing Guide: Residential Square Foot Costs 2008

Now available in one concise volume, all you need to know to plan and budget the cost of new homes. If you are looking for a quick reference, the model home section contains costs for over 250 different sizes and types of residences, with hundreds of easily applied modifications. If you need even more detail, the Assemblies Section lets you build your own costs or modify the model costs further. Hundreds of graphics are provided, along with forms and procedures to help you get it right.

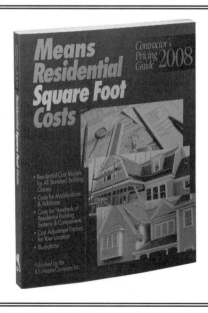

$39.95 per copy
Available Nov. 2007
Catalog no. 60328

Annual Cost Guides

For more information
visit the RSMeans Website
at www.rsmeans.com

RSMeans Building Construction Cost Data 2008

Available in Softbound, Looseleaf, and Spanish Versions

Many customers enjoy the convenience and flexibility of the looseleaf binder, which increases the usefulness of *RSMeans Building Construction Cost Data 2008* by making it easy to add and remove pages. You can insert your own cost information pages, so everything is in one place. Copying pages for faxing is easier also. Whichever edition you prefer—softbound, looseleaf, or the new Spanish version—you'll be eligible to receive *RSMeans Quarterly Update Service* FREE. Current subscribers can receive *RSMeans Quarterly Update Service* via e-mail.

Unit prices now updated to MasterFormat 2004!

$149.95 per copy (English or Spanish)
Catalog no. 60018 (English) Available Oct. 2007
Catalog no. 60718 (Spanish) Available Dec. 2007

$187.95 per copy, looseleaf
Available Oct. 2007
Catalog no. 61018

RSMeans Building Construction Cost Data 2008

Now available in Spanish!

Offers you unchallenged unit price reliability in an easy-to-use arrangement. Whether used for complete, finished estimates or for periodic checks, it supplies more cost facts better and faster than any comparable source. Over 20,000 unit prices for 2008. The City Cost Indexes and Location Factors cover over 930 areas, for indexing to any project location in North America. Order and get *RSMeans Quarterly Update Service* FREE. You'll have year-long access to the RSMeans Estimating **HOTLINE** FREE with your subscription. Expert assistance when using RSMeans data is just a phone call away.

$149.95 per copy (English or Spanish)
Catalog no. 60018 (English) Available Oct. 2007
Catalog no. 60718 (Spanish) Available Dec. 2007

Unit prices now updated to MasterFormat 2004!

RSMeans Metric Construction Cost Data 2008

A massive compendium of all the data from both the *RSMeans Building Construction Cost Data* AND *Heavy Construction Cost Data*, in **metric** format! Access all of this vital information from one complete source. It contains more than 600 pages of unit costs and 40 pages of assemblies costs. The Reference Section contains over 200 pages of tables, charts, and other estimating aids. A great way to stay in step with today's construction trends and rapidly changing costs.

$179.95 per copy
Available Dec. 2007
Catalog no. 63018

For more information
visit the RSMeans Website
at www.rsmeans.com

Annual Cost Guides

RSMeans Mechanical Cost Data 2008

- **HVAC**
- **Controls**

Total unit and systems price guidance for mechanical construction. . . materials, parts, fittings, and complete labor cost information. Includes prices for piping, heating, air conditioning, ventilation, and all related construction.

Plus new 2008 unit costs for:

- Over 2,500 installed HVAC/controls assemblies components
- "On-site" Location Factors for over 930 cities and towns in the U.S. and Canada
- Crews, labor, and equipment

$149.95 per copy
Available Oct. 2007
Catalog no. 60028

Unit prices now updated to MasterFormat 2004!

RSMeans Plumbing Cost Data 2008

Comprehensive unit prices and assemblies for plumbing, irrigation systems, commercial and residential fire protection, point-of-use water heaters, and the latest approved materials. This publication and its companion, *RSMeans Mechanical Cost Data*, provide full-range cost estimating coverage for all the mechanical trades.

Now contains more lines of no-hub CI soil pipe fittings, more flange-type escutcheons, fiberglass pipe insulation in a full range of sizes for 2-1/2" and 3" wall thicknesses, 220 lines of grease duct, and much more.

$149.95 per copy
Available Oct. 2007
Catalog no. 60218

RSMeans Electrical Cost Data 2008

Pricing information for every part of electrical cost planning. More than 13,000 unit and systems costs with design tables; clear specifications and drawings; engineering guides; illustrated estimating procedures; complete labor-hour and materials costs for better scheduling and procurement; and the latest electrical products and construction methods.

- A variety of special electrical systems including cathodic protection
- Costs for maintenance, demolition, HVAC/ mechanical, specialties, equipment, and more

$149.95 per copy
Available Oct. 2007
Catalog no. 60038

Unit prices now updated to MasterFormat 2004!

RSMeans Electrical Change Order Cost Data 2008

RSMeans Electrical Change Order Cost Data provides you with electrical unit prices exclusively for pricing change orders—based on the recent, direct experience of contractors and suppliers. Analyze and check your own change order estimates against the experience others have had doing the same work. It also covers productivity analysis and change order cost justifications. With useful information for calculating the effects of change orders and dealing with their administration.

$149.95 per copy
Available Nov. 2007
Catalog no. 60238

RSMeans Square Foot Costs 2008

It's Accurate and Easy To Use!

- **Updated price information** based on nationwide figures from suppliers, estimators, labor experts, and contractors
- "How-to-Use" sections, with **clear examples** of commercial, residential, industrial, and institutional structures
- Realistic graphics, offering true-to-life illustrations of building projects
- Extensive information on using square foot cost data, including sample estimates and alternate pricing methods

$163.95 per copy
Available Nov. 2007
Catalog no. 60058

RSMeans Repair & Remodeling Cost Data 2008

Commercial/Residential

Use this valuable tool to estimate commercial and residential renovation and remodeling.

Includes: New costs for hundreds of unique methods, materials, and conditions that only come up in repair and remodeling, PLUS:

- Unit costs for over 15,000 construction components
- Installed costs for over 90 assemblies
- Over 930 "on-site" localization factors for the U.S. and Canada.

Unit prices now updated to MasterFormat 2004!

$128.95 per copy
Available Nov. 2007
Catalog no. 60048

Annual Cost Guides

For more information
visit the RSMeans Website
at www.rsmeans.com

RSMeans Facilities Construction Cost Data 2008

For the maintenance and construction of commercial, industrial, municipal, and institutional properties. Costs are shown for new and remodeling construction and are broken down into materials, labor, equipment, and overhead and profit. Special emphasis is given to sections on mechanical, electrical, furnishings, site work, building maintenance, finish work, and demolition.

More than 43,000 unit costs, plus assemblies costs and a comprehensive Reference Section are included.

$357.95 per copy
Available Nov. 2007
Catalog no. 60208

Unit prices now updated to MasterFormat 2004!

RSMeans Light Commercial Cost Data 2008

Specifically addresses the light commercial market, which is a specialized niche in the construction industry. Aids you, the owner/designer/contractor, in preparing all types of estimates—from budgets to detailed bids. Includes new advances in methods and materials.

Assemblies Section allows you to evaluate alternatives in the early stages of design/planning.

Over 11,000 unit costs ensure that you have the prices you need. . . when you need them.

$128.95 per copy
Available Nov. 2007
Catalog no. 60188

RSMeans Residential Cost Data 2008

Contains square foot costs for 30 basic home models with the look of today, plus hundreds of custom additions and modifications you can quote right off the page. With costs for the 100 residential systems you're most likely to use in the year ahead. Complete with blank estimating forms, sample estimates, and step-by-step instructions.

Now contains line items for cultured stone and brick, PVC trim lumber, and TPO roofing.

$128.95 per copy
Available Oct. 2007
Catalog no. 60178

Unit prices now updated to MasterFormat 2004!

RSMeans Site Work & Landscape Cost Data 2008

Includes unit and assemblies costs for earthwork, sewerage, piped utilities, site improvements, drainage, paving, trees & shrubs, street openings/ repairs, underground tanks, and more. Contains 57 tables of assemblies costs for accurate conceptual estimates.

Includes:
• Estimating for infrastructure improvements
• Environmentally-oriented construction
• ADA-mandated handicapped access
• Hazardous waste line items

$149.95 per copy
Available Nov. 2007
Catalog no. 60288

RSMeans Assemblies Cost Data 2008

RSMeans Assemblies Cost Data takes the guesswork out of preliminary or conceptual estimates. Now you don't have to try to calculate the assembled cost by working up individual component costs. We've done all the work for you.

Presents detailed illustrations, descriptions, specifications, and costs for every conceivable building assembly—240 types in all—arranged in the easy-to-use UNIFORMAT II system. Each illustrated "assembled" cost includes a complete grouping of materials and associated installation costs, including the installing contractor's overhead and profit.

$245.95 per copy
Available Oct. 2007
Catalog no. 60068

Unit prices now updated to MasterFormat 2004!

RSMeans Open Shop Building Construction Cost Data 2008

The latest costs for accurate budgeting and estimating of new commercial and residential construction. . . renovation work. . . change orders. . . cost engineering.

RSMeans Open Shop "BCCD" will assist you to:
• Develop benchmark prices for change orders
• Plug gaps in preliminary estimates and budgets
• Estimate complex projects
• Substantiate invoices on contracts
• Price ADA-related renovations

$149.95 per copy
Available Dec. 2007
Catalog no. 60158

For more information
visit the RSMeans Website
at www.rsmeans.com

Annual Cost Guides

RSMeans Building Construction Cost Data 2008
Western Edition

This regional edition provides more precise cost information for western North America. Labor rates are based on union rates from 13 western states and western Canada. Included are western practices and materials not found in our national edition: tilt-up concrete walls, glu-lam structural systems, specialized timber construction, seismic restraints, and landscape and irrigation systems.

$149.95 per copy
Available Dec. 2007
Catalog no. 60228

Unit prices now updated to MasterFormat 2004!

RSMeans Heavy Construction Cost Data 2008

A comprehensive guide to heavy construction costs. Includes costs for highly specialized projects such as tunnels, dams, highways, airports, and waterways. Information on labor rates, equipment, and materials costs is included. Features unit price costs, systems costs, and numerous reference tables for costs and design.

$149.95 per copy
Available Dec. 2007
Catalog no. 60168

RSMeans Construction Cost Indexes 2008

What materials and labor costs will change unexpectedly this year? By how much?
- Breakdowns for 316 major cities
- National averages for 30 key cities
- Expanded five major city indexes
- Historical construction cost indexes

$325.00 per year (subscription)
Catalog no. 50148

$81.25 individual quarters
Catalog no. 60148 A,B,C,D

RSMeans Interior Cost Data 2008

Provides you with prices and guidance needed to make accurate interior work estimates. Contains costs on materials, equipment, hardware, custom installations, furnishings, and labor costs. . . for new and remodel commercial and industrial interior construction, including updated information on office furnishings, and reference information.

Unit prices now updated to MasterFormat 2004!

$149.95 per copy
Available Nov. 2007
Catalog no. 60098

RSMeans Concrete & Masonry Cost Data 2008

Provides you with cost facts for virtually all concrete/masonry estimating needs, from complicated formwork to various sizes and face finishes of brick and block—all in great detail. The comprehensive Unit Price Section contains more than 7,500 selected entries. Also contains an Assemblies [Cost] Section, and a detailed Reference Section that supplements the cost data.

Unit prices now updated to MasterFormat 2004!

$136.95 per copy
Available Dec. 2007
Catalog no. 60118

RSMeans Labor Rates for the Construction Industry 2008

Complete information for estimating labor costs, making comparisons, and negotiating wage rates by trade for over 300 U.S. and Canadian cities. With 46 construction trades listed by local union number in each city, and historical wage rates included for comparison. Each city chart lists the county and is alphabetically arranged with handy visual flip tabs for quick reference.

$326.95 per copy
Available Dec. 2007
Catalog no. 60128

RSMeans Facilities Maintenance & Repair Cost Data 2008

RSMeans Facilities Maintenance & Repair Cost Data gives you a complete system to manage and plan your facility repair and maintenance costs and budget efficiently. Guidelines for auditing a facility and developing an annual maintenance plan. Budgeting is included, along with reference tables on cost and management, and information on frequency and productivity of maintenance operations.

The only nationally recognized source of maintenance and repair costs. Developed in cooperation with the Civil Engineering Research Laboratory (CERL) of the Army Corps of Engineers.

$326.95 per copy
Available Dec. 2007
Catalog no. 60308

Reference Books

For more information
visit the RSMeans Website
at www.rsmeans.com

Value Engineering: Practical Applications

For Design, Construction, Maintenance & Operations

by Alphonse Dell'Isola, PE

A tool for immediate application—for engineers, architects, facility managers, owners, and contractors. Includes making the case for VE—the management briefing; integrating VE into planning, budgeting, and design; conducting life cycle costing; using VE methodology in design review and consultant selection; case studies; VE workbook; and a life cycle costing program on disk.

$79.95 per copy
Over 450 pages, illustrated, softcover
Catalog no. 67319A

Facilities Operations & Engineering Reference

by the Association for Facilities Engineering and RSMeans

An all-in-one technical reference for planning and managing facility projects and solving day-to-day operations problems. Selected as the official certified plant engineer reference, this handbook covers financial analysis, maintenance, HVAC and energy efficiency, and more.

$54.98 per copy
Over 700 pages, illustrated, hardcover
Catalog no. 67318

The Building Professional's Guide to Contract Documents

3rd Edition

by Waller S. Poage, AIA, CSI, CVS

A comprehensive reference for owners, design professionals, contractors, and students

- Structure your documents for maximum efficiency.
- Effectively communicate construction requirements.
- Understand the roles and responsibilities of construction professionals.
- Improve methods of project delivery.

$32.48 per copy, 400 pages
Diagrams and construction forms, hardcover
Catalog no. 67261A

Building Security: Strategies & Costs

by David Owen

This comprehensive resource will help you evaluate your facility's security needs, and design and budget for the materials and devices needed to fulfill them.

Includes over 130 pages of RSMeans cost data for installation of security systems and materials, plus a review of more than 50 security devices and construction solutions.

$44.98 per copy
350 pages, illustrated, hardcover
Catalog no. 67339

Cost Planning & Estimating for Facilities Maintenance

In this unique book, a team of facilities management authorities shares their expertise on:

- Evaluating and budgeting maintenance operations
- Maintaining and repairing key building components
- Applying *RSMeans Facilities Maintenance & Repair Cost Data* to your estimating

Covers special maintenance requirements of the ten major building types.

$89.95 per copy
Over 475 pages, hardcover
Catalog no. 67314

Life Cycle Costing for Facilities

by Alphonse Dell'Isola and Dr. Steven Kirk

Guidance for achieving higher quality design and construction projects at lower costs! Cost-cutting efforts often sacrifice quality to yield the cheapest product. Life cycle costing enables building designers and owners to achieve both. The authors of this book show how LCC can work for a variety of projects — from roads to HVAC upgrades to different types of buildings.

$99.95 per copy
450 pages, hardcover
Catalog no. 67341

Planning & Managing Interior Projects 2nd Edition

by Carol E. Farren, CFM

Expert guidance on managing renovation & relocation projects.

This book guides you through every step in relocating to a new space or renovating an old one. From initial meeting through design and construction, to post-project administration, it helps you get the most for your company or client. Includes sample forms, spec lists, agreements, drawings, and much more!

$34.98 per copy
200 pages, softcover
Catalog no. 67245A

Builder's Essentials: Best Business Practices for Builders & Remodelers

An Easy-to-Use Checklist System

by Thomas N. Frisby

A comprehensive guide covering all aspects of running a construction business, with more than 40 user-friendly checklists. Provides expert guidance on increasing your revenue and keeping more of your profit, planning for long-term growth, keeping good employees, and managing subcontractors.

$29.95 per copy
Over 220 pages, softcover
Catalog no. 67329

For more information
visit the RSMeans Website
at www.rsmeans.com

Reference Books

Interior Home Improvement
Costs 9th Edition

Updated estimates for the most popular remodeling and repair projects—from small, do-it-yourself jobs to major renovations and new construction. Includes: kitchens & baths; new living space from your attic, basement, or garage; new floors, paint, and wallpaper; tearing out or building new walls; closets, stairs, and fireplaces; new energy-saving improvements, home theaters, and more!

$24.95 per copy
250 pages, illustrated, softcover
Catalog no. 67308E

Exterior Home Improvement
Costs 9th Edition

Updated estimates for the most popular remodeling and repair projects—from small, do-it-yourself jobs, to major renovations and new construction. Includes: curb appeal projects—landscaping, patios, porches, driveways, and walkways; new windows and doors; decks, greenhouses, and sunrooms; room additions and garages; roofing, siding, and painting; "green" improvements to save energy & water.

$24.95 per copy
Over 275 pages, illustrated, softcover
Catalog no. 67309E

Builder's Essentials: Plan Reading & Material Takeoff
For Residential and Light Commercial Construction

by Wayne J. DelPico

A valuable tool for understanding plans and specs, and accurately calculating material quantities. Step-by-step instructions and takeoff procedures based on a full set of working drawings.

$35.95 per copy
Over 420 pages, softcover
Catalog no. 67307

Means Unit Price Estimating Methods
New 4th Edition

This new edition includes up-to-date cost data and estimating examples, updated to reflect changes to the CSI numbering system and new features of RSMeans cost data. It describes the most productive, universally accepted ways to estimate, and uses checklists and forms to illustrate shortcuts and timesavers. A model estimate demonstrates procedures. A new chapter explores computer estimating alternatives.

$59.95 per copy
Over 350 pages, illustrated, softcover
Catalog no. 67303B

Total Productive Facilities Management
by Richard W. Sievert, Jr.

Today, facilities are viewed as strategic resources. . . elevating the facility manager to the role of asset manager supporting the organization's overall business goals. Now, Richard Sievert Jr., in this well-articulated guidebook, sets forth a new operational standard for the facility manager's emerging role. . . a comprehensive program for managing facilities as a true profit center.

$29.98 per copy
275 pages, softcover
Catalog no. 67321

Means Environmental Remediation Estimating Methods 2nd Edition
by Richard R. Rast

Guidelines for estimating 50 standard remediation technologies. Use it to prepare preliminary budgets, develop estimates, compare costs and solutions, estimate liability, review quotes, negotiate settlements.

$49.98 per copy
Over 750 pages, illustrated, hardcover
Catalog no. 64777A

Concrete Repair and Maintenance Illustrated
by Peter Emmons

Hundreds of illustrations show users how to analyze, repair, clean, and maintain concrete structures for optimal performance and cost effectiveness. From parking garages to roads and bridges to structural concrete, this comprehensive book describes the causes, effects, and remedies for concrete wear and failure. Invaluable for planning jobs, selecting materials, and training employees, this book is a must-have for concrete specialists, general contractors, facility managers, civil and structural engineers, and architects.

$69.95 per copy
300 pages, illustrated, softcover
Catalog no. 67146

Reference Books

For more information
visit the RSMeans Website
at www.rsmeans.com

Means Illustrated Construction
Dictionary Condensed, 2nd Edition

The best portable dictionary for office or field use—an essential tool for contractors, architects, insurance and real estate personnel, facility managers, homeowners, and anyone who needs quick, clear definitions for construction terms. The second edition has been further enhanced with updates and hundreds of new terms and illustrations . . . in keeping with the most recent developments in the construction industry.

Now with a quick-reference Spanish section. Includes tools and equipment, materials, tasks, and more!

$59.95 per copy
Over 500 pages, softcover
Catalog no. 67282A

Means Repair & Remodeling
Estimating New 4th Edition
By Edward B. Wetherill and RSMeans

This important reference focuses on the unique problems of estimating renovations of existing structures, and helps you determine the true costs of remodeling through careful evaluation of architectural details and a site visit.

New section on disaster restoration costs.

$69.95 per copy
Over 450 pages, illustrated, hardcover
Catalog no. 67265B

Facilities Planning &
Relocation
by David D. Owen

A complete system for planning space needs and managing relocations. Includes step-by-step manual, over 50 forms, and extensive reference section on materials and furnishings.

New lower price and user-friendly format.

$89.95 per copy
Over 450 pages, softcover
Catalog no. 67301

Means Square Foot &
UNIFORMAT Assemblies
Estimating Methods 3rd Edition

Develop realistic square foot and assemblies costs for budgeting and construction funding. The new edition features updated guidance on square foot and assemblies estimating using UNIFORMAT II. An essential reference for anyone who performs conceptual estimates.

$69.95 per copy
Over 300 pages, illustrated, softcover
Catalog no. 67145B

Means Electrical Estimating
Methods 3rd Edition

Expanded edition includes sample estimates and cost information in keeping with the latest version of the CSI MasterFormat and UNIFORMAT II. Complete coverage of fiber optic and uninterruptible power supply electrical systems, broken down by components, and explained in detail. Includes a new chapter on computerized estimating methods. A practical companion to *RSMeans Electrical Cost Data.*

$64.95 per copy
Over 325 pages, hardcover
Catalog no. 67230B

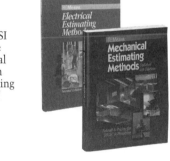

Means Mechanical
Estimating Methods 4th Edition

Completely updated, this guide assists you in making a review of plans, specs, and bid packages, with suggestions for takeoff procedures, listings, substitutions, and pre-bid scheduling for all components of HVAC. Includes suggestions for budgeting labor and equipment usage. Compares materials and construction methods to allow you to select the best option.

$64.95 per copy
Over 350 pages, illustrated, softcover
Catalog no. 67294B

Means ADA Compliance Pricing
Guide New 2nd Edition
by Adaptive Environments and
RSMeans

Completely updated and revised to the new 2004 *Americans with Disabilities Act Accessibility Guidelines,* this book features more than 70 of the most commonly needed modifications for ADA compliance. Projects range from installing ramps and walkways, widening doorways and entryways, and installing and refitting elevators, to relocating light switches and signage.

$79.95 per copy
Over 350 pages, illustrated, softcover
Catalog no. 67310A

Project Scheduling &
Management for Construction
New 3rd Edition
by David R. Pierce, Jr.

A comprehensive yet easy-to-follow guide to construction project scheduling and control—from vital project management principles through the latest scheduling, tracking, and controlling techniques. The author is a leading authority on scheduling, with years of field and teaching experience at leading academic institutions. Spend a few hours with this book and come away with a solid understanding of this essential management topic.

$64.95 per copy
Over 300 pages, illustrated, hardcover
Catalog no. 67247B

For more information
visit the RSMeans Website
at www.rsmeans.com

Reference Books

The Practice of Cost Segregation Analysis

by Bruce A. Desrosiers and Wayne J. DelPico

This expert guide walks you through the practice of cost segregation analysis, which enables property owners to defer taxes and benefit from "accelerated cost recovery" through depreciation deductions on assets that are properly identified and classified.

With a glossary of terms, sample cost segregation estimates for various building types, key information resources, and updates via a dedicated Web site, this book is a critical resource for anyone involved in cost segregation analysis.

$99.95 per copy
Over 225 pages
Catalog no. 67345

Preventive Maintenance for Multi-Family Housing

by John C. Maciha

Prepared by one of the nation's leading experts on multi-family housing.

This complete PM system for apartment and condominium communities features expert guidance, checklists for buildings and grounds maintenance tasks and their frequencies, a reusable wall chart to track maintenance, and a dedicated Web site featuring customizable electronic forms. A must-have for anyone involved with multi-family housing maintenance and upkeep.

$89.95 per copy
225 pages
Catalog no. 67346

How to Estimate with Means Data & CostWorks

New 3rd Edition

by RSMeans and Saleh A. Mubarak, Ph.D.

New 3rd Edition—fully updated with new chapters, plus new CD with updated *CostWorks* cost data and MasterFormat organization. Includes all major construction items—with more than 300 exercises and two sets of plans that show how to estimate for a broad range of construction items and systems—including general conditions and equipment costs.

$59.95 per copy
272 pages, softcover
Includes CostWorks CD
Catalog no. 67324B

Job Order Contracting

Expediting Construction Project Delivery

by Allen Henderson

Expert guidance to help you implement JOC—fast becoming the preferred project delivery method for repair and renovation, minor new construction, and maintenance projects in the public sector and in many states and municipalities. The author, a leading JOC expert and practitioner, shows how to:

• Establish a JOC program

• Evaluate proposals and award contracts

• Handle general requirements and estimating

• Partner for maximum benefits

$89.95 per copy
192 pages, illustrated, hardcover
Catalog no. 67348

Builder's Essentials: Estimating Building Costs

For the Residential & Light Commercial Contractor

by Wayne J. DelPico

Step-by-step estimating methods for residential and light commercial contractors. Includes a detailed look at every construction specialty—explaining all the components, takeoff units, and labor needed for well-organized, complete estimates. Covers correctly interpreting plans and specifications, and developing accurate and complete labor and material costs.

$29.95 per copy
Over 400 pages, illustrated, softcover
Catalog no. 67343

Building & Renovating Schools

This all-inclusive guide covers every step of the school construction process—from initial planning, needs assessment, and design, right through moving into the new facility. A must-have resource for anyone concerned with new school construction or renovation. With square foot cost models for elementary, middle, and high school facilities, and real-life case studies of recently completed school projects.

The contributors to this book—architects, construction project managers, contractors, and estimators who specialize in school construction—provide start-to-finish, expert guidance on the process.

$99.95 per copy
Over 425 pages, hardcover
Catalog no. 67342

Reference Books

For more information
visit the RSMeans Website
at www.rsmeans.com

Residential & Light Commercial Construction Standards 2nd Edition

by RSMeans and contributing authors

This book provides authoritative requirements and recommendations compiled from the nation's leading professional associations, industry publications, and building code organizations.

It's an all-in-one reference for establishing a standard for workmanship, quickly resolving disputes, and avoiding defect claims.

$59.95 per copy
600 pages, illustrated, softcover
Catalog no. 67322A

Means Illustrated Construction Dictionary
Unabridged 3rd Edition, with CD-ROM

Long regarded as the industry's finest, *Means Illustrated Construction Dictionary* is now even better. With the addition of over 1,000 new terms and hundreds of new illustrations, it is the clear choice for the most comprehensive and current information. The companion CD-ROM that comes with this new edition adds many extra features: larger graphics, expanded definitions, and links to both CSI MasterFormat numbers and product information.

$99.95 per copy
Over 790 pages, illustrated, hardcover
Catalog no. 67292A

Designing & Building with the IBC 2nd Edition

by Rolf Jensen & Associates, Inc.

This updated, comprehensive guide helps building professionals make the transition to the 2003 International Building Code®. Includes a side-by-side code comparison of the IBC 2003 to the IBC 2000 and the three primary model codes, a quick-find index, and professional code commentary. With illustrations, abbreviations key, and an extensive Resource section.

$99.95 per copy
Over 875 pages, softcover
Catalog no. 67328A

Means Plumbing Estimating Methods 3rd Edition

by Joseph Galeno and Sheldon Greene

Updated and revised! This practical guide walks you through a plumbing estimate, from basic materials and installation methods through change order analysis. *Plumbing Estimating Methods* covers residential, commercial, industrial, and medical systems, and features sample takeoff and estimate forms and detailed illustrations of systems and components.

$29.98 per copy
330+ pages, softcover
Catalog no. 67283B

Understanding & Negotiating Construction Contracts

by Kit Werremeyer

Take advantage of the author's 30 years' experience in small-to-large (including international) construction projects. Learn how to identify, understand, and evaluate high risk terms and conditions typically found in all construction contracts—then negotiate to lower or eliminate the risk, improve terms of payment, and reduce exposure to claims and disputes. The author avoids "legalese" and gives real-life examples from actual projects.

$69.95 per copy
300 pages, softcover
Catalog no. 67350

Means Estimating Handbook
2nd Edition

Updated Second Edition answers virtually any estimating technical question—all organized by CSI MasterFormat. This comprehensive reference covers the full spectrum of technical data required to estimate construction costs. The book includes information on sizing, productivity, equipment requirements, code-mandated specifications, design standards, and engineering factors.

$99.95 per copy
Over 900 pages, hardcover
Catalog no. 67276A

Means Spanish/English Construction Dictionary 2nd Edition

by RSMeans and the International Code Council

This expanded edition features thousands of the most common words and useful phrases in the construction industry with easy-to-follow pronunciations in both Spanish and English. Over 800 new terms, phrases, and illustrations have been added. It also features a new stand-alone "Safety & Emergencies" section, with colored pages for quick access.

Unique to this dictionary are the systems illustrations showing the relationship of components in the most common building systems for all major trades.

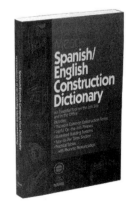

$23.95 per copy
Over 400 pages
Catalog no. 67327A

For more information
visit the RSMeans Website
at www.rsmeans.com

Seminars

Means CostWorks® Training

This *one-day* seminar has been designed with the intention of assisting both new and existing users to become more familiar with the *Means CostWorks* program. The class is broken into two unique sections: (1) A one-half day presentation on the function of each icon; and each student will be shown how to use the software to develop a cost estimate. (2) Hands-on estimating exercises that will ensure that each student thoroughly understands how to use *CostWorks*. You must bring your own laptop computer to this course.

Means CostWorks Benefits/Features:
- Estimate in your own spreadsheet format
- Power of RSMeans National Database
- Database automatically regionalized
- Save time with keyword searches
- Save time by establishing common estimate items in "Bookmark" files
- Customize your spreadsheet template
- Hot Key to Product Manufacturers' listings and specs
- Merge capability for networking environments
- View crews and assembly components
- AutoSave capability
- Enhanced sorting capability

Unit Price Estimating

This interactive *two-day* seminar teaches attendees how to interpret project information and process it into final, detailed estimates with the greatest accuracy level.

The single most important credential an estimator can take to the job is the ability to visualize construction in the mind's eye, and thereby estimate accurately.

Some of what you'll learn:
- Interpreting the design in terms of cost
- The most detailed, time-tested methodology for accurate "pricing"
- Key cost drivers—material, labor, equipment, staging, and subcontracts
- Understanding direct and indirect costs for accurate job cost accounting and change order management

Who should attend: Corporate and government estimators and purchasers, architects, engineers... and others needing to produce accurate project estimates.

Square Foot and Assemblies Estimating

This *two-day* course teaches attendees how to quickly deliver accurate square foot estimates using limited budget and design information.

Some of what you'll learn:
- How square foot costing gets the estimate done faster
- Taking advantage of a "systems" or "assemblies" format
- The RSMeans "building assemblies/square foot cost approach"
- How to create a very reliable preliminary and systems estimate using bare-bones design information

Who should attend: Facilities managers, facilities engineers, estimators, planners, developers, construction finance professionals... and others needing to make quick, accurate construction cost estimates at commercial, government, educational, and medical facilities.

Repair and Remodeling Estimating

This *two-day* seminar emphasizes all the underlying considerations unique to repair/remodeling estimating and presents the correct methods for generating accurate, reliable R&R project costs using the unit price and assemblies methods.

Some of what you'll learn:
- Estimating considerations—like labor-hours, building code compliance, working within existing structures, purchasing materials in smaller quantities, unforeseen deficiencies
- Identifying problems and providing solutions to estimating building alterations
- Rules for factoring in minimum labor costs, accurate productivity estimates, and allowances for project contingencies
- R&R estimating examples calculated using unit price and assemblies data

Who should attend: Facilities managers, plant engineers, architects, contractors, estimators, builders... and others who are concerned with the proper preparation and/or evaluation of repair and remodeling estimates.

Mechanical and Electrical Estimating

This *two-day* course teaches attendees how to prepare more accurate and complete mechanical/electrical estimates, avoiding the pitfalls of omission and double-counting, while understanding the composition and rationale within the RSMeans Mechanical/Electrical database.

Some of what you'll learn:
- The unique way mechanical and electrical systems are interrelated
- M&E estimates–conceptual, planning, budgeting, and bidding stages
- Order of magnitude, square foot, assemblies, and unit price estimating
- Comparative cost analysis of equipment and design alternatives

Who should attend: Architects, engineers, facilities managers, mechanical and electrical contractors... and others needing a highly reliable method for developing, understanding, and evaluating mechanical and electrical contracts.

Green Building Planning & Construction

In this *two-day* course, learn about tailoring a building and its placement on the site to the local climate, site conditions, culture, and community. Includes information to reduce resource consumption and augment resource supply.

Some of what you'll learn:
- Green technologies, materials, systems, and standards
- Energy efficiencies with energy modeling tools
- Cost vs. value of green products over their life cycle
- Low-cost strategies and economic incentives and funding
- Health, comfort, and productivity goals and techniques

Who should attend: Contractors, project managers, building owners, building officials, healthcare and insurance professionals.

Facilities Maintenance and Repair Estimating

This *two-day* course teaches attendees how to plan, budget, and estimate the cost of ongoing and preventive maintenance and repair for existing buildings and grounds.

Some of what you'll learn:
- The most financially favorable maintenance, repair, and replacement scheduling and estimating
- Auditing and value engineering facilities
- Preventive planning and facilities upgrading
- Determining both in-house and contract-out service costs
- Annual, asset-protecting M&R plan

Who should attend: Facility managers, maintenance supervisors, buildings and grounds superintendents, plant managers, planners, estimators... and others involved in facilities planning and budgeting.

Practical Project Management for Construction Professionals

In this *two-day* course, acquire the essential knowledge and develop the skills to effectively and efficiently execute the day-to-day responsibilities of the construction project manager.

Covers:
- General conditions of the construction contract
- Contract modifications: change orders and construction change directives
- Negotiations with subcontractors and vendors
- Effective writing: notification and communications
- Dispute resolution: claims and liens

Who should attend: Architects, engineers, owner's representatives, project managers.

Life Cycle Costing for Facilities

This *two-day* course teaches attendees how to plan and conduct life cycle cost analysis studies.

Some of what you'll learn:
- Initial project feasibility
- Developing guidelines for LCC studies and their accomplishment
- Selecting the best design
- Applying the latest economic models for energy conservation and greening of the environment

Who should attend: Professionals involved in planning, programming, real estate development, maintenance, operation, procurement, design, specifying, and construction.

For more information
visit the RSMeans Website
at www.rsmeans.com

Scheduling and Project Management

This *two-day* course teaches attendees the most current and proven scheduling and management techniques needed to bring projects in on time and on budget.

Some of what you'll learn:
- Crucial phases of planning and scheduling
- How to establish project priorities and develop realistic schedules and management techniques
- Critical Path and Precedence Methods
- Special emphasis on cost control

Who should attend: Construction project managers, supervisors, engineers, estimators, contractors... and others who want to improve their project planning, scheduling, and management skills.

Understanding & Negotiating Construction Contracts

In this *two-day* course, learn how to protect the assets of your company by justifying or eliminating commercial risk through negotiation of a contract's terms and conditions.

Some of what you'll learn:
- Myths and paradigms of contracts
- Scope of work, terms of payment and scheduling
- Dispute resolution
- Why clients love CLAIMS!
- Negotiating issues and much more

Who should attend: Contractors & subcontractors, material suppliers, project managers, risk & insurance managers, procurement managers, owners and facility managers, corporate executives.

Site Work & Heavy Construction Estimating

This *two-day* course teaches attendees how to estimate earthwork, site utilities, foundations, and site improvements, using the assemblies and the unit price methods.

Some of what you'll learn:
- Basic site work and heavy construction estimating skills
- Estimating foundations, utilities, earthwork, and site improvements
- Correct equipment usage, quality control, and site investigation for estimating purposes

Who should attend: Project managers, design engineers, estimators, and contractors doing site work and heavy construction.

Assessing Scope of Work for Facility Construction Estimating

This *two-day* course is a practical training program that addresses the vital importance of understanding the SCOPE of projects in order to produce accurate cost estimates in a facility repair and remodeling environment.

Some of what you'll learn:
- Discussions on site visits, plans/specs, record drawings of facilities, and site-specific lists
- Review of CSI divisions, including means, methods, materials, and the challenges of scoping each topic
- Exercises in SCOPE identification and SCOPE writing for accurate estimating of projects
- Hands-on exercises that require SCOPE, take-off, and pricing

Who should attend: Corporate and government estimators, planners, facility managers, and others who need to produce accurate project estimates.

2008 RSMeans Seminar Schedule

Note: Call for exact dates and details.

Location	Dates
Las Vegas, NV	March
Washington, DC	April
Denver, CO	May
San Francisco, CA	June
Washington, DC	September
Dallas, TX	September
Las Vegas, NV	October
Orlando, FL	November
Atlantic City, NJ	October
San Diego, CA	December

1-800-334-3509, ext. 5115

For more information
visit the RSMeans Website
at www.rsmeans.com

Registration Information

Register early... Save up to $100! Register 30 days before the start date of a seminar and save $100 off your total fee. *Note: This discount can be applied only once per order. It cannot be applied to team discount registrations or any other special offer.*

How to register Register by phone today! The RSMeans toll-free number for making reservations is **1-800-334-3509, ext. 5115.**

Individual seminar registration fee - $935. *Means CostWorks®* **training registration fee - $375.** To register by mail, complete the registration form and return, with your full fee, to: Seminar Division, Reed Construction Data, RSMeans Seminars, 63 Smiths Lane, Kingston, MA 02364.

Federal government pricing All federal government employees save 25% off the regular seminar price. Other promotional discounts cannot be combined with the federal government discount.

Team discount program for two to four seminar registrations. Call for pricing: 1-800-334-3509, ext. 5115

Multiple course discounts When signing up for two or more courses, call for pricing.

Refund policy Cancellations will be accepted up to ten days prior to the seminar start. There are no refunds for cancellations received later than ten working days prior to the first day of the seminar. A $150 processing fee will be applied for all cancellations. Written notice of cancellation is required. Substitutions can be made at any time before the session starts. **No-shows are subject to the full seminar fee.**

AACE approved courses Many seminars described and offered here have been approved for 14 hours (1.4 recertification credits) of credit by the AACE International Certification Board toward meeting the continuing education requirements for recertification as a Certified Cost Engineer/Certified Cost Consultant.

AIA Continuing Education We are registered with the AIA Continuing Education System (AIA/CES) and are committed to developing quality learning activities in accordance with the CES criteria. Many seminars meet the AIA/CES criteria for Quality Level 2. AIA members may receive (14) learning units (LUs) for each two-day RSMeans course.

NASBA CPE sponsor credits We are part of the National Registry of CPE sponsors. Attendees may be eligible for (16) CPE credits.

Daily course schedule The first day of each seminar session begins at 8:30 a.m. and ends at 4:30 p.m. The second day begins at 8:00 a.m. and ends at 4:00 p.m. Participants are urged to bring a hand-held calculator, since many actual problems will be worked out in each session.

Continental breakfast Your registration includes the cost of a continental breakfast, a morning coffee break, and an afternoon break. These informal segments will allow you to discuss topics of mutual interest with other members of the seminar. (You are free to make your own lunch and dinner arrangements.)

Hotel/transportation arrangements RSMeans has arranged to hold a block of rooms at most host hotels. To take advantage of special group rates when making your reservation, be sure to mention that you are attending the RSMeans seminar. You are, of course, free to stay at the lodging place of your choice. **(Hotel reservations and transportation arrangements should be made directly by seminar attendees.)**

Important Class sizes are limited, so please register as soon as possible.

Note: Pricing subject to change.

Registration Form

Call 1-800-334-3509, ext. 5115 to register or FAX 1-800-632-6732. Visit our Web site: www.rsmeans.com

Please register the following people for the RSMeans construction seminars as shown here. We understand that we must make our own hotel reservations if overnight stays are necessary.

☐ Full payment of $_____ enclosed.

☐ Bill me

Name of registrant(s)

(To appear on certificate of completion)

_____

_____

_____

_____

P.O. #: _____
GOVERNMENT AGENCIES MUST SUPPLY PURCHASE ORDER NUMBER OR TRAINING FORM.

Firm name_____

Address_____

City/State/Zip_____

Telephone no._____ Fax no._____

E-mail address_____

Charge our registration(s) to: ☐ MasterCard ☐ VISA ☐ American Express ☐ Discover

Account no._____ Exp. date_____

Cardholder's signature_____

Seminar name_____

City _____ Dates _____

Please mail check to: Seminar Division, Reed Construction Data, RSMeans Seminars, 63 Smiths Lane, P.O. Box 800, Kingston, MA 02364 USA

MeansData™

CONSTRUCTION COSTS FOR SOFTWARE APPLICATIONS
Your construction estimating software is only as good as your cost data.

A proven construction cost database is a mandatory part of any estimating package. The following list of software providers can offer you MeansData™ as an added feature for their estimating systems. See the table below for what types of products and services they offer (match their numbers). Visit online at **www.rsmeans.com/demosource/** for more information and free demos. Or call their numbers listed below.

1. **3D International**
   713-871-7000
   venegas@3di.com

2. **4Clicks-Solutions, LLC**
   719-574-7721
   mbrown@4clicks-solutions.com

3. **ArenaSoft Estimating**
   888-370-8806
   info@arenasoft.com

4. **Beck Technology**
   214-303-6293
   stewartcarroll@beckgroup.com

5. **BSD - Building Systems Design, Inc.**
   888-273-7638
   bsd@bsdsoftlink.com

6. **Building Explorer LLC**
   949-500-9773
   info@buildingexplorer.com

7. **CMS - Computerized Micro Solutions**
   800-255-7407
   cms@proest.com

8. **Corecon Technologies, Inc.**
   714-895-7222
   sales@corecon.com

9. **CorVet Systems**
   301-622-9069
   sales@corvetsys.com

10. **Digital Alchemy**
    206-779-6308
    info@DigitalAlchemyPro.com

11. **Earth Tech**
    303-771-3103
    kyle.knudson@earthtech.com

12. **Estimating Systems, Inc.**
    800-967-8572
    esipulsar@adelphia.net

13. **MC² - Management Computer**
    800-225-5622
    vkeys@mc2-ice.com

14. **Maximus Asset Solutions**
    800-659-9001
    assetsolutions@maximus.com

15. **PrioSoft**
    888-394-0252
    sales@priosoft.com

16. **Sage Timberline Office**
    800-628-6583
    productinfo.timberline@sage.com

17. **SchoolDude.com**
    877-868-3833
    info@schooldude.com

18. **US Cost, Inc.**
    800-372-4003
    sales@uscost.com

19. **Vanderweil Facility Advisors**
    617-451-5100
    info@VFA.com

20. **WinEstimator, Inc.**
    800-950-2374
    sales@winest.com

TYPE	1	2	3	4	5	6	7	8	9	10	11	12	13	14	15	16	17	18	19	20
BID			•		•		•		•				•			•				•
Estimating		•	•	•	•		•	•	•		•	•	•		•	•		•		•
DOC/JOC/SABER		•	•		•				•			•		•		•				•
ID/IQ		•							•			•		•						•
Asset Mgmt.														•			•		•	•
Facility Mgmt.	•													•			•		•	
Project Mgmt.	•	•						•	•						•	•				
TAKE-OFF			•				•	•	•		•		•			•		•		
EARTHWORK								•			•		•							
Pipe Flow																				
HVAC/Plumbing			•				•		•											
Roofing			•				•		•											
Design	•		•	•		•				•						•				•
Other Offers/Links:																				
Accounting/HR		•	•										•							
Scheduling			•													•		•		•
CAD				•		•				•						•				•
PDA																•		•		•
Lt. Versions		•					•									•		•		•
Consulting	•	•	•	•			•		•		•			•		•	•	•	•	•
Training		•	•	•	•	•	•	•	•	•	•	•	•	•		•	•	•	•	•

Qualified re-seller applications now being accepted. Call Carol Polio, ext. 5107.

FOR MORE INFORMATION
CALL 1-800-448-8182, EXT. 5107 OR FAX 1-800-632-6732

For more information
visit the RSMeans Website
at www.rsmeans.com

New Titles

How Your House Works
by Charlie Wing

A must-have reference for every homeowner, handyman, and contractor—for repair, remodeling, and new construction. This book uncovers the mysteries behind just about every major appliance and building element in your house—from electrical, heating and AC, to plumbing, framing, foundations and appliances. Clear, "exploded" drawings show exactly how things should be put together and how they function—what to check if they don't work, and what you can do that might save you having to call in a professional.

$21.95 per copy
160 pages, softcover
Catalog no. 67351

Green Building: Project Planning & Cost Estimating 2nd Edition

This new edition has been completely updated with the latest in green building technologies, design concepts, standards, and costs. Now includes a 2008 Green Building *CostWorks* CD with more than 300 green building assemblies and over 5,000 unit price line items for sustainable building. The new edition is also full-color with all new case studies—plus a new chapter on deconstruction, a key aspect of green building.

$129.95 per copy
350 pages, softcover
Catalog no. 67338A

Complete Book of Framing
by Scot Simpson

This straightforward, easy-to-learn method will help framers, carpenters, and handy homeowners build their skills in rough carpentry and framing. Shows how to frame all the parts of a house: floors, walls, roofs, door & window openings, and stairs—with hundreds of color photographs and drawings that show every detail. The book gives beginners all the basics they need to go from zero framing knowledge to a journeyman level. And it provides valuable tips and tables for the experienced carpenter—plus "framer-friendly" tips and a dedicated Website to access framing formulas.

$29.95 per copy
352 pages, softcover
Catalog no. 67353

Means Landscape Estimating Methods
New 5th Edition

Answers questions about preparing competitive landscape construction estimates, with up-to-date cost estimates and the new MasterFormat classification system. Expanded and revised to address the latest materials and methods, including new coverage on approaches to green building that save water, reduce maintenance costs, and provide other benefits. Includes:

- Step-by-step explanation of the estimating process and a sample estimate for a major project.
- Sample forms and worksheets that save time and prevent errors—now available on a new companion Website.

$64.95 per copy
Over 350 pages, softcover
Catalog no. 67295C

Construction Business Management
by Nick Ganaway

Only 43% of construction firms stay in business after four years. Make sure your company thrives with valuable guidance from a pro with 25 years of success as a commercial contractor. Find out what it takes to build all aspects of a business that is profitable, enjoyable, and enduring. With a bonus chapter on retail construction.

$49.95 per copy
200 pages, softcover
Catalog no. 67352

The Homeowner's Guide to Mold By Michael Pugliese

Expert guidance to protect your health and your home.

Mold, whether caused by leaks, humidity or flooding, is a real health and financial issue—for homeowners and contractors. This full-color book explains:

- Construction and maintenance practices to prevent mold
- How to inspect for and remove mold
- Mold remediation procedures and costs
- What to do after a flood
- How to deal with insurance companies if you're thinking of submitting a mold damages claim

$21.95 per copy
144 pages, softcover
Catalog no. 67344

Qty.	Book no.	COST ESTIMATING BOOKS	Unit Price	Total
	60068	Assemblies Cost Data 2008	$245.95	
	60018	Building Construction Cost Data 2008	149.95	
	61018	Building Const. Cost Data–Looseleaf Ed. 2008	187.95	
	60718	Building Const. Cost Data–Spanish 2008	149.95	
	60228	Building Const. Cost Data–Western Ed. 2008	149.95	
	60118	Concrete & Masonry Cost Data 2008	136.95	
	50148	Construction Cost Indexes 2008 (subscription)	325.00	
	60148A	Construction Cost Index–January 2008	81.25	
	60148B	Construction Cost Index–April 2008	81.25	
	60148C	Construction Cost Index–July 2008	81.25	
	60148D	Construction Cost Index–October 2008	81.25	
	60348	Contr. Pricing Guide: Resid. R & R Costs 2008	39.95	
	60338	Contr. Pricing Guide: Resid. Detailed 2008	39.95	
	60328	Contr. Pricing Guide: Resid. Sq. Ft. 2008	39.95	
	60238	Electrical Change Order Cost Data 2008	149.95	
	60038	Electrical Cost Data 2008	149.95	
	60208	Facilities Construction Cost Data 2008	357.95	
	60308	Facilities Maintenance & Repair Cost Data 2008	326.95	
	60168	Heavy Construction Cost Data 2008	149.95	
	60098	Interior Cost Data 2008	149.95	
	60128	Labor Rates for the Const. Industry 2008	326.95	
	60188	Light Commercial Cost Data 2008	128.95	
	60028	Mechanical Cost Data 2008	149.95	
	63018	Metric Construction Cost Data 2008	179.95	
	60158	Open Shop Building Const. Cost Data 2008	149.95	
	60218	Plumbing Cost Data 2008	149.95	
	60048	Repair and Remodeling Cost Data 2008	128.95	
	60178	Residential Cost Data 2008	128.95	
	60288	Site Work & Landscape Cost Data 2008	149.95	
	60058	Square Foot Costs 2008	163.95	
	62018	Yardsticks for Costing (2008)	149.95	
	62017	Yardsticks for Costing (2007)	136.95	
		REFERENCE BOOKS		
	67310A	ADA Compliance Pricing Guide, 2nd Ed.	79.95	
	67330	Bldrs Essentials: Adv. Framing Methods	12.98	
	67329	Bldrs Essentials: Best Bus. Practices for Bldrs	29.95	
	67298A	Bldrs Essentials: Framing/Carpentry 2nd Ed.	24.95	
	67298AS	Bldrs Essentials: Framing/Carpentry Spanish	24.95	
	67307	Bldrs Essentials: Plan Reading & Takeoff	35.95	
	67342	Building & Renovating Schools	99.95	
	67339	Building Security: Strategies & Costs	44.98	
	67353	Complete Book of Framing	29.95	
	67146	Concrete Repair & Maintenance Illustrated	69.95	
	67352	Construction Business Management	49.95	
	67314	Cost Planning & Est. for Facil. Maint.	89.95	
	67328A	Designing & Building with the IBC, 2nd Ed.	99.95	
	67230B	Electrical Estimating Methods, 3rd Ed.	64.95	
	64777A	Environmental Remediation Est. Methods, 2nd Ed.	49.98	
	67343	Estimating Bldg. Costs for Resi. & Lt. Comm.	29.95	

Qty.	Book no.	REFERENCE BOOKS (Cont.)	Unit Price	Total
	67276A	Estimating Handbook, 2nd Ed.	$99.95	
	67318	Facilities Operations & Engineering Reference	54.98	
	67301	Facilities Planning & Relocation	89.95	
	67338A	Green Building: Proj. Planning & Cost Est., 2nd Ed.	129.95	
	67349	Home Addition & Renovation Project Costs	29.95	
	67308E	Home Improvement Costs–Int. Projects, 9th Ed.	24.95	
	67309E	Home Improvement Costs–Ext. Projects, 9th Ed.	24.95	
	67344	Homeowner's Guide to Mold	21.95	
	67324B	How to Est. w/Means Data & CostWorks, 3rd Ed.	59.95	
	67351	How Your House Works	21.95	
	67282A	Illustrated Const. Dictionary, Condensed, 2nd Ed.	59.95	
	67292A	Illustrated Const. Dictionary, w/CD-ROM, 3rd Ed.	99.95	
	67348	Job Order Contracting	89.95	
	67347	Kitchen & Bath Project Costs	29.95	
	67295C	Landscape Estimating Methods, 5th Ed.	64.95	
	67341	Life Cycle Costing for Facilities	99.95	
	67294B	Mechanical Estimating Methods, 4th Ed.	64.95	
	67245A	Planning & Managing Interior Projects, 2nd Ed.	34.98	
	67283B	Plumbing Estimating Methods, 3rd Ed.	29.98	
	67345	Practice of Cost Segregation Analysis	99.95	
	67337	Preventive Maint. for Higher Education Facilities	149.95	
	67346	Preventive Maint. for Multi-Family Housing	89.95	
	67326	Preventive Maint. Guidelines for School Facil.	149.95	
	67247B	Project Scheduling & Management for Constr. 3rd Ed.	64.95	
	67265B	Repair & Remodeling Estimating Methods, 4th Ed.	69.95	
	67322A	Resi. & Light Commercial Const. Stds., 2nd Ed.	59.95	
	67327A	Spanish/English Construction Dictionary, 2nd Ed.	23.95	
	67145B	Sq. Ft. & Assem. Estimating Methods, 3rd Ed.	69.95	
	67321	Total Productive Facilities Management	29.98	
	67350	Understanding and Negotiating Const. Contracts	69.95	
	67303B	Unit Price Estimating Methods, 4th Ed.	59.95	
	67319A	Value Engineering: Practical Applications	79.95	

MA residents add 5% state sales tax		
Shipping & Handling**		
Total (U.S. Funds)*		

Prices are subject to change and are for U.S. delivery only. *Canadian customers may call for current prices. **Shipping & handling charges: Add 7% of total order for check and credit card payments. Add 9% of total order for invoiced orders.

Send order to: **ADDV-1000**

Name (please print) _____

Company _____

☐ **Company**

☐ **Home   Address** _____

_____

City/State/Zip _____

Phone # _____ P.O. # _____

(Must accompany all orders being billed)

Mail to: RSMeans, P.O. Box 800, Kingston, MA 02364-0800

Reed Construction Data, Inc.

Reed Construction Data, Inc. is a leading worldwide provider of total construction information solutions. The company's portfolio of information products and services is designed specifically to help construction industry professionals advance their businesses with timely, accurate, and actionable project, product, and cost data. Reed Construction Data is a division of Reed Business Information, a member of the Reed Elsevier PLC group of companies.

Cost Information

RSMeans, the undisputed market leader in construction costs, provides current cost and estimating information through its innovative MeansCostworks.com® web-based solution. In addition, RSMeans publishes annual cost books, estimating software, and a rich library of reference books. RSMeans also conducts a series of professional seminars and provides construction cost consulting for owners, manufacturers, designers, and contractors to sharpen personal skills and maximize the effective use of cost estimating and management tools.

Project Data

Reed Construction Data assembles one of the largest databases of public and private project data for use by contractors, distributors, and building product manufacturers in the U.S. and Canadian markets. In addition, Reed Construction Data is the North American construction community's premier resource for project leads and bid documents. Reed Bulletin and Reed CONNECT™ provide project leads and project data through all stages of construction for many of the country's largest public sector, commercial, industrial, and multi-family residential projects.

Building Product Information

Reed First Source™ in the U.S. and BuildCore in Canada are the only integrated building product information systems offered to the commercial construction industry for searching, selecting, and specifying building products. Written by industry professionals and organized using CSI MasterFormat™ 2004 criteria, the design and construction community uses this information to make better, more informed design decisions.

Research and Analytics

Reed Construction Data's forecasting tools cover most aspects of the construction business in the U.S. and Canada. Our vast network of resources makes us uniquely qualified to give you the information you need to keep your business profitable.

Associated Construction Publications (ACP)

Reed Construction Data's regional construction magazines cover the nation through a network of 14 regional magazines. Serving the construction market for more than 100 years, our magazines are a trusted source of news and information in the local and national construction communities.

For more information, please visit our website at www.reedconstructiondata.com

Reed Construction Data, Inc.
30 Technology Parkway South
Norcross, GA 30092-2912
(800) 322-6996
(800) 895-8661 (fax)
Email: info@reedbusiness.com